MW01016593

French English Frequency Dictionary Essential Vocabulary

2.500 most used words & 548 most common verbs

Handwritten notes:

4:00 AM Portland

1:00 PM - FRANCE

9 hrs DIFFERENCE

!!!

#1034 LA VIE EST UNE MALADIE MORTELLE SEXUELLEMENT TRANSMISSIBLE
LIFE IS A FATAL SEXUALLY TRANSMITTED DISEASE

FUNNY SENTENCES
#'S 1034, 5, 1046

First Printing, 2016

Jolie Laide LTD
12/F, 67 Percival Street, Hong Kong

www.MostUsedWords.com

Index

1. Why this dictionary was created

This dictionary was created because I needed a word list of the most frequent used words & verbs in Spanish, to help me learn that language in the shortest amount of time possible.

I started passing it around to friends and got great feedback on it, so I decided to turn it into a book.

I applied the same principals to different languages, and aim to create series of all major languages. This way everyone is able to learn a new language in a fast and efficient way.

I hope you find this book as useful as it was for my friends and me.

Why study by frequency?

If you´re not familiar with the importance of frequency word lists when it comes to language learning, here is a short summary:

Language learning is fun, but can be overwhelming. Almost every language as hundreds of thousands different words, but most of them you will rarely use. That's why it makes sense to study only the words you actually need to know to have conversations and read in your desired language.

Frequency dictionaries are usually either text based, or speech based. The unique advantage of using subtitles as a method of frequency sorting is that it covers both speaking and reading (73% and 83% respectively).

By only studying the words you will actually use, it is possible to gain a good grasp of a language in a short amount of time. By knowing 2500 words, you can express yourself in everyday situations and be fluent enough have conversations with locals.

On average, you only use 1000 words in any language on a daily spoken basis. This translates to roughly 95% of all words you use daily speech. When it comes to reading, 2500 words will get you to understand around 85% of all words used in written text.

This is idea is based on the Pareto Principle.

You might have heard about it. Pareto was an Italian economist who discovered that 80% of the output comes from only 20% of the input (or material, or effort).

It also applies to language learning. To understand 95% of a foreign language, and become fluent enough in everyday speaking and reading, it might take 3 months of applied learning.

But to get to a 98% understanding might take 10 years. Talk about diminishing returns!

I´m not promising you to speak like a native. That is completely up to you. But, in my opinion, it´s a waste of time. The goal of acquiring a new language is **to be able to communicate**. Not to speak without errors. Most natives don't even speak without making mistakes.

When you acquired your first language as an infant, did your parents give you hours and hours of detailed grammar study? (I hope not)

Build your vocabulary, learn basic grammar and go out there and speak. Make mistakes, have a laugh and learn from them. Good luck!

2. Study tips

While you are free to do whatever you want with this dictionary, I would like to give you some pointers. **By learning just 28 new words a day, you can build up your vocabulary to fluency in three months**. If you dedicate yourself and learn 43 new words daily, two months is possible. Here are a couple of tips to build up your vocabulary fast, and to keep remembering what you previously learned.

Spaced repetition

Hack your brains ability to store and recall information. The most efficient way of studying is by incorporating the system of spaced repetition. This way you can store information faster, and for a longer amount of time. Paul Pimsleur published a paper in 1968 on spaced repetition. He came up with the following intervals: 5 seconds, 25 seconds, 2 minutes, 10 minutes, 1 hour, 5 hours, 1 day, 5 days, 25 days, 4 months, and 2 years.

You do not need to time yourself with a stopwatch, as there are upper and lower bounds to the intervals. Just revisited the words you have previously learned from time to timey.

 (Interactive language learning software and audio courses are based on this principle, and they **can** work really well. To see which ones are great investments, and which ones are terrible, read our reviews of different 3rd party language learning methods, audio courses, software and apps on www.mostusedwords.com/reviews)

Mnemonics

By giving creating a little story with a word, it's easier to remember. The more visual it is, the easier it is to remember. My favorite is , caber. Caber means to fit. Now picture in your mind a bear and a cab. The bear wants to get in the cab, but it's having difficulties. After all, it's really hard *to fit a bear in a cab*. By creating little visual stories like these, it's much easier to remember vocabulary.

Cognates

Instant vocabulary doesn't get any better than this. Cognates are words that share a common etymological origin. French and English, fortunately, share a lot of these words. "absolute, to abuse, major" would be "absolute, abuser , mayor" . Use these word to your advantage. We listed some rule of thumbs on the next page.

English words ending in:		French words ending in:		English	French	notes
1	—al	=	—al	e.g.	animal	animal	Words ending in—al are usually the same in French. Words ending in —al are usually adjectives
2	—ance	=	—ance	e.g.	distance	distance	Words ending in —ance are usually the same in French. Often feminine nouns.
3	—ary	—>	—aire	e.g.	anniversary	anniversaire	Words can be adjectives or nouns
4	—ist	—>	—iste	e.g.	tourist	touriset	Nouns that keep the same ending for masculine and feminine
5	—ble	=	—ble	e.g.	adorable	adorable	These words are generally adjectives
6	—tion	=	—tion	e.g.	conversation	conversation	Generally the same in French. Usually feminine nouns
7	—ct	=	—ct	e.g.	correct	correct	Usually the same. Can be nouns or adjectives
8	—ent	=	—ent	e.g.	different	different	Usually the same in French. Words can be nouns or adjectives
9	—ical	—>	—ique	e.g.	practical	pratique	These words are often adjectives
10	—ence	=	—ence	e.g.	violence	violence	Same ending in French. Usually feminine nouns

Read

What also helps greatly with building your vocabulary AND developing a sense of grammar, is by actively reading. Read out loud. Hear what you're reading. Get used to the way the language sounds, and you will also get a grasp for the endings of verb conjugations this way. Reading helps solidify your vocabulary, because you are using the method of spaced repetition while reading. When you read, and don´t know a word, you can usually discover it by the context. For some reason, words discovered through context are more easily remembered than when you study them from a list.

Anyway, you can get bilingual books from either a bookstore or from www.mostusedwords.com/parallel-texts. Our selection is ever expanding, so check for updates regularly. It currently spans the range from English to French, Portuguese, French, Italian Dutch and German etc.

Listen

Turn on the French (internet) radio, download songs in French, and watch French series. Conversing along with your favorite soap opera is a great way of getting around a new language.

Watch

Change your phone and/or computer into French. Nothing helps you acquire a new language as much as necessity.

3. How to use this dictionary

Adverb	=	*adv*
Article	=	*art*
Conjunction	=	*conj*
Determiners	=	*adj*
Interjection	=	*int*
Feminine	=	*f*
Masculine	=	*m*
Intervariable	=	*i*
Noun, masculine and feminine (same meaning)	=	*nmf*
Noun, feminine	=	*nf*
Noun, masculine	=	*nm*
Noun, invariable	=	*ni*
Noun, masculine and feminine (different meanings, (masc form given))	=	*nm/f*
Numeral	=	*num*
Plural	=	*pl*
Singular	=	*sg*
Informal	=	*fam*
Formal	=	*form*
Preposition	=	*prep*
Pronoun	=	*pron*
Subject	=	*subj*
Object	=	*obj*
Direct object	=	*dir-obj*
Indirect object	=	*indir-obj*
Verb	=	*v*

On Part of Speech definitions

We made the decision to give the most common use(s) of a word as the part of speech. It does however, not mean that this is the only part of speech the word can be used for. Certain verbs (or conjugations thereof) can be used as adjectives, and certain words can be verbs as well as nouns. Some words can be adverbs, adjectives and pronouns, etc.

International Phonetic Alphabet (IPA)

In the beginning, pronounctution can be tricky. The IPA entries for each term can help you, by telling you how to pronounce a word the right way. For more information and instructions on pronunciation of the IPA, visit www.internationalphoneticalphabet.org. It's quick to gain an understanding of the IPA pronunciations if you are already familiar with the sounds and way of speech of the language you're learning.

rench – English Frequency Dictionary

ench	English Translation
Part of Speech	**French Example Sentence**
IPA	*English Translation Sentence*

1 de, du, de la, de l', des — of, from, some, any

det, prep

Ils ont pris deux semaines de vacances sur l'île de Phuket dans le sud de la Thaïlande par l'intermédiaire d'une agence de tourisme.

də, dy, də la, də ɛl', de

They took a two week vacation on Phuket island in the south of Thailand through a travel agency.

2 je, j´ — I

pron

~~PARTIR À - TO LEAVE FOR ; PARTIR DE - LEAVE FROM~~

Parfois je pars au travail à pied, parfois à vélo, car j'habite près de mon lieu de travail. ~~SOMETIMES I LEAVE FOR WORK BY FOOT, SOMETIMES BY BIKE...~~

ʒə, ʒi´

Sometimes I walk home from work and sometimes I cycle, because I live close to where I work.

3 être — to be; being ~~SUPPOSED TO, REPUTED TO BE (ADJ)~~

nm, verb

~~976~~
Je ne suis pas censé être vulgaire, mais ses commentaires arrogants m'emmerdent vraiment. ~~EMMERDENT = PRESENT TENSE~~

ɛtʁ

I don't mean to be vulgar, but your arrogant comments have really annoyed me. ~~But HIS ARROGANT COMMENT TRUELY ANNOY/BOTHER ME.~~

4 pas — not; footstep

adv, nm[pl]

~~AMUSEMENT~~
Ce n'est pas que je n'aime pas le divertissement, mais je n'ai pas de temps pour ça.

pa

It's not that I don't like to have fun, but I don't have time for that.

5 le, la, les, l´ — the; him, her, it, them

det, pron

Un des plus gros problèmes dans notre société moderne, c'est que les gens ne voient pas le monde comme moi.

lə, la, le, ɛl´

One of the biggest problems in our modern society is that the people don't see the world as I do.

6 vous — you (form & pl)

pron

Vous devrez apporter deux photos de vous au format identité prises sur un fond blanc. ~~IN THE IDENTITY FORMAT~~

vu

You will need to bring two passport-sized photos of yourself taken with a white background. ~~LE FOND = BOTTOM, BACK, FAR-END, CORE~~

7 là — there, here

adv, int

Personne ne m'avait dit que Tom serait là.

la

Nobody told me Tom would be here. ~~THERE~~

8 tu — you (fam)

pron

Penses-tu que n'importe quelle personne intelligente soit en soi intéressée par les langues ?

ty

Do you think that any really smart person is inherently interested in languages?

9	**que, qu'**	**that, which, who, whom, as**
	adv, conj, pron	Avoir le droit de faire une chose n'est pas du tout la même chose que d'avoir raison de le faire.
	kə, k'	*To have a right to do a thing is not at all the same thing as to be right in doing it.*
10	**un, une, des**	**a, an, one**
	adj, det, nm, pron, num	Si un mec te paie un verre dans un bar, tu peux être sûre qu'il cherche à coucher avec toi.
	œ̃, yn, de	*If a man buys you a drink in a bar, he definitely wants to sleep with you.*
11	**il**	**he, it**
	pron	Tu as vu son travail ? Il aurait voulu mal le faire qu'il ne s'y serait pas pris autrement.
	il	*Did you see his work? Would he have wanted to do it badly, he wouldn't have proceeded otherwise.*
12	**et**	**and**
	conj	Ils étaient aux antipodes l'un de l'autre : l'un était honnête et fiable tandis que l'autre était imprévisible et irresponsable.
	e	*They were polar opposites: one was honest and reliable whilst the other was unpredictable and irresponsable.*
13	**à, au, aux**	**to, at, in**
	det, prep	Le magazine s'adresse aux adolescents
	a, o, o	*The magazine is aimed at teenagers*
14	**avoir**	**asset, to have**
	nm, verb	Avoir un téléphone l'a aidée à trouver plus de clients
	avwaʁ	*Having a telephone helped her find more clients*
15	**ne, n´**	**not**
	adv	Le contribuable ne doit pas supporter financièrement les dommages commis par autrui.
	nə, ɛn´	*The taxpayer should not have to support financially the damage caused by others.*
16	**ce, cet, cette, ces**	**this, that**
	det, pron	Les aptitudes de mon fils en mathématiques ont progressé cette année
	sə, sɛt, sɛt, se	*My son's ability at math has improved this year.*
17	**en**	**in, by**
	adv, prep, pron	Elle a dit qu'elle n'avait pas de blessures. En fait, elle était terriblement blessée.
	ã	*She said she was OK. In fact, she was terribly injured.*
18	**on**	**one, we**
	pron	On mange et puis on va tout de suite se coucher.
	ɔ̃	*We will eat, and then go straight to bed.*
19	**cela**	**that, it**
	pron	Si, pour une raison quelconque, cela devait advenir, que feriez-vous ?
	səla	*If for some reason that should happen, what would you do?*
20	**pour**	**to, for, in order to,**

MEC = GUY
MÉCHANT = BAD, MEAN

	prep	Pour ne pas être obligée d'aller à l'école, Marie fit comme si elle était malade
	puʁ	*Mary pretended she was sick to avoid going to school.*
21	**moi**	**me**
	nm, pron	Passe-moi un coup de fil quand tu décideras de m'épouser.
	mwa	*Give me a ring when you decide to marry me*
22	**qui**	**who, whom**
	pron	Je ne négligerai aucun détail pour découvrir qui a fait ça.
	ki	*I'll leave no stone unturned to find out who did this.*
23	**nous**	**we, us**
	pron	Nous ne sommes pas sûr de que ce qu'il est en train de se passer
	nu	*We're not sure what's going on.*
24	**mais**	**but**
	adv, conj, int	D'un côté nous avons essuyé une lourde perte, mais d'un autre côté nous avons beaucoup appris de cette expérience.
	mɛ	*On the one hand we suffered a heavy loss, but on the other hand we learned a great deal from the experience.*
25	**y**	**there**
	adv, ni, pron	« Serez-vous à ma soirée, demain ? » « J'essaierai d'y être. »
	i	*"Will you be at my party tomorrow night?" "I'll try to be there."*
26	**me, m'**	**me, to me, myself**
	pron	J'ai glissé et je suis tombé mais je ne me suis pas fait mal.
	mə, ɛm'	*I slipped and fell but did not hurt myself.*
27	**dans**	**in, into, from**
	prep	Le moine prie pendant une heure pendant que la moinesse fait bouillir l'herbe dans la cuisine.
	dã	*The monk prays for an hour, while the nun boils the herb in the kitchen.*
28	**bien**	**well**
	adj(i), adv, nm	Vous savez bien que l'Autriche n'a pas de bord de mer.
	bjɛ̃	*You are well aware that Austria has no coast.*
29	**elle**	**she, her**
	pron	Elle n'a pas eu de mal à apprendre le poème par cœur.
	ɛl	*She had no difficulty in learning the poem by heart.*
30	**si**	**if, whether** *ni = noun invariable*
	adv, conj, ni	Si tu ne tardes pas trop, j'attendrai ici pour toi toute ma vie.
	si	*If you are not too long, I will wait here for you all my life.*
31	**tout**	**all, very**
	adv, det, nm, adj, pron	Il est hors de question d'apprendre toutes ces phrases par cœur.
	tu	*It is out of the question to learn all these sentences by heart.*
32	**plus**	**more, no**
	adv	Tom a dit qu'il avait des choses plus importantes à faire.
	ply	*Tom said he had more important things to do.*
33	**non**	**no, not**
	adv	« Je vais acheter une maison neuve. Et vous ? » « Non, je ne vais pas en acheter. »

	nɔ̃		"I shall buy a new house. How about you?" "No, I will not buy one."

34 mon, ma, mes — **my**
det
mɔ̃, ma, me
Je suis devenue connue parce que mon nom est Kardashian.
I became famous because my name is Kardashian.

35 suivre — **to follow**
verb
sɥivʁ
Tom a trouvé relativement facile de suivre Mary sans être vu.
Tom found it fairly easy to follow Mary without being seen.

36 te, t´ — **you, to you, from you**
pron
tə, te´
C'est avec plaisir qu'on te donnera un coup de main.
We're willing to help you.

37 avec — **with**
prep
avɛk
Qu'est-ce qu'une langue ? C'est un dialecte avec une armée et une marine.
What is a language? It's a dialect with an army and a navy.

38 oui — **yes**
adv, ni
wi
Il est souvent plus facile de dire "oui" que de dire "non".
It's often easier to say "yes", than to say "no".

39 aller — **to go**
nm, verb
ale
Je lui ai demandé si elle voulait aller se promener.
I asked her if she wanted to go for a walk.

40 toi — **you, yourself**
nm, pron
twa
Si tu souhaites te comprendre toi-même, alors regarde comment les autres le font.
If you want to understand yourself, just look how the others carry on

41 faire — **to do, make**
nm, verb
fɛʁ
Toi seul peux le faire, mais tu ne peux le faire seul.
You alone can do it, but you can't do it alone.

42 se, s´ — **oneself, himself, herself, itself, themselves**
pron
sə, əs´
Il a réussi à se sortir de sa situation difficile.
He managed to get himself out of his predicament.

43 comme — **like, as**
adv, conj
kɔm
Elle prend toujours des airs, agissant comme si elle était une reine.
She's always putting on airs, acting as if she were a queen.

44 sur — **on, upon**
adj, prep
syʁ
Tom et Mary sont assis tous les deux sur le canapé.
Tom and Mary are both sitting on the couch.

45 quoi — **what**
pron
kwa
Nous ne sommes pas trop jeunes pour dire à quoi l'amour ressemble.
We are not too young to tell what love is like.

46 ici — **here**
adv
isi
Je vous suggère de nettoyer un tantinet, avant que votre mère n'arrive ici.
I'd suggest that you clean up a bit before your mother gets here.

47 savoir — **to know**
nm, verb
savwaʁ
Savoir ce qu'il adviendra est plus important que de savoir ce qu'il est advenu.
Knowing what will happen is more important than knowing what has happened.

48	**lui**	**him, her**
	pron	Surtout ne lui achète rien : ce mec est un arnaqueur de première !
	lɥi	*Above all, don't buy anything from him: he's a blithering swindler.*
49	**vouloir**	**to want**
	nm, verb	Maman veut aller là-bas, mais papa veut regarder la télé à la maison.
	vulwaʁ	*Mom wants to go there, but Dad wants to watch TV at home.*
50	**là**	**there, here**
	adv, int	Et si tu y vas et qu'elle n'est pas là et qu'en plus il pleuve ?
	la	*So what if you show up and she's not there and then it starts to pour?*
51	**rien**	**nothing**
	adv, nm, pron	Il a fait mine de me parler mais n'a rien dit.
	ʁjɛ̃	*He made as if to speak to me but said nothing.*
52	**dire**	**to say**
	nm, verb	Le docteur dit que je suis en bonne santé.
	diʁ	*The doctor says that I am in good health.*
53	**où**	**where**
	adv, pron	Y a-t-il une banque où je peux changer des yens contre des dollars ?
	u	*Is there a bank where I can exchange yen for dollars?*
54	**votre**	**your**
	det	Voyez-vous un inconvénient à ce que je me joigne à votre escapade à la campagne ?
	vɔtʁ	*Do you mind if I join your trip to the country?*
55	**pourquoi**	**why**
	adv, conj, ni	Je pense que nous savons toutes deux pourquoi je suis ici.
	puʁkwa	*I think we both know why I'm here.*
56	**quand**	**when**
	adv, conj	Tout ce qui se trouvait sur la table commença à s'entrechoquer quand le tremblement de Terre arriva.
	kɑ̃	*Everything on top of the table started rattling when the earthquake hit.*
57	**par**	**by**
	prep	Le présent accord est produit en deux exemplaires signés par les deux parties.
	paʁ	*The present agreement is put forth in two copies, signed by the two parties.*
58	**son, sa, ses**	**his, her, its; sound; bran**
	det, nm	L'une de ses trois voitures est bleue et les autres sont blanches.
	sɔ̃, sa, se	*One of her three cars is blue and the others are white.*
59	**ton, ta, tes**	**your; tone**
	det, nm	Tu n'es bien sûr pas obligé de le dire à tes parents.
	tɔ̃, ta, te	*You don't have to tell that to your parents.*
60	**pouvoir**	**can, to be able to**
	nm, verb	Non, tu ne peux pas te mettre la passoire sur la tête ; tu feras l'astronaute après que j'aurai égoutté les pâtes.
	puvwaʁ	*No, you may not put the colander on your head; you can be an astronaut after I drain the pasta.*
61	**alors**	**then, so**

	adv	Si Dieu est avec nous, alors qui est contre nous ?
	aloʁ	*If God is with us, then who is against us?*
62	**comment**	**how**
	adv, conj, int, ni	Comment a eu lieu l'accident de chemin de fer à la gare de Tokyo ?
	kɔmã	*How did the railway accident at Tokyo Station happen?*
63	**bon**	**good**
	adj, adv, int, nm	Rien qu'en regardant ton visage, je sais que tu as de bonnes nouvelles.
	bõ	*Just by looking at your face, I know that you have good news.*
64	**ou**	**where**
	adv, pron	C'est la gare où je prends mon train tous les matins.
	u	*This is the station where I take my train every morning.*
65	**très**	**very**
	adv	Je suis très occupé, alors ne comptez pas sur moi.
	tʁɛ	*I'm very busy so don't count on me.*
66	**même**	**same, even, self**
	adj(f), adv, pron	Je ne peux même pas me souvenir de mon propre nom.
	mɛm	*I can't even remember my own name.*
67	**merci**	**thank you; favor**
	int, nm, nf	Merci pour ton mail, hier. Désolée de pas t'avoir répondu.
	mɛʁsi	*Thanks for the email yesterday. Sorry I didn't reply.*
68	**jamais**	**never**
	adv	Je ne suis jamais allée à un match de base-ball professionnel.
	ʒamɛ	*I've never been to a professional baseball game.*
69	**aussi**	**too, also, as**
	adv, conj	J'aimerais pouvoir jouer de la guitare aussi bien que vous.
	osi	*I wish I could play the guitar as well as you do.*
70	**chose**	**thing**
	adj(f), nf	Tu n'as jamais le temps pour les choses importantes !
	ʃoz	*You never have time for important things!*
71	**voir**	**to see**
	verb	Tu vois la couleur ? Ça veut dire que tu es enceinte !
	vwaʁ	*Do you see the color? It means you're pregnant!*
72	**deux**	**two, couple**
	det, num	Voyez-vous un inconvénient à ce que je vous pose une ou deux questions ?
	dø	*Do you mind if I ask you a couple of questions?*
73	**falloir**	**to take, require, need**
	verb	Il va me falloir plus de trois heures pour lire le document.
	falwaʁ	*It will take me more than three hours to look over the document.*
74	**autre**	**other**
	adj(f), pron	Qui est l'homme qui est assis à l'autre bout de la table ?
	otʁ	*Who is the man sitting at the other end of the table?*
75	**maintenant**	**now**
	adv	S'il n'y avait pas eu de guerre civile, ils auraient été riches maintenant.
	mɛ̃tnã	*If it had not been for civil war, they would be wealthy now.*

76	**encore**	**again, yet**
	adv	Même si je suis fauché, j'ai encore acheté un livre.
	ãkɔʁ	*Even though I don't have any money, I bought a book again.*
77	**peu**	**little**
	adv	Elle a encore un peu d'argent, mais pas beaucoup.
	pø	*She still has a little money, but not much.*
78	**vraiment**	**truly, really, very**
	adv	Je veux que tu me dises ce que tu penses vraiment de moi.
	vʁɛmã	*I want you to tell me what you really think of me.*
79	**temps**	**time**
	nm[pl]	Ce que l'on passe son temps à faire durant son enfance, affecte le reste de sa vie.
	tã	*What you spend time doing in your childhood affects the rest of your life.*
80	**toujours**	**always**
	adv	Comment se fait-il que vous soyez toujours aussi énergique ?
	tuʒuʁ	*How come you're always so energetic?*
81	**notre**	**our**
	det	Le climat joue beaucoup sur notre corps et notre esprit.
	nɔtʁ	*The climate has much to do with our mind and body.*
82	**vie**	**life**
	nf	Qui n'aime point le vin, les femmes ni les chants, restera un sot toute sa vie durant.
	vi	*Who loves not women, wine and song remains a fool his whole life long.*
83	**oh**	**oh**
	int	Oh non ! Je ne faisais pas attention et j'ai laissé mon téléphone portable au restaurant.
	o	*Oh no! I wasn't paying attention and left my cell phone in the restaurant!*
84	**juste**	**just, only; fair**
	adv, nm, adj(f)	Je n'ai pas extraordinairement faim quand on pense que j'ai juste mangé une tranche de pain de toute la journée.
	ʒyst	*Considering all I've eaten all day is just one slice of bread, I'm not really all that hungry.*
85	**sans**	**without**
	prep	L'homme naît sans dents, sans cheveux et sans illusions, et il meurt de même, sans cheveux, sans dents et sans illusions.
	sã	*Man is born without teeth, without hair, and without illusions. And he dies the same way: without teeth, without hair, and without illusions.*
86	**quelque**	**some**
	adv, adj, det	Si je devais échouer pour quelque raison que ce soit, j'essaierais de nouveau.
	kɛlk	*If for some reason I failed, I'd try again.*
87	**monde**	**world, people**
	nm	Il y a beaucoup de monde, aussi, aujourd'hui, nous avons opté pour la formule buffet.
	mɔ̃d	*There are a lot of people so today we've gone for buffet style.*
88	**accord**	**agreement**

	nm	Je me trouve en partie d'accord avec chacune de ces deux thèses.
	akɔʁ	*I find myself in partial agreement with both of these arguments.*
89	**fois**	**time, times**
	nf[pl]	Je vous le dis pour la énième fois : Non !
	fwa	*I'm telling you for the umpteenth time - No!*
90	**trop**	**too much, too many**
	adv	'ai commandé beaucoup trop. Je ne pense pas pouvoir tout manger.
	tʁo	*I ordered way too much. I don't think I can eat it all.*
91	**venir**	**to come**
	verb	Si tu as besoin de changer de rythme, pourquoi ne viens-tu pas pour une visite ?
	vəniʁ	*If you need a change of pace, why don't you come for a visit?*
92	**croire**	**to believe**
	verb	Je ne crois pas la moitié de ce qu'on m'a dit sur vous.
	kʁwaʁ	*I don't believe half of what I've been told about you.*
93	**devoir**	**to have to, owe; duty**
	nm, verb	Je dois aller à un autre rendez-vous ennuyeux, demain.
	dəvwaʁ	*I've got to go to another dreary meeting tomorrow.*
94	**père**	**father**
	nm	Mon père lit toujours le journal avant le petit déjeuner.
	pɛʁ	*My father always reads the newspaper before breakfast.*
95	**dieu**	**god**
	int, nm	Le corps et l'esprit sont des jumeaux, Dieu seul sait les reconnaître.
	djø	*Body and spirit are twins: God only knows which is which.*
96	**homme**	**man**
	nm	Un homme de peu de volonté est la cible des critiques ; même ses amis le harcèleront en corrigeant ses défauts.
	ɔm	*A man of weak will is the target of criticism; even his friends would badger him into correcting his defects.*
97	**sûr**	**on, upon**
	adj, prep	L'étudiant doit rédiger un essai sur l'art moderne.
	syʁ	*The student must write an essay about modern art.*
98	**leur**	**them, their, theirs**
	det, adj(f), pron	Je ne veux pas leur dire pourquoi je suis en retard.
	lœʁ	*I don't want to tell them why I'm late.*
99	**avant**	**before**
	adj(i), adv, nm, prep	En France, il faut mettre un espace avant un point d'exclamation.
	avã	*In France, you must put a space before an exclamation point*
100	**besoin**	**need**
	nm	Nous avons besoin de trouver quelqu'un qui peut nous aider.
	bəzwɛ̃	*We need to find somebody who can help us.*
101	**femme**	**woman, wife**
	nf	Tom marcha sur la pointe des pieds jusqu'à la chambre pour éviter de réveiller sa femme.

	fam	*Tom tiptoed into the bedroom to avoid waking up his wife.*
102	**personne**	**person, people, anybody, anyone nobody, no-one**
	nf, pron	J'ai le sentiment que personne ici ne nous dit la vérité.
	pɛʁsɔn	*I get the feeling that no one here is telling us the truth.*
103	**aimer**	**to like, love, wish**
	verb	J'aimerais pouvoir jouer de la guitare aussi bien que toi.
	eme	*I wish I could play the guitar as well as you do.*
104	**chez**	**at, with**
	prep	Je me demande ce qui ne va pas chez lui, il a l'air inquiet.
	ʃe	*I wonder what is wrong with him, he looks worried.*
105	**vrai**	**true**
	adv, nm, adj	Les dictionnaires servent à trouver le vrai sens d'un mot.
	vʁɛ	*Dictionaries are used to find the true meaning of a word.*
106	**an**	**year**
	nm	Tom va chez le coiffeur moins de quatre fois par an.
	ã	*Tom goes to the barber less than four times a year.*
107	**mal**	**bad, sore**
	adj(i), adv, nm	J'ai mal au dos du fait que je sois assis de longues heures devant l'ordinateur.
	mal	*I have a sore back from sitting in front of the computer too many hours.*
108	**parler**	**to speak, talk**
	nm, verb	Nous étions en train de parler de Jim quand il est entré dans la pièce.
	paʁle	*We had been talking about Jim when he entered the room.*
109	**après**	**after**
	adv	Il a commencé le jardinage après avoir pris sa retraite.
	apʁɛ	*He took up gardening after he retired.*
110	**mort**	**dead; death**
	adj, nf	Ce que les médecins devraient faire c'est sauver des vies et lutter contre la mort.
	mɔʁ	*What doctors should do is to save lives and fight against death.*
111	**parce que**	**because**
	conj	Marie est en colère contre moi parce qu'elle pense que j'ai piqué son petit ami.
	paʁsə kə	*Mary is mad at me because she thinks I stole her boyfriend.*
112	**mieux**	**better**
	adj(i)[pl], adv, nm	Si me blâmer te fait te sentir mieux, vas-y.
	mjø	*If blaming me makes you feel better, go right ahead.*
113	**petit**	**small, little**
	adv, nm, adj	Les microbes sont très petits et invisibles à l'œil nu.
	pəti	*Microbes are very small and invisible to the naked eye.*
114	**beaucoup**	**much, a lot of, many**
	adv	Beaucoup de phrases de ce projet ne sont pas encore traduites.
	boku	*Many frases from this project aren't translated yet.*
115	**monsieur**	**mister, sir, gentleman**

	nm	Est-ce que, ces derniers temps, vous étiez en contact avec monsieur Leblanc ?	
	məsjø	*Have you been in contact with Mr. Leblanc lately?*	

116 voilà — right, there, here; that's
prep — Voilà une des choses les plus bizarres qu'il m'ait été donné de voir.
vwala — *That's one of the weirdest things I've ever seen.*

117 depuis — since, for , in
adv, prep — C'est parti pour être l'été le plus chaud depuis trente-six ans.
dəpyi — *This is going to be the hottest summer in thirty-six years.*

118 devoir — must, have to
verb — Tu dois acquérir au plus vite une bonne connaissance de l'anglais commercial.
dəvwaʁ — *You must acquire as soon as possible a good knowledge of business English.*

119 mère — mother
nf — J'ai demandé à ma mère si le petit-déjeuner était prêt.
mɛʁ — *I asked my mother if breakfast was ready.*

120 quel — which, what
det, adj, pron — Il dit à toute occasion qui se présente quel type formidable il est.
kɛl — *He says at every opportunity what a great guy he is.*

121 fille — girl, daughter
nf — En tant que fille, Elisa adorait jouer à la nourrice avec ses poupées.
fij — *As a girl, Elisa loved to play nurse with her dolls.*

122 déjà — already, ever
adv — Avez-vous déjà entendu parler d'un poète qui s'appelle Tom ?
deʒa — *Have you ever heard of a poet by the name of Tom?*

123 gens — people
nmpl — À chaque fois que je vais à Paris, je vais au Sacré-Cœur m'asseoir sur les marches pour écouter les gens chanter, jouer de la musique.
ʒã — *Every time I go to Paris, I visit the Sacred Heart Basilica, sit on the steps, and listen to the people below singing and playing musical instruments.*

124 donc — so, then, therefore, thus
conj — Bill n'avait pas étudié suffisamment, il a donc échoué.
dɔ̃k — *Bill didn't work hard enough and so he failed.*

125 jour — day
nm — Nos combattants ont effectué une moyenne de 430 missions par jour.
ʒuʁ — *Our fighters averaged 430 missions a day.*

126 soir — evening
nm — Lorsque, hier soir, je suis venu à la maison, j'étais fourbu.
swaʁ — *I was dog tired when I got home last night.*

127 ouais — yeah
int — « On est bien mardi, aujourd'hui ? » « Ouais. » « Mais pourquoi c'est aussi bondé ? »
wɛ — *"Today's Tuesday, right?" "Yeah." "Why's it so crowded?"*

128 argent — money, silver
nm — As-tu déjà dépensé l'argent que Tom t'avait donné ?

	aʁʒɑ̃	*Have you already spent the money Tom gave you?*
129	**maison**	**house**
	nf	Tom et Mary veulent acheter une maison avec au moins trois chambres.
	mɛzɔ̃	*Tom and Mary want to buy a house with at least three bedrooms.*
130	**nom**	**name**
	nm	Je suis devenue connue parce que mon nom est Kardashian.
	nɔ̃	*I became famous because my name is Kardashian.*
131	**bonjour**	**hello**
	nm	Si vous voyez les Popescu, s'il vous plaît, dites bonjour pour nous.
	bɔ̃ʒuʁ	*When you see the Popescus, please say hello from us.*
132	**penser**	**to think**
	nm, verb	Je pense que c'est le bon moment pour présenter le produit.
	pɑ̃se	*I think that it is the right time to introduce the product.*
133	**nuit**	**night**
	nf	Tu as pleuré toute la nuit ? Tes yeux sont gonflés.
	nɥi	*Have you been crying all night? Your eyes are all puffy.*
134	**merde**	**sh*t, crap**
	int, nf	Ah merde, la date limite de consommation est dépassée, c'est pour ça que tu as vomi !
	mɛʁd	*Oh crap, it's past the consume-by date. That's why you threw up!*
135	**papa**	**dad, daddy**
	nm	À chaque fois que je tombe amoureux, Papa me dit que la fille est ma demi-sœur.
	papa	*Every time I fall in love, Dad tells me the girl is my half sister.*
136	**maman**	**mom**
	nf	Ma sœur aidait Maman à s'occuper de moi lorsque j'étais bébé.
	mamɑ̃	*My sister used to help mum look after me when I was a baby.*
137	**rester**	**to stay**
	verb	Je vous promets de rester avec vous jusqu'à ce que votre père arrive.
	ʁɛste	*I promise you I'll stay with you until your father arrives.*
138	**peur**	**fear**
	nf	Je n'espère rien, je n'ai peur de rien ; je suis libre.
	pœʁ	*I hope for nothing, I fear for nothing, I am free.*
139	**désolé**	**sorry, afraid**
	adj	« Je suis désolé ! » « Tout va bien. Ne t'inquiète pas. »
	dezɔle	*I'm sorry! - It's OK. Don't worry.*
140	**salut**	**salute, hi, bye**
	int, nm	Salut tout le monde ! Je m'appelle Mary.
	saly	*Hello everyone! My name is Mary.*
141	**seul**	**alone, only**
	adj	Personne ne peut surpasser ma générosité, mais je suis seulement un peu vantard
	sœl	*Nobody can outdo my generosity, but I am only a little boastful.*
142	**arriver**	**to arrive, happen**
	verb	Je ne veux en aucune manière qu'il arrive quoi que ce soit à Tom.

	aʀive	I'd just hate to see anything happen to Tom.
143	**vite**	**fast, quickly**
	adv	Elle lui recommanda de ne pas conduire trop vite mais il refusa de l'écouter.
	vit	She advised him not to drive too fast, but he wouldn't listen to her.
144	**prendre**	**to take**
	verb	Je sais que je ne peux pas prendre la place de Tom.
	pʀɑ̃dʀ	I know I can't take Tom's place.
145	**regarder**	**to look, watch**
	verb	Regarde aux alentours et dis-moi ce que tu vois.
	ʀəgaʀde	Look around you and tell me what you see.
146	**soit**	**either...or**
	adv, conj	De même, la CLIA communique surtout des renseignements généraux aux clients, soit par téléphone, soit par le biais du service.
	swa	CLIA also primarily provides general information to clients, either through direct calls to the office or through the Law Line
147	**air**	**air, appearance**
	nm	Fermez ou retirez l'alimentation d'air pour éviter tout dommage à l'équipement ou blessure.
	ɛʀ	Shut off or deplete the air supply to prevent equipment damage or personal injury.
148	**passer**	**to pass, go**
	verb	Les trois années sont passées comme trois jours, comme dans un rêve !
	pase	These three years have gone by like three days, just like a dream!
149	**trois**	**three**
	det, num	Tom a joué du piano pendant trois heures sans prendre de pause.
	tʀwa	Tom played the piano for three hours without taking a break.
150	**plaire**	**to please, like**
	verb	Je suis las de tout; la seule chose qui me plairait, ce serait d'être aux Canaries.
	plɛʀ	I'm tired of everything; I would like nothing more than to be in the Canary Islands.
151	**chose**	**thing**
	adj(f), nf	Apprendre par cœur n'est pas la meilleure façon pour se rappeler des choses.
	ʃoz	Learning by heart is not the best way how to remember things.
152	**fil**	**thread, wire**
	nm	Si tu touches ce fil, tu recevras une décharge.
	fil	If you touch that wire, you'll get a shock.
153	**ah**	**ah, oh**
	int	Ah ! Si j'étais riche, je m'achèterais une maison en Espagne.
	a	Ah! If I were rich, I'd buy myself a house in Spain.
154	**bas**	**low; bass; stockings**
	adv, nm&f, adj[pl], nm[pl]	Lorsque les vaches volent haut et les bœufs volent bas, c'est qu'il y a probablement une tornade.
	ba	When the cow flies high and the ox flies low, there probably is a twister.

155	**moins**	**less**
	adj(i)[pl], adv, nm[pl], prep	La musique est l'une de ces choses qui nous font nous sentir quelque peu moins seuls dans le monde.
	mwɛ̃	*Music is one of those things that make us feel a little less alone in the world.*
156	**entre**	**between**
	prep	Il prit le papillon entre le pouce et l'index.
	ɑ̃tʁ	*He picked up a butterfly between his thumb and forefinger.*
157	**passe**	**pass, past**
	nf, adj, prep	Oublions le passé et parlons de l'avenir.
	pas	*Let's forget the past and talk about the future.*
158	**demain**	**tomorrow**
	adv, nm	Dites à Tom qu'il lui faut porter une cravate demain.
	dəmɛ̃	*Tell Tom that he needs to wear a tie tomorrow.*
159	**appeler**	**to call**
	verb	Je suis content que vous n'ayez pas appelé Tom.
	aple	*I'm glad you didn't call Tom.*
160	**grand**	**great, older girl or boy, tall**
	adv, nm/f, adj	Vous pouvez facilement le reconnaître étant donné qu'il est très grand
	gʁɑ̃	*You can easily identify him because he is very tall.*
161	**tête**	**head**
	nf	Guillaume Tell a tiré une flèche dans la pomme posée sur la tête de son fils.
	tɛt	*William Tell shot an arrow at the apple on his son's head.*
162	**arrêter**	**to stop, arrest**
	verb	De même, les plus fortes raisons d'arrêter sont en général les bénéfices à court terme (par exemple, se sentir en meilleure santé et plus séduisant).
	aʁete	*Similarly, the strongest reasons for stopping are usually the short-term benefits (for example, feeling healthier and more attractive).*
163	**hein**	**eh, huh**
	int	On dirait que le temps se gâte, hein.
	ɛ̃	*Looks like the weather's gotten worse, eh?*
164	**attendre**	**to wait**
	verb	Si tu ne tardes pas trop, j'attendrai ici pour toi toute ma vie.
	atɑ̃dʁ	*If you are not too long, I will wait here for you all my life.*
165	**raison**	**reason**
	nf	La raison pour laquelle j'ai eu une mauvaise note, c'est parce que je n'ai pas révisé.
	ʁɛzɔ̃	*The reason why I got a bad grade is that I did not study.*
166	**enfant**	**child**
	nm, nf, adj(f)	Maintenant que tu es grand, tu ne dois pas te comporter comme un enfant.
	ɑ̃fɑ̃	*Now that you are grown up, you must not behave like a child.*
167	**assez**	**enough**
	adv	Ma sœur est assez vieille pour aller à un cours d'aérobic par elle-même.
	ase	*My sister is old enough to go to a workout studio by herself.*

168 moment — moment
nm
Enfin nous nous rencontrons ! J'ai longtemps attendu ce moment.
/mɔmɑ̃/
So, we finally meet! I've waited so long for this moment.

169 amour — love
nm
Quand je te vois, mon cœur me dit que je suis amoureux.
/amuʁ/
Whenever I see you, my heart tells me that I'm in love.

170 heure — hour
nf
Nous étions très fatiguées par le voyage de cinq heures.
/œʁ/
We were very tired from the five-hour trip.

171 puis — then, so
adv
Ajouter la farine et la levure chimique, puis le beurre et le restant du lait. Laisser reposer 15 min.
/pɥi/
Add the flour and baking powder, then the butter and leftover milk; let stand for 15 min.

172 tard — late
adv
Tom n'est arrivé que lorsqu'il était déjà trop tard.
/taʁ/
Tom didn't arrive until it was already too late.

173 tuer — to kill
verb
À Nanaimo, d'après ce que j'ai compris, on les brûle, on les chauffe jusqu'à une température donnée pour tuer la maladie.
/tɥe/
In Nanaimo, I understand they burn them to a certain degree of heat to kill the disease.

174 eh — hey, uh
int
Eh, ce n'est pas ainsi que ça fonctionne !
/e/
Hey, it doesn't work that way.

175 ami — friend
nm/f, adj
L'homme qui conduit le bus est un bon ami à moi.
/ami/
The man driving the bus is a good friend of mine.

176 partir — to leave
verb
Il est parti pour New York il y a une semaine.
/paʁtiʁ/
He left for New York a week ago.

177 connaître — to know
verb
Meg est curieuse de tout connaître sur le Japon.
/kɔnɛtʁ/
Meg is curious to know everything about Japan.

178 aider — to help, assist
verb
Nous avons besoin de trouver quelqu'un qui peut nous aider.
/ede/
We need to find somebody who can help us.

179 gars — guy
nm[pl]
Je suis le gars qui a donné à Tom ce chapeau.
/ga/
I'm the guy who gave Tom that hat.

180 chance — luck; chance
nf
Je veux croire qu'il y a encore une chance, pour nous, d'être heureux ensemble.

	ʃɑ̃s		*I want to believe there's still a chance for us to be happy together.*

181 combien — **how much, how many**

adv, conj — Tom pense savoir combien d'argent Mary gagne, mais Mary se fait bien plus que ce que Tom pense.

kɔ̃bjɛ̃ — *Tom thinks he knows how much money Mary makes, but Mary makes quite a bit more than Tom thinks she does.*

182 tant — **so much, so many**

adv — Je n'ai jamais imaginé que tant de gens viendraient à ma fête.

tɑ̃ — *I never imagined so many people would come to my party.*

183 part — **share**

nf — Autant en donner, alors, une part à ceux qui sont dans le besoin.

paʁ — *Therefore, he would be as well to give a share of it to those who are in need.*

184 voiture — **car**

nf — Tom lave sa voiture au moins une fois par semaine.

vwatyʁ — *Tom washes his car at least once a week.*

185 problème — **problem**

nm — Au cœur de cette question se pose le problème de la modernisation.

pʁɔblɛm — *Central to this issue is the problem of modernization.*

186 coup — **coup, blow, knock, stroke**

nm — M. Duff a-t-il porté un coup à M. Watson et relégué ce dernier au second rang au sein du groupe libéral ?

ku — *Did Mr Duff strike a blow and relegate Mr Watson to the second row of the Liberal Group?*

187 porte — **door**

nf — Accueillir quelqu'un, c'est lui ouvrir la porte de son cœur, lui donner de l'espace.

pɔʁt — *To welcome someone is to open the heart's door and make room for him.*

188 travail — **work**

nm — Ne devrais-tu pas être au travail en ce moment ?

tʁavaj — *Shouldn't you be at work now?*

189 famille — **family**

nf — Seuls les plats les plus irréprochables sont servis à la famille royale.

famij — *Only the most impeccable dishes are served to the royal family.*

190 sens — **sense, meaning**

nm[pl] — Si vous ne comprenez pas un certain mot dans la phrase, ignorez-le. La traduction prend tout son sens sans lui.

sɑ̃s — *If you don't understand a particular word in a sentence, ignore it. The translation will make perfect sense without it.*

191 putain — **whore, bitch; stupid**

nf — Les politiciens sont appelés des putains parce qu'ils écoutent les gens qui ne sont pas d'accord avec nous.

pytɛ̃ — *Politicians are called whores because they listen to people who don't agree with us.*

192 idée — **idea**

nf — As-tu la moindre idée de ce qu'il y a dans la boite ?

	ide	*Do you have any idea what's in the box?*
193	**ni**	**nor , neither**
	conj, adv	La compétition en soi n'est ni bonne ni mauvaise.
	ni	*Competition is neither good nor evil in itself.*
194	**contre**	**against**
	adv, nm, prep	Les minorités ethniques se battent contre les préjugés et la pauvreté.
	kɔ̃tʁ	*Ethnic minorities struggle against prejudice and poverty.*
195	**revoir**	**to see again, revise, meet**
	verb	J'ai hâte de vous revoir tous après tout ce temps.
	ʁəvwaʁ	*I'm looking forward to meeting you all after such a long time.*
196	**entendre**	**to hear**
	verb	Les enfants veulent entendre la même histoire encore et encore.
	ãtãdʁ	*Children want to hear the same story over and over again.*
197	**comprendre**	**to understand**
	verb	Il est important de comprendre que chaque pays a sa propre culture.
	kɔ̃pʁãdʁ	*It is important to understand that each country has its own culture.*
198	**pendre**	**to hang down**
	verb	Laissez votre pied pendre depuis votre cheville.
	pãdʁ	*Let your foot hang down from your ankle.*
199	**trouver**	**to find**
	verb	Je me suis creusé la tête pour trouver une solution à l'énigme mais j'ai finalement échoué pour en trouver une.
	tʁuve	*I racked my mind to find a solution to the riddle but eventually failed to find one.*
200	**vieux**	**old**
	adj[pl], nm[pl]	Il n'est pas encore assez vieux pour aller là tout seul.
	vjø	*He is still not old enough to go there all alone.*
201	**attention**	**attention**
	nf	Il ne fait pas attention aux sentiments des autres.
	atãsjɔ̃	*He pays no attention to others' feelings.*
202	**demander**	**to ask for**
	verb	En outre, un membre du Conseil peut demander qu'il soit vérifié que les votes favorables représentent au moins 62 % de la population totale de l'UE.
	dəmãde	*In addition, a Council member may ask for confirmation that the votes in favour represent at least 62% of the EU population.*
203	**chercher**	**to look for**
	verb	Tom a demandé à Mary qui elle était en train de chercher.
	ʃɛʁʃe	*Tom asked Mary who she was looking for.*
204	**sous**	**under**
	prep	Les branches de saule ne cassent pas sous le poids de la neige.
	su	*Willow branches don't break under the weight of snow.*
205	**voici**	**here is, here are, this is, these are**
	prep	Michael, voici le restaurant où ton père et moi avons eu notre premier rendez-vous.
	vwasi	*Michael, this is the restaurant where your father and I had our first date.*

206	**sang**	**blood**
	nm	Un diabétique a trop de sucre dans son sang et dans son urine.
	sɑ̃	*A diabetic has too much sugar in his blood and in his urine.*
207	**histoire**	**history, story**
	nf	Les enfants étaient assis autour du feu de camp et écoutaient Tom qui racontait des histoires de fantômes.
	istwaʁ	*The children sat around the campfire and listened to Tom tell ghost stories.*
208	**sortir**	**to go out, leave**
	verb	Il faut éteindre la lumière avant de sortir d'une pièce.
	sɔʁtiʁ	*You must turn off the light before you go out.*
209	**question**	**question**
	nf	Il est hors de question d'apprendre toutes ces phrases par cœur.
	kɛstjɔ̃	*It is out of the question to learn all these sentences by heart.*
210	**frère**	**brother**
	nm	Je ne suis pas aussi grand que mon frère, mais je suis plus grand que mon père.
	fʁɛʁ	*I am not as big as my brother, but I am bigger than my dad.*
211	**ville**	**city**
	nf	Les gens disent qu'il est l'homme le plus riche de la ville.
	vil	*They say he's the richest person in the city.*
212	**finir**	**to finish**
	verb	« Tu as fini ? » « Au contraire, je viens juste de commencer. »
	finiʁ	*"Have you finished it?" "On the contrary, I've just begun."*
213	**nouveau**	**new**
	adj, nm	J'ai commencé un nouveau blog. Je vais m'efforcer de ne pas laisser tomber !
	nuvo	*I started a new blog. I'll do my best to keep it going.*
214	**eux**	**them**
	pron	Le pardon ça se passe entre eux et Dieu, moi je me charge de organiser le rendez-vous.
	ø	*Forgiveness is between them and God, it's my job to arrange the meeting.*
215	**truc**	**trick; (that) thing (what I can't recall)**
	nm	Le diable nous enseigne à faire ses trucs, mais pas à les cacher.
	tʁyk	*The devil teaches us his tricks but not how to hide them.*
216	**tenir**	**to hold**
	verb	J'ai tenu la main de mon fils pour traverser la route.
	təniʁ	*I held my son's hand to cross the road.*
217	**œil**	**eye**
	nm	Mon oncle a un œil de verre et une jambe de bois.
	œj	*My uncle has a glass eye and a wooden leg.*
218	**moi**	**me**
	nm, pron	Dieu, qu'est-ce qui ne va pas avec moi aujourd'hui ?
	mwa	*God, what's wrong with me today?*
219	**laisser**	**to leave**
	verb	Cela met en colère Mary quand Tom laisse le siège des toilettes relevé.
	lese	*It irritates Mary when Tom leaves the toilet seat up.*

220	**mec**	**guy**
	nm	Le grand mec en train de fumer un cigare là-bas est un réalisateur célèbre.
	mɛk	*The tall guy smoking a cigar over there is a famous director.*
221	**longtemps**	**a long time, a long while**
	adv	Cela faisait longtemps que je ne m'étais pas autant amusé.
	lɔ̃tɑ̃	*I haven't had this much fun in a long time.*
222	**beau**	**handsome, fine, right**
	adj, nm	Il paraît que le nouveau prof d'anglais est un beau gosse qui ressemble à Tom Cruise.
	bo	*I heard that the new English teacher is a handsome guy who looks like Tom Cruise.*
223	**police**	**police**
	nf	Tom s'efforça de dissuader Marie d'aller à la police.
	pɔlis	*Tom tried to prevent Mary from going to the police.*
224	**seulement**	**only**
	adv	Seuls les plats les plus irréprochables sont servis à la famille royale.
	sœlmɑ̃	*Only the most impeccable dishes are served to the royal family.*
225	**importer**	**to import; to be important**
	verb	Notre entreprise importe des meubles d'Italie.
	ɛ̃pɔʁte	*Our company imports furniture from Italy.*
226	**eau**	**water**
	nf	Tom a oublié de nous dire de ne pas boire l'eau du robinet.
	o	*Tom forgot to tell us not to drink the tap water.*
227	**car**	**because**
	conj, nm	J'ai eu beaucoup de difficultés au Mexique, car je ne comprenais pas du tout l'espagnol.
	kaʁ	*I had a difficult time in Mexico because I couldn't understand all of the Spanish.*
228	**super**	**great**
	adj(i), nm	Est-ce que ça ne sens pas super bon ?
	sypɛʁ	*Doesn't that smell great?*
229	**chaque**	**each, every**
	det, adj	Notre professeur de français nous donne un contrôle chaque lundi.
	ʃak	*Our French teacher gives us a test every Monday.*
230	**cas**	**case**
	nm[pl]	Comme c'est souvent le cas, Henry n'était pas chez lui.
	ka	*Henry was not at home, as is often the case with him.*
231	**terre**	**earth, world, soil, land**
	nf	Les deux tiers de la surface de la terre sont couverts d'eau.
	tɛʁ	*Two-thirds of the earth's surface is covered with water.*
232	**placer**	**to place**
	verb	Placez ce questionnaire dans une enveloppe affranchie.
	plase	*Place this questionnaire in postage paid envelope.*
233	**main**	**hand**
	nf	Je sentais mes mains trembler et mon cœur s'emballer.
	mɛ̃	*I felt my hands shaking and my heart beating fast.*

234 **ensemble**   **together**
adv, nm   Nous avons passé tant de bons moments ensemble.
ãsãbl   *We had so many good times together.*

235 **type**   **type; guy**
nm   Il dit à toute occasion qui se présente quel type formidable il est.
tip   *He says at every opportunity what a great guy he is.*

236 **pardon**   **forgiveness**
nm   Le pardon ça se passe entre eux et Dieu, moi je me charge de organiser le rendez-vous.
paʁdɔ̃   *Forgiveness is between them and God, it's my job to arrange the meeting.*

237 **vers**   **toward; verse**
nm[pl], prep   L'expiation est le premier pas vers la réhabilitation.
vɛʁ   *Making amends is the first step toward rehabilitation.*

238 **aucun**   **none, either, neither, not any**
det, adj, pron   Aucune d'entre elles ne voulait discuter.
okœ̃   *None of them wanted to talk.*

239 **guerre**   **war**
nf   Des guerres civiles éclatent dans de nombreux pays.
gɛʁ   *Civil wars are occurring in many countries.*

240 **suite**   **result, follow-up, rest**
nf   Avez-vous vraiment reçu toutes les réponses nécessaires et quelles suites allez-vous donner à ce questionnaire?
sɥit   *Have you really received all of the necessary replies and how are you going to follow up on that questionnaire?*

241 **prier**   **to pray**
verb   La femme allait à l'église afin de prier tous les après-midis.
pʁije   *Every afternoon, the woman went to church to pray.*

242 **devant**   **in front, ahead**
adv, nm, prep   J'ai mal au dos du fait que je sois assis de longues heures devant l'ordinateur.
dəvã   *I have a sore back from sitting in front of the computer too many hours.*

243 **arrivé**   **arrived, happen**
adj   Il est la meilleure chose qui me soit arrivée.
aʁive   *He's the best thing that ever happened to me.*

244 **mettre**   **to put, place**
verb   En France, il faut mettre un espace avant un point d'exclamation.
mɛtʁ   *In France, you must put a space before an exclamation point.*

245 **matin**   **morning**
nm   Thomas disait qu'il avait vu quelque chose de suspect, le matin où Marie est morte.
matɛ̃   *Tom said he saw something suspicious on the morning Mary died.*

246 **aide**   **help, assistance**
nm, nf   Je suis presque sûr que je vais avoir besoin d'aide.
ɛd   *I'm pretty sure I'm going to need some help.*

247 **dessus**   **above, on top**

	adv, nm[pl], prep	La montagne s'élève à approximativement 3 000 mètres au-dessus du niveau de la mer.
	dəsy	*The mountain is about 3000 meters above sea level.*
248	**genre**	**type, kind, sort**
	nm	Je n'ai jamais fait ce genre d'erreurs auparavant.
	ʒɑ̃ʁ	*I've never made this kind of mistake before.*
249	**fin**	**end; gist, clever person**
	adj, adv, nf, nm	Le pont a été bombardé seulement à la fin du conflit.
	fɛ̃	*The bridge was bombed only at the end of the conflict.*
250	**perdre**	**to lose**
	verb	Mon docteur m'a dit que j'avais besoin de perdre du poids.
	pɛʁdʁ	*My doctor told me that I needed to lose some weight.*
251	**jeune**	**young**
	nmf adj(f)	Être jeune, c'est avoir un esprit qui calcule et un cœur qui ne calcule pas.
	ʒœn	*To be young is to have a head which calculates and a heart which doesn't calculate.*
252	**chéri**	**darling, love, dear**
	noun, adj	En vous regardant, votre chéri oubliera vite la défaite de son équipe !
	ʃeʁi	*As soon as your darling sees you, he'll forget all about his team's crushing defeat!*
253	**premier**	**first, premier, first,**
	det, nm&f, adj	Est-ce la première fois que vous mangez de la nourriture japonaise ?
	pʁəmje	*Is this the first time you've eaten Japanese food?*
254	**donner**	**to give**
	verb	Je ne veux pas que Tom donne des conseils à Mary.
	dɔne	*I don't want Tom giving Mary advice.*
255	**droit**	**right**
	adj, adv, nm	Toute personne, sans aucune forme discriminatoire, a le droit de toucher un salaire égal pour un travail égal.
	dʁwa	*Everyone, without any discrimination, has the right to equal pay for equal work.*
256	**côté**	**coast**
	nf	Les touristes viennent par exemple sur les côtes de ma région pour la pêche au crabe.
	kote	*Tourists come to my coast, for example, for the crabs.*
257	**chambre**	**bedroom, chamber**
	nf	Tom marcha sur la pointe des pieds jusqu'à la chambre pour éviter de réveiller sa femme.
	ʃɑ̃bʁ	*Tom tiptoed into the bedroom to avoid waking up his wife.*
258	**loin**	**far**
	adv, nm	Nous prévoyons de nous rendre aussi loin que nous le pouvons.
	lwɛ̃	*We plan to go as far as we can.*
259	**feu**	**fire**
	adj(f), nm	Ses joues étaient teintées de rouge par la chaleur du feu.
	fø	*Her cheeks were tinged with red by the warmth of fire.*
260	**jouer**	**to play**

	verb	J'aimerais pouvoir jouer de la guitare aussi bien que vous.
	ʒwe	*I wish I could play the guitar as well as you do.*

261 train — **train**
nm
tʁɛ̃
Par erreur je suis monté dans le train qui allait dans la direction opposée.
By mistake I boarded a train going in the opposite direction.

262 gros — **big, whoiesale, heavy**
adv, nm, adj[pl]
gʁo
La violence à l'école est un gros problème.
School violence is a big problem.

263 compter — **to count**
verb
kɔ̃te
Il ne faut pas compter sur l'œuf dans le cul d'une poule.
Do not count your chickens before they are hatched.

264 mourir — **to die**
verb
muʁiʁ
Le vieux monsieur sait qu'il va bientôt mourir.
The old man knows that he will die soon.

265 dernier — **last**
nm&f, adj
dɛʁnje
Je vais lui demander où il est allé dimanche dernier.
I will ask him where he went last Sunday.

266 minute — **minute**
nf
minyt
Peux-tu me consacrer quelques minutes ? J'aimerais te dire un mot.
Can you spare me a few minutes? I'd like to have a word with you.

267 mari — **husband**
nm
maʁi
C'est le mari de ma sœur. C'est mon beau-frère.
He's my sister's husband. He's my brother-in-law.

268 enfin — **at last, finally**
adv
ɑ̃fɛ̃
D'abord ils vous ignorent, ensuite ils vous raillent, ensuite ils vous combattent et enfin, vous gagnez.
First they pay no attention. Then they ridicule you. Then they fight you. And finally, you win.

269 madame — **madam, lady**
nf
madam
Excusez-moi, madame, je suis honteuse de pleurer comme ça devant vous, mais je ne peux pas retenir mes larmes.
Pardon me, madam, I'm ashamed to be crying like this in front of you, but I can't hold my tears.

270 façon — **way, manner**
nf
fasɔ̃
La façon dont elle parle me tape sur les nerfs.
The way she talks gets on my nerves.

271 film — **film, movie**
nm
film
De tous les films que tu as vus cette année, lequel as-tu préféré ?
Out of all the movies you saw this year, which one was your favorite?

272 fort — **strong**
adv, adj, nm
fɔʁ
Généralement, les hommes sont plus forts que les femmes.
Generally speaking, men are stronger than women.

273 écoute — **listening**
nf
Vous devez adapter vos aptitudes à l'écoute pour maximiser vos possibilités professionnelles.

ekut · *You need to adapt your listening skills to make the most of your career opportunities.*

274 pays — **country**
nm[pl]
Le précédent président des États-Unis est le seul Américain à connaître le président de tous les pays.
pei · *The former president of the United States is the only American who knows the president of every country.*

275 affaire — **case, matter, business**
nf, adj
J'ai besoin de davantage d'information quant à cette affaire.
afɛʁ · *I need more information on this matter.*

276 endroit — **place, spot**
nm
Je pense que ce doit être l'endroit où Tom habite.
ɑ̃dʁwa · *I think this must be the place where Tom lives.*

277 corps — **body**
nm[pl]
Descartes pensait que l'esprit et le corps se rejoignaient dans la glande pinéale.
kɔʁ · *Descartes thought that the mind and body were joined in the pineal gland.*

278 fou — **mad, crazy**
adj, nm
Quasiment fou de terreur, je me suis précipité hors de la cabane.
fu · *Practically mad with fear, I rushed out of the cabin.*

279 vivre — **to live**
nm, verb
Nous ne pouvons vivre sans eau, même pour un jour.
vivʁ · *We can't live without water for even one day.*

280 prêt — **ready**
adj, nm
La vie commence lorsque tu es prêt à la vivre.
pʁɛ · *Life begins when you're ready to live it.*

281 dont — **whose, of which**
pron
Ne commettez jamais l'erreur de débattre avec des gens dont vous n'avez pas de respect pour les opinions.
dɔ̃ · *Never make the mistake of arguing with people for whose opinions you have no respect.*

282 espérer — **to hope**
verb
J'espère que tu sais que la dernière chose que je veuille faire est de te blesser.
ɛspeʁe · *I hope you know that the last thing I want to do is hurt you.*

283 cause — **cause**
nf
Les dons ont été utilisés pour des causes de bienfaisance.
koz · *The donations were used for charitable causes.*

284 point — **point**
adv, nm
Le but d'une «conclusion » est de reprendre et résumer les points essentiels d'un document.
pwɛ̃ · *The purpose of a conclusion is to sum up the main points of the essay.*

285 dehors — **outside**
adv, nm[pl], prep
De nos jours les enfants ne jouent pas dehors.
dəɔʁ · *Nowadays children do not play outdoors.*

286	**hier**	**yesterday**
	adv	Toute la journée d'hier, j'ai appris par cœur des mots anglais.
	ijɛʁ	*I learned English words by heart all day yesterday.*
287	**boulot**	**work, job**
	adj, nm	J'ai besoin de trouver un boulot au pas de course pour payer mes factures.
	bulo	*I need to find a better job on the double to pay my bills.*
288	**garçon**	**boy**
	nm	Aucun autre garçon dans notre classe n'est plus studieux que Jack.
	gaʁsɔ̃	*No other boy in our class is more studious than Jack.*
289	**près**	**near, nearby, close by**
	adv, prep	S'il vous plaît veillez à ce que cet enfant n'aille pas trop près de la mare.
	pʁɛ	*Please see to it that the child does not go near the pond.*
290	**cinq**	**five**
	det, nm[pl]	Il vaut mieux être lâche durant cinq minutes que mort durant toute une vie.
	sɛ̃k	*It is better to be a coward for five minutes than dead for the rest of your life.*
291	**chef**	**head, leader, chief**
	nm	Le chef du gouvernement doit inspirer la foi du peuple.
	ʃɛf	*The head of the government must inspire the faith of the people.*
292	**ainsi**	**thus**
	adv	L'équipe a marqué un but et a donc gagné le match.
	ɛ̃si	*The team scored a goal, thus winning the match.*
293	**haut**	**top, high**
	adv, adj	Beurrer les moules à madeleines, et verser la préparation dedans (mais pas jusqu'en haut, les madeleines vont gonfler !).
	o	*Grease the madeleine molds and pour in the batter (but not all the way to the top; the madeleines will rise!)*
294	**celui**	**that, the one, he, him**
	pron	Nous nous référons au principe le plus général de toute la physique classique, celui de la conservation de l'énergie.
	səlɥi	*We are referring to the most general principle in all classical physics, that of conservation of energy.*
295	**bébé**	**baby**
	nmf, adj(f)	Mon bébé a aussi huit mois, il est en bonne santé et il grandit à vue d'œil.
	bebe	*My baby is also eight months old, is healthy and is growing by leaps and bounds.*
296	**possible**	**possible**
	adj(f)	Pourriez-vous, s'il vous plaît, parler le plus lentement possible ?
	pɔsibl	*Could you speak as slowly as possible?*
297	**école**	**school**
	nf	Il regrette de ne pas avoir travaillé plus dur à l'école.
	ekɔl	*He regrets not having worked harder at school.*
298	**plein**	**full**
	adv, nm, adj, prep	Je suis entré dans la salle, qui était pleine de monde.

	plɛ̃	*entered the room, which was full of people.*
299	**année**	**year**
	nf	La fête de la mi-automne tombe un lundi cette année, non ?
	ane	*Does the mid-autumn festival fall on Monday this year?*
300	**manger**	**to eat**
	nm, verb	Je n'aimerais autant pas manger la viande d'un animal qui a été cloné.
	mɑ̃ʒe	*I'd rather not eat the meat from an animal that was cloned.*
301	**docteur**	**doctor**
	nm	Le docteur recommanda à ce patient de cesser de fumer.
	dɔktœʁ	*The doctor urged the patient to stop smoking.*
302	**tour**	**tower; turn; tour**
	nm, nf	Le vieux couple s'est embarqué pour un tour du monde.
	tuʁ	*The old couple embarked on a tour around the world.*
303	**quatre**	**four**
	det, num	Le docteur sauva les quatre personnes blessées dans l'accident.
	katʁ	*The doctor saved the four people injured in the accident.*
304	**plutôt**	**rather**
	adv	Je préférerais sortir plutôt que de rester à l'intérieur.
	plyto	*I would rather go out than stay indoors.*
305	**marcher**	**to walk**
	verb	Elle lui a conseillé de marcher plutôt que de prendre le bus.
	maʁʃe	*She advised him to walk instead of taking a bus.*
306	**semaine**	**week**
	nf	Nous sommes impatients de partir en randonnée la semaine prochaine.
	səmɛn	*We are looking forward to going on a hike next week.*
307	**vérité**	**truth**
	nf	La plupart des gens ne veulent qu'entendre leur propre vérité.
	veʁite	*Most people only want to hear their own truth.*
308	**envier**	**to envy**
	verb	Parfois, j'envie ceux de mon cours qui pratique ce que nous avons étudié.
	ɑ̃vje	*At times I envy all the ones on our course practicing what we studied for.*
309	**capitaine**	**captain**
	nm	Le vieux sergent n'était pas moins ému que le capitaine
	kapitɛn	*The old sergeant was not less moved than the captain.*
310	**affaire**	**business, matter**
	nf	J'ai besoin de davantage d'information quant à cette affaire.
	afɛʁ	*I need more information on this matter.*
311	**bientôt**	**soon**
	adv	Je suis sûre que Tom sera bientôt à la maison.
	bjɛ̃to	*I'm sure Tom will be home soon.*
312	**instant**	**instant, moment**
	adj, nm	Les feux éblouissants nous éblouirent pendant un instant.
	ɛ̃stɑ̃	*The glaring headlights dazzled us for a moment.*
313	**essayer**	**to try**
	verb	Je vais arrêter d'essayer d'être amicale à votre égard.

eseje
I'm going to stop trying to be friendly with you.

314 **tellement**   **so much**
adv
Je croyais tellement à ce projet que j'ai tout misé sur sa réussite.
tɛlmɑ̃   *I believed in this project so much that I staked everything on its success.*

315 **derrière**   **last; behind**
adv, nm, prep
Soudain, je tendis l'oreille au faible son de pas venant de derrière moi.
dɛʁjɛʁ   *Suddenly, I raised my ears to the faint sound of footsteps coming from behind me.*

316 **tomber**   **to fall**
verb
Vint l'automne et les feuilles se mirent à tomber.
tɔ̃be   *Autumn came and the leaves started to fall.*

317 **presque**   **almost**
adv
Ma télé a presque 15 ans, mais l'image est encore bonne.
pʁɛsk   *My TV set is almost 15 years old, but it still has a good picture.*

318 **meilleur**   **best, better,**
nmf, adj, adv
Pour le meilleur ou pour le pire, il n'y a rien d'autre à faire que de laisser le problème entre ses mains.
mɛjœʁ   *For better or worse, there is nothing for it but to leave the matter in his hands.*

319 **numéro**   **number**
nm
J'ai noté son numéro de téléphone sur un morceau de papier.
nymeʁo   *I wrote down his phone number on a scrap of paper.*

320 **journée**   **day**
nf
Merci pour tout ce que vous avez fait pour rendre si mémorable cette journée spéciale pour moi.
ʒuʁne   *Thanks for all you've done to make my special day such a memorable one.*

321 **dollar**   **dollar**
nm
Tu as encore besoin de dix dollars pour acheter cet appareil photo.
dɔlaʁ   *You need another ten dollars to buy that camera.*

322 **confiance**   **confidence, trust**
nf
En ce qui me concerne, je ne lui fais pas du tout confiance.
kɔ̃fjɑ̃s   *As for me, I don't trust him at all.*

323 **garde**   **guard**
nm, nf
Je veux des gardes postés ici et je les veux maintenant !
gaʁd   *I want guards posted here and I want them here now.*

324 **souvenir**   **memory; to remember**
nm, verb
Je ne peux même pas me souvenir de mon propre nom.
suvəniʁ   *I can't even remember my own name.*

325 **dur**   **hard**
adv, nm&f, adj
Je ne peux toujours pas formater mon disque dur.
dyʁ   *I still couldn't format my hard disk.*

326 **bureau**   **office, desk**
nm
Il a pour règle d'arriver au bureau le matin vers huit heures et demie.
byʁo   *As a rule, he arrives at the office about eight-thirty in morning.*

327 **abord**   **manner; approach, access, environs**

nm

Le règlement ne renfermait pas de normes relativement au tracé en plan général des abords routiers ou à leur largeur.

abɔʁ

The regulations did not contain standards for the general horizontal alignment or width of road approaches.

328 important   **important**

nm, adj

J'avais une conscience aiguë de l'importance primordiale de l'enseignement des mathématiques.

ɛ̃pɔʁtɑ̃

I was acutely aware of how very important mathematical education was.

329 ben   **well**

adv

T'es pas enceinte, non ? Bon ben arrête de boire !

bɛ̃

Aren't you pregnant? Well, stop drinking then!

330 peiner   **to toil, labor, struggle**

verb

Vu les considérations qui précèdent, le SPT continue de peiner pour mener à bien sa mission.

pene

In the light of the above considerations, the SPT has continued to struggle to carry out its work.

331 cours   **course**

nfpl, nm[pl]

Un cours de cuisine devrait être obligatoire à l'école.

kuʁ

A cooking course should be mandatory in schools.

332 seigneur   **lord**

nm

Le seigneur démon perdit enfin connaissance et tomba au sol avec un bruit sourd.

sɛɲœʁ

The demon lord finally lost conciousness and fell to the floor with a thud.

333 suffire   **to be sufficient, suffice**

verb

Le moment venu, il sera indispensable d'utiliser les moyens dont nous disposons et qui, en principe, devraient suffire.

syfiʁ

It is essential when the case warrants it to state the means that are available, and which obviously have to be sufficient.

334 route   **road**

nf

J'ai découvert à qui était la voiture qui est sortie de la route.

ʁut

I found out whose car went off the road.

335 cul   **bum, arse, ass**

nm

Mon cœur est français mais mon cul est international !

ky

My heart is French, but my ass is international!

336 minute   **minute**

nf

Elle s'évanouit mais revint à elle après quelques minutes.

minyt

She fainted, but came to after a few minutes.

337 bonsoir   **good evening**

nm

Bonsoir,' dis-je, 'je suis ravi que vous soyez venu si tôt.

bɔ̃swaʁ

Good evening', I said, 'I am pleased that you have come so early.

338 jeu   **game**

nm

À peine le jeu avait-il débuté, que commença la pluie.

ʒø

As soon as the game started, it began to rain.

339 ferme   **shut, closed, locked**

adj

Marie s'est enfermée dans la chambre, avec toutes les fenêtres fermées.

	fɛʁm	*Mary shut herself up in the room, with all the windows closed.*
340	**plaisir**	**pleasure**
	nm	Traduire est un grand plaisir pour moi. Je ne voudrais pas faire autrement.
	pleziʁ	*Translating is a great pleasure for me. I wouldn't do it otherwise.*
341	**heureux**	**happy, lucky, fortunate**
	adj[pl]	Je ne peux pas vous dire à quel point je suis heureux que vous soyez venus nous rendre visite.
	øʁø	*I can't tell you how happy I am that you've come to visit us.*
342	**mot**	**word**
	nm	Est-ce que vous pourriez vous présenter en quelques mots ?
	mo	*Can you introduce yourself in a few words?*
343	**musique**	**music**
	nf	La musique peut se définir comme l'art d'émouvoir par la combinaison des sons.
	myzik	*Music can be defined as the art of producing emotion by the combination of sounds.*
344	**chien**	**dog**
	nm	Vous n'êtes pas autorisés à amener des chiens dans ce bâtiment.
	ʃjɛ̃	*You are not permitted to bring dogs into this building.*
345	**messieurs**	**gentlemen**
	nmpl	Mesdames et Messieurs, nous avons maintenant atterri à l'aéroport international de Tokyo.
	mesjø	*Ladies and Gentlemen, we have now landed at Tokyo International Airport.*
346	**calme**	**composure, calm**
	nm, adj(f)	Nous avons une meilleure chance de survie si nous restons calmes.
	kalm	*We'll have a better chance of surviving if we stay calm.*
347	**parent**	**parent**
	nm&f, adj	Les parents ont la priorité pour choisir le genre d'éducation que leurs enfants recevront.
	paʁɑ̃	*Parents have a prior right to choose the kind of education that shall be given to their children.*
348	**dedans**	**inside, indoors**
	adv, nm[pl], prep	Mais tout cela n'est rien comparé à la raison pour laquelle je me sens si malade au-dedans, car ce n'est pas à mon sujet que j'ai mal.
	dədɑ̃	*But all that is minor as to why I feel so sick inside because it is not about myself that I hurt.*
349	**mariage**	**marriage, wedding**
	nm	Au sein de nombreux groupes ethniques, on offre traditionnellement de l'argent en guise de cadeau de mariage.
	maʁjaʒ	*Many ethnic groups traditionally give money as a wedding gift.*
350	**entrer**	**to enter, go in, come in, get in**
	verb	Elle venait à peine d'entrer dans le bain que le facteur sonnait à la porte avec un colis.
	ɑ̃tʁe	*Hardly had she got in the bath when the postman knocked on the door with a parcel.*

351	**rentrer**	**to go in, come in, come back, return**
	verb	Elle voulait rentrer chez elle, mais elle se perdit.
	ʀɑ̃tʀe	*She wanted to return home, but she got lost.*
352	**lit**	**bed**
	nm	Tom retira les draps du lit et les mit à la machine à laver.
	li	*Tom took the sheets off the bed and put them into the washing machine.*
353	**autant**	**as much, as many**
	adv	Elle n'a pas autant de patience que toi.
	otɑ̃	*She doesn't have as much patience as you do.*
354	**revenir**	**to come back**
	verb	Dans ce film d'horreur, les morts peuvent revenir à la vie.
	ʀəvəniʀ	*In this horror movie, it is possible for the dead to come back to life.*
355	**parfait**	**perfect**
	nm, adj, int	Tu viens de me faire manquer le coup parfait quand tu as crié.
	paʀfɛ	*You just made me miss the perfect shot when you hollered.*
356	**cœur**	**heart**
	nm	Tant que nous vivons, notre cœur ne cesse de battre.
	kœʀ	*As long as we live, our heart never stops beating.*
357	**ceci**	**this**
	pron	J'ai pensé que vous voudriez que je vous rende ceci.
	səsi	*I thought you wanted this back.*
358	**service**	**service**
	nm	Un signe qu'on a affaire à une célébrité est souvent que son nom vaut plus que ses services.
	sɛʀvis	*A sign of a celebrity is often that his name is worth more than his services.*
359	**téléphoner**	**to telephone, phone, call**
	verb	Il lui téléphona dès qu'il rentra à la maison.
	telefɔne	*He phoned her as soon as he came home.*
360	**pauvre**	**poor**
	nmf, adj(f)	Un tel plan économique sacrifiera les pauvres et aidera les riches.
	povʀ	*Such an economic program will help the rich at the expense of the poor.*
361	**mademoiselle**	**Miss**
	nf	Mademoiselle Ethel Bond est une jeune fille victorienne typique.
	madmwazɛl	*Miss Ethel Bond is a more typical Victorian.*
362	**drôle**	**funny, strange**
	adj(f), nm	Qu'une blague soit ressentie comme drôle dépend fortement du milieu culturel.
	dʀol	*Whether a joke is found to be funny depends strongly on the culture.*
363	**parfois**	**sometimes**
	adv	Parfois, les choses sont plus belles quand on les regarde sous un angle différent.
	paʀfwa	*Sometimes, things are more beautiful when you look at them from a different angle.*
364	**retour**	**return**
	nm	La perspective de son retour m'insuffla du courage.
	ʀətuʀ	*The hope of his return encouraged me.*

365	**verre**	**glass**
	nm	L'histoire du verre est extrêmement longue et commence dans l'Orient antique.
	vɛʁ	*The history of glass is extremely long, and begins in the ancient Orient.*
366	**six**	**six**
	det, num	Il faut huit heures pour un vol de Zurich à Boston, mais seulement six pour le retour.
	sis	*It takes eight hours to fly from Zurich to Boston, but only six for the return trip.*
367	**ci**	**this one, here**
	adv, pron	J'ai besoin d'un nouveau balai, celui-ci est foutu.
	si	*I need a new broom. This one's shot.*
368	**impossible**	**impossible**
	nm, adj(f)	Il nous est impossible de visualiser des objets en quatre dimensions.
	ɛ̃pɔsibl	*It's impossible for us to visualise four-dimensional objects.*
369	**payer**	**to pay**
	verb	Comme c'est un homme de parole, il te paiera sûrement ce qu'il te doit.
	peje	*As he is a man of his word, he will surely pay what he owes to you.*
370	**facile**	**easy**
	adj(f)	Ce n'est pas la raison pour laquelle je disais que le travail n'était pas facile.
	fasil	*That's not the reason why I said the job wasn't easy.*
371	**maître**	**master**
	nm	L'esprit devrait être un bon serviteur, mais c'est au cœur d'être le maître.
	mɛtʁ	*The mind should be a good servant, but the heart should be the master.*
372	**mauvais**	**bad, wrong**
	adv, nm, adj[pl]	De ses nombreux enfants, quelques-uns sont bons et d'autres mauvais.
	movɛ	*Some of her children are good, some are bad.*
373	**général**	**general**
	nm, adj	En raison du peu de présents, on doit remettre l'assemblée générale.
	ʒeneʁal	*Due to the lack of attendees, we have to postpone the general assembly.*
374	**doute**	**doubt**
	nm	La vérité est belle, sans doute; mais de même des mensonges.
	dut	*Truth is beautiful, without doubt; but so are lies.*
375	**prison**	**prison, jail**
	nf	Quiconque a volé l'argent devrait être interpellé, être obligé à le rembourser et aller en prison.
	pʁizɔ̃	*Whoever stole the money should be caught, made to pay it back, and go to jail.*
376	**adorer**	**to adore, worship**
	verb	Il ne nous reste qu'à nous agenouiller et à adorer en silence ce grand mystère de la foi.
	adɔʁe	*We can only fall to our knees and silently adore this supreme mystery of faith.*
377	**faute**	**mistake, error, fault**
	nf	Comme elle est prudente, elle fait peu de fautes.
	fot	*She is very careful, so she seldom makes mistakes.*

378	**oublier**	**to forget**
	verb	J'ai oublié d'apporter mon parapluie et ai fini trempé sur le chemin de la maison.
	ublije	*I forgot to bring my umbrella and ended up getting drenched on the way home.*
379	**bras**	**arm**
	nm[pl]	Un colorant a été injecté dans une veine du bras du patient.
	bʁa	*A dye was injected into a vein of the patient's arm.*
380	**exactement**	**exactly**
	adv	Je pense que vous savez exactement de quoi je parle.
	ɛgzaktəmã	*I think you know exactly what I'm talking about.*
381	**fêter**	**to celebrate**
	verb	Plus que jamais, nous formons à présent une seule Europe, unie dans toute notre diversité, et c'est quelque chose que nous devons fêter.
	fete	*More than ever before, we are now one Europe, united in all our diversity, and that is something we should celebrate.*
382	**café**	**coffee, café**
	nm	Combien de tasses de café avez-vous déjà bues aujourd'hui ?
	kafe	*How many cups of coffee did you drink today?*
383	**gentil**	**nice, kind**
	adj	Il a l'air très gentil, mais il est désagréable.
	ʒãti	*He looks very kind, but he is unpleasant.*
384	**valoir**	**to be worth**
	verb	Tom n'a pas été payé autant qu'il pensait valoir.
	valwaʁ	*Tom didn't get paid as much as he thought he was worth.*
385	**lieu**	**place**
	nm	Il y avait beaucoup de restes humains dans ce lieu.
	ljø	*There were a lot of human remains in that place.*
386	**malade**	**mental patient; ill, sick**
	nmf, adj(f)	Je pense que vous êtes trop malade pour aller à l'école.
	malad	*I think you're too sick to go to school.*
387	**changer**	**to change**
	verb	Peu importe ce qui arrive, je ne changerai pas d'idée.
	ʃãʒe	*No matter what happens, I won't change my mind.*
388	**roi**	**king**
	nm	Alfred, Roi d'Angleterre, fut un grand érudit autant qu'un grand dirigeant.
	ʁwa	*Alfred, King of England, was a great scholar as well as a great ruler.*
389	**commencer**	**to begin, start**
	verb	Elle a commencé à lui courir après avant qu'il ne devienne célèbre.
	kɔmãse	*She started pursuing him before he became famous.*
390	**président**	**president**
	nm	Ils ont dit que c'était exactement ce que le président voulait.
	pʁezidã	*They said it was exactly what the president wanted.*
391	**travailler**	**to work**
	verb	Tom et Mary acceptèrent de travailler ensemble sur le projet.
	tʁavaje	*Tom and Mary agreed to work together on the project.*

392	**partout**	**everywhere, all over the place**
	adv	Je ne sais pas ce qu'il s'est passé, mais il y a des plumes partout.
	paʁtu	*I don't know what happened, but there are feathers all over the place.*
393	**cher**	**expensive**
	adj, adv	La guitare est tellement chère que je ne peux pas me la payer.
	ʃɛʁ	*The guitar is so expensive that I can't afford it.*
394	**rendre**	**to render, return, yield, give up**
	verb	Demain je vais te rendre la carte que tu m'as prêtée.
	ʁɑ̃dʁ	*Tomorrow I am going to return the map that you lent me.*
395	**écrire**	**to write**
	verb	Parler est une chose, et écrire en est une autre.
	ekʁiʁ	*To speak is one thing and to write is another.*
396	**équipe**	**team**
	nf	Quelle équipe a le plus de chance de gagner le championnat ?
	ekip	*Which team is the most likely to win the championship?*
397	**sinon**	**otherwise, or else, or**
	conj	Maintenant, sois un bon garçon et sinon, je t'enverrai sur Obéron.
	sinɔ̃	*Now be a good boy or I'm going to send you to Oberon.*
398	**esprit**	**mind, spirit**
	nm	J'ai eu beaucoup de choses à l'esprit, ces derniers temps.
	ɛspʁi	*I've had a lot on my mind lately.*
399	**plan**	**plan**
	adj, nm	Jusqu'à présent, nous n'avons fait aucun plan pour les vacances.
	plɑ̃	*As yet we have not made any plans for the holidays.*
400	**montrer**	**to show**
	verb	Je te montrerai que l'on peut renaître de ses cendres.
	mɔ̃tʁe	*I will show that it's possible to be reborn from one's ashes.*
401	**boire**	**to drink**
	nm, verb	Tom n'avait pas franchement envie de sortir boire un verre avec les autres.
	bwaʁ	*Tom didn't really feel like going out drinking with the guys.*
402	**propre**	**particular; clean, proper**
	nm, adj(f)	Les chambres de cet hôtel ne sont pas aussi propres que les chambres de celui-là.
	pʁɔpʁ	*The rooms in this hotel are not as clean as the rooms in that hotel.*
403	**état**	**state**
	nm	La marijuana thérapeutique est légale dans cet État.
	eta	*Medical marijuana is legal in this state.*
404	**bois**	**wood**
	nm[pl]	Il s'est perdu en se promenant dans les bois.
	bwa	*He got lost while walking in the woods.*
405	**essayer**	**to try**
	verb	Il semble que la victime ait essayé d'écrire le nom du meurtrier de son propre sang.
	eseje	*It appears that the victim tried to write the murderer's name with his own blood.*
406	**dès**	**from, as soon**

		prep	J'ai éclaté de rire dès que je l'ai vu.
		dɛ	*As soon as I saw him, I burst into laughter.*
407	**sembler**		**to seem**
	verb	Au début, tu n'appréciais pas l'idée, mais il semble qu'à présent, tu sois contente.
	sãble	*At the beginning you had disliked the idea, but now you seem to be content.*
408	**dix**		**ten**
	det, num	Lorsque tu avais deux ans, tu pouvais déjà compter jusqu'à dix.
	dis	*When you were two years old, you could already count to ten.*
409	**génial**		**inspired, great, brilliant**
	adj	Aucun autre élève de la classe n'est aussi génial que lui.
	ʒenjal	*No other student in the class is as brilliant as he is.*
410	**sécurité**		**security, safety, health**
	nf	Le lac était entouré d'une clôture, de toute évidence pour des raisons de sécurité.
	sekyʁite	*The lake was ringed by a fence, apparently for health and safety reasons.*
411	**tôt**		**early**
	adj(i), adv	Je veux aller dormir tôt parce qu'il me faut me lever tôt, demain.
	to	*I want to go to sleep soon because I need to get up early tomorrow.*
412	**rêver**		**to dream**
	verb	Je tins le manteau de fourrure près de ma joue et je rêvai au jour où j'aurais les moyens de l'acheter.
	ʁeve	*I held the fur coat close to my cheek and dreamt of the day I would be able to afford it.*
413	**armer**		**to arm**
	verb	Son échec complet à la dernière conférence pour la paix, lui a appris à s'armer jusqu'aux dents avec de nouvelles techniques et tactiques.
	aʁme	*His utter failure at the last peace conference has taught him to arm himself to the teeth with new tricks and tactics.*
414	**avis**		**opinion, mind**
	nm[pl]	Du reste, je suis d'avis que Carthage doit être détruite.
	avi	*Moreover, I am of the opinion that Carthage must be destroyed.*
415	**surtout**		**especially, above all**
	adv, nm	C'est dur de faire des prédictions, surtout concernant le futur !
	syʁtu	*It's tough to make predictions, especially about the future!*
416	**difficile**		**difficult**
	adj(f)	Il est difficile de comprendre pourquoi vous voulez vous en aller.
	difisil	*It is difficult to understand why you want to go.*
417	**dormir**		**to sleep**
	verb	Je sais que je devrais être en train de dormir, à l'heure qu'il est.
	dɔʁmiʁ	*I know that I should be sleeping now.*
418	**ensuite**		**next** , AFTER, AFTERWARDS, THEN, IN THE NEXT PLACE
	adv	S'il vous plait, dites nous ce qu'il faut faire ensuite.
	ãsɥit	*Please tell us what to do next.*
419	**pire**		**worse, worst**

	adj(f), nm	Il n'y a rien de pire que de faire les choses à demi !
	piʁ	*There's nothing worse than doing things by halves!!*
420	**simple**	**simple, single**
	adj(f)	De nombreuses erreurs auraient pu être évitées par de simples expérimentations. "DE" ⇒ "SOME"?
	sɛ̃pl	*Many mistakes could have been avoided through simple experiments.*
421	**paix**	**peace**
	nf[pl]	Toute personne qui cherche à contrôler sa destinée ne trouvera jamais la paix.
	pɛ	*He who seeks to control fate shall never find peace.*
422	**sujet**	**subject, topic**
	nm	Le contenu de son discours était sans rapport avec le sujet.
	syʒɛ	*The content of his speech is not relevant to the subject.*
423	**retard**	**delay, late**
	nm	Je vous dois des excuses pour mon retard.
	ʁətaʁ	*I must offer you an apology for coming late.*
424	**livre**	**book; pound**
	nm, nf	Combien de livres puis-je prendre en une seule fois ?
	livʁ	*How many books can I take out at one time?*
425	**apprendre**	**to learn**
	verb	Tom est allé dans une école pour apprendre l'accordage de piano.
	apʁɑ̃dʁ	*Tom went to school to learn how to tune pianos.*
426	**sale**	**dirty**
	adj(f)	Tom a laissé de la vaisselle sale dans l'évier.
	sal	*Tom left some dirty dishes in the sink.*
427	**souvent**	**often**
	adv	De petites choses ont souvent de grandes conséquences.
	suvɑ̃	*Little things often have big consequences.*
428	**sauf**	**except**
	adj, prep	Les mathématiciens sont des poètes, sauf qu'ils doivent démontrer ce que leur fantaisie crée.
	sof	*Mathematicians are poets, except that they have to prove what their fantasy creates.*
429	**choix**	**choice**
	nm[pl]	Nous n'avons d'autre choix que de continuer.
	ʃwa	*We have no choice but to carry on.*
430	**sûrement**	**surely**
	adv	Lentement mais sûrement, nous entrevoyons le succès.
	syʁmɑ̃	*Slowly but surely, we are seeing success.*
431	**or**	**gold; hence, thus**
	conj, nm	Qu'est-ce qui est le plus lourd, le plomb ou l'or ?
	ɔʁ	*Which is heavier, lead or gold?*
432	**visage**	**face**
	nm	En regardant simplement ton visage, je sais que tu apportes de bonnes nouvelles.
	vizaʒ	*Just by looking at your face, I know that you have good news.*

433	**ordre**	**order**
	nm	Il n'a pas d'autre choix que d'accepter les ordres de son patron.
	ɔʁdʁ	*He cannot help accepting his boss's order.*
434	**noir**	**black (wo)man, black**
	nmf adj	Tom a deux chats. L'un est blanc et l'autre est noir.
	nwaʁ	*Tom has two cats. One is white and the other is black.*
435	**dîner**	**dinner; to dine**
	nm, verb	Je me demande quoi faire à manger pour dîner.
	dine	*I'm wondering what to cook for dinner.*
436	**âge**	**age**
	nm	Beaucoup de jeunes de ton âge travaillent déjà et ont fondé une famille.
	aʒ	*A lot of young people your age are already working and have a family.*
437	**chemin**	**path, way**
	nm	Certaines personnes superstitieuses en Amérique, croient que si un chat noir croise votre chemin, vous aurez de la malchance.
	ʃəmɛ̃	*Some superstitious people in America believe that if a black cat crosses your path, you'll have bad luck.*
438	**bouillir**	**to boil**
	verb	Ils sont en train de faire bouillir l'eau pour le thé.
	bujiʁ	*They are boiling water for tea.*
439	**face**	**front, side, face**
	nf	Je voulais m'entretenir avec eux en face à face.
	fas	*I wanted to talk to them face to face.*
440	**rue**	**street**
	nf	Si vous vous perdez en rue, demandez à un agent de police !
	ʁy	*If you get lost in the street, ask a policeman.*
441	**inquiet**	**worried, anxious**
	adj	J'étais d'autant plus inquiet de son silence.
	ɛ̃kjɛ	*I was all the more worried for her silence.*
442	**photo**	**photo**
	nf	Quand la photo que je voulais faire agrandir sera-t-elle prête ?
	fɔto	*When will that picture I wanted enlarged be ready?*
443	**sérieux**	**seriousness, serious**
	nm, adj[pl]	Je n'ai pas pris conscience que tu étais sérieux.
	seʁjø	*I didn't realize you were serious.*
444	**ciel**	**sky**
	nm	Nous avons vu la première étoile briller dans le ciel.
	sjɛl	*We saw the first star shining in the sky.*
445	**honneur**	**honor**
	nm	Je sentais que mon honneur en tant qu'homme était en jeu.
	ɔnœʁ	*I felt that my honor was at stake.*
446	**force**	**force**
	adv, nf	Ce fut le triomphe de la civilisation sur la force.
	fɔʁs	*It was the triumph of civilization over force.*
447	**garder**	**to keep**

	.rb	Pourquoi avoir gardé un si bon vin en réserve jusque-là ?
	gaʁde	*Why have you kept such an excellent wine back till now?*
448	**tirer**	**to pull, fire**
	verb	Je compte jusqu'à trois, et ensuite, je tire.
	tiʁe	*I will count to three, and then I will fire!*
449	**million**	**million**
	nm	Le dictionnaire contient approximativement 2 millions de mots.
	miljɔ̃	*There are approximately 2 million words in the dictionary.*
450	**grave**	**serious, grave**
	adv, adj(f), nm	La croissance de la délinquance juvénile est un problème grave.
	gʁav	*The increase in juvenile delinquency is a serious problem.*
451	**voix**	**voice**
	nf[pl]	"Oui !", murmura-t-il dans mon oreille de sa voix ravissante.
	vwa	*"Yes!", he whispered in my ear with his charming voice.*
452	**courant**	**current**
	adj, nm	J'ai transféré de l'argent sur mon compte courant.
	kuʁɑ̃	*I transferred money to my current account.*
453	**propos**	**remark**
	nm[pl]	Ce genre de propos est tout simplement déplacé.
	pʁɔpo	*That kind of a remark is simply inappropriate here.*
454	**bateau**	**boat, ship**
	nm	Ça ressemble à un bateau de plaisance à vapeur.
	bato	*It looks like there's a pleasure boat.*
455	**con**	**stupid**
	adj, nmf	On doit taper un code à la con à chaque fois que vous vous connectez
	kɔ̃	*You have to enter a stupid code every time you're going to play*
456	**gauche**	**left**
	nf, adj(f)	La France semble pencher à gauche, la Grande-Bretagne vers la droite.
	goʃ	*France seems to be swinging left - Britain to the right.*
457	**content**	**glad, pleased, happy**
	adj	Je veux juste dire que je suis contente que vous soyez ici.
	kɔ̃tɑ̃	*I just want to say I'm glad you're here.*
458	**prix**	**price; prize**
	nm[pl]	J'étais loin d'imaginer remporter le premier prix.
	pʁi	*I never dreamed that I would win first prize.*
459	**rouge**	**red**
	nm, adj(f)	Elle était vêtue d'une chemise rouge et d'une jupe noire.
	ʁuʒ	*She wore a red shirt and a black skirt.*
460	**faim**	**hungry**
	nf	J'ai très faim. À quelle heure la nourriture sera-t-elle prête ?
	fɛ̃	*I'm very hungry. What time will the food be ready?*
461	**avion**	**plane**
	nm	Comme notre avion était parti de Narita en retard de deux heures, on a manqué notre correspondance à Hong Kong.

	avjɔ̃	*Our plane took off from Narita two hours late, so we missed our flight in Hong Kong.*
462	**devenir**	**to become**
	nm, verb	Même si leurs langues et leurs coutumes sont différentes, tous les gens peuvent devenir amis.
	dəvəniʁ	*All people can become friends, even if their languages and customs are different.*
463	**prochain**	**next; fellow man**
	adj, nm	Nous rendrons visite à notre instituteur la semaine prochaine.
	pʁɔʃɛ̃	*We will visit our teacher next week.*
464	**acheter**	**to buy**
	verb	J'ai trouvé un endroit où l'on peut acheter des fruits bon marché.
	aʃte	*I found out where to buy fruit cheaply.*
465	**voyage**	**trip, journey**
	nm	Au milieu de notre voyage, nous nous aperçûmes que nous n'avions pas emporté assez d'argent.
	vwajaʒ	*Midway through our trip we realized that we hadn't brought enough money.*
466	**sorte**	**sort, kind**
	nf	Les fleurs de cette sorte ne poussent pas dans mon jardin.
	sɔʁt	*This kind of flower doesn't grow in my garden.*
467	**long**	**long, lengthy, length**
	adv, adj, nm	Ce ne sera plus long avant de pouvoir voyager vers Mars.
	lɔ̃	*It won't be long before we can travel to Mars.*
468	**espèce**	**species**
	nf	Ce n'est pas l'espèce la plus forte, qui survit, ni la plus intelligente, mais la plus réactive aux changements.
	ɛspɛs	*It is not the strongest of the species that survive, not the most intelligent, but the one most responsive to change.*
469	**idiot**	**idiot, fool, stupid**
	nmf, adj	Vous devez penser que je suis une parfaite idiote.
	idjo	*You must think I'm a complete idiot.*
470	**gueule**	**mouth, trap**
	nf	Ne réfléchis-tu jamais avant d'ouvrir ta grande gueule ?
	gœl	*Do you ever think before you open your big mouth?*
471	**début**	**beginning**
	nm	J'ai trouvé ce livre intéressant du début à la fin.
	deby	*I found this book interesting from beginning to end.*
472	**bouger**	**to move, shift, budge**
	verb	La cloche retentit, et le train commença à bouger.
	buʒe	*The bell rang, and the train began to move.*
473	**continu**	**continuous**
	adj	La société a enregistré une baisse continue des ventes.
	kɔ̃tiny	*The company recorded a continuous drop in sales*
474	**hôpital**	**hospital**

	nm	Tom a refusé que j'appelle une ambulance alors je l'ai amené à l'hôpital par moi-même.
	ɔpital	*Tom wouldn't let me call an ambulance so I drove him to the hospital myself.*
475	**grâce**	**thanks, grace, favor**
	nf	Grâce à Internet, le monde commence à se détourner de la centralisation des ressources et du pouvoir qui a caractérisé la révolution industrielle.
	gʁas	*Thanks to the Internet, the world is beginning to turn away from the centralization of resources and power that characterized the Industrial Revolution.*
476	**message**	**message**
	nm	Je ferai en sorte que Tom reçoive votre message.
	mesaʒ	*I'll make sure Tom gets your message.*
477	**certain**	**certain, sure**
	adj, det, nm, pron	Le voleur est certain de se faire prendre, au bout du compte.
	sɛʁtɛ̃	*The thief is certain to be caught eventually.*
478	**patron**	**boss**
	nm	La recommandation de la part de mon patron a fait toute la différence.
	patʁɔ̃	*The recommendation from my boss made all the difference.*
479	**recevoir**	**to receive**
	verb	Vous devriez les recevoir à la fin de la semaine.
	ʁəsəvwaʁ	*You should receive them by the end of the week.*
480	**ouvrir**	**to open**
	verb	Avez-vous été en mesure de vous ouvrir et de parler ?
	uvʁiʁ	*Were you able to open up and talk?*
481	**promettre**	**to promise**
	verb	Je ne peux rien promettre, mais je vais faire de mon mieux.
	pʁɔmɛtʁ	*I can't promise anything, but I'll do my best.*
482	**oncle**	**uncle**
	nm	Mon oncle était impliqué dans un accident de la circulation.
	ɔ̃kl	*My uncle was involved in the traffic accident.*
483	**euh**	**er, um, uh**
	int	"Tu es, euh..., Mo..." "Je te trompe déjà de la première lettre !"
	ø	*"Let's see, you're ... er, um ... M-" "You're wrong from the first letter!!"*
484	**bienvenue**	**welcome**
	nf, adj	Bienvenue sur Wikipédia, le projet d'encyclopédie libre que vous pouvez améliorer.
	bjɛ̃vəny	*Welcome to Wikipedia, the free encyclopedia that anyone can edit.*
485	**occuper**	**to occupy**
	verb	La famille a fait un puzzle pour occuper les enfants.
	ɔkype	*The family did a puzzle to occupy the children.*
486	**camp**	**camp**
	nm	La principale cause de mortalité dans les camps de réfugiés est la pénurie de nourriture.
	kɑ̃	*The principal cause of death in refugee camps is the lack of nourishment.*

487 manquer
verb
mɑ̃ke

to miss
Cette conférence est très importante. Ne la manquez pas.
This conference is very important. Don't miss it.

488 soleil
nm
sɔlɛj

sun
La température à la surface du Soleil est estimée à environ 6000 °C.
The surface temperature of the sun is assumed to be about 6000°C.

489 cheveu
nm
ʃəvø

hair
Tout d'abord, ils passent à un cheveu de perdre leur siège.
First, they come within a hair of losing their seat.

490 arme
adj

aʁm

armed
Et surtout, ils votent contre un meilleur appui financier aux valeureux membres de nos forces armées.
Above all, they are voting against improved financial support for the brave men and women of our armed forces.

491 salle
nf
sal

room
Lorsque vous quittez la salle de réunion, éteignez la lumière s'il vous plait.
When you leave the meeting room, please, switch off the light.

492 bizarre
adj(f)
bizaʁ

strange, odd
Cela ne vous vient-il pas à l'esprit que c'est bizarre ?
Doesn't that strike you as odd?

493 gagner
verb
gaɲe

to win, earn
Outre le fait de gagner de l'argent, je n'ai aucun intérêt dans l'immobilier.
Apart from earning money, I have no interest in real estate.

494 fondre
verb

fɔ̃dʁ

to melt, merge
Je me demande si le niveau de la mer montera vraiment quand la glace au pôle Nord fondra.
I wonder if the sea level really will rise when the ice at the North Pole melts.

495 sauver
verb

sove

to rescue, save
Aucun pécheur n'est jamais sauvé après les vingt premières minutes d'un sermon.
No sinner is ever saved after the first twenty minutes of a sermon.

496 pièce
nf
pjɛs

piece, part, component; room
Mon chien me suit, chaque fois que je quitte la pièce.
My dog follows me whenever I leave the room.

497 erreur
nf
eʁœʁ

mistake, error
Nous sommes conscients de l'erreur et travaillons à une solution.
We are aware of the error and are working on a solution.

498 ailleurs
adv
ajœʁ

elsewhere, somewhere else
Elle s'assit près de lui en souhaitant qu'elle fut ailleurs.
She sat next to him wishing she were somewhere else.

499 rapport
nm
ʁapɔʁ

relationship, report
Selon le rapport balistique, cette arme à feu ne peut être l'arme du crime
According to the ballistics report, this gun can't be the murder weapon.

500 froid
nm, adj

cold
Nous trouvâmes le randonneur perdu, transi de froid.

ʁwa   *We found the lost hiker numb with cold.*

501   scène   **scene**

nf   Un détective est arrivé sur la scène du crime.

sɛn   *A detective arrived upon the scene of the crime.*

502   secret   **secret**

nm, adj   Je ne peux pas te le dire. C'est un secret et si je te le disais, ce ne serait plus un secret.

səkʁɛ   *I can't tell you. It's a secret and if I told you, it wouldn't be a secret anymore.*

503   sac   **bag, sack**

nm   L'Union Européenne envisage d'interdire les sacs plastiques.

sak   *The European Union is considering banning plastic bags.*

504   second   **second**

adj, det, nm   La course n'était pas égale, car le gagnant avait une avance au départ de dix secondes.

səgɔ̃   *The race wasn't fair because the winner had a ten-second head start.*

505   cru   **vintage, raw, crude**

adj   En général les occidentaux ne mangent pas de poisson cru.

kʁy   *Generally speaking, Westerners don't eat fish raw.*

506   allô   **hello**

conj   Allô ! Avec qui je parle ? Tu ne me reconnais pas ? C'est moi, Aldo !

alo   *Hello! With whom am I speaking? You don't recognize me? It's me, Aldo!*

507   battre   **to beat, hit**

verb   Pour ce qui est de l'anglais, personne ne peut me battre.

batʁ   *As far as English is concerned, nobody can beat me.*

508   hôtel   **hotel**

nm   S'il te plaît, viens me chercher en voiture devant l'hôtel.

otɛl   *Please pick me up by car in front of the hotel.*

509   soirée   **evening**

nf   Nous avons passé une soirée sympa au restaurant.

swaʁe   *We spent a nice evening at the restaurant.*

510   sœur   **sister**

nf   Elles l'ont pris en train de faire une farce à sa sœur.

sœʁ   *They caught him playing a trick on his sister.*

511   pied   **foot**

nm   Au pied de la colline se trouve un très joli lac.

pje   *At the foot of the hill is a beautiful lake.*

512   carte   **card**

nf   J'ai interrompu toutes mes cartes de crédit sauf une.

kaʁt   *I cut up all but one of my credit cards*

513   joli   **pretty, attractive**

adj   Un homme qui peut conduire prudemment en embrassant une jolie dame ne consacre tout simplement pas au baiser l'attention qu'il mérite.

ʒɔli   *Any man who can drive safely while kissing a pretty lady is simply not giving the kiss the attention it deserves.*

514	**groupe**	**group**
	nm	Les deux groupes se répartissent de manière égale dans la société.
	ɡʁup	*The two groups share equally in the company.*
515	**monter**	**to go up, rise, assemble**
	verb	Le prix de l'essence ne cesse de monter.
	mɔ̃te	*The cost of petrol keeps on going up.*
516	**agent**	**agent**
	nm, nf	Dan a échoué en tant qu'en agent de Voyage.
	aʒɑ̃	*Dan failed as a travel agent.*
517	**effet**	**effect**
	nm	Pourquoi donc ces comprimés doivent-ils toujours avoir des effets secondaires ?
	efɛ	*Why do these pills always have to have side effects?*
518	**libre**	**free**
	adj(f)	Qu'appréciez-vous faire pendant votre temps libre ?
	libʁ	*What do you enjoy doing in your free time?*
519	**foutre**	**to f*ck, shove off, piss off**
	verb, nm	Pourquoi ne vas-tu pas simplement te faire foutre ?
	futʁ	*Why don't you just piss off?*
520	**bordel**	**brothel, mess, chaos**
	nm	Elle m'a aidé à nettoyer le bordel.
	bɔʁdɛl	*She helped me clean up the mess*
521	**neuf**	**nine; new**
	det, adj, ni	Tu ferais mieux d'en acheter un neuf plutôt que d'essayer de le réparer.
	nœf	*You will be better off buying a new one than trying to fix it.*
522	**faux**	**false; scythe**
	adv, adj[pl], nm[pl], nf[pl]	Les faux amis sont des paires de mots dans deux langues qui sont similaires en orthographe ou en prononciation mais dont les significations sont différentes.
	fo	*False friends are pairs of words in two languages that are similar in spelling or pronunciation, but differ in meaning.*
523	**situation**	**situation**
	nf	Nous devons être capables de différencier entre les objets et les situations.
	sitɥasjɔ̃	*We must be able to differentiate between objects and situations.*
524	**taire**	**to keep quiet, hold ones tongue**
	verb	Celui qui a rendu un service doit se taire ; c'est à celui qui l'a reçu de parler.
	tɛʁ	*The one who has rendered a service should hold his tongue; it is up to the one who has received it to speak.*
525	**lumière**	**light**
	nf	Tu ne devrais pas lire par une lumière aussi faible.
	lymjɛʁ	*You shouldn't read in such poor light.*
526	**debout**	**standing**
	adv	Es-tu capable de sauter par dessus une chaise à partir de la station debout ?
	dəbu	*Can you jump over a chair from a standing position?*
527	**Noël**	**Christmas**

nm

Je soulevai ma fille de telle sorte qu'elle puisse placer l'étoile au haut de l'arbre de Noël.

nɔɛl

I lifted my daughter up so she could put the star on top of the Christmas tree.

528 cheval — **horse**

nm

Le cheval est la plus noble conquête que l'homme ait jamais faite.

ʃəval

The horse is the noblest conquest ever made by man.

529 intérieur — **interior, inside**

nm adj

Les grands polatouches nidifient à l'intérieur des arbres.

ɛ̃teʁjœʁ

Northern flying squirrels nest inside trees.

530 écouter — **to listen to**

verb

J'aime écouter de la musique italienne toutes les nuits.

ekute

I like to listen to Italian music every night.

531 loi — **law**

nf

Le clergé tout entier est contre la nouvelle loi.

lwa

All the clergy are against the new law.

532 incroyable — **incredible, amazing, unbelievable**

adj(f)

C'est incroyable qu'il a gagné le championnat à l'âge de 19 ans.

ɛ̃kʁwajabl

It's amazing that he won the championship at the age of nineteen.

533 lettre — **letter**

nf

Il déchira sa lettre en petits morceaux et les jeta par la fenêtre.

lɛtʁ

He tore up his letter into small bits and threw them out the window.

534 présent — **present**

nm, adj

Tous les membres n'étaient pas présents à la réunion d'hier.

pʁezɑ̃

All the members were not present at the meeting yesterday.

535 absolument — **absolutely**

adv

Qu'est cette chose ? Je n'en ai absolument aucune idée.

apsɔlymɑ̃

What's that thing? I have absolutely no idea.

536 dame — **lady**

int, nf

Une vieille dame nous a guidé à travers le château.

dam

An old lady guided us through the castle.

537 professeur — **professor, teacher**

nm, nf

Son professeur lui suggéra de lire de plus en plus de livres.

pʁɔfesœʁ

Her teacher advised her to read more and more novels.

538 fric — **cash, money, dough**

nm

Y a-t-il assez de fric pour acheter une bouteille de vin ?

fʁik

Is there enough money to get a bottle of wine?

539 retrouver — **to find, recall**

verb

J'ai eu du mal à retrouver le chemin du retour jusqu'à mon hôtel hier soir.

ʁətʁuve

I had trouble finding my way back to my hotel last night.

540 coin — **corner**

nm

Le magasin au coin vend des fruits à très bon prix.

kwɛ̃

The shop on the corner sells fruit at a very good price.

541 table — **table**

nf

Je veux quelques belles fleurs à mettre sur la table.

	tabl	*I want some beautiful flowers to put on the table.*
542	**colonel**	**colonel**
	nm	Le colonel dit que la situation est sous contrôle.
	kɔlɔnɛl	*The Colonel said the situation is under control.*
543	**âme**	**soul**
	nf	Une maison sans amour n'est pas plus une maison qu'un corps sans âme n'est un homme.
	am	*A home without love is not a home any more than a body without a soul is a man.*
544	**dos**	**back**
	nm[pl]	Pourriez-vous me mettre un peu de crème solaire dans le dos?
	do	*Could you put a little sunscreen on my back?*
545	**magnifique**	**magnificent**
	adj(f)	Elle aimait se vanter des magnifiques lustres dans sa maison.
	maɲifik	*She liked to boast about the magnificent chandeliers in her house.*
546	**rencontrer**	**to meet**
	verb	Si tu rencontres un ours, fais semblant d'être mort.
	ʁɑ̃kɔ̃tʁe	*If you should meet a bear, pretend to be dead.*
547	**réussir**	**to succeed**
	verb	Qu'il réussisse ou qu'il échoue, il doit faire de son mieux.
	ʁeysiʁ	*Whether he succeeds or fails, he has to do his best.*
548	**rappeler**	**to recall, call back, remember**
	verb	J'avais beau me triturer les méninges, je ne pouvais me rappeler son nom.
	ʁaple	*No matter how I racked my brain, I couldn't remember that name.*
549	**tranquille**	**quiet**
	adj(f)	Tu peux rester ici si tu veux, aussi longtemps que tu restes tranquille
	tʁɑ̃kil	*You may stay here if you like, as long as you keep quiet.*
550	**chaud**	**warm, hot**
	adv, nm, adj	Un verre d'eau froide est très rafraîchissant lorsqu'il fait chaud.
	ʃo	*A glass of cold water is very refreshing in hot weather.*
551	**agir**	**to act**
	verb	Maintenant je sais ce que me réserve l'avenir et je peux agir en conséquence.
	aʒiʁ	*Now I know what's in store for me and can act accordingly.*
552	**doucement**	**gently, softly**
	adv	La soutane du prêtre gonflait doucement au vent.
	dusmɑ̃	*The priest's cassock billowed gently in the wind.*
553	**pareil**	**similar, likewise; peer, equal; the same**
	adj, nm	Vous pouvez maintenant faire pareil avec vos photos
	paʁɛj	*Now you can do the same with your photos.*
554	**accident**	**accident**
	nm	Ils se sont précipités sur le lieu de l'accident.
	aksidɑ̃	*They hurried to the scene of the accident.*
555	**appel**	**call, phone call**
	nm	Les appels téléphoniques peuvent décharger la batterie.
	apɛl	*Phone calls may discharge the battery.*

556	**anniversaire**	**anniversary, birthday**
	nm, adj(f)	L'anniversaire de Mary est bientôt. Je vais lui préparer un gâteau.
	anivɛʀsɛʀ	*Mary's birthday will be soon. I am going to bake a cake for her.*
557	**blanc**	**white**
	adj, nm	Le mois dernier, il a fait peindre sa maison en blanc.
	blã	*Last month he had his house painted white.*
558	**risque**	**risk**
	nm	Être un mâle est de loin le plus grand facteur de risque de violence.
	ʀisk	*Maleness is by far the biggest risk factor for violence.*
559	**moyen**	**means, way; medium**
	adj, nm	Ils trouveraient moyen de faire ce qu'ils veulent, de toutes manières.
	mwajɛ̃	*They'd find a way to do whatever they want to do anyway.*
560	**terminer**	**to finish, end,**
	verb	Nous ne nous attendions pas à ce qu'il termine le travail en si peu de temps.
	tɛʀmine	*We did not expect him to finish the task in so short a time.*
561	**complètement**	**completely, fully**
	adv	A cause d'une forte pluie, mes projets sont complètement tombés à l'eau.
	kɔ̃plɛtmã	*Due to the rain, my plans were completely mixed up.*
562	**clair**	**clear**
	adv, adj	C'est clair qu'il y a un désaccord assez fort entre les deux.
	klɛʀ	*It's clear that there's a rather strong disagreement between the two.*
563	**meurtre**	**murder**
	nm	Tom n'a pas laisse de note de suicide, alors la police suspecte un meurtre.
	mœʀtʀ	*Tom didn't leave a suicide note, so the police suspect murder.*
564	**toucher**	**to touch**
	nm, verb	Si vous touchez cet interrupteur, les rideaux s'ouvriront automatiquement.
	tuʃe	*If you touch this switch, it will open the curtains automatically.*
565	**dejeuner**	**lunch, to eat lunch**
	nm, verb	Il y avait quelques hommes en train de déjeuner sous les arbres devant la bibliothèque.
	dəʒœne	*There were some men eating their lunches under the trees in front of the library.*
566	**envoyer**	**to send**
	verb	Faites bien attention à mettre le bon objet avant de m'envoyer votre e-mail, autrement il finira dans le dossier "pourriel".
	ãvwaje	*Take care to indicate the right object before sending me your email, otherwise it will end up in the spam folder.*
567	**lire**	**to read; italian lira**
	nf, verb	Mon père avait l'habitude de me lire des livres au moment du coucher.
	liʀ	*My father used to read books to me at bedtime.*
568	**avance**	**advance**
	nf	Il est impossible de leur accorder un prêt ou une avance sur salaire.
	avãs	*They cannot be granted a loan or an advance on their salary.*
569	**detester**	**to hate, detest**
	verb	Je suis parti avec ma vieille voiture, bien que je déteste ça.

dətɛste *I parted with my old car, though I hated to do so.*

570 forme **form**

nf Il y a des gens dans le monde si affamés que Dieu ne peut pas leur apparaître, sauf sous forme de pain.

fɔʀm *There are people in the world so hungry, that God cannot appear to them except in the form of bread.*

571 bord **edge, side**

nm Étrangement, je me fatiguai rapidement et m'assis sur le bord d'un rocher.

bɔʀ *As was unusual for me, I got tired quickly and I sat down on the edge of a rock.*

572 decider **to decide**

verb Ainsi nous devions decider de partir ou de revenir au temple.

dəside *So we had to decide to leave or to go back to the temple.*

573 mer **sea**

nf En été, je vais à la mer et en hiver à la montagne.

mɛʀ *In summer I go to the sea, in winter to the mountains.*

574 medecin **physician, doctor**

nm Est-ce correct pour un médecin de décider quand quelqu'un doit mourir ?

mədsɛ̃ *Is it right for a doctor to decide when someone should die?*

575 midi **noon**

nm Aujourd'hui à midi nous mangerons des cerises d'Italie.

midi *Today at noon we'll eat cherries from Italy.*

576 porter **to wear, carry**

nm, verb Porter des vêtements de seconde main est désormais répandu chez les jeunes.

pɔʀte *Wearing second-hand clothes is now popular among young people.*

577 ignorer **to ignore**

verb Si le téléphone sonne de nouveau, j'ai l'intention de l'ignorer.

iɲɔʀe *If the phone rings again, I plan to ignore it.*

578 silence **silence**

nm Le silence est un argument qu'on peut difficilement réfuter.

silɑ̃s *Silence is an argument which is difficult to counter.*

579 diable **devil**

int, nm Le diable que tu connais vaut mieux que le diable que tu ne connais pas.

djabl *Better the devil you know than the devil you don't.*

580 cadeau **present, gift**

nm Je cherche un cadeau pour ma mère. Avez-vous quelque chose à l'esprit ?

kado *I'm looking for a present for my mother. Do you have anything in mind?*

581 supposer **to suppose, assume**

verb Je ne me souviens pas exactement mais je suppose que c'était vendredi dernier.

sypoze *I don't remember exactly, but I suppose it was Friday last week.*

582 flic **cop**

nm, nf Les flics recherchent la planque de la bande.

flik *The cops are looking for the gang's hideout.*

583 avocat **lawyer**

	nm	Il n'y a pas si longtemps, nous entendîmes un père, dire en présence de sa famille étendue : « Je veux qu'aucun de mes garçons ne soit avocat. »
	avɔka	*Not long ago we heard a father say in the presence of his large family, "I don't want any of my boys to be lawyers."*
584	**jurer**	**to swear**
	verb	Lorsqu'ils se sont mariés, ils ont tous deux juré de ne plus jamais mentir.
	ʒyʁe	*When they got married, they both swore to never lie.*
585	**anglais**	**English**
	nm, adj[pl]	Vous pouvez écouter l'anglais sur la chaîne 1 et le japonais sur la chaîne 7.
	ãglɛ	*You can hear English on Channel 1, and Japanese on Channel 7.*
586	**sept**	**seven**
	det, num	Pourriez-vous nous appeler à sept heures pour nous réveiller ?
	sɛt	*Could you call us at seven to wake us?*
587	**moitié**	**half**
	nf	Près de la moitié des hommes en Grande-Bretagne offrent régulièrement du chocolat à leur partenaire comme cadeau, notamment pour leur anniversaire.
	mwatje	*Almost half the men in Great Britain regularly give chocolate to their partner, especially for their birthday.*
588	**surprendre**	**to surprise**
	verb	Au risque de vous surprendre, il m'arrive de travailler.
	syʁpʁãdʁ	*At the risk of surprising you, I happen to work*
589	**chacun**	**each**
	pron	Chacun de ses enfants dispose de sa propre chambre.
	ʃakœ̃	*Each of his children has his own room.*
590	**exact**	**exact, correct**
	adj	J'aimerais savoir le taux exact du change pour le yen.
	ɛgzakt	*I'd like to know the exact exchange rate for yen.*
591	**commander**	**to order, command**
	verb	C'est moins cher si vous les commandez à la douzaine.
	kɔmãde	*It's cheaper if you order these by the dozen.*
592	**télé**	**TV**
	nf	Pour commencer, vous devez prouvez votre connaissance des séries télé.
	tele	*First of all, you have to prove your TV series knowledge*
593	**autour**	**around**
	adv, nm	J'ai flirté avec l'idée de tout bazarder et de faire un long voyage tranquille autour du monde.
	otuʁ	*I've been toying with the idea of selling everything and taking a long, slow trip around the world.*
594	**disparaître**	**to disappear, vanish**
	verb	De nombreuses formes de vie sont en train de disparaître.
	dispaʁɛtʁ	*Many forms of life are disappearing.*
595	**ligne**	**line**
	nf	N'importe quel politicien qui ne suit pas les grandes lignes de son parti sera reconnu comme un traître.

liɲ | Any politician who does not toe the main party line would be branded a renegade.

596 expliquer — **to explain**
verb
Je peux te l'expliquer mais je ne peux pas le comprendre à ta place !
ɛksplike
I can explain it to you, but I can't understand it for you!

597 arrivée — **arrival**
nf
L'arrivée du nouveau chien a comblé un vide dans ma vie.
aʁive
The new dog's arrival has filled a gap in my life.

598 simplement — **simply, just**
adv
La candidature requiert simplement de remplir un formulaire.
sɛ̃pləmɑ̃
The application just requires filling in a form.

599 mission — **mission**
nf
Je ne veux pas interrompre la mission à l'heure actuelle.
misjɔ̃
I don't want to abort the mission now.

600 balle — **ball, bullet**
nf
Mon chien adore jouer avec la balle jaune.
bal
My dog loves to play with the yellow ball.

601 quitter — **to leave**
verb
À quand remonte la dernière fois que vous avez quitté le travail plus tôt?
kite
When was the last time you left work early?

602 selon — **according to**
prep
Leur maison est organisée selon les préceptes du Feng Shui.
səlɔ̃
Their house is organized according to Feng Shui.

603 classe — **class**
nf
Découvrez tous les services et avantages de la première classe.
klas
Discover all the services and advantages of first class.

604 pari — **bet, wager**
nm
Phileas Fogg avait gagné son pari. Il avait accompli en quatre-vingts jours ce voyage autour du monde !
paʁi
Phileas Fogg had won his wager. He had made his journey around the world in eighty days!

605 peuple — **people**
nm
Les hommes qui se sont occupés du bonheur des peuples ont rendu leurs proches bien malheureux.
pœpl
Those who have given themselves the most concern about the happiness of people have made their friends very miserable.

606 habitude — **habit**
nf
Tu devrais prendre l'habitude d'utiliser ton dictionnaire.
abityd
You should try to form the habit of using your dictionaries.

607 voie — **road, lane, route, track, way**
nf
Je pense que tu es sur la bonne voie.
vwa
I think you're on the right track.

608 dangereux — **dangerous**
adj[pl]
Il est dangereux de se baigner dans cette rivière.
dɑ̃ʒʁø
It is dangerous to bathe in this river.

609	**pote**	**mate**
	nm	Il se trouva qu'un bon pote s'enfermait constamment dans son local afin de faire du son
	pɔt	*It so happened that a good mate was constantly locking himself in his appartment to make music*
610	**contrôle**	**control**
	nm	Un jour, les robots prendront le contrôle, soyez-en sûr.
	kɔ̃tʁol	*The robots will gain control one day, be sure of that.*
611	**honte**	**shame**
	nf	On appelle parfois cela le défilé de la honte.
	ɔ̃t	*This is sometimes called the walk of shame.*
612	**impression**	**impression**
	nf	Elle a fait une très bonne première impression.
	ɛ̃pʁesjɔ̃	*She made a very good first impression.*
613	**fou**	**mad, crazy**
	adj, nm	Es-tu fou de penser que tu devrais faire une telle chose ?
	fu	*Are you mad that you should do such a thing?*
614	**suivre**	**to follow**
	verb	Tout ce que vous avez à faire est de suivre son avis.
	sɥivʁ	*All that you have to do is to follow his advice.*
615	**retourner**	**to return, go back**
	verb	Je me suis levée à quatre heures, ai mangé un peu de nourriture et puis suis retournée dormir.
	ʁətuʁne	*I got up at 4:00, ate some food, then went back to sleep.*
616	**offrir**	**to offer**
	verb	Je ne peux rien offrir d'autre que du sang, des efforts, des larmes et de la sueur.
	ɔfʁiʁ	*I have nothing to offer but blood, toil, tears and sweat.*
617	**chanson**	**song, tune**
	nf	Je me souviens avoir entendu cette chanson, auparavant.
	ʃɑ̃sɔ̃	*I remember hearing this tune before.*
618	**trou**	**hole**
	nm	Les poèmes se font à peu près comme les canons : on prend un trou, et on met quelque chose autour.
	tʁu	*Poems are made in about the same way that we make guns. We take a hole, and we put something around it*
619	**arriere**	**back, rear**
	adj(i), adv, nm	Un ballon a frappé l'arrière de ma tête lorsque je jouais au foot.
	aʁiʁ	*A ball hit the back of my head while I was playing soccer.*
620	**poste**	**post, position, job; post office**
	nm, nf	Je n'arrive pas à croire que tu aies refusé ce poste.
	pɔst	*I can't believe you turned down that job.*
621	**huit**	**eight**
	det, num	Appelez-moi entre sept et huit heures, s'il vous plaît.
	ɥit	*Please call me up between seven and eight.*

622 **radio** **radio**
adj(i), nm, nf En écoutant les programmes en anglais à la radio, tu peux apprendre l'anglais gratuitement.
ʁadjo *If you listen to English programs on the radio, you can learn English for nothing.*

623 **ressembler** **to look like, resemble**
verb Ça ressemble à une blessure par balle tirée à bout portant.
ʁəsɑ̃ble *This looks like a close-range gunshot wound.*

624 **attaque** **attack**
nf Le programme nucléaire iranien vient de faire l'objet d'une attaque par un maliciel.
atak *The Iranian nuclear program has just been attacked by malware.*

625 **baiser** **to kiss**
nm, verb Vous devez vous agenouiller à mes pieds, me baiser la main et jurer que je suis un ange.
beze *You must kneel at my feet, kiss my hand and swear that I am an angel.*

626 **pourtant** **yet, nonetheless, nevertheless**
adv Pourtant, nombreux sont ceux qui choisissent la retraite anticipée.
puʁtɑ̃ *Nevertheless, many are choosing early retirement.*

627 **réponse** **answer, response**
nf Jusqu'à ce jour, nous n'avons obtenu aucune réponse de sa part.
ʁepɔ̃s *As of today, we haven't had an answer from him.*

628 **connard** **shithead, asshole**
nm Putain, quel est le connard qui ose m'appeler au milieu de la nuit ! ?
kɔnaʁ *Fuck, what kind of asshole calls people in the middle of the night?*

629 **pute** **whore, bitch, prostitute**
nf La seule différence entre une chaudasse et une pute, c'est le paiement.
pyt *The only difference between a bimbo and a prostitute is payment.*

630 **bande** **band, strip**
nf Ma mère a utilisé une bande de tissu pour réparer ma robe.
bɑ̃d *My mother used a strip of cloth to repair my dress.*

631 **enfer** **hell**
nm Vénus est pareille à l'enfer. Sa température de surface, telle une fournaise, s'élève à plus de quatre-cent-cinquante degrés Celsius.
ɑ̃fɛʁ *Venus is like Hell. The oven-like surface temperature hovers over 450 degrees Celsius.*

632 **triste** **sad**
adj(f) Quand j'étais adolescente, mes parents ne me laissaient jamais sortir avec des garçons, alors j'étais toujours triste.
tʁist *When I was a teenager, my parents would never allow me to go out with boys so I was always sad.*

633 **tel** **such**
adj, det, pron Je ne peux m'empêcher de rire en entendant une telle histoire.
tɛl *I cannot help laughing to hear such a story.*

634 **bravo** **bravo, well done**

	int, nm	Il y avait de nombreux journalistes qui saluaient Ogawa d'un " bravo, bonne performance !"
	bʀavo	*There were many journalists who praised Ogawa with, "bravo, good show!"*
635	**plusieurs**	**several**
	det, adj, pron	La température a été en dessous de zéro depuis plusieurs jours.
	plyzjœʀ	*The temperature has been below freezing for several days.*
636	**exister**	**to exist**
	verb	Si ce n'était du Soleil, aucun être vivant ne pourrait exister sur Terre.
	ɛgziste	*If it were not for the sun, no living creatures could exist on the earth.*
637	**rire**	**to laugh**
	nm, verb	Je ne peux m'empêcher de rire quand je pense à ça.
	ʀiʀ	*I can't help but laugh when I think about that.*
638	**compagnie**	**company**
	nf	Il a décidé de louer sa propriété à cette compagnie.
	kɔ̃paɲi	*He decided to rent his property to that company.*
639	**étrange**	**strange, odd**
	adj(f)	Mais je ne pense pas que ce soit du tout étrange.
	etʀɑ̃ʒ	*But I don't think that it's strange at all.*
640	**exemple**	**example**
	nm	Je crois que les phrases d'exemples font partie intégrante de l'assistance aux apprenants en langues.
	ɛgzɑ̃pl	*I believe example sentences are an integral aid for language learners.*
641	**combat**	**fight, combat, battle**
	nm	Les soldats qui sont revenus ont été loués pour leur bravoure au combat.
	kɔ̃ba	*The returning soldiers were commended for their bravery in battle.*
642	**secours**	**help, aid, assistance**
	nm[pl]	Docteur, donnez les premiers secours à cet enfant s'il vous plaît.
	səkuʀ	*Doctor, please give this child first aid.*
643	**connerie**	**crap, bullsh*t, stupidity**
	nf	Sauf votre respect, je pense que c'est une connerie.
	kɔnʀi	*With all due respect, I think it's bullshit.*
644	**visiter**	**to visit**
	verb	La dernière fois que je suis allé en Chine, j'ai visité Shanghai.
	vizite	*The last time I went to China, I visited Shanghai.*
645	**coucher**	**lie down, sleep**
	nm, verb	Longtemps, je me suis couché de bonne heure
	kuʃe	*Over a long period of time, I had the habit of going to sleep early.*
646	**imaginer**	**to imagine**
	verb	Maintenant, je voudrais que tu t'imaginies une carte de la Grande-Bretagne.
	imaʒine	*Now, I would like you to imagine a map of Great Britain.*
647	**merveilleux**	**marvellous, wonderful**
	adj[pl]	Ah que voici une journée merveilleuse pour un pique-nique.
	mɛʀvɛjø	*It's a wonderful day for a picnic.*
648	**continuer**	**to continue**

	verb	Nous pouvons continuer à jouer pour autant que nous ne fassions pas trop de bruit.
	kɔ̃tinɥe	*We can continue playing, as long as we don't make too much noise.*
649	**voler**	**to steal, rob**
	verb	Comment peux-tu être sûr que c'est Tom qui a volé le vélo ?
	vɔle	*What makes you so sure Tom was the one who stole your bicycle?*
650	**lune**	**moon**
	nf	J'ai entendu dire qu'ils avaient trouvé un objet extraterrestre sur la lune.
	lyn	*I heard they found an alien artifact on the moon.*
651	**bouche**	**mouth**
	nf	Dès qu'il ouvre la bouche, c'est pour se plaindre.
	buʃ	*He never opens his mouth without complaining about something.*
652	**sud**	**south**
	adj(i), nm	Après la guerre, il se débrouilla pour s'enfuir en Amérique du Sud.
	syd	*After the war, he managed to escape to South America.*
653	**danser**	**to dance**
	verb	J'étais tellement effrayée que personne ne voulut m'inviter à danser.
	dɑ̃se	*I was so afraid that no one would ask me to dance.*
654	**ennui**	**boredom, trouble, worry**
	nm	Pour contrer l'ennui, les Innus se regroupent dans un même endroit et s'adonnent à toutes sortes de travaux
	ɑ̃nɥi	*To keep boredom at bay, Innu get together and make all kinds of objects.*
655	**but**	**goal, aim, objective, purpose**
	nm	Mes collègues partagent le même but, à savoir la réussite.
	by	*My colleagues share the same goal, namely success.*
656	**hors**	**except, outside**
	adv, prep	Les problèmes de pollution sur Terre nécessitèrent de trouver des habitats hors de la Terre.
	ɔʁ	*Pollution problems on Earth necessitated finding homes outside of Earth.*
657	**sortie**	**exit**
	nf	Les points de sortie doivent aussi faire l'objet d'un contrôle au même titre, sinon davantage, que les points d'entrée
	sɔʁti	*Exit points must be controlled in the same way as - if not more so than - entry points*
658	**boîte**	**box**
	nf	Le contenu de la boîte est indiqué sur l'étiquette.
	bwat	*The contents of the box are listed on the label.*
659	**vol**	**flight, theft**
	nm	Lors d'un vol long tu devrais te lever une fois de temps en temps pour t'étirer les jambes.
	vɔl	*On a long flight you should get up every once in a while to stretch your legs*
660	**public**	**public, audience**
	nm, adj	Tu ne devrais pas dire de telles choses en public.
	pyblik	*You ought not to say such things in public.*
661	**lieutenant**	**lieutenant**

	nm	Lieutenant, ma patience est plus courte que mon épée.
	ljøtnã	*Lieutenant, my patience is shorter than my sword.*
662	**système**	**system**
	nm	L'étoile la plus proche de notre système solaire est Proxima du Centaure.
	sistɛm	*The nearest star to our solar system is Proxima Centauri.*
663	**époque**	**era, period**
	nf	La révolution industrielle a annoncé le début d'une nouvelle époque.
	epɔk	*The industrial revolution marked the beginning of a new era.*
664	**bête**	**animal, beast; stupid**
	nf, adj(f)	L'homme primitif était effrayé à la vue d'une bête sauvage.
	bɛt	*The primitive man was frightened at the sight of a savage beast.*
665	**vendre**	**to sell**
	verb	Peter était un joueur de jeux vidéo altruiste ; il donnait des objets aux gens qui en avaient besoin, plutôt que de les vendre par intérêt personnel.
	vãdʁ	*Peter was an altruistic video game player; he would give items to people who needed them, rather than selling them for personal profit.*
666	**avenir**	**future**
	nm	Il y aura une crise énergétique dans l'avenir proche.
	avniʁ	*There will be an energy crisis in the near future.*
667	**santé**	**health**
	nf	Mieux vaut être pauvre et en santé que riche et malade.
	sãte	*It's better to be poor and in good health than rich and ill.*
668	**amoureux**	**lover; in love, amorous**
	nmf, adj[pl]	Tout le monde tombe amoureux au moins une fois dans sa vie.
	amuʁø	*Everybody falls in love at least once in their lives.*
669	**cuisine**	**cooking, kitchen**
	nf	Depuis cette porte, on accède à la cuisine.
	kɥizin	*The door gives access to the kitchen.*
670	**normal**	**normal**
	adj	Je pense que je suis un gars plutôt normal.
	nɔʁmal	*I think I'm a pretty normal guy.*
671	**danger**	**danger**
	nm	Ils considéraient cet homme comme un danger pour la société.
	dãʒe	*They regarded the man as a danger to society.*
672	**gouvernement**	**government**
	nm	Les gouvernements tyranniques mettent fréquemment leurs opposants politiques en prison.
	guvɛʁnəmã	*Tyrannical governments frequently put their political opponents in prison.*
673	**village**	**village**
	nm	Les grandes rues de nombreux villages ont été pratiquement abandonnées à cause, en grande partie, de géants comme Wal-Mart.
	vilaʒ	*The main streets of many villages have in fact been abandoned. The main reason is the advance of big stores like Wal-Mart.*
674	**poser**	**to put, pose, ask**
	verb	Ne pose pas de questions dont tu ne veux pas connaître la réponse.

poze   *Don't ask questions that you don't want to know the answer to.*

675 ouvrir   **to open**

verb   Tu peux ouvrir les yeux. Je sais que tu fais semblant de dormir.

uvʁiʁ   *You can open your eyes. I know you're just pretending to be asleep.*

676 journal   **newspaper, paper**

nm   Le scandale politique a occupé toute la première page du journal.

ʒuʁnal   *The political scandal took up the whole first page of the newspaper.*

677 approche   **approach**

nf   Mon approche est étonnamment simple mais très effective.

apʁɔʃ   *My approach is amazingly simple but very effective.*

678 dommage   **damage, harm; too bad, a pity**

nm   C'est dommage que nous n'ayons pas rendu visite à Tom lorsque nous en avons eu l'occasion.

dɔmaʒ   *It's a pity we didn't visit Tom when we had the chance.*

679 peau   **skin**

nf   Est-il vrai que les hommes ont la peau plus grasse que les femmes ?

po   *Is it true that men have oilier skin than women?*

680 nez   **nose**

nm[pl]   Jusqu'à quelle profondeur arrives-tu à t'enfoncer le doigt dans le nez ?

ne   *How far can you stick your finger up your nose?*

681 servir   **to serve**

verb   La nourriture chinoise fut servie en petites portions qui ne nécessitaient pas d'être coupées avec un couteau ou une fourchette.

sɛʁviʁ   *Chinese food was served in small portions which did not require cutting with a knife or fork.*

682 sympa   **friendly, nice, kind**

adj   Il a été trop sympa de nous amener sur l'île avec son bateau.

sɛ̃pa   *He was kind enough to take us over to the island in his boat.*

683 mille   **thousand**

det, nm, num   Il a vendu sa maison cent cinquante mille euros.

mil   *He sold his house for a hundred fifty thousand euro.*

684 héros   **hero**

nm[pl]   Vous avez remarqué que les héros de films d'action semblent n'être jamais à court de munitions ?

eʁo   *Notice how the hero in an action flick never seems to run out of ammo?*

685 banque   **bank**

nf   Il reçoit un salaire raisonnable en tant qu'employé de banque.

bɑ̃k   *He gets a reasonable salary as a bank clerk.*

686 clé   **key**

nf   Je crois bien que j'ai oublié mes clés de bureau dans la poche de mon imperméable.

kle   *I'm pretty sure that I've left the keys to my office in my raincoat pocket.*

687 seconde   **second**

det, nf   Un second miroir est suspendu à côté de la porte.

səgɔ̃d   *A second mirror is hanging next to the door.*

688	**nord**	**north**
	adj(i), nm	Il est contraire à la loi de ne pas attacher sa ceinture en Amérique du Nord.
	nɔʁ	*In North America it is against the law to fail to fasten your seatbelt.*
689	**inspecteur**	**inspector**
	nm	L'inspecteur Dan Anderson n'a pas trouvé d'empreintes digitales sur le marteau.
	ɛ̃spɛktœʁ	*Inspector Dan Anderson found no fingerprints on the hammer.*
690	**liberté**	**liberty, freedom**
	nf	La liberté est si fondamentale que nous ne saurions en exagérer l'importance.
	libɛʁte	*Freedom is so fundamental that its importance cannot be overemphasized.*
691	**salaud**	**bastard**
	nm	C'est ce salaud de Metternich qui gouverne en fait.
	salo	*It's that bastard Metternich that's really in charge*
692	**cour**	**yard, court**
	nf	Je vis le chien de mon voisin courir dans ma cour.
	kuʁ	*I saw my neighbor's dog running in my yard.*
693	**juge**	**judge**
	nm, nf	Des circonstances atténuantes ont conduit le juge à prononcer une peine plus clémente.
	ʒyʒ	*Extenuating circumstances led the judge to pass a more lenient sentence.*
694	**terrible**	**terrible, dreadful**
	adj(f)	Le voyage a été annulé à cause d'une terrible tempête.
	teʁibl	*The trip was canceled because of a terrible storm.*
695	**paraître**	**to appear**
	verb	L'accusé paraîtra devant la cour vendredi.
	paʁɛtʁ	*The accused is to appear before the court on Friday.*
696	**crime**	**crime**
	nm	Tom a commis des crimes, mais n'a jamais été condamné.
	kʁim	*Tom committed crimes, but was never convicted.*
697	**asseoir**	**to sit**
	verb	Si tu peux juste t'asseoir tranquillement, je pense que je peux démêler les nœuds de tes cheveux.
	aswaʁ	*If you'll just sit still I think I can comb out the knots in your hair.*
698	**thé**	**tea**
	nm	Je bois toujours mon thé avec du sucre.
	te	*I always take my tea with sugar.*
699	**bonheur**	**happiness**
	nm	La recherche du bonheur te rend seulement malheureux.
	bɔnœʁ	*Trying to find happiness only makes you unhappy.*
700	**tas**	**pile, lots of, heap**
	nm[pl]	Des lettres d'admiratrices étaient posées en tas sur le bureau.
	ta	*Fan letters lay in a heap on the desk.*
701	**travers**	**breadth, across; fault, amiss**
	nm[pl]	Le son d'une détonation résonna à travers la gorge.
	tʁavɛʁ	*The sound of a gunshot echoed across the canyon.*

702	**stupide**	**stupid, silly, bemused**
	adj(f)	Je pense que ce que Tom a fait a été très stupide.
	stypid	*I think what Tom did was very stupid.*
703	**blague**	**joke**
	nf	Christophe Colomb a répété la même blague 256 fois en une seule journée ; tout son équipage en est mort... de rire.
	blag	*Christopher Columbus once used the same joke 256 times in one day... thereby causing his entire crew to die of laughter.*
704	**préférer**	**to prefer**
	verb	Ces tasses ne me plaisent pas, je préfère celles qui sont sur la table.
	pʁefeʁe	*I don't like these cups; I prefer those on the table.*
705	**conseil**	**advice, counsel, council**
	nm	Cela ne sert à rien de lui donner des conseils.
	kɔ̃sɛj	*It is no use giving her advice.*
706	**protéger**	**to protect**
	verb	J'ai de la sympathie pour mon amie qui déclare n'être qu'une immigrante qui essaie de protéger la langue anglaise de ses locuteurs natifs.
	pʁɔteʒe	*I sympathize with my friend who says that she's only an immigrant trying to protect the English language from its native speakers.*
707	**rêve**	**dream**
	nm	Ne laisse pas des gens étroits d'esprit te convaincre que tes rêves sont trop grands.
	ʁɛv	*Don't let narrow-minded people convince you that your dreams are too big.*
708	**pitié**	**pity, mercy**
	nf	L'évêque eu pitié des étrangers dans le désespoir.
	pitje	*The bishop took pity on the desperate immigrants.*
709	**vin**	**wine**
	nm	Quels sont les aliments qu'on mange habituellement avec du vin rouge ?
	vɛ̃	*What are some foods you usually eat with red wine?*
710	**don**	**gift**
	nm	L'étudiant en traduction possédait un don pour les langues.
	dɔ̃	*The translation student had a gift for languages.*
711	**sol**	**floor, ground**
	nm	L'avion en papier plana lentement vers le sol.
	sɔl	*The paper aeroplane slowly glided to the ground.*
712	**vent**	**wind**
	nm	Le vent transporte les graines sur de longues distances.
	vã	*The wind carries seeds for great distances.*
713	**club**	**club**
	nm	Seuls les membres du club sont autorisés à utiliser cette pièce.
	klœb	*Only members of the club are entitled to use this room.*
714	**gamin**	**kid**
	nm	J'aime bien réaliser des tours de magie pour les gamins, mais ils tombent parfois à plat.
	gamɛ̃	*I like to perform magic tricks for kids, but they sometimes fall flat.*

715	**tante**	**aunt**
	nf	Ma tante montre beaucoup d'affection pour ses enfants.
	tɑ̃t	*My aunt displays much affection for her children.*
716	**bar**	**bar**
	nm	Après la mort de son père, John s'est mis à passer son temps dans les bars.
	baʁ	*After his father's death, John took to spending his time in bars.*
717	**milieu**	**middle**
	nm	La voiture au milieu du chemin est très gênante.
	miljø	*That car in the middle of the path is an inconvenience.*
718	**reine**	**queen**
	nf	La reine a pris ombrage des remarques faites dans la presse à propos de son insensibilité à la mort de la princesse.
	ʁɛn	*The queen took umbrage at remarks made in the press about her insensitivity to the death of the princess.*
719	**signer**	**to sign**
	verb	La France avait signé une alliance secrète avec l'Espagne.
	siɲe	*France had signed a secret treaty with Spain.*
720	**centre**	**center, centre**
	nm	Là où était la limite de la science se trouve maintenant son centre.
	sɑ̃tʁ	*Where the frontier of science once was is now the centre.*
721	**probablement**	**probably**
	adv	L'origine de l'univers, ne sera probablement pas éclaircie pour l'éternité.
	pʁɔbabləmɑ̃	*The origin of the universe will probably never be explained.*
722	**bière**	**beer, coffin**
	nf	Je ne bois pas de bière, je bois seulement de l'alcool.
	bjɛʁ	*I don't drink beer, only spirits.*
723	**dingue**	**crazy, mad, wild, nutty**
	adj	Lorsque nous nous souvenons que nous sommes tous dingues, les mystères disparaissent et la vie se trouve expliquée.
	dɛ̃g	*When we remember we are all mad, the mysteries disappear and life stands explained.*
724	**inutile**	**useless**
	adj(f)	La moitié de ce que nous écrivons est nuisible, l'autre moitié est inutile.
	inytil	*Half of what we write is harmful; the other half is useless.*
725	**nul**	**nil, null**
	adj, det, pron	Votre capital est garanti mais le rendement pourrait être nul.
	nyl	*Your capital is guaranteed but the return may be nil.*
726	**sentir**	**to feel, smell**
	verb	Je me suis senti très soulagé après avoir dit tout ce que j'avais à dire.
	sɑ̃tiʁ	*I felt quite relieved after I had said all I wanted to say.*
727	**différent**	**different**
	adj	En Amérique, les gens jouent à différentes versions du Mahjong.
	difeʁɑ̃	*In America, people play a different version of mahjong.*
728	**emmener**	**to take**
	verb	Veux-tu que je t'emmène chez le médecin ?

		ãmne	*Do you want me to take you to the doctor?*

729 vêtement — **garment, item or article of clothing**

nm

Il porte des vêtements de femme et mange des petits pains au beurre pour le thé.

vɛtmã — *He puts on women's clothing, and has buttered scones for tea.*

730 liste — **list**

nf

Dan fit une liste des choses qu'il voulait réaliser dans sa vie.

list — *Dan made a list of things he wanted to achieve in life.*

731 unir — **to unite, come to terms with**

verb

Nous avons ambitionné de nous unir avec eux.

yniʁ — *We sought to come to terms with them.*

732 société — **society**

nf

La société humaine est une fonction de toute l'humanité. Ceux qui en profitent le plus devraient payer le plus pour le bénéfice qu'ils en retirent.

sɔsjete — *Human society is a function of all humanity, those who profit most from it should pay the most for the benefit they gain.*

733 soin — **care**

nm

Ne vous faites pas de souci pour votre chien. J'en prendrai soin.

swɛ̃ — *Don't worry about your dog. I'll take care of him.*

734 pierre — **stone**

nf

Il brisa la fenêtre en jetant une pierre.

pjɛʁ — *He broke the window by throwing a stone.*

735 utiliser — **to use**

verb

Penses-tu que je puisse utiliser mon téléphone portable dans la douche ?

ytilize — *Do you think I can use my cellphone in the shower?*

736 lequel — **who, whom, which**

pron

Le langage est le moyen par lequel les gens communiquent entre eux.

ləkɛl — *Language is the means by which people communicate with others.*

737 ficher — **to file; to make fun of, not care, not give a damn**

verb

Je me fiche de combien tu le veux. Je ne vais pas te le donner.

fiʃe — *I don't care how much you want it. I'm not going to give it to you.*

738 parole — **word**

nf

Je lui ai donné ma parole que je serai de retour pour neuf heures.

paʁɔl — *I gave her my word I would be back home by nine.*

739 marier — **to marry**

verb

Être amoureux et être marié sont deux choses différentes.

maʁje — *Falling in love is one thing; getting married is another.*

740 départ — **departure**

nm

Le jour du départ, les chambres devraient être libérées pour onze heures.

depaʁ — *Rooms should be left vacant by eleven a.m. on the day of departure.*

741 ennemi — **enemy**

nmf, adj

Le progrès est un joli mot. Son moteur en est le changement. Et le changement a ses ennemis.

ɛnmi — *Progress is a lovely word. But its driving force is change, and change has its enemies.*

742	**spectacle**	**sight, show**
	nm	À quelle heure le spectacle a-t-il pris fin ?
	spɛktakl	*At what time did the show finish?*
743	**recherche**	**research, search**
	nf	Avant de prendre sa retraite, elle travaillait en tant que secrétaire du Directeur d'une école de recherche de l'université.
	ʁəʃɛʁʃ	*Before she retired, she worked as a secretary to a director of a research school at a university.*
744	**choisir**	**to choose**
	verb	Il a choisi de ne pas se présenter à l'élection présidentielle.
	ʃwaziʁ	*He chose not to run for the presidential election.*
745	**intérêt**	**interest**
	nm	Elle me dit que sans moi la vie n'avait plus d'intérêt.
	ɛ̃teʁɛ	*She told me that, without me, this life had nothing of interest for her.*
746	**intéresser**	**to interest, involve**
	verb	« Vous vous intéressez à cette sorte de choses ? » « Non, pas vraiment. »
	ɛ̃teʁese	*"You're interested in this sort of thing?" "No, not really."*
747	**rôle**	**role**
	nm	Kate a eu l'occasion de jouer un rôle important dans un film.
	ʁol	*Kate has been given an opportunity to play a major role in a movie.*
748	**félicitations**	**congratulations**
	nf	Veuillez accepter nos félicitations pour le mariage de votre fils.
	felisitasjɔ̃	*Please accept our heartiest congratulations on the marriage of your son.*
749	**descendre**	**to go down, come down**
	verb	Nous lui avons demandé à l'interphone s'il pouvait descendre rapidement.
	desãdʁ	*We asked him on the interphone if he could come downstairs quickly.*
750	**tourner**	**to turn, to spin**
	verb	La toupie tournait dangereusement près du bord de la table.
	tuʁne	*The top spun perilously close to the edge of the table.*
751	**position**	**position**
	nf	Les soldats avancèrent sur la position ennemie sous couvert de l'obscurité.
	pozisjɔ̃	*The soldiers advanced on the enemy's position under cover of darkness.*
752	**blessé**	**injured; injured person, causualty**
	adj, nmf	Un animal peut être bien plus dangereux lorsqu'il est blessé.
	blese	*An animal can be much more dangerous when injured.*
753	**humain**	**human**
	nm, adj	Combien de fois me faudra-t-il te dire que Tatoeba n'est pas un être humain ?
	ymɛ̃	*How many times do I have to tell you that Tatoeba is not a human being?*
754	**match**	**match, game**
	nm	Tom aime regarder les matchs de baseball à la télé.
	matʃ	*Tom likes to watch baseball games on TV.*
755	**coupable**	**guilty**
	nmf, adj(f)	Le chien s'est senti coupable d'avoir mangé le devoir.
	kupabl	*The dog felt guilty about eating the homework.*

756	**environ**	**about, thereabouts, or so**
	adv, prep, nm	La production d'acier a atteint environ 100 millions de tonnes l'année dernière.
	ãviʁɔ̃	*Steel production reached an estimated 100 million tons last year.*
757	**art**	**art**
	nm	Où puis-je me rendre pour acquérir des livres et des catalogues d'art ?
	aʁ	*Where can I go to buy art books and catalogs?*
758	**espoir**	**hope**
	nm	Il était incapable d'abandonner complètement ses espoirs de l'épouser.
	ɛspwaʁ	*He was unable to completely give up on his hopes of marrying her.*
759	**mur**	**wall**
	nm	Elle affirme être en mesure de voir à travers les murs.
	myʁ	*She says that she can see through walls.*
760	**église**	**church**
	nf	Nous fauchâmes les herbes, bonnes et mauvaises, autour de l'église.
	egliz	*We cut away all the grass and weeds around the church.*
761	**salope**	**slut**
	nf	Pourquoi les mecs qui couchent sont-ils des étalons et les filles qui couchent des salopes ?
	salɔp	*Why is it that guys who sleep around are studs and girls who sleep around are sluts?*
762	**beauté**	**beauty**
	nf	Marie est allée au salon de beauté pour se faire manucurer.
	bote	*Mary went to the beauty salon to get a manicure.*
763	**lâche**	**loose**
	adj	Le mucus est lâche et peut facilement être craché.
	laʃ	*The mucus is loose and can easily be coughed up*
764	**adresser**	**to address**
	verb	L'article 104, paragraphe 5, du traité impose à la Commission d'adresser un avis au Conseil
	adʁese	*Article 104(5) of the Treaty requires the Commission to address an opinion to the Council*
765	**sauter**	**to jump**
	verb	Il a été effrayé lorsque le singe lui a sauté dessus.
	sote	*He was scared when the monkey jumped at him.*
766	**colère**	**anger, wrath**
	nf	Nous étions pleins de colère contre le meurtrier.
	kɔlɛʁ	*We were filled with anger against the murderer.*
767	**directeur**	**director**
	nmf, adj	Le directeur de l'école veut fermer la cantine et créer une nouvelle salle récréative pour les élèves.
	diʁɛktœʁ	*The director of the school wants to close the canteen and create a new recreation room for the students.*
768	**adieu**	**goodbye, farewell, adieu**
	int, nm	Après le discours d'adieu de Jane, nous devînmes très tristes.

	adjø	*After saying goodbye to Jane, we were very sad.*
769	**parier**	**to bet**
	verb	J'ai parié cent dollars avec mon copain qu'il ne mangerait pas un cafard vivant. J'ai perdu !
	paʁje	*I bet my friend $100 that he wouldn't eat a live cockroach. I lost!*
770	**tort**	**wrong**
	nm	Je pensais que vous seriez tué. Je me réjouis d'avoir eu tort.
	tɔʁ	*I thought you'd been killed. I'm glad I was wrong.*
771	**conduire**	**to lead, drive**
	verb	Vous pouvez conduire ma voiture pour autant que vous conduisiez prudemment.
	kɔ̃dɥiʁ	*You can use my car if you drive carefully.*
772	**américain**	**American, American English,**
	adj, nm	On dit que les Américains considèrent le revenu d'un homme comme critère majeur de ses capacités.
	ameʁikɛ̃	*Americans are said to regard the amount of money a man makes as a criterion of his ability.*
773	**revenu**	**income**
	nm	Si j'avais 25% de plus de revenu, je serais plus satisfait de ma vie.
	ʁəvəny	*If I had 25% more income, I'd be more satisfied with my life.*
774	**justice**	**justice**
	nf	Pour lui rendre justice, il a fait de son mieux avec des ressources et des effectifs limités.
	ʒystis	*To do him justice, he did his best with his limited men and supplies.*
775	**soldat**	**soldier**
	nm	Les soldats faisaient à chaque ferme et à chaque village une pause.
	sɔlda	*The soldiers stopped at every farm and village.*
776	**expérience**	**experience**
	nf	Je préférerais mourir que de vivre une expérience aussi terrible.
	ɛkspeʁjɑ̃s	*I would rather die than have such a terrible experience.*
777	**cerveau**	**brain**
	nm	Il y a des jours où j'ai l'impression que mon cerveau veut m'abandonner.
	sɛʁvo	*There are days where I feel like my brain wants to abandon me.*
778	**fenêtre**	**window**
	nf	Elle s'est levée et s'est dirigée vers la fenêtre.
	fənɛtʁ	*She stood up and walked to the window.*
779	**quartier**	**district, quarter**
	nm	Une usine ne convient pas dans un quartier résidentiel.
	kaʁtje	*A factory is not suitable for a residential district.*
780	**prince**	**prince**
	nm	Qui vole une agrafe est mis à mort, qui vole une principauté en devient le prince.
	pʁɛ̃s	*He who steals a belt buckle will be executed; he who steals a state becomes a prince.*
781	**riche**	**rich**
	adj(f)	Si j'avais acheté ce tableau autrefois, maintenant je serais riche.

ʁiʃ   *If I had bought the painting then, I would be rich now.*

782   **fleur**   **flower**

nf   Elle est curieuse de savoir qui a envoyé les fleurs.

flœʁ   *She wants to know who sent the flowers.*

783   **présenter**   **to present**

verb   Il présenta un argument en faveur de la guerre.

pʁezɑ̃te   *He presented an argument for the war.*

784   **presse**   **press**

nf   Les directeurs généraux millionnaires étaient traités en héros par la presse, mais plus maintenant.

pʁɛs   *Millionaire CEOs used to be lionized in the press, but no more.*

785   **ridicule**   **ridiculousness, silly**

nm, adj(f)   Elle s'habille si outrageusement ; ça a l'air complètement ridicule !

ʁidikyl   *She dresses so outrageously; it looks completely ridiculous!*

786   **preuve**   **proof**

nf   La réponse en est bien plus facilement découverte que la preuve.

pʁœv   *The answer is far more easily discovered than the proof.*

787   **épouser**   **to marry, wed**

verb   Je ne peux interdire à quelqu'un d'épouser plusieurs femmes car cela ne contredit pas les écritures.

epuze   *I cannot forbid a person to marry several wives, for it does not contradict Scripture.*

788   **intéressant**   **interesting**

adj   As-tu mangé quelque part d'intéressant, ces derniers temps ?

ɛ̃teʁesɑ̃   *Have you eaten anywhere interesting lately?*

789   **gosse**   **kid**

nm, nf   Il est temps pour moi d'y aller, les gosses !

gɔs   *It's time for me to go, kids.*

790   **rose**   **pink; rose**

adj(f), nf   Elle a choisi un chandail rose pour que je puisse l'essayer.

ʁoz   *She picked out a pink shirt for me to try on.*

791   **nature**   **nature**

nf   J'ai toujours pensé qu'un infarctus était la manière dont la nature t'indique qu'il est temps de mourir.

natyʁ   *I always thought that a stroke was one of nature's ways to tell you that it's time to die.*

792   **vide**   **empty; vacuum**

adj(f), nm   La police suivit toutes ses pistes mais revint les mains vides.

vid   *The police followed up all their leads, but came up empty handed.*

793   **responsable**   **responsible**

adj(f), nmf   À partir de maintenant, tu dois être responsable de tes actes.

ʁɛspɔ̃sabl   *From now on, you must be responsible for what you do.*

794   **courage**   **courage**

nm   Je n'ai pas le courage de demander à mon patron qu'il me prête sa voiture.

kuʁaʒ   *I do not have the courage to ask my boss to lend me his car.*

795	**capable**	**able, capable**
	adj(f)	Les chances sont telles qu'il est capable de remporter un prix Nobel.
	kapabl	*The chances are he will be able to win a Nobel prize.*
796	**cinéma**	**cinema**
	nm	Mon père ? Il se rend à la bibliothèque, au cinéma, au théâtre. Il est très actif.
	sinema	*My father? He goes to the library, to the cinema, to the theatre. He's very active.*
797	**décision**	**decision**
	nf	J'ai dû disposer de tous les faits avant de pouvoir prendre une décision.
	desizjɔ̃	*I had to get all the facts before I could make a decision.*
798	**taxi**	**taxi**
	nm	Nous avons pris un taxi pour arriver là-bas à l'heure.
	taksi	*We took a taxi so as to reach there on time.*
799	**chanter**	**to sing**
	verb	Ce bel oiseau ne faisait rien d'autre que chanter jour après jour.
	ʃɑ̃te	*That pretty bird did nothing but sing day after day.*
800	**excuser**	**to excuse**
	verb	Veuillez m'excuser de vous appeler si tôt le matin.
	ɛkskyze	*Please excuse me for calling you so early in the morning.*
801	**fier**	**to rely on; proud**
	adj, verb	Il est fier que son père ait été un scientifique renommé.
	fjɛʁ	*He is proud that his father was a famous scientist.*
802	**deuxième**	**second**
	det, nm, nf	Le football était joué en Chine pendant le deuxième siècle.
	døzjɛm	*Football was played in China in the second century.*
803	**appartement**	**apartment, flat**
	nm	Tom, avec qui je partageais l'appartement, a déménagé le mois dernier.
	apaʁtəmɑ̃	*Tom, who I shared the apartment with, moved out last month.*
804	**contact**	**contact**
	nm	À peine étais-je entré en contact avec lui que je décidai de bien faire sa connaissance.
	kɔ̃takt	*No sooner had I come into contact with him than I determined to get to know him well.*
805	**cacher**	**to hide**
	verb	Ma veste comporte une poche secrète où je peux cacher de l'argent ou d'autres objets de valeur.
	kaʃe	*My jacket has a secret pocket where I can hide money or other valuables.*
806	**répondre**	**to answer**
	verb	Pourriez-vous simplement répondre à la question, s'il vous plaît ? Nous n'avons pas toute la journée !
	ʁepɔ̃dʁ	*Could you just please answer the question? We don't have all day.*
807	**manière**	**manner, way**
	nf	Et bien sûr, un orateur communique habituellement de deux manières : oralement aussi bien qu'à travers ses gestes.

manjɛʁ

And of course, a speaker usually communicates in two ways, orally as well as through gestures.

808	**jambe**	**leg**
	nf	J'étire toujours les muscles de mes jambes avant de jouer au tennis.
	ʒɑ̃b	*I always stretch my leg muscles before playing tennis.*
809	**occasion**	**chance, opportunity**
	nf	Je suis content d'avoir cette occasion de travailler avec vous.
	ɔkazjɔ̃	*'m glad to have this opportunity to work with you.*
810	**défense**	**defence**
	nf	Nos troupes réussirent à passer les défenses de l'ennemi.
	defɑ̃s	*Our army broke through the enemy defenses.*
811	**longue**	**long**
	adj	Je n'ai pas pu faire mes devoirs la nuit dernière, à cause d'une longue panne d'électricité.
	lɔ̃g	*Last night I could not do my homework on account of a long blackout.*
812	**jeter**	**to throw**
	verb	Il décida de jeter l'éponge malgré nos encouragements.
	ʒəte	*In spite of our encouragement, he decided to throw in the towel.*
813	**formidable**	**tremendous, considerable, great**
	adj(f)	La vie n'est-elle pas simplement formidable ?
	fɔʁmidabl	*Isn't life just great?*
814	**base**	**base**
	nf	Les étudiants sont jugés sur la base de leurs résultats d'examens
	baz	*Students are judged on the basis of their test results.*
815	**glace**	**ice, ice cream; mirror**
	nf	Si tu me paies une glace, je te donnerai un baiser.
	glas	*If you buy me an ice cream, I'll give you a kiss.*
816	**dent**	**tooth**
	nf	Si ta dent te fait mal, tu devrais aller voir un dentiste.
	dɑ̃	*If your tooth hurts, you should see a dentist.*
817	**parmi**	**among**
	prep	Il y avait un petit nombre d'étrangers parmi les visiteurs du musée.
	paʁmi	*There was a sprinkling of foreigners among the visitors in the museum.*
818	**immediatement**	**immediately**
	adv	Si tu expliques tout en jargon médical, il est impossible que tout le monde comprenne immédiatement.
	imdjatmɑ̃	*If you explain everything in medical jargon, it's impossible that everyone understands immediately.*
819	**paie**	**pay, payroll**
	nf	Cette situation a entraîné une pénurie de personnel expérimenté et bien formé au service de la paie.
	pɛ	*This has led to a shortage of experienced and properly trained payroll staff.*
820	**machine**	**machine**
	nf	Peux-tu m'aider ? J'ignore comment je peux démarrer cette machine.

	maʃin	*Can you help me? I can't make out how to start this machine.*
821	**vacance**	**vacancy; vacation ; holiday**
	nf	Pendant que nous étions en vacances, un voisin s'est occupé de notre chat.
	vakãs	*While we were on holiday, a neighbor took care of our cat.*
822	**monstre**	**monster**
	nm adj(f)	Tous les monstres commencent comme les bébés de quelqu'un.
	mõstʁ	*Every monster starts off as someone's baby.*
823	**tueur**	**killer, hit man**
	nm	Malheureusement, la police a dû attendre qu'il y ait une autre victime avant de tenter d'en savoir plus sur le tueur en série.
	tɥœʁ	*Unfortunately, the police had to wait until there was another victim to try to find more about the serial killer.*
824	**naitre**	**to be born**
	verb	Chacun de nous quitte la vie avec le sentiment qu'il vient à peine de naître.
	nɛtʁ	*Each of us leaves life with the feeling that they were just born.*
825	**francais**	**French**
	nm, adj[pl]	Je suis sûr que tu seras heureux d'apprendre le français en compagnie de Tom.
	fʁãkɛ	*I'm sure you'll enjoy studying French with Tom.*
826	**course**	**race, shopping**
	nf	Aujourd'hui un de mes camarades t'a vu faire les courses à Auchan.
	kuʁs	*Today, my classmate saw you guys shopping at Auchan.*
827	**majeste**	**majesty**
	nf	Le Conseil consultatif travaille avec S.M. le Roi et est présidé directement par Sa Majesté elle- même
	maʒɛst	*The Advisory Council works with His Majesty the King and is chaired directly by His Majesty.*
828	**mien**	**mine**
	pron	Ta voiture va vite, mais la mienne va encore plus vite.
	mjɛ̃	*Your car is fast, but mine is faster.*
829	**type**	**type; guy**
	nm	Oublie ce type. Il y a plein d'hommes meilleurs que lui en ce monde.
	tip	*Forget about this guy. There are a lot of men better than him in this world.*
830	**certainement**	**certainly**
	adv	Je peux certainement vous aider par rapport à vos problèmes d'argent
	sɛʁtɛnmã	*With respect to your money problems, I can certainly help.*
831	**couper**	**to cut**
	verb	Coupez les poivrons en lamelles de cinq centimètres.
	kupe	*Cut the bell peppers into two-inch strips.*
832	**ha**	**oh**
	int	Encore une fois, on disait de nous: « Ah, ces gens-là sont insensés »
	a	*Once again, everybody said, "Oh, those people are crazy"*
833	**importance**	**importance**
	nf	Le docteur a souligné l'importance du sommeil pour être en bonne santé.
	ɛ̃pɔʁtãs	*The doctor emphasized the importance of sleep for good health*

834 ouest — **west**

adj(i), nm — Des rebelles libyens ont pénétré dans deux villes stratégiques, qui contrôlent l'accès à la capitale par l'ouest et le sud.

wɛst — *Libyan rebels have advanced into two strategic towns controlling access to the capital from the west and the south.*

835 chat — **cat; chat**

nm — Les chats sont plus malins que tu ne penses.

ʃa — *Cats are smarter than you think.*

836 degager — **to free, clear**

verb — Le ciel est dégagé. Pas un nuage en vue.

dəgaʒe — *The sky is clear. Not a cloud in sight.*

837 chier — **to sh*t, piss off, get pissed off**

verb — Mon dieu, tu fais chier. Tu as vraiment gâché le moment.

ʃje — *God, you piss me off. You completely ruined the moment.*

838 ravir — **to delight, rob**

verb — Je serais ravie s'ils me demandaient de prononcer un discours.

ʁaviʁ — *I'd be delighted if they asked me to give a speech.*

839 joie — **joy**

nf — Il éprouvait la joie la plus céleste qu'il eût éprouvée depuis sa naissance.

ʒwa — *He felt the most divine joy that he had experienced since his birth.*

840 lorsque — **when**

conj — Tu es supposée aider tes amis lorsqu'ils ont des ennuis.

lɔʁsk — *You're supposed to help your friends when they're in trouble.*

841 superbe — **arrogance; superb, magnificent**

nf, adj(f) — I y a une superbe vue depuis le toit de cet immeuble. Vous voulez aller voir ?

sypɛʁb — *There's a great view from the rooftop of that building. Want to go see?*

842 bain — **bath, bathing**

nm — La première chose que tu as à faire est prendre un bain.

bɛ̃ — *The first thing you have to do is take a bath.*

843 horrible — **horrible, terrible, dreadful, hideous**

adj(f) — Mourir n'est pas terrible. Mais… ne plus la revoir jamais… Voilà l'horrible !

ɔʁibl — *Dying is not so terrible. But… to never see her again… That's what's horrible!*

844 court — **short**

adj, adv, nm — Je ne peux pas vérifier si votre courriel est correct ou pas parce qu'il est trop court.

kuʁ — *I can't check to see if your email is correct or not because it's too short.*

845 deranger — **to disturb, bother**

verb — Je suis désolé de te déranger, mais il y a un appel téléphonique pour toi.

dəʁãʒe — *I'm sorry to disturb you, but there's a phone call for you.*

846 bombe — **bomb**

nf — Le groupe terroriste fut responsable de l'explosion de la bombe à l'extérieur de l'ambassade.

bɔ̃b — *The terrorist group was responsible for the bomb explosion outside the embassy.*

847	**ramener**	**to bring back, return, take back**
	verb	La curiosité tue le chat, mais la satisfaction le ramène à la vie.
	ʁamne	*Curiosity killed the cat, but satisfaction brought it back to life.*
848	**realite**	**reality**
	nf	Comment se fait-ce que nos espoirs soient en contradiction avec la réalité ?
	ʁilit	*From what stems this contradiction between our hopes and our reality?*
849	**enqueter**	**to investigate, hold inquiry, conduct a survey**
	verb	Charles Walcot a enquêté sur le compas magnétique des pigeons.
	ãkte	*Charles Walcot investigated the magnetic compass bearing sense in pigeons.*
850	**camion**	**truck**
	nm	Le camion chargé d'essence percuta les portes et explosa.
	kamjõ	*The gasoline truck ran into the gate and blew up.*
851	**signifier**	**to mean**
	verb	Marie voulait un tatouage qui signifiât « Amour et fidélité » mais il signifie en vérité « Imbécile d'étranger » en chinois.
	siɲifje	*Mary wanted a tattoo that meant "Love and Fidelity", but it really means "Stupid Foreigner" in Chinese.*
852	**cent**	**one hundred, cent**
	det, nm	Ils ont bâti leur empire au Pérou il y a environ cinq cents ans.
	sã	*They built their empire in Peru about five hundred years ago.*
853	**rencontre**	**meeting**
	nm	Tu arrives trop tard. La rencontre est terminée depuis trente minutes.
	ʁãkõtʁ	*You are late. The meeting finished thirty minutes ago.*
854	**excellent**	**excellent**
	adj	Cette une excellente érudite et elle est reconnue partout comme telle.
	ɛksɛlã	*She is an excellent scholar, and is recognized everywhere as such.*
855	**respect**	**respect**
	nm	Les supérieurs et les employés se traitent avec respect.
	ʁɛspɛ	*Superiors and employees treat one another with respect.*
856	**terrain**	**ground, terrain**
	nm	C'est un terrain horriblement accidenté ; j'espère qu'on ne va pas foutre en l'air la transmission.
	teʁɛ̃	*This is awfully hilly terrain; I hope we don't screw up the transmission.*
857	**projet**	**project**
	nm	Si ce n'est pas maintenant, quand pensez-vous commencer le projet ?
	pʁɔʒɛ	*If not now, when do you plan to start the project?*
858	**eviter**	**to avoid**
	verb	Aujourd'hui je quitte le travail un peu plus tard, afin d'éviter d'être surchargé de travail demain matin.
	əvite	*Today I'm working a little late so as to avoid a rush in the morning.*
859	**poisson**	**fish**
	nm	Vouloir me protéger de moi-même, c'est aussi ingénieux que sauver un poisson de la noyade.

pwasɔ̃ | *Wanting to protect me from myself is about as ingenious as saving a fish from drowning.*

860	**plupart**	**the majority , most**
	most,	C'est un petit pays dont la plupart des gens n'ont jamais entendu parler.
	plypaʁ	*It's a tiny country that most people have never heard of.*
861	**joyeux**	**merry, joyful, happy**
	adj[pl]	De beaux feux d'artifices conclurent ces deux journées joyeuses.
	ʒwajø	*Beautiful fireworks conclude these two joyful days.*
862	**empecher**	**to prevent**
	verb	Un pare-feu empêche le feu de se propager dans la forêt.
	ɑ̃pʃe	*A firebreak prevents fire from spreading in the forest.*
863	**envers**	**towards**
	nm[pl], prep	L'entreprise a une obligation de diligence envers ses employés
	ɑ̃vɛʁ	*The company has a duty of care towards its employees.*
864	**kilometre**	**kilometer**
	nm	Nous livrons votre commande gratuitement dans un rayon de 30 kilomètres.
	kilɔmɛtʁ	*We deliver your order free of charge within a 30-kilometer limit.*
865	**ange**	**angel**
	nm	J'ai connu ta mère sur Facebook. Donc si Facebook n'existait pas, tu n'existerais pas non plus, mon petit ange.
	ɑ̃ʒ	*I met your mother through Facebook. So, if Facebook didn't exist, neither would you, my little angel.*
866	**copine**	**girlfriend**
	nf	Ma copine travaille à une école de langues et adore ça.
	kɔpin	*My girlfriend works at a language school and loves it very much.*
867	**chaussure**	**shoe, sneakers**
	nf	Ce n'est pas trop de te demander de nettoyer tes chaussures, Tom.
	ʃosyʁ	*t's not too much to ask of you, to clean your own shoes, Tom.*
868	**dossier**	**file, record; case**
	nm	Après analyse de votre dossier, nous vous prions de nous excuser pour les désagréments encourus.
	dosje	*After looking through your file, we ask that you excuse us for any inconveniences caused.*
869	**règle**	**regular, steady, well-ordered, ruled**
	adj	Il y a quelques cas auxquels cette règle ne s'applique pas.
	ʁɛgl	*There are some cases where this rule does not apply.*
870	**animal**	**animal**
	nm, adj	Les chiens, les chats et les chevaux sont des animaux.
	animal	*The dogs, the cats, and the horses are animals.*
871	**langue**	**language, tongue**
	nf	La conquête normande de l'Angleterre eut beaucoup d'influence sur la langue anglaise
	lɑ̃g	*The Norman victory over England had a big impact on the English language*
872	**imbécile**	**imbecile, fool**

	adj, nf	Tu peux le traiter d'imbécile mais pas de poule mouillée.
	ɛ̃besil	*You may call him a fool, but you cannot call him a coward.*
873	**princesse**	**princess**
	nf	Ne sachant avec quel prétendant elle voulait se marier, la princesse hésitait, nommant tantôt l'un, tantôt l'autre.
	pʁɛ̃sɛs	*Unsure of which suitor she wanted to marry, the princess vacillated, saying now one, now the other.*
874	**zone**	**zone, area**
	nf	Le petit-déjeuner en terrasse est largement pratiqué dans les zones urbaines de la France.
	zon	*Patio dining for breakfast is widely practiced in urban areas of France.*
875	**droguer**	**to drug, take drugs**
	verb	Ils m'ont kidnappé, ils m'ont drogué et alors ils m'ont lavé le cerveau.
	dʁɔge	*They kidnapped me, drugged me, and then brainwashed me.*
876	**charge**	**to charge, load**
	nf	Le vieil homme chargea son mulet avec des sacs de sables.
	ʃaʁʒ	*The old man loaded his mule with bags full of sand.*
877	**enfoiré**	**bastard**
	nm	Si vous êtes un enfoiré, vous pouvez cracher sur le cadavre du vieillard.
	ɑ̃fwaʁe	*If you are a bastard, you can spit on the corpse.*
878	**nourriture**	**food**
	nf	Il n'y a pas assez de nourriture pour nous toutes.
	nuʁityʁ	*There's not enough food for all of us.*
879	**pont**	**bridge**
	nm	Je ne connais pas la longueur exacte de ce pont.
	pɔ̃	*I don't know the exact length of this bridge.*
880	**refuser**	**to refuse**
	verb	Je vais vous faire une proposition que vous ne pouvez pas refuser.
	ʁəfyze	*I'm going to make you an offer that you can't refuse.*
881	**contraire**	**opposite, contrary**
	nm, adj(f)	L'absence de preuve du contraire est elle-même la preuve que votre théorie est probablement vraie.
	kɔ̃tʁɛʁ	*The lack of evidence to the contrary is itself evidence that your theory is probably right.*
882	**enchanter**	**to delight, enchant, rejoice**
	verb	Chris était sûr que Beth serait enchantée de son progrès.
	ɑ̃ʃɑ̃te	*Chris was confident that Beth would be delighted with his improvement.*
883	**douleur**	**pain**
	nf	La douleur était au-delà de ce qu'il pouvait supporter.
	dulœʁ	*The pain was more than he could stand.*
884	**politique**	**politician; politics; political**
	nm, nf, adj(f)	Les circonstances politiques du pays vont de mal en pis.
	pɔlitik	*The political circumstances in the country got worse and worse.*
885	**fait**	**done, fact**
	adj, nm	L'éducation ne consiste pas à apprendre beaucoup de faits.

	fɛ	*Education doesn't consist of learning a lot of facts.*
886	**magasin**	**store, shop**
	nm	J'ai entendu dire qu'un magasin de barbe à papa vient juste d'ouvrir. Allons-y, les mecs.
	magazɛ̃	*I heard a cotton candy shop has just opened. Let's go, dudes.*
887	**entier**	**whole, full**
	nm, adj	Elle profita de notre hospitalité et resta un mois entier sans rien nous payer.
	ɑ̃tje	*She took advantage of our hospitality and stayed a whole month without paying us anything.*
888	**chapeau**	**hat**
	nm	Voir la femme au chapeau jaune m'a remémoré une histoire.
	ʃapo	*Seeing the woman with the yellow hat reminded me of a story.*
889	**raconter**	**to tell**
	verb	Le propriétaire m'a raconté toute une histoire pour expliquer pourquoi nous n'avions pas de chauffage depuis trois jours.
	ʁakɔ̃te	*The landlord told me a cock and bull story about why we didn't have heat for three days.*
890	**discuter**	**to discuss, debate; to question**
	verb	Je voulais en discuter avec vous, hier, mais vous ne sembliez pas disposées à écouter.
	diskyte	*I wanted to discuss this with you yesterday, but you didn't seem to want to listen.*
891	**papier**	**paper**
	nm	Faisons faire aujourd'hui la vaisselle à celui qui perd à roche-papier-ciseaux !
	papje	*Let's have the one who loses at rock-paper-scissors do the dishwashing today!*
892	**action**	**action**
	nf	À chaque action correspond une réaction égale et opposée.
	aksjɔ̃	*For every action there is an equal and opposite reaction.*
893	**permettre**	**to allow**
	verb	Le médecin ne me permettrait pas de prendre part au marathon.
	pɛʁmɛtʁ	*The doctor wouldn't allow me to take part in the marathon.*
894	**rapide**	**fast, quick; rapids, fast train**
	adj(f), nm	L'empereur romain Caligula avait un cheval nommé «Incitatus», qui veut dire rapide.
	ʁapid	*Roman Emperor Caligula had a horse called Incitatus which means fast.*
895	**frais**	**cool, fresh; fee, expense**
	adj[pl], adv, nm[pl]	Je voulais aller dehors et prendre un bol d'air frais.
	fʁɛ	*I wanted to go outside and get a breath of fresh air.*
896	**réunion**	**meeting, reunion**
	nf	Elle fit clairement savoir qu'elle ne pourrait pas être à temps à la réunion.
	ʁeynjɔ̃	*She made it clear that she couldn't make it in time for the meeting.*
897	**île**	**island**

	nf	Les premiers rayons du soleil déchirèrent le voile nuageux et les contours d'une île rocheuse apparurent.
	il	*The first rays of the sun tore the cloudy veil and the outline of a rocky island appeared.*
898	**toilette**	**washing, toilet, lavatory, bathroom, restroom**
	nf	« Je peux aller aux toilettes ? » « Oui. Je t'attends là, alors. »
	twalɛt	*"Is it OK if I go to the restroom?" "Sure. I'll wait here for you then."*
899	**coder**	**to code, encode**
	verb	L'agent secret a codé le message.
	kɔde	*The secret agent enocded the message.*
900	**opération**	**operation**
	nf	Le chirurgien m'a convaincue de subir une opération de transplantation.
	ɔpeʁasjɔ̃	*The surgeon persuaded me to undergo an organ transplant operation.*
901	**spécial**	**special**
	adj	J'aime les films de Terminator parce que les effets spéciaux sont fantastiques.
	spesjal	*I like the Terminator films because the special effects are fantastic.*
902	**planète**	**planet**
	nf	Il y a environ sept milliards d'habitants, sur notre planète.
	planɛt	*Approximately seven billion people inhabit our planet.*
903	**champ**	**field, realm**
	nm	Du côté droit se trouve un champ d'orge, tandis qu'à gauche se trouve un champ de blé.
	ʃɑ̃	*On the right, there is a field of barley; while on the left, there is a field of wheat.*
904	**couleur**	**color**
	nf	À la campagne, les couleurs du ciel et du feuillage sont entièrement différentes de celles qu'on voit en ville.
	kulœʁ	*In the country, the colors of the sky and of the foliage are entirely different from those seen in the city.*
905	**pain**	**bread**
	nm	Donne-nous notre pain quotidien et pardonne-nous nos offenses, comme nous pardonnons aussi à ceux qui nous ont offensés.
	pɛ̃	*Give us this day our daily bread, and forgive us our debts, as we also have forgiven our debtors.*
906	**destin**	**fate, destiny**
	nm	Crois-tu que notre destin soit régi par les étoiles ?
	dɛstɛ̃	*Do you believe our destinies are controlled by the stars?*
907	**découvrir**	**to discover, find out**
	verb	Ça surprend la plupart des gens de découvrir que le directeur de la prison est une femme.
	dekuvʁiʁ	*It surprises most people to find out that the prison warden is a woman.*
908	**puisque**	**since**
	conj	Puisque tu n'as rien à voir avec cette affaire, tu ne dois pas te faire de souci.
	pɥisk	*Since you have nothing to do with this matter, you don't have to worry.*

909	**tailler**	**to cut, carve, engrave, sharpen, trim**
	verb	C'était taillé dans un morceau de bois de pin, sculpté et poncé en forme de cœur.
	taje	*It was carved from a piece of pine wood, cut and sanded into the shape of a heart.*
910	**vaisseau**	**ship, vessel**
	nm	Une société sans religion est comme un vaisseau sans boussole.
	vɛso	*A society without religion is like a ship without a compass.*
911	**sexe**	**sex**
	nm	Je me demande si vous pourriez porter plainte contre quelqu'un du même sexe que vous pour harcèlement sexuel.
	sɛks	*I wonder if you can sue someone of the same sex for sexual harassment?*
912	**sacré**	**sacred**
	adj	S'il y a quelque chose de sacré, le corps humain est sacré.
	sakʁe	*If anything is to be called sacred, it's the human body.*
913	**repas**	**meal**
	nm[pl]	Y a-t-il un café où je puisse manger un repas léger ?
	ʁəpa	*Is there a cafe where I can have a light meal?*
914	**contrat**	**contract**
	nm	Leur contrat vient à expiration à la fin de ce mois.
	kɔ̃tʁa	*Their contract is to run out at the end of this month.*
915	**nécessaire**	**necessary, required**
	nm, adj(f)	Le talent, c'est comme l'argent. Il n'est pas nécessaire d'en avoir pour en parler.
	nesesɛʁ	*Talent is like money. It's not necessary to have any to talk about it.*
916	**client**	**client, customer**
	nm	Le client est resté pendu au téléphone pendant deux heures avec le vendeur.
	klijã	*The customer has been on the phone with the salesman for two hours.*
917	**détruire**	**to destroy**
	verb	A certain égard, j'ai aussi peur des gens; ils ont le pouvoir de vous détruire.
	detʁɥiʁ	*To some degree I am also afraid of people, they have the power to destroy you.*
918	**lait**	**milk**
	nm	Verriez-vous un inconvénient à ce que je boive le reste du lait ?
	lɛ	*Would you mind if I drank the rest of the milk?*
919	**mémoire**	**memory**
	nm, nf	Smith a passé des années à étudier l'effet du sommeil et du manque de sommeil sur la mémoire et l'apprentissage.
	memwaʁ	*Smith has spent years studying the effects of sleep and sleep loss on memory and learning.*
920	**pleurer**	**to cry**
	verb	Il essaya de la consoler, mais elle n'arrêtait pas de pleurer.
	plœʁe	*He tried to comfort her, but she kept crying.*
921	**copain**	**friend, buddy, mate**
	nm	C'est amusant de passer du temps sur la plage avec des copains.

		kɔpɛ̃	*Spending time with friends on the beach is fun.*
922	**reste**		**rest**
	nm		Je dormis le reste de la journée.
		ʁɛst	*I slept the rest of the day.*
923	**personnel**		**personnel, personal**
	noun, adj		Mettez votre CV dans l'enveloppe et adressez-le au service du personnel.
		pɛʁsɔnɛl	*Enclose your resume in this envelope and submit it to the personnel department.*
924	**doubler**		**to double, pass; to dub**
	verb		Grâce à l'innovation technologique, le maximum de rendement de l'usine a doublé.
		duble	*Thanks to technological innovations, maximum outputs of the factory have doubled.*
925	**mignon**		**cute**
	adj		Qui est ce mignon garçon avec lequel je vous ai vu hier ?
		miɲɔ̃	*Who's that cute guy I saw you with yesterday?*
926	**couteau**		**knife**
	nm		Le voleur a tenté de plonger le couteau dans le corps du garçon.
		kuto	*The robber tried to plunge the knife into the boy.*
927	**témoin**		**witness**
	nm		Des témoins ont rapporté avoir vu Dan presque partout dans la ville.
		temwɛ̃	*Witnesses reported seeing Dan almost everywhere in the town.*
928	**foi**		**faith**
	nf		Ils commençaient à perdre foi en leur commandant.
		fwa	*They were beginning to lose faith in their commander.*
929	**remercier**		**to thank**
	verb		Je ne te remercierai jamais assez pour ta gentillesse.
		ʁəmɛʁsje	*I cannot thank you enough for your kindness.*
930	**direction**		**direction, management**
	nf		La direction prend toutes les décisions importantes d'une entreprise.
		diʁɛksjɔ̃	*The management makes all the important decisions in a company.*
931	**malin**		**smart, shrewd, cunning**
	noun, adj		S'il est capable de foirer un truc pareil, c'est qu'il n'est pas bien malin.
		malɛ̃	*He can't be smart if he can screw up something like that.*
932	**niveau**		**level**
	nm		Les prix descendirent à des niveaux incroyablement bas.
		nivo	*Prices went to amazingly low levels.*
933	**remettre**		**to deliver, replace, set, put back**
	verb		L'idée est d'enlever le bouchon, se laver les mains et puis le remettre en place.
		ʁəmɛtʁ	*The idea is you remove the stick stopper, wash hands and then put it back in place.*
934	**habiter**		**to live**
	verb		Il habite une grande ville dans le sud de l'Espagne.
		abite	*He lives in a big city in the south of Spain.*
935	**apporter**		**to bring**

		verb	Dès que nous fûmes assis, elle nous a apporté le café.
		apɔʁte	*As soon as we sat down, she brought us coffee.*
936	**procès**	**trial, proceedings**	
		nm[pl]	Elle alla au procès accusée du meurtre de son mari.
		pʁɔsɛ	*She went on trial charged with murdering her husband.*
937	**doux**	**soft, sweet**	

937 **doux** adv, noun, adj[pl] — Souvenez-vous que le nom d'une personne est pour elle le son le plus doux et le plus important dans quelque langue que ce soit.

du — *Remember that a person's name is to that person the sweetest and most important sound in any language.*

938 **solution** solution

nf — Il doit y avoir un moyen d'arriver à une solution diplomatique.

sɔlysjɔ̃ — *There must be a way to arrive at a diplomatic solution.*

939 **fermer** to close, shut

verb — La café le plus proche de l'école est fermé à l'heure du déjeuner.

fɛʁme — *The café nearer to the school is closed at lunch hours.*

940 **goût** taste

nm — Ces cookies ne coûtent pas cher mais ils ont bon goût.

gu — *These cookies aren't expensive, but they taste good.*

941 **amuser** to amuse

verb — Marie et moi, qui sommes jumelles, avions pour habitude de nous amuser en échangeant nos identités et en trompant tout le monde.

amyze — *Mary and I, who are twins, used to amuse ourselves by exchanging identities and fooling everyone.*

942 **différence** difference

nf — La différence entre un « mot juste » et un « mot presque juste » est comme la différence entre la foudre et le foudre.

difeʁɑ̃s — *The difference between the right word and almost the right word is the difference between lightning and the lightning bug.*

943 **stop** stop

nm, int — Un panneau STOP au Japon a trois côtés alors qu'aux États-Unis, les panneaux STOP en ont huit.

sto — *A stop sign in Japan has 3 sides, whereas a stop sign in the U.S. has 8 sides.*

944 **réfléchir** to reflect

verb — Un enseignement du débat est de réfléchir à un concept global de sécurité des approvisionnements

ʁefleʃiʁ — *One message of the debate is to reflect on a global concept of security of supply.*

945 **enceinte** pregnant; enclosure

adjf, nf — J'ai tout le temps envie de dormir parce que je suis enceinte.

ɑ̃sɛ̃t — *I always feel like sleeping because I'm pregnant.*

946 **université** university, college

nf — Je suis allé en Australie une fois alors que j'étais à l'université.

ynivɛʁsite — *I have been to Australia once when I was in college.*

947 **bleu** blue

	adj, nm	Ce sont les myrtilles les plus bleues que j'ai jamais vues. Elles ont l'air d'un bleu quasi artificiel.
	blø	*These are the bluest blueberries I have ever seen. They're almost unnaturally blue.*
948	**mètre**	**meter**
	nm	Elle partit dernière à la course de 100 mètres mais rattrapa rapidement les autres participantes.
	mɛtʁ	*In a hundred meter dash she started last but soon caught up with the others.*
949	**marre**	**fed up, to have enough**
	nf	J'en ai tout à fait marre de ses plaisanteries.
	maʁ	*I have had quite enough of his jokes.*
950	**mentir**	**to lie**
	verb	Son histoire a été confortée par un journaliste, qui découvrit que le policier avait menti.
	mɑ̃tiʁ	*Her story was vindicated by a reporter, who found that the police officer had been lying.*
951	**courir**	**to run**
	verb	Il a dit qu'il pouvait courir 200 kilomètres en une journée et il l'a fait.
	kuʁiʁ	*He said he would run 200 kilometers in a day and he did.*
952	**arranger**	**to arrange**
	verb	Je m'arrangerai pour que quelqu'un vienne vous chercher chez vous.
	aʁɑ̃ʒe	*I'll arrange for someone to pick you up at your home.*
953	**officier**	**officer; officiate**
	nm, nf, verb	L'officier de police de service sentit un vieil homme s'approcher derrière lui.
	ɔfisje	*The police officer on duty sensed an elderly man coming up behind him.*
954	**espace**	**space**
	nm, nf	Dans un vaste espace laissé libre entre la foule et le feu, une jeune fille dansait.
	ɛspas	*In a vast space left empty between the crowd and the fire, a young girl danced.*
955	**sourire**	**smile; to smile**
	nm, verb	J'aime toujours la manière que tu as de me sourire.
	suʁiʁ	*I still love the way you smile at me.*
956	**mérite**	**merit**
	nm	Ces propositions visent une directive dont le mérite apparaît également évident.
	meʁit	*The merit of the directive that such proposals aim to achieve is also clear.*
957	**lettre**	**letter**
	nf	S'il te plaît, rappelle-moi d'écrire une lettre demain.
	lɛtʁ	*Please remind me to write a letter tomorrow.*
958	**accepter**	**to accept, admit**
	verb	Il est difficile d'accepter l'idée à soi-même qu'on est un échec.
	aksɛpte	*It's hard to admit to yourself that you are a failure.*
959	**failli**	**bankrupt**

	adj	Le syndic de faillite se servira du numéro d'inscription pour rendre compte des activités de la succession du failli.
	faji	*The trustee in bankruptcy will use the registration number to report and account for activities of the estate of the bankrupt.*
960	**angleterre**	**England**
	nf	Mon frère vit en Angleterre ça fait déjà plus de trente ans.
	ɑ̃glətɛʁ	*My brother has lived in England for more than thirty years.*
961	**vitesse**	**speed**
	nf	La vitesse de la lumière est bien plus importante que celle du son.
	vitɛs	*The speed of light is much greater than that of sound.*
962	**jambe**	**leg**
	nf	L'infirmière enroula un bandage autour de ma jambe.
	ʒɑ̃b	*The nurse wound my leg with a bandage.*
963	**camera**	**camera**
	nf	Je ne peux pas acheter une camera de plus de 300 dollars.
	kamʁa	*I cannot afford a camera above 300 dollars.*
964	**arbre**	**tree**
	nm	Des vents forts dépouillèrent l'arbre de ses feuilles.
	aʁbʁ	*Strong winds stripped the tree of its leaves.*
965	**force**	**force**
	adv, nf	Cette résolution des Nations Unies appelle au retrait des forces armées israéliennes de territoires occupés dans le récent conflit.
	fɔʁs	*This United Nations resolution calls for the withdrawal of Israel armed forces from territories occupied in the recent conflict.*
966	**trésor**	**treasure, treasury**
	nm	Ils explorèrent le désert à la recherche du trésor enfoui.
	tʁezɔʁ	*They explored the desert in quest of buried treasure.*
967	**victime**	**victim**
	nf	En dépit de la protection du gouvernement, il fut la victime d'une tentative d'assassinat qui le tua.
	viktim	*Despite the government's protection, he was the victim of an assassination attempt which killed him.*
968	**énergie**	**energy**
	nf	Si tu manges un déjeuner léger, tu éviteras probablement une baisse d'énergie en milieu d'après-midi.
	enɛʁʒi	*If you eat a light lunch, you're likely to avoid a mid-afternoon energy slump.*
969	**énorme**	**enormous, huge**
	adj(f)	Nous avons fait exploser un énorme rocher à la dynamite.
	enɔʁm	*We blew up a huge rock with dynamite.*
970	**appartenir**	**to belong**
	verb	Au camp d'été, elle avait la responsabilité du groupe auquel j'appartenais.
	apaʁtəniʁ	*At the summer camp, she was in charge of the group I belonged to.*
971	**préparer**	**to prepare**
	verb	Il n'est pas nécessaire que vous prépariez un discours formel.
	pʁepaʁe	*There's no need for you to prepare a formal speech.*

972	regretter	to regret
	verb	Je regrette de ne pas avoir beaucoup étudié pour le test.
	ʁəgʁete	*I regret not having studied hard for the test.*
973	finalement	finally, eventually
	adv	Je pense qu'il se pourrait que vous changiez finalement d'avis.
	finalmã	*I think you might eventually change your mind.*
974	inviter	to invite
	verb	Aussi bien lui que sa sœur sont invités à la fête.
	ɛ̃vite	*He, as well as his sister, are invited to the party.*
975	moindre	lesser, least, slightest
	adj(f)	La moindre petite chose peut rendre les enfants heureux
	mwɛ̃dʁ	*The least little thing can make children happy.*
976	censé	supposed (TO); REPUTED TO BE
	adj	Nous ne sommes pas censés boire de l'alcool dans ce théâtre.
	sãse	*We are not supposed to drink in this theater.*
977	image	picture, image
	nf	Si tu veux être élu, tu vas devoir soigner ton image. LOOK AFTER, TAKE CARE OF, TO TREAT 185
	imaʒ	*If you want to get elected, you're going to have to improve your public image.*
978	justement	exactly, rightly, precisely
	adv	Cette situation est justement la cause du retard économique et de la pauvreté du pays
	ʒystəmã	*This situation is precisely the cause for the backwardness and poverty of the country.*
979	enlever	to remove, to take off
	verb	J'ai enlevé mes souliers et les ai mis sous le lit.
	ãlve	*I took my shoes off and put them under the bed.*
980	chasse	chase, hunt, hunting
	nf	Nous sommes allés l'autre jour ensemble à la chasse aux ours.
	ʃas	*We went bear hunting together the other day.*
981	unique	unique
	adj(f)	Plus une personne est unique, plus elle contribue à la sagesse des autres.
	ynik	*The more unique each person is, the more he contributes to the wisdom of others.*
982	arrêt	stop
	nm	Il y a une bousculade à l'arrêt de bus à l'heure de pointe.
	aʁɛ	*There is a crush at the bus stop during rush hour.*
983	filer	to spin, run, get out
	verb	J'utilise un rouet pour filer de la laine.
	file	*I use a spinning wheel to spin wool.*
984	balle	ball, bullet
	nf	Le verre à l'épreuve des balles garantit la sécurité, mais il n'est pas beaucoup diffusé en raison de son prix élevé.
	bal	*Bullet-proof glass ensures safety but isn't widely available due to its high cost.*
985	dimanche	Sunday

	nm	Cette année, l'anniversaire de mon père tombe un dimanche.
	dimɑ̃ʃ	*My father's birthday falls on Sunday this year.*
986	**lycée**	**high school**
	nm	Quand j'étais au lycée, j'avais l'habitude de me faire de l'argent de poche en gardant des enfants.
	lise	*When I was in high school, I used to earn extra money babysitting.*
987	**fil**	**thread, wire**
	nm	Elle a utilisé une bobine de fil noir pour coudre sa robe.
	fil	*She used a reel of black thread to sew her dress.*
988	**morceau**	**piece, bit**
	nm	La souris fut attirée dans le piège à l'aide d'un gros morceau de fromage.
	mɔʁso	*The mouse was lured into the trap by a big piece of cheese.*
989	**durant**	**during, for**
	prep	Les indigènes d'Australie ont mangé du kangourou durant des millénaires.
	dyʁɑ̃	*Indigenous Australians have eaten kangaroos for millenia.*
990	**casser**	**to break**
	verb	Presque toutes les poignées de porte de cet appartement étaient cassées.
	kase	*Nearly all the doorknobs in this apartment were broken.*
991	**doigt**	**finger**
	nm	Mes doigts sont tellement engourdis par le froid que je n'arrive pas à jouer du piano.
	dwa	*My fingers are so numb with cold that I can't play the piano.*
992	**vérifier**	**to check, verify**
	verb	Je vérifierai mon agenda mais, à ce stade, je devrais être en mesure d'y parvenir la semaine prochaine.
	veʁifje	*I'll check my diary, but, at this stage, I should be able to make it next week.*
993	**appareil**	**apparatus, device**
	nm	J'ai trouvé cet appareil qui a l'air bizarre chez un antiquaire. Qu'en pensez-vous ?
	apaʁɛj	*I found this odd-looking device in an antique shop. What do you make of it?*
994	**piste**	**track, trail, path**
	nf	La piste mène à travers la forêt.
	pist	*The path leads through the forest.*
995	**troisième**	**third**
	det, nm, nf	« Où est ma salle de classe ? » - « Elle est au troisième étage. »
	tʁwazjɛm	*"Where is my classroom?" "It's on the third floor."*
996	**dépendre**	**to depend**
	verb	Tu ne devrais pas trop dépendre d'autres gens pour t'aider.
	depɑ̃dʁ	*You shouldn't depend too much on other people to help you.*
997	**programme**	**program**
	nm	Ils paraissaient déterminés à faire avancer leur programme de réforme.
	pʁɔgʁam	*They seem determined to press forward with their program of reform.*
998	**honnête**	**honest, decent, fair**
	adj(f)	Je prends pour argent comptant que les gens sont honnêtes.
	ɔnɛt	*I take it for granted that people are honest.*

999	**voiture**	**car**
	nf	Aller à l'église ne fait pas davantage de toi un Chrétien que te tenir dans un garage ne fait de toi une voiture.
	vwatyʁ	*Going to church doesn't make you a Christian any more than standing in a garage makes you a car.*
1000	**régler**	**to pay, adjust, settle**
	verb	Régler la commande de volume de la guitare au niveau désiré.
	ʁegle	*Adjust the volume control on your guitar to desired level.*
1001	**aveugle**	**blind**
	noun, adj(f)	Si par exemple, soudainement, tu devenais aveugle, que ferais-tu?
	avœgl	*If you became blind suddenly, what would you do?*
1002	**présence**	**presence**
	nf	Je t'ai dit de ne pas parler de l'affaire en sa présence.
	pʁezɑ̃s	*I told you not to talk about the matter in her presence.*
1003	**crise**	**crisis**
	nf	Une crise en France pourrait être mauvaise pour l'Amérique
	kʁiz	*A crisis in France could be bad for the United States.*
1004	**amener**	**to bring**
	verb	Je ne les ai pas achetés, mais après quelqu'un a amené trois chatons à la fondation Gorira.
	amne	*Well, I didn't buy them, but later someone brought three baby kittens to the Gorilla Foundation.*
1005	**interdire**	**to forbid, prohibit, ban**
	verb	Le conseil d'école local ferait tout pour interdire ce livre.
	ɛ̃tɛʁdiʁ	*The local school board would go to any length to ban that book.*
1006	**lever**	**to lift, raise**
	verb	Lever les mains est devenu un symbole de protestation.
	ləve	*Raised hands have become a symbol of protest.*
1007	**obtenir**	**to get, obtain**
	verb	Il tente de s'immiscer sur mon territoire et d'obtenir une part du gâteau.
	ɔptəniʁ	*He's trying to muscle in on my territory and get a piece of the action.*
1008	**pluie**	**rain**
	nf	Nous avons eu beaucoup de pluie l'année dernière.
	plчi	*We had a lot of rain last year.*
1009	**récupérer**	**to get back, recover, recuperate**
	verb	On s'est débrouillé pour la récupérer sans qu'elle le sache.
	ʁekypeʁe	*We managed to get it back without her knowing.*
1010	**prouver**	**to prove**
	verb	Une banque est un endroit où on vous prêtera de l'argent, si vous pouvez prouver que vous n'en avez pas besoin.
	pʁuve	*A bank is a place that will lend you money, if you can prove that you don't need it.*
1011	**souris**	**mouse**
	nf[pl]	La molette de la souris permet de défiler vers le bas.
	suʁi	*The mouse wheel can be used to scroll down.*

1012	**restaurer**	**to restore, feed**
	verb	L'ensemble de la communauté mondiale devrait agir pour restaurer la santé des océans.
	ʁɛstɔʁe	*All citizens should act to restore ocean health.*
1013	**regard**	**look, glance**
	nm	L'enfant a jeté un regard implorant à sa mère.
	ʁəgaʁ	*The child gave his mother an appealing look.*
1014	**intention**	**intention**
	nf	Te blesser n'était pas dans mes intentions.
	ɛ̃tɑ̃sjɔ̃	*It was not my intention to hurt your feelings.*
1015	**cou**	**neck**
	nm	Il tendit le cou dans l'espoir d'entendre ce qu'elles chuchotaient.
	ku	*He craned his neck a bit in hopes of hearing what they were whispering.*
1016	**proche**	**nearby, close**
	adv, noun, adj(f), prep	Je t'ai toujours considérée comme une amie proche.
	pʁɔʃ	*I have always considered you a close friend.*
1017	**urgence**	**emergency**
	nf	Où dois-je me rendre pour être admis en salle des urgences ?
	yʁʒɑ̃s	*Where should I go to be admitted into the emergency room?*
1018	**folie**	**madness, folly, insanity**
	nf	Le génie et la folie ne sont séparés que par le succès.
	fɔli	*Genius and madness are separated only by success.*
1019	**ancien**	**ancient; former**
	adj, nm	La Bulgarie est le seul pays d'Europe où un ancien souverain ait été élu Premier ministre.
	ɑ̃sjɛ̃	*Bulgaria is the only country in Europe where a former monarch has been elected prime minister.*
1020	**relation**	**relationship**
	nf	La relation entre Tom et Marie me paraît être la plus louche.
	ʁəlasjɔ̃	*The relationship between Tom and Mary seems to me to be the most suspicious.*
1021	**bouteille**	**bottle**
	nf	J'ai pensé que tu pourrais te sentir seule alors je suis venu avec une bouteille de vin.
	butɛj	*I thought you might be lonely, so I came over with a bottle of wine.*
1022	**étager**	**floor**
	nm	L'ascenseur est en panne alors nous devrons emprunter l'escalier. Au moins, il n'y a que deux étages !
	etaʒe	*The elevator's out of order, so we'll have to take the stairs. At least it's only two floors!*
1023	**rejoindre**	**to rejoin, reunite**
	verb	Le moment est largement venu pour eux d'être autorisés à rejoindre la famille européenne.
	ʁəʒwɛ̃dʁ	*The time is long overdue for them to be allowed to rejoin the European family.*

1024	**cassé**	**broken**
	adj	Dans un magasin si vous cassez quelque chose vous devez le payer.
	kase	*In a store if you break something you must pay for it.*
1025	**jardin**	**garden**
	nm	Si vous avez un bon jardin, cela augmentera la valeur de votre maison.
	ʒaʁdɛ̃	*If you have a good garden, it will enhance the value of your house.*
1026	**malgré**	**despite, in spite of**
	prep	Il a fait un très bon travail, malgré son jeune âge.
	malgʁe	*Despite his young age, he did a very good job.*
1027	**oiseau**	**bird**
	nm	Le chasseur mit l'oiseau en joue, mais le manqua.
	wazo	*The hunter aimed at the bird, but missed.*
1028	**frappé**	**strike, striking, stamp, impression, punch**
	nf	Je suis frappé de sentir combien le reste du monde est convaincu que demain sera meilleur
	fʁape	*I am struck by the way the rest of the world is confident of a better future*
1029	**nombre**	**number**
	nm	Bien que le nombre des étudiants augmente, en tout, moins de bourses ont été versées
	nɔ̃bʁ	*Even though student numbers are increasing, on the whole, fewer scholarships have been granted.*
1030	**sentiment**	**feeling**
	nm	J'ai le sentiment que tu ne veux pas vraiment que je parte.
	sãtimã	*I get the feeling you don't really want me to go.*
1031	**toit**	**roof**
	nm	Le vent a arraché le toit de notre immeuble.
	twa	*The wind ripped the roof off our building.*
1032	**lors**	**at the time of, during**
	adv	Il fut fait prisonnier et tué lors de la Révolution.
	lɔʁ	*He was imprisoned and killed during the revolution.*
1033	**métier**	**job, occupation, trade**
	nm	Le métier de contrôleur aérien est un métier qui procure énormément de stress.
	metje	*Air traffic controller is an extremely high pressure job.*
1034	**maladie**	**illness, disease**
	nf	La vie est une maladie mortelle sexuellement transmissible.
	maladi	*Life is a fatal sexually transmitted disease.*
1035	**poche**	**pocket**
	nf	Il mit sa main dans sa poche et sentit son portefeuille.
	pɔʃ	*He stuck his hand in his pocket and felt for his wallet.*
1036	**frapper**	**to hit, strike, knock**
	verb	Je fus tout à coup frappé de ce que la fille essayait de cacher quelque chose.
	fʁape	*It struck me that the girl was trying to hide something.*
1037	**succès**	**success**

	nm[pl]	Les chances de succès sont plus grandes si l'homme d'affaire s'y connaît et aussi s'il dispose de davantage de fonds
	syksɛ	*The chances of success are greater if the business man knows the ropes, and also has more funds at his disposal.*
1038	**dessous**	**underneath, below, bottom, underside**
	adv, nm[pl], prep	La température est encore aujourd'hui en dessous de zéro.
	dəsu	*The temperature is below zero today, too.*
1039	**théâtre**	**theater**
	nm	On ne peut pas prendre de photos dans le théâtre sans permission.
	teatʁ	*You cannot take pictures in the theater without permission.*
1040	**chinois**	**Chinese**
	noun, adj[pl]	Comme ils parlaient en chinois, je ne comprenais pas un seul mot.
	ʃinwa	*Their conversation being in Chinese, I did not understand one word.*
1041	**craindre**	**to fear, be afraid of**
	verb	L'homme passe sa vie à raisonner sur le passé, à se plaindre du présent, à craindre l'avenir.
	kʁɛ̃dʁ	*Man spends his life in reasoning with the past, in complaining about the present, in fearing the future.*
1042	**afin**	**order to, so that, so as**
	in	Ils ont mis en œuvre une politique de communication afin de promouvoir leur nouveau concept.
	afɛ̃	*They implemented a communication policy so as to promote their new concept.*
1043	**gare**	**station, railway station; beware**
	int, nf	J'ai rencontré par hasard mon vieil ami à la gare de Tokyo.
	gaʁ	*I ran into an old friend at Tokyo Station.*
1044	**billet**	**ticket**
	nm	J'ai eu des difficultés à me procurer un billet pour le concert.
	bijɛ	*I had difficulty getting a ticket for the concert.*
1045	**remarquer**	**to remark; to notice, point out**
	verb	Tom remarqua que Mary ne portait pas la bague qu'il lui avait donnée.
	ʁəmaʁke	*Tom noticed Mary wasn't wearing the ring he'd given her.*
1046	**paradis**	**paradise, heaven**
	nm[pl]	Je veux aller au paradis mais je ne veux pas mourir pour y parvenir !
	paʁadi	*I want to go to heaven, but I don't want to die to get there!*
1047	**étranger**	**foreigner; foreign**
	noun, adj	Mon école propose un hébergement gratuit pour les étudiants étrangers.
	etʁɑ̃ʒe	*My school provides free accommodation for foreign students.*
1048	**campagne**	**countryside**
	nf	En vivant comme il le faisait dans une campagne éloignée, il montait rarement à la ville.
	kɑ̃paɲ	*Living as he did in the remote countryside, he seldom came into town.*
1049	**alcool**	**alcohol**
	nm	L'alcool a fait de gros dégâts sur son corps.

	alkɔl	*Alcohol has done great mischief to his body.*
1050	**samedi**	**Saturday**
	nm	Nous jouions au tennis tous les samedis après les cours.
	samdi	*We played tennis after school every Saturday.*
1051	**produire**	**to product**
	verb	Avec un peu de chance, je peux produire plusieurs pièces par jour.
	pʁɔdɥiʁ	*I can produce several pieces a day if I'm lucky.*
1052	**répéter**	**to repeat**
	verb	Je n'ai pas le temps de le répéter alors écoutez avec attention !
	ʁepete	*I don't have time to say this twice, so listen carefully.*
1053	**souhaiter**	**to wish**
	verb	Je souhaiterais vraiment pouvoir être là, avec vous.
	swete	*I really wish I could be there with you.*
1054	**odeur**	**smell, odor**
	nf	L'odeur du gazon fraîchement coupé évoque l'image de chauds après-midi d'été.
	ɔdœʁ	*The smell of cut grass summons up images of hot summer afternoons.*
1055	**vôtre**	**your (form & pl)**
	det	Son explication de cette affaire concorde avec la vôtre.
	votʁ	*Her explanation concerning that matter matches yours.*
1056	**attendant**	**meanwhile**
	adv	Il ne faisait que se plaindre ; en attendant, j'ai trouvé une solution.
	atɑ̃dɑ̃	*All he did was complain; meanwhile, I found a solution.*
1057	**montagne**	**mountain**
	nf	Je crois que c'est dangereux d'escalader cette montagne seul.
	mɔ̃taɲ	*I think it's dangerous to climb that mountain alone.*
1058	**fantastique**	**fantastic, terrific, great, weird, eerie**
	noun, adj(f)	Je viens de découvrir ce site web et je pense qu'il est fantastique !
	fɑ̃tastik	*I just discovered this website and I think it's fantastic!*
1059	**victoire**	**victory**
	nf	Notre équipe est rentrée à la maison après une immense victoire.
	viktwaʁ	*Our team returned home after a huge victory.*
1060	**carrière**	**career**
	nf	Penses-tu sérieusement à poursuivre une carrière de pilote de course automobile ?
	kaʁjeʁ	*Are you seriously thinking about pursuing a career as a race car driver?*
1061	**fatiguer**	**to tire, get**
	verb	Ses questions étaient toujours aussi perspicaces, mais mon maître me dit de ne pas la fatiguer et de partir sans tarder.
	fatige	*She was very shrewd in her questions, but my leader said not to tire her any longer and to leave soon.*
1062	**rater**	**to miss, misfire**
	verb	J'ai couru aussi vite que j'ai pu, mais j'ai quand même raté le bus.
	ʁate	*I ran as fast as I could, but I missed the bus.*
1063	**règle**	**regular, steady, well-ordered, ruled**

		adj	Mes papiers sont en règle
		ʁɛgl	*My papers are in order.*
1064	**assurer**		**to assure, insure**
		verb	Le souscripteur a décidé de ne pas assurer le demandeur.
		asyʁe	*The underwriter decided not to insure the applicant.*
1065	**queue**		**tail, handle, stalk, stem, rear**
		nf	La petite sirène gémit et regarda tristement sa queue de poisson.
		kø	*The little mermaid sighed and looked sadly at her fish tail.*
1066	**viande**		**meat**
		nf	On n'arrive pas à faire une bonne soupe avec de la viande de mauvaise qualité.
		vjɑ̃d	*You can't make good soup with cheap meat.*
1067	**rivière**		**river**
		nf	Les gens du coin nomment cette rivière "la mangeuse d'hommes" et la craignent.
		ʁivjɛʁ	*The locals call this river the man-eating river and fear it.*
1068	**suivant**		**following**
		noun, adj, prep	Le mode de fonctionnement de la commande de pompes 2 est expliqué plus en détail dans le diagramme suivant.
		sɥivɑ̃	*The function of the pump control 2 is shown in detail in the following diagram.*
1069	**obliger**		**to require, force, oblige, to have to**
		verb	Vous n'êtes pas obligés d'y aller, à moins que vous ne le vouliez.
		ɔbliʒe	*You don't have to go unless you want to.*
1070	**fusil**		**rifle, gun**
		nm	Tom gardait son fusil pointé vers Mary et lui dit de ne pas bouger.
		fyzi	*Tom kept his gun pointed at Mary and told her not to move.*
1071	**passager**		**passenger, temporary**
		noun, adj	Un passager fit un malaise mais l'hôtesse de l'air le ranima.
		pasaʒe	*A passenger fainted, but the stewardess brought him round.*
1072	**hasard**		**chance, luck**
		nm	J'ai trouvé par hasard le livre chez ce libraire.
		azaʁ	*I found the book at that bookstore by chance.*
1073	**neige**		**snow**
		nf	Cette année, il a encore plus neigé que l'an dernier.
		nɛʒ	*This year we had more snow than last year.*
1074	**parfaitement**		**perfectly**
		adv	La fête s'est déroulée parfaitement et les enfants étaient tous joyeux
		paʁfɛtmɑ̃	*The party went perfectly and the children were all jolly.*
1075	**journal**		**newspaper, paper**
		nm	D'après les journaux il y a eu un tremblement de terre à Mexico.
		ʒuʁnal	*According to the newspaper there was an earthquake in Mexico.*
1076	**échapper**		**to escape**
		verb	Le garçon a échappé de justesse à la noyade.
		eʃape	*The boy narrowly escaped drowning.*
1077	**plage**		**beach**

		nf	J'entends dire que beaucoup de filles portent des bikinis sur cette plage.
		plaʒ	*I hear a lot of girls wear bikinis at that beach.*
1078	**signal**	**signal**	
		nm	Aux premiers temps, les hommes communiquaient par signaux de fumée.
		siɲal	*In the early days people communicated by smoke signals.*
1079	**crétin**	**dumbass**	
		nm	N'importe quel crétin avec un appareil photo, pense qu'il est photographe.
		kʁetɛ̃	*Every dumbass with a camera thinks he is a photographer.*
1080	**vidéo**	**video**	
		adj(i), nf	Certains pensent, à tort, que les jeux vidéo sont la source de nos maux.
		video	*There are those who think, falsely, that video games are the source of all our ills.*
1081	**coffrer**	**trunk, boot, chest**	
		nm	Les portes refusaient de s'ouvrir et je dus donc monter par le coffre.
		kɔfʁe	*The doors wouldn't open, so I had to get in through the trunk.*
1082	**pression**	**pressure**	
		nf	Je pense que je comprends la pression que tu subis.
		pʁesjɔ̃	*I think I understand the pressures you are under.*
1083	**costume**	**suit, costume, dress**	
		nm	Essaie ce nouveau costume pour voir s'il te va bien.
		kɔstym	*Try on this new suit to see if it fits well.*
1084	**information**	**information**	
		nf	Toute conversation implique l'encodage et le décodage d'information.
		ɛ̃fɔʁmasjɔ̃	*All conversation involves the encoding and decoding of information.*
1085	**futur**	**future**	
		noun, adj	Le futur appartient au peu d'entre nous qui n'ont toujours pas peur de se salir les mains.
		fytyʁ	*The future belongs to the few among us who are still willing to get their hands dirty.*
1086	**univers**	**universe**	
		nm[pl]	L'observation d'ondes gravitationnelles inaugurera une nouvelle étape dans l'étude de l'univers.
		ynivɛʁ	*The observation of gravitational waves will start a new phase in the study of the universe.*
1087	**volonté**	**will**	
		nf	Je n'ai aucune force de volonté lorsqu'il s'agit de faire de l'exercice.
		vɔlɔ̃te	*I have no will power when it comes to exercising.*
1088	**attendu**	**expected**	
		adj	Énoncez ce que vous allez faire et définissez le résultat attendu.
		atɑ̃dy	*Name what you're going to do and define the expected outcome.*
1089	**excuse**	**excuse, apology**	
		nf	Il a toujours une bonne excuse pour ses retards.
		ɛkskyz	*He always has a good excuse for being late.*
1090	**faible**	**weak**	

	noun, adj(f)	La compétitivité du Japon est très forte pour les produits industriels mais faible pour les produits agricoles.
	fɛbl	*Japan's competitiveness is very strong in industrial products, but weak in agricultural products.*
1091	**attraper**	**to catch, get, pick up**
	verb	Jim a été attrapé alors qu'il trichait à l'examen.
	atʁape	*Jim was caught cheating in the examination.*
1092	**inquiéter**	**to worry, disturb**
	verb	Ne t'inquiète pas ! Même si je bois, ça n'affecte pas ma capacité à conduire.
	ẽkjete	*Don't worry! Even if I drink, it doesn't have an effect on my driving.*
1093	**cesse**	**constantly, always**
	adv	Eh bien, elle a sans cesse la diarrhée et elle s'absente de l'école.
	sɛs	*Well, she is always having diarrhoea and missing school.*
1094	**ministre**	**minister**
	nm, nf	Golda Meir a été Premier Ministre durant les années mille-neuf-cent-soixante-neuf à mille-neuf-cent-soixante-quatorze.
	ministʁ	*Golda Meir served as prime minister during the years 1969-1974.*
1095	**naissance**	**birth**
	nf	Je me demande ce que pense une personne aveugle de naissance lorsqu'elle entend les mots «bleu» ou «vert».
	nɛsãs	*I wonder what a person blind from birth thinks of when they hear the words "blue" or "green".*
1096	**utile**	**useful**
	adj(f)	Plus il y aura de contributeurs, plus Tatoeba sera utile !
	ytil	*The more contributors there are, the more useful Tatoeba will become!*
1097	**gaz**	**gas**
	nm[pl]	N'oubliez pas de couper le gaz avant de quitter la maison.
	gaz	*Don't forget to turn off the gas before leaving the house.*
1098	**bataille**	**battle**
	nf	Perdre une bataille ne signifie pas perdre la guerre !
	bataj	*Losing a battle doesn't mean losing the war!*
1099	**voleur**	**thief, light-fingered**
	noun, adj	Je suis monté sur un vélo, et j'ai poursuivi le voleur.
	vɔlœʁ	*I got on a bicycle and chased after the thief.*
1100	**poids**	**weight**
	nm[pl]	Comment fais-tu pour manger ainsi, sans prendre de poids ?
	pwa	*How do you eat like that without gaining weight?*
1101	**discourir**	**to discuss, to discourse, ramble**
	verb	Comme vous le voyez, je suis capable de discourir longtemps, et probablement de prendre tout le temps qui est réservé aux autres.
	diskuʁiʁ	*As you can see, I have the ability to ramble and probably take up everybody's time here.*
1102	**star**	**star**
	nf	Il est captivé par l'idée de devenir une star du rock.

	staʁ	*He's enamored of the idea of becoming a rock star.*
1103	**gâteau**	**cake**
	noun, adj	Nous avons besoin de farine, de sucre et d'œufs pour élaborer ce gâteau.
	gato	*We need flour, sugar and eggs to make this cake.*
1104	**ventre**	**belly, stomach**
	nm	Étendez-vous sur le ventre, sur la table d'examen.
	vãtʁ	*Lie on your stomach on the examination table.*
1105	**connaissance**	**knowledge**
	nf	Nous avons maintenant des politiciens qui n'ont même pas la connaissance qu'aurait un enfant du gouvernement.
	kɔnɛsãs	*We now have politicians who lack a child's knowledge of government.*
1106	**vif**	**lively**
	noun, adj	Le rapporteur a souligné que ce rapport a fait l'objet d'un vif débat au sein du groupe ALDE
	vif	*The rapporteur pointed out that the report has been the subject of lively debate in the ALDE Group.*
1107	**assassin**	**murderer, assassin**
	noun, adj	L'assassin purge une peine de prison de dix ans.
	asasɛ̃	*The murderer is serving a ten-year prison sentence.*
1108	**vendredi**	**Friday**
	nm	Habituellement, ils vont à l'école du lundi au vendredi.
	vãdʁədi	*They usually go to school from Monday to Friday.*
1109	**couple**	**couple**
	nm, nf	On s'attend à ce que cent cinquante mille couples se marient à Shanghai en 2006.
	kupl	*One hundred and fifty thousand couples are expected to get married in Shanghai in 2006.*
1110	**sérieusement**	**seriously**
	adv	Cependant, les activités de la LNP continuent à être sérieusement ralenties par le manque d'équipements de base.
	seʁjøzmã	*The operations of the LNP, however, continue to be seriously hampered by the lack of basic equipment.*
1111	**militaire**	**military**
	noun, adj(f)	Il est responsable de la logistique de l'opération militaire.
	militɛʁ	*He is in charge of the logistics of the military operation.*
1112	**date**	**date**
	nf	Date à laquelle cette page a été mise à jour pour la dernière fois : le 03/11/2010.
	dat	*Date of last revision of this page: 2010-11-03*
1113	**titre**	**title**
	nm	Je n'ai pas réussi à me rappeler du titre de la chanson.
	titʁ	*I wasn't able to remember the title of that song.*
1114	**génie**	**genius**
	nm	Il a une intelligence extraordinaire, c'est un génie.
	ʒeni	*His intelligence is truly extraordinary, he is a genius.*
1115	**autrement**	**differently, something else, otherwise**

	adv	Elle était partie, autrement nous lui aurions rendu visite.
	otʁəmã	*She was away, otherwise we would have visited her.*
1116	**amener**	**to bring**
	verb	Je veux juste savoir pourquoi tu m'as amenée ici.
	amne	*I just want to know why you brought me here.*
1117	**os**	**bone**
	nm[pl]	Le mur autour de la hutte était fait d'os humains et sur son faîte, se trouvaient des crânes.
	ɔs	*The wall around the hut was made of human bones and on its top were skulls.*
1118	**valeur**	**value, worth**
	nf	J'accorde davantage de valeur à notre amitié qu'à quoi que ce soit d'autre.
	valœʁ	*I consider our friendship to be worth more than any other.*
1119	**puissant**	**powerful**
	noun, adj	Beaucoup de gens rêvent de devenir riches et puissants.
	pɥisã	*Many people dream of becoming rich and powerful.*
1120	**style**	**style**
	nm	Tous les grands écrivains sont dotés de leurs propres styles.
	stil	*All great writers have their own personal styles.*
1121	**vert**	**green**
	noun, adj	La chaleur du soleil tombe en plein sur le champ de blé vert.
	vɛʁ	*The warm sunlight is full upon the green wheat field.*
1122	**fortune**	**fortune**
	nf	Il a accumulé une fortune immense au cours de l'après-guerre.
	fɔʁtyn	*He accumulated a tremendous fortune during the post war.*
1123	**poulet**	**chicken**
	nm	Lorsque je suis entré dans la cuisine, elle faisait un curry au poulet avec du riz
	pulɛ	*When I entered the kitchen, she was making chicken curry with rice.*
1124	**embrasser**	**to kiss, embrace**
	verb	Je n'arrive pas à croire que je sois en train de t'embrasser.
	ãbʁase	*I can't believe I'm kissing you.*
1125	**genou**	**knee**
	nm	Tom s'est blessé au genou gauche à l'entraînement, alors Jean a dû jouer à sa place.
	ʒənu	*Tom hurt his left knee during practice, so John had to play the game in his place.*
1126	**célèbre**	**famous**
	adj(f)	Washington était l'homme le plus célèbre des États-Unis d'Amérique.
	selɛbʁ	*Washington was the most famous man in the United States.*
1127	**cibler**	**to target**
	verb	La campagne cible un public jeune.
	sible	*The campaign targets a young audience.*
1128	**cousin**	**cousin**
	nm	Mon cousin n'est pas le genre de personne qui romprait jamais une promesse.

kuzɛ̃

My cousin isn't the kind of person who'd ever break a promise.

1129 conscience | **conscience, consciousness**

nf

Une conscience sans tache est le meilleur des oreillers.

kɔ̃sjɑ̃s

A clear conscience is the best pillow.

1130 prévenir | **to prevent, warn; to notify**

verb

Des mesures drastiques doivent être prises afin de prévenir une plus grande propagation du virus.

pʁevəniʁ

Drastic measures must be taken to prevent the further spread of the virus.

1131 article | **article**

nm

Cet article n'a pas fait l'objet d'une révision par des pairs.

aʁtikl

This article is not peer-reviewed.

1132 étoile | **star**

nf

Il y a plusieurs étoiles plus grandes que le soleil dans l'univers.

etwal

There are a lot of stars which are larger than our sun.

1133 millier | **thousand**

nm

Des milliers de personnes sont allés à la plage pour voir le dauphin.

milje

Thousands of people went to the beach to see the dolphin.

1134 reprendre | **to resume, recover, start again, take back**

verb

Après une courte pause, ils ont repris les négociations.

ʁəpʁɑ̃dʁ

After a short break, they resumed negotiations.

1135 mine | **appearance, look, skin**

nf

Ce complément de soin confère un spectaculaire effet bonne mine !

min

This extra treatment makes your skin look spectacularly healthy!

1136 charmant | **charming**

adj

Ce charmant village est niché entre l'océan et les dernières crêtes des Pyrénées.

ʃaʁmɑ̃

This charming village is nestling between the ocean and the Western end of the Pyrenees.

1137 reposer | **to rest**

verb

La prospérité d'une nation repose largement sur ses jeunes générations.

ʁəpoze

The prosperity of a nation largely rests to its young men.

1138 noter | **to note, notice, write down**

verb

Je n'ai pas pu noter le numéro d'immatriculation de la voiture.

nɔte

I was unable to write down the number of the car.

1139 agréable | **pleasant, nice, agreeable**

noun, adj(f)

Il eut un mot gentil et un sourire agréable à l'intention de chacun.

agʁeabl

He had a kind word and a pleasant smile for everyone.

1140 château | **castle**

nm

La ville dans laquelle je suis né est connue pour ses vieux châteaux.

ʃato

The town in which I was born is famous for its old castle.

1141 bal | **ball**

nm

« Veux-tu aller au bal avec moi ? » « Je suis vraiment désolée, mais je ne peux pas. »

bal

"Do you want to go to the ball with me?" "I'm really sorry, but I can't."

1142 oreille | **ear**

| | nf | Ils ont des yeux, mais ne voient pas; des oreilles, mais n'entendent pas. |

ɔʀɛj — *They have eyes but they do not see - ears, and they do not hear.*

1143 apparemment — **apparently**

adv — Apparemment, mon entretien s'est bien passé puisque j'ai reçu une offre d'emploi.

apaʀamɑ̃ — *Apparently, my interview went well since I received a job offer.*

1144 zéro — **zero**

nm — Sans perte de généralité, on peut supposer que la suite converge vers zéro.

zeʀo — *Without loss of generality, we can say that the sequence converges to zero.*

1145 saint — **saint, holy**

noun, adj — Chacun sait que ce n'est pas un saint. En le défendant, nous accepterions et encouragerions ses points de vue.

sɛ̃ — *Everyone knows that he's no saint. By defending him, we'd be accepting and encouraging his views.*

1146 marrant — **funny, funny guy**

noun, adj — On commence par refuser gentiment mais nous finissons par accepter en se disant que ca pourrait être marrant.

maʀɑ̃ — *First we refuse nicely but we finally accept thinking it could be funny.*

1147 joue — **cheek**

nf — Sommes-nous pour la loi du talion ou tendons-nous l'autre joue ?

ʒu — *Do we subscribe to retaliation or do we turn the other cheek?*

1148 salon — **lounge, living room**

nm — Nous nous trouvions dans le salon lorsque nous avons entendu le coup de feu.

salɔ̃ — *We were in the living room when we heard the gunshot.*

1149 lève — **survey**

nf — Un levé de terrain révèle que le seuil de la piste 27 se trouve à 1 712 pieds au-dessus du niveau de la mer

lɛv — *A survey determined that the threshold of runway 27 is 1 712 feet above sea level*

1150 conversation — **conversation**

nf — C'est souvent qu'il s'immisce en plein milieu d'une conversation.

kɔ̃vɛʀsasjɔ̃ — *He often breaks into the middle of a conversation.*

1151 piloter — **to fly, pilot, drive**

verb — Une chose dont j'ai toujours eu envie, c'est d'apprendre à piloter un avion.

pilɔte — *One thing I've always wanted to do is learn to fly an airplane.*

1152 fer — **iron**

nm — Cette étude confirme l'effet bienfaisant possible d'une consommation modérée d'alcool sur le taux de fer dans le sang.

fɛʀ — *The study rather confirms the more likely beneficial effect of moderate alcohol consumption for blood iron levels.*

1153 gorge — **throat**

nf — Avaler et s'éclaircir la gorge peut être un signe que quelqu'un ment.

gɔʀʒ — *Swallowing and throat-clearing can be a sign that someone is lying.*

1154 victime — **victim**

nf — Ils nous demandèrent de faire quelque chose pour aider les victimes.

	viktim	They called on us to do something to help the victims.
1155	**détail**	**detail**
	nm	Il est préférable de prendre les choses avec calme que de se stresser sur chaque petit détail.
	detaj	*It's better to take things in stride than to stress out over every little detail.*
1156	**priver**	**to deprive**
	verb	En pareil cas, il ne serait pas opportun de priver le travailleur de la possibilité que la juridiction de son lieu de travail soit compétente.
	pʁive	*It would not be appropriate to deprive the employee of the alternative forum of his place of work in such cases.*
1157	**violence**	**violence**
	nf	La paix n'est pas l'absence de violence mais la présence de justice.
	vjɔlɑ̃s	*Peace is not the absence of violence but the presence of justice.*
1158	**nerveux**	**nervous, irritable**
	noun, adj[pl]	Avec autant de personnes autour de lui, il devint naturellement un peu nerveux.
	nɛʁvø	*With so many people around he naturally became a bit nervous.*
1159	**aéroport**	**airport**
	nm	Je me rendis à l'aéroport pour rencontrer mon père.
	aeʁɔpɔʁ	*I went to the airport to meet my father.*
1160	**direct**	**direct**
	noun, adj	Tu as désobéi à un ordre direct et tu dois en payer les conséquences.
	diʁɛkt	*You disobeyed a direct order and must pay the consequences.*
1161	**tribunal**	**court**
	nm	L'attitude du tribunal envers les jeunes criminels est différente de celle qu'il a envers les criminels adultes.
	tʁibynal	*The attitude of the court toward young criminals is different from its attitude toward adult criminals.*
1162	**paquet**	**packet**
	nm	Ce livre est l'équivalent littéraire des bonbons Haribo : on veut juste en goûter un, et on finit par dévorer le paquet tout entier.
	pakɛ	*This book is the literary equivalent of Haribo sweets: you only want to eat one, but end up devouring the whole packet.*
1163	**fumer**	**to smoke**
	verb	Après de vives discussions, un compromis a été adopté à l'effet que les fumeurs pourront maintenant fumer dans le coin pour fumeurs.
	fyme	*After a heated discussion, a compromise was adopted. Smokers will be allowed to smoke in the smoking corner.*
1164	**aise**	**comfort, joy, pleasure, ease**
	noun, adj(f)	Je me sens à l'aise avec mes beaux-parents.
	ɛz	*I feel at ease with my parents-in-law.*
1165	**emmerder**	**to bug, bother**
	verb	Il doit cesser de nous emmerder avec ses propos ridicules et ses remarques tout à fait déplacées.
	ãmɛʁde	*He must stop bugging us with his ludicrous statements and his inept comments*

1166	**joindre**	**to join**
	verb	Je serais ravi si tu pouvais te joindre à nous pour déjeuner.
	ʒwɛ̃dʁ	*I'd be delighted if you could join us for dinner.*
1167	**lance**	**lance, spear**
	nf	Les chevaliers avaient souvent des lances pour combattre.
	lɑ̃s	*Knights often had spears to fight.*
1168	**usiner**	**factory**
	nf	De nouvelles usines et zones industrielles furent érigées.
	yzine	*New factories and industrial centers were built.*
1169	**défendre**	**to defend, forbid**
	verb	Nous devons défendre notre liberté coûte que coûte.
	defɑ̃dʁ	*We must defend our freedom at all cost.*
1170	**forêt**	**forest**
	nf	En Amérique, il y a de très nombreux feux de forêt.
	fɔʁɛ	*There are a great many forest fires in America.*
1171	**champion**	**champion**
	noun, adj	On attendait du champion de l'année dernière qu'il remportât Wimbledon.
	ʃɑ̃pjɔ̃	*Last year's champion was expected to win Wimbledon.*
1172	**horreur**	**horror**
	nf	Le réalisme de leur jeu rappelait à chacun l'horreur de la crucifixion.
	ɔʁœʁ	*The realism brought home to everyone the horror of the crucifixion.*
1173	**test**	**test**
	nm	C'était un test si difficile que nous n'avons pas eu le temps de finir.
	tɛst	*It was such a hard test that we did not have time to finish.*
1174	**désormais**	**from now on, henceforth**
	adv	Désormais, cet institut devrait devenir une Agence européenne des droits de l'Homme.
	dezɔʁmɛ	*Henceforth, this institute shall become a European Human Rights Agency*
1175	**extérieur**	**exterior**
	noun, adj	Les murs extérieurs de cette maison sont recouverts de chaux.
	ɛksteʁjœʁ	*The exterior walls of this house are covered with lime.*
1176	**désert**	**desert, wilderness**
	adj, nm	La dernière partie de l'excursion fut un parcours à travers le désert.
	dezɛʁ	*The last part of the trip was across the desert.*
1177	**intelligent**	**intelligent, clever, bright, smart**
	adj	Je ne suis pas aussi intelligent que les gens le pensent.
	ɛ̃teliʒɑ̃	*I'm not as smart as people think I am.*
1178	**hum**	**um, uh, Hmm**
	int	Hum. J'ai le sentiment que je vais me perdre, quelle que soit la route que je prenne
	œm	*Hmm. I have a feeling I'm going to get lost whichever road I take.*
1179	**compte**	**account, count**
	nm	Je n'ai pas besoin d'un compte Facebook pour avoir des amis.
	kɔ̃t	*I don't need a Facebook account in order to have friends.*
1180	**mode**	**mode, way, fashion**

		nm, nf	Les jupes courtes ne sont déjà plus à la mode.
		mɔd	*Short skirts have already gone out of fashion.*
1181	**série**	**series**
		nf	L'entraîneur a préparé une série d'exercices pour les athlètes.
		seʁi	*The coach prepared a series of exercises for the athletes.*
1182	**pis**	**worse**
		adv, nm[pl]	Les circonstances politiques du pays vont de mal en pis.
		pi	*The country's political circumstances are going from bad to worse.*
1183	**sage**	**wise, good, sound, sensible**
		noun, adj(f)	Me voici pauvre fou maintenant et pas plus sage qu'auparavant
		saʒ	*Me voici pauvre fou maintenant et pas plus sage qu'auparavant*
1184	**concerner**	**to concern**
		verb	Tom ergotait à propos des phrases le concernant alors que Mary faisait du mieux qu'elle pouvait pour les traduire.
		kɔ̃sɛʁne	*Tom was quibbling about the sentences concerning him, while Mary was doing her best to translate them.*
1185	**grandir**	**to grow, increase, expand**
		verb	En voyant les choses d'un point de vue nouveau, nous avons une occasion excitante de grandir en nombre et en services.
		gʁɑ̃diʁ	*By looking at things from a new point of view, we have an exciting opportunity to grow, both in numbers and in service.*
1186	**pousser**	**to push**
		verb	Nous nous plaçâmes derrière la voiture et poussâmes.
		puse	*We got behind the car and pushed.*
1187	**vache**	**cow**
		adj(f), nf	Le lait de vache est plus savoureux que le lait de soja.
		vaʃ	*Cow's milk is tastier than soy milk.*
1188	**repos**	**rest**
		nm[pl]	Je veux que vous preniez une bonne nuit de repos.
		ʁəpo	*I want you to get a good night's rest.*
1189	**ordinateur**	**computer**
		noun, adj	L'ordinateur de Tom est si vieux qu'il tourne encore sous Windows 98.
		ɔʁdinatœʁ	*Tom's computer is so old that it still runs Windows 98.*
1190	**rock**	**rock music**
		nm	Je pense que la plupart des jeunes aiment la musique rock.
		ʁɔk	*I think that most young people like rock music.*
1191	**ombre**	**shade, shadow**
		nm, nf	Le souci dote souvent une petite chose d'une grande ombre.
		ɔ̃bʁ	*Worry often gives a small thing a large shadow.*
1192	**russe**	**Russian**
		noun, adj(f)	Le chapitre sur la révolution russe m'a vraiment affecté.
		ʁys	*The chapter on the Russian Revolution really blew me away.*
1193	**minuit**	**midnight**
		nm	C'était une nuit torride que je n'ai pu m'endormir avant minuit.
		minɥi	*It was such a hot night that I could not sleep till midnight.*

1194	**amusant**	**funny, amusing, entertaining**
	noun, adj	Tous les visiteurs, surtout les enfants, ont trouvé le clown amusant.
	amyzɑ̃	*All visitors, especially the children, found the clown funny*
1195	**membre**	**member**
	nm	Les membres de la famille prenaient soin du patient à tour de rôle.
	mɑ̃bʁ	*The family members nursed the patient in turns.*
1196	**ouvert**	**open**
	adj	Peter voit que la porte du garage est ouverte.
	uvɛʁ	*Peter sees that the garage door is open.*
1197	**nombreux**	**numerous**
	adj[pl]	Le chanteur a reçu de nombreuses lettres de ses fans
	nɔ̃bʁø	*The singer received numerous letters from his fans.*
1198	**également**	**also, too, as well, equally**
	adv	La candidature peut également être soumise par e-mail.
	egalmɑ̃	*The application can also be submitted via e-mail.*
1199	**mince**	**thin, slim, slender**
	adj(f), int	Il y a beaucoup de pression sur les femmes pour qu'elles soient minces.
	mɛ̃s	*There is a lot of pressure on women to be thin.*
1200	**essence**	**gas, petrol**
	nf	Notre voiture tomba en panne d'essence dix minutes plus tard.
	esɑ̃s	*Our car ran out of gas after ten minutes.*
1201	**maire**	**mayor**
	nm	Il a représenté le maire lors de la cérémonie.
	mɛʁ	*He represented the mayor at a ceremony.*
1202	**lundi**	**Monday**
	nm	Je veux votre papier sur mon bureau d'ici lundi.
	lœ̃di	*Have your paper on my desk by Monday.*
1203	**moteur**	**motor**
	noun, adj	Il a vidé l'huile du moteur.
	mɔtœʁ	*He drained the oil from the motor.*
1204	**réparer**	**to repair, fix, correct, make up**
	verb	Il faut que je fasse venir quelqu'un pour réparer ma télé.
	ʁepaʁe	*I must get the television fixed.*
1205	**franchement**	**frankly**
	adv	Franchement, ma chère, c'est le cadet de mes soucis.
	fʁɑ̃ʃmɑ̃	*Frankly, my dear, I don't give a damn.*
1206	**cigarette**	**cigarette**
	nf	Veuillez éteindre vos cigarettes avant de pénétrer dans le musée.
	sigaʁɛt	*Please put out your cigarettes before entering the museum.*
1207	**partager**	**to share**
	verb	Pourquoi voudrais-tu partager ce type d'information avec des gens que tu connais à peine ?
	paʁtaʒe	*Why would you want to share this type of information with people you hardly know?*
1208	**puissance**	**power**

	nf	Une part toujours croissante de la population n'est pas en mesure d'exploiter à fond la puissance d'expression de la langue allemande.
	pɥisɑ̃s	*An increasingly greater part of the population is not capable of fully utilizing the power of expression of the German language.*
1209	**hiver**	**winter**
	nm	Il devrait être plutôt fou pour escalader la montagne en hiver.
	ivɛʁ	*He'd be crazy to climb the mountain in winter.*
1210	**souffle**	**breath, puff**
	nm	Il fait si froid que je peux voir mon propre souffle.
	sufl	*It is so cold that I can see my own breath.*
1211	**tenter**	**to tempt, try**
	verb	Il m'a fallu un moment pour comprendre ce qu'elle tentait de dire.
	tɑ̃te	*It took me a while to understand what she was trying to say.*
1212	**vingt**	**twenty**
	det, num	L'Australie est environ vingt fois plus grande que le Japon.
	vɛ̃	*Australia is about twenty times as large as Japan.*
1213	**miracle**	**miracle**
	nm	C'est dommage qu'on ne puisse pas acheter des miracles comme on achète des pommes de terre.
	miʁakl	*It's a pity that you can't buy miracles like you would buy potatoes.*
1214	**apprécier**	**to appreciate**
	verb	Les clients apprécient l'excellent service de la firme.
	apʁesje	*Customers appreciate the firm's excellent service.*
1215	**artiste**	**artist**
	noun, adj(f)	Picasso est un artiste célèbre que tout le monde connaît.
	aʁtist	*Picasso is a famous artist whom everyone knows.*
1216	**créer**	**to create**
	verb	Les chercheurs ont créé des chatons qui luisent dans l'obscurité.
	kʁee	*The researchers have created kittens that can glow in the dark.*
1217	**lac**	**lake**
	nm	Nous effectuâmes un tour complet du lac en marchant.
	lak	*We've walked all around the lake.*
1218	**sommeil**	**sleep, sleepiness**
	nm	On m'a dit que j'avais besoin de prendre suffisamment de sommeil.
	sɔmɛj	*I was told that I needed to get enough sleep.*
1219	**réveiller**	**to wake up**
	verb	Hier le réveil n'a pas sonné et Kurt ne s'est pas réveillé.
	ʁeveje	*Yesterday the alarm clock didn't go off and Kurt didn't wake up.*
1220	**leçon**	**lesson**
	nf	« Parles-tu le grec ? » - « Pas encore, c'est ma première leçon ! »
	ləsɔ̃	*Do you speak Greek? - Not yet, that's my first lesson!*
1221	**chemise**	**shirt, folder**
	nf	Ces chemises sont pareilles. Elles sont de la même taille.
	ʃəmiz	*These shirts are the same. They are the same size.*
1222	**fantôme**	**ghost, phantom**

	nm	Y a-t-il beaucoup de gens en Europe qui croient encore aux fantômes ?
	fɑ̃tom	*Are there many people in Europe who believe in ghosts even now?*
1223	**acteur**	**actor**
	nm	L'homme qui demeure à côté de chez nous est un acteur célèbre.
	aktœʁ	*The man who lives next door to us is a famous actor.*
1224	**parc**	**park**
	nm	Je suis allé au parc pour profiter du beau temps.
	paʁk	*I went to the park to enjoy the fine weather.*
1225	**chair**	**flesh**
	nf	La guerre, c'est simple : c'est faire entrer un morceau de fer dans un morceau de chair.
	ʃɛʁ	*War is simple: it's driving a piece of iron through a piece of flesh.*
1226	**rue**	**street**
	nf	Descendez la rue pendant 5 minutes et vous verrez le magasin sur votre droite.
	ʁy	*Go down the street for about five minutes, and you will see the department store to the right.*
1227	**reculer**	**to move back, back up, move backward**
	verb	Nous insistons pour progresser plutôt que reculer dans le domaine de la sécurité aérienne.
	ʁəkyle	*We are insisting that we move forward to enhance aviation safety, not move backward.*
1228	**japonais**	**Japanese**
	noun, adj[pl]	Marie vit au Japon depuis assez longtemps. Ne pensez-vous pas qu'il est temps qu'elle s'adapte aux coutumes japonaises ?
	ʒapɔnɛ	*Mary's been living in Japan so long. Don't you think it's time she adjusted to Japanese customs?*
1229	**coûter**	**to cost**
	verb	Cette affaire m'a coûté de nombreuses nuits blanches.
	kute	*The affair cost me many sleepless nights.*
1230	**semblant**	**semblance, pretence**
	nm	Est-il sage selon vous, Mesdames et Messieurs les Députés, de faire semblant que ce problème n'existe pas ?
	sɑ̃blɑ̃	*Ladies and gentlemen, in your opinion, is it wise to pretend that the problem does not exist?*
1231	**annoncer**	**to announce**
	verb	J'ai perdu mon chat et mon boulot en un jour, et pour enfoncer le clou ma femme m'a annoncé qu'elle me quittait.
	anɔ̃se	*I lost my cat and job on the same day, and on top of it all, my wife announced that she was leaving me.*
1232	**échange**	**exchange**
	nm	Les participants au séminaire ont l'intention d'échanger des expériences et ainsi d'apprendre les uns des autres.
	eʃɑ̃ʒ	*The seminar participants intend on exchanging experiences and in doing so learn from each other.*
1233	**payer**	**to pay**

	verb	Les personnes qui n'ont pas payé leur cotisation sont priées de venir me voir à la fin du cours.
	peje	*Those who have not paid their dues are asked to see me at the end of class.*
1234	**débarrasser**	**to clear, get rid of**
	verb	Le gouvernement essaie de se débarrasser de la pollution.
	debaʁase	*The government is trying to get rid of pollution.*
1235	**fuir**	**to flee**
	verb	Le bruit a fait fuir tous les animaux.
	fɥiʁ	*The noise caused all the animals to flee.*
1236	**supplier**	**to beg, implore, plead**
	verb	Elle le supplia de rester un petit peu plus longtemps.
	syplije	*She pleaded with him to stay a little bit longer.*
1237	**gouverneur**	**governor**
	nm, nf	Il a osé rendre visite au gouverneur de l'État de New-York.
	guvɛʁnœʁ	*He dared to visit the governor of New York State.*
1238	**mark**	**mark**
	nm	Si l'euro est une devise faible, le mark était alors tout bonnement anémique.
	maʁk	*If the euro is a weak currency, than the Mark was positively anaemic.*
1239	**chauffeur**	**driver, chauffeur**
	nm	J'ai besoin d'un chauffeur pour me conduire à la gare. Il pleut.
	ʃofœʁ	*I need a driver to take me to the station. It's raining.*
1240	**marquer**	**to mark**
	verb	L'invention des ordinateurs a marqué l'avènement d'une nouvelle ère
	maʁke	*The invention of computers marked the coming of a new era.*
1241	**rapidement**	**quickly, rapidly**
	adv	Les vieilles coutumes sont en train de disparaître rapidement aujourd'hui.
	ʁapidmã	*Ancient customs are dying out quickly today.*
1242	**unité**	**unity; unit**
	nf	Les scientifiques ont depuis longtemps cessé de croire que l'atome est la plus petite unité de matière.
	ynite	*Scientists long ago ceased to believe that the atom is the smallest unit of matter.*
1243	**fesser**	**to spank**
	verb	Enfant, j'étais fessé si je faisais quelque chose de mal.
	fese	*When I was a child, I was spanked if I did something wrong.*
1244	**souci**	**worry, concern, care**
	nm	Les touristes laissent leurs soucis derrière eux quand ils voyagent.
	susi	*Tourists leave their cares behind when they travel.*
1245	**manteau**	**coat, overcoat**
	nm	Ma sœur, portant son manteau rouge favori, est sortie aujourd'hui.
	mãto	*My sister, wearing her favorite red coat, went out today.*
1246	**allemand**	**German**
	noun, adj	Non seulement parle-t-elle anglais, mais aussi allemand.
	almã	*Not only does she speak English, but also German.*
1247	**pantalon**	**trousers, pants**

	nm		Que vais-je mettre: un pantalon ou une jupe ?
	pɑ̃talɔ̃		*What shall I put on: trousers or a skirt?*
1248	**policier**	**policeman**	
	noun, adj		Les émeutiers frappèrent de nombreux policiers à mort.
	pɔlisje		*The rioters beat many policemen to death.*
1249	**innocent**	**innocent**	
	noun, adj		Plus on devient vieux, moins on devient innocent.
	inɔsɑ̃		*The older we grow, the less innocent we become.*
1250	**véritable**	**real, TRUE**	
	adj(f)		Le véritable amour ne s'est jamais déroulé sans heurts.
	veʁitabl		*The course of true love never did run smooth.*
1251	**caisse**	**till, cash desk, cashier**	
	nf		C'est comme changer l'étiquette de prix d'un vêtement
	kɛs		*It's like switching the price tag on an item before bringing it to the cashier.*
1252	**lunette(s)**	**sg: telescope; pl: glasses**	
	nf		Elle a mis des lunettes noires pour protéger ses yeux du soleil.
	lynetɛ)		*She put on dark glasses to protect her eyes from the sun.*
1253	**patient**	**patient**	
	noun, adj		Si tu avais été un peu plus patient, tu aurais pu réussir.
	pasjɑ̃		*If you had been a little more patient, you could have succeeded.*
1254	**menteur**	**liar**	
	nm		Dans ma vie, j'ai toujours été un menteur. C'est pourquoi les gens m'appréciaient.
	mɑ̃tœʁ		*In my life I always was a liar. That's why people liked me.*
1255	**perte**	**loss**	
	nf		On doit compenser les pertes d'une manière ou d'une autre.
	pɛʁt		*We must make up for the loss in some way.*
1256	**menace**	**threat**	
	nf		Elle était tentée de le prendre au mot, croyant à peine qu'il mettrait sa menace à exécution.
	mənas		*She was tempted to call his bluff, hardly believing that he would carry out his threat.*
1257	**émission**	**transmision, broadcasting, programme**	
	nf		Nous avons vu une émission intéressante à la télévision hier.
	emisjɔ̃		*We saw an interesting program on television yesterday.*
1258	**abandonner**	**to give up, abandon**	
	verb		Les projets qui nuisent à l'environnement devraient être systématiquement abandonnés.
	abɑ̃dɔne		*Environmentally damaging projects should be abandoned systematically.*
1259	**permission**	**permission, leave**	
	nf		On ne laisse entrer personne sans permission spéciale.
	pɛʁmisjɔ̃		*They don't let anyone enter without special permission.*
1260	**herbe**	**grass, herb**	
	nf		Les vaches se mouvaient très lentement à travers les grandes herbes vertes.
	ɛʁb		*The cows were moving very slowly through the long green grass.*

1261	**front**	**front, forehead**
	nm	Ton front est très chaud ; je pense que tu as de la fièvre.
	fʁɔ̃	*Your forehead is quite hot. I think you have a fever.*
1262	**juif**	**Jew, Jewish**
	noun, adj	Il y avait des juifs dans les pays arabes avant le partage de la Palestine.
	ʒɥif	*There were Jews in Arab countries before the partition of Palestine*
1263	**chouette**	**owl, nice, awesome!**
	nf, adj, int	C'était chouette de votre part de faire tout ce chemin pour me voir.
	ʃwɛt	*It was nice of you to come all this way to see me.*
1264	**chaise**	**chair**
	nf	Est-ce qu'il y a toujours assez de chaises pour tout le monde ?
	ʃɛz	*Are there still enough chairs for everyone?*
1265	**suicider**	**to commit suicide**
	verb	Une femme a écrit 30 livres sur comment être heureux, et après s'est suicidée.
	sɥiside	*A woman wrote 30 books about how to become happy, and then committed suicide.*
1266	**malheureusement**	**unfortunately**
	adv	Malheureusement, je n'ai pas eu l'occasion de voir le château.
	maløʁøzmɑ̃	*Unfortunately, I didn't get the chance to see the castle.*
1267	**chocolat**	**chocolate**
	adj(i), nm	Le gâteau préféré de Tom est celui avec trois couches de chocolat.
	ʃɔkɔla	*Tom's favorite is the triple-layer chocolate cake.*
1268	**mouvement**	**movement**
	nm	Le mouvement de résistance est entré dans la clandestinité.
	muvmɑ̃	*The resistance movement has gone underground.*
1269	**identité**	**identity**
	nf	Un emploi du temps, c'est une carte d'identité du temps, seulement, si on n'a pas d'emploi du temps, le temps n'est pas là.
	idɑ̃tite	*A schedule is an identity card for time, but, if you don't have a schedule, the time isn't there.*
1270	**douche**	**shower, douche**
	nf	Je ne peux pas arrêter la douche. Pourriez-vous la vérifier pour moi ?
	duʃ	*I can't turn the shower off. Could you check it for me?*
1271	**chaleur**	**heat**
	nf	Il ne pouvait pas dormir à cause de la chaleur.
	ʃalœʁ	*He could not sleep because of the heat.*
1272	**lèvre**	**lip**
	nf	Ordener pressa religieusement sur ses lèvres ce présent de sa bien-aimée.
	lɛvʁ	*Ordener religiously pressed this gift from his beloved against his lips.*
1273	**étude**	**study**
	nf	La méthode proposée est appliquée à trois études de cas basées sur des simulations.
	etyd	*The proposed methodology is applied to three simulated case studies.*

1274	faveur	favor
	nf	En récompense de mon aide pour vos études, j'aimerais vous demander une petite faveur.
	favœʁ	*In return for helping you with your studies, I'd like to ask a small favor of you.*
1275	totalement	totally
	adv	Mais avoir enseigné à un martyr est quelque chose de totalement différent.
	tɔtalmã	*But to learn that one of our students is a martyr is something totally different.*
1276	pause	break, pause
	nf	Tom a joué du piano pendant trois heures sans prendre de pause.
	poz	*Tom played the piano for three hours without taking a break.*
1277	mai	May
	nm	C'est une vieille coutume d'offrir du muguet en cadeau le premier mai.
	mɛ	*It's an old custom to give a gift of lilies of the valley on the first of May.*
1278	soudain	sudden, suddenly
	adj, adv	Soudainement, la fille aînée s'exclama : "Je veux des bonbons."
	sudɛ̃	*Suddenly the eldest daughter spoke up, saying, "I want candy."*
1279	heureusement	fortunately, luckily
	adv	Heureusement ou malheureusement, cet échec est partagé par la société civile en général
	øʁøzmã	*Luckily or regretfully, this failure is shared by civil society in general.*
1280	choc	shock, clash
	nm	Ma fille était sous le choc lorsqu'elle a rencontré son idole.
	ʃɔk	*My daughter was in shock when she met her idol.*
1281	note	note, grade
	nf	Il me faut m'entretenir avec toi de tes notes.
	nɔt	*I need to talk to you about your grades.*
1282	piéger	to trap, booby-trap
	verb	Une fosse profonde, une plate-forme en béton ou bois et terre, un abri et une conduite d'aération pour piéger les mouches.
	pjeʒe	*A deep pit, a concrete or wood and earth platform, a shelter, and a vent pipe to trap flies.*
1283	malheur	misfortune
	nm	Elle a eu le malheur de naître femme et elle a eu la malheur d'épouser un Blanc.
	malœʁ	*She had the misfortune of being born a girl and then marrying a white man.*
1284	attaquer	to attack
	verb	Les chiens ne mordent que rarement, sauf s'ils sont attaqués.
	atake	*A dog seldom bites unless it is attacked.*
1285	mars	March; Mars
	nm[pl]	Nous sommes actuellement, dans la première partie du mois de mars, en pleine saison du vêlage.
	maʁs	*We were the first part of March, in the middle of calving season.*

1286	**fonctionner**	**to function, work**
	verb	L'ordinateur a cessé de fonctionner après une mise à jour système automatique.
	fɔ̃ksjɔne	*The computer stopped working after an automatic system update.*
1287	**portable**	**portable, wearable; cell phone**
	adj(f), nm	Oh non ! Je ne faisais pas attention et j'ai laissé mon téléphone portable au restaurant.
	pɔʁtabl	*Oh no! I wasn't paying attention and left my cell phone in the restaurant!*
1288	**secrétaire**	**secretary**
	nm, nf	Cette secrétaire s'est révélée être une espionne.
	səkʁetɛʁ	*The secretary proved to be a spy.*
1289	**mensonge**	**lie**
	nm	Un homme aussi honnête que John ne pourrait dire un mensonge.
	mɑ̃sɔ̃ʒ	*Such an honest man as John cannot have told a lie.*
1290	**nettoyer**	**to clean**
	verb	Seriez-vous prêts à m'aider à nettoyer le garage ?
	netwaje	*Would you be willing to help me clean the garage?*
1291	**gloire**	**glory, fame**
	nf	La gloire suit la vertu comme si elle était son ombre.
	glwaʁ	*Glory follows virtue as if it were its shadow.*
1292	**accès**	**access**
	nm[pl]	Zone d'Accès Contrôlé : Entrée interdite sans autorisation.
	aksɛ	*Controlled Access Zone: No entry without permission.*
1293	**changement**	**change**
	nm	Le changement climatique est vu par beaucoup comme le problème crucial de notre temps.
	ʃɑ̃ʒmɑ̃	*Climate change is seen by many as the defining issue of our time.*
1294	**poupée**	**doll, dolly, puppet**
	nf	Alors, les yeux de la petite poupée se mettaient à briller, tels des vers luisants, et elle s'animait.
	pupe	*Then the little doll's eyes would begin to shine like glowworms, and it would become alive.*
1295	**bref**	**brief, short**
	adj, adv, nm	Nous allons débuter par un bref tour de table
	bʁɛf	*We will begin with a short round table discussion.*
1296	**réel**	**real**
	noun, adj	Les dragons n'existent pas dans le monde réel.
	ʁeɛl	*Dragons do not exist in the real world.*
1297	**ballon**	**ball**
	nm	Le ballon de rugby a à peu près une forme d'œuf.
	balɔ̃	*The rugby ball is shaped something like an egg.*
1298	**abri**	**shelter**
	nm	Il apporta de la nourriture à son invité et lui procura un abri.
	abʁi	*He brought food to his guest and provided him shelter.*
1299	**corde**	**rope, cord, string**

	nf	Je me tins fermement à la corde de sorte que je ne tombe pas.
	kɔʁd	*I held on to the rope tightly so I wouldn't fall.*
1300	**respirer**	**to breathe**
	verb	Il a monté l'escalier en respirant très difficilement.
	ʁɛspiʁe	*He ran up the stairs breathing very hard.*
1301	**plat**	**dish, flat**
	adj, nm	Nous ferions tout aussi bien de manger de la nourriture pour chien qu'un tel plat.
	pla	*We might as well eat dog food as eat such a dish.*
1302	**emploi**	**employment, work, use**
	nm	Il a trouvé un emploi et n'a plus à mendier pour manger.
	ɑ̃plwa	*He found work and no longer has to beg to eat.*
1303	**ennuyer**	**to bore, worry, bother**
	verb	Elle avait l'air de s'ennuyer pendant que nous faisions l'amour.
	ɑ̃nɥije	*She looked bored while we were making love.*
1304	**attrape**	**catch**
	nf	Un joueur lance la balle et l'autre joueur l'attrape.
	atʁap	*One player throws the ball and the other player catches it.*
1305	**foule**	**crowd**
	nf	Une fille s'approcha du roi à travers la foule.
	ful	*A girl approached the king from among the crowd.*
1306	**larme**	**tear**
	nf	Quand as-tu, pour la dernière fois, essuyé les larmes de quelqu'un ?
	laʁm	*When did you last wipe someone's tears away?*
1307	**siècle**	**century**
	nm	Les lunes galiléennes sont les quatre lunes découvertes par Galileo Galilei au 17e siècle.
	sjɛkl	*The Galilean moons are the four moons of Jupiter that were discovered by Galileo Galilei in the 17th century.*
1308	**atteindre**	**to reach**
	verb	Après que John fut devenu directeur, il m'a dit qu'il n'avait jamais pensé atteindre un poste aussi haut placé.
	atɛ̃dʁ	*After John became manager, he told me he would never have expected to reach such a high position.*
1309	**veste**	**jacket**
	nf	Il remarqua un trou dans sa veste, mais essaya de l'ignorer.
	vɛst	*He noticed a hole in his jacket, but he tried to ignore it.*
1310	**couverture**	**blanket**
	nf	Nous devrions utiliser les couvertures électriques chauffantes ce soir.
	kuvɛʁtyʁ	*We should use the electric blankets tonight.*
1311	**fac**	**uni, university**
	nf	Alors, la question que je me pose est la suivante: que va-t-il se passer une fois ces jeunes iront à la Fac?
	fak	*Now the question is: what will happen to these young people once they reach the University?*

1312	**mener**	**to lead, live**
	verb	Mon rêve est de mener une vie tranquille à la campagne.
	məne	*My dream is to live a quiet life in the country.*
1313	**lancer**	**to throw, launch, start**
	nm, verb	Si tu vas lancer une nouvelle affaire, tu as besoin d'un plan d'affaire.
	lɑ̃se	*If you're going to start a new business, you need a business plan.*
1314	**piano**	**piano**
	adv, nm	Quelle est la différence entre un piano et un poisson ?
	pjano	*What is the difference between a piano and a fish?*
1315	**source**	**source, spring**
	nf	Si la source n'est pas mentionnée, une citation n'est pas une citation mais du plagiat.
	suʁs	*If the source is not specified, a quote is not a quote but plagiarism.*
1316	**camarade**	**friend, comrade, pal, mate**
	nm, nf	Parmi les délits mineurs, le plus grave est de voler un camarade.
	kamaʁad	*Among minor offences, the most serious was stealing from a comrade*
1317	**couche**	**layer, coat**
	nf	Le dessert a deux couches de fruits et une couche de crème.
	kuʃ	*The dessert has two layers of fruit and one layer of cream.*
1318	**prêtre**	**priest**
	nm	Le prêtre fit le signe de croix tandis que le cercueil était descendu dans le sol.
	pʁɛtʁ	*The priest made the sign of the cross as the casket was lowered into the ground.*
1319	**saison**	**season**
	nf	Se moucher sans cesse le nez pendant la saison des allergies.
	sɛzɔ̃	*Constantly blowing his nose in allergy season.*
1320	**mesurer**	**to measure**
	verb	L'architecte a soigneusement mesuré la largeur de la chambre
	məzyʁe	*The architect carefully measured the width of the bedroom.*
1321	**entreprendre**	**to begin, start, undertake**
	verb	Je veux entreprendre un voyage autour du monde.
	ɑ̃tʁəpʁɑ̃dʁ	*I want to undertake a journey around the world.*
1322	**supporter**	**to support, endure**
	nm, verb	Le fort a été construit pour supporter des attaques répétées
	sypɔʁte	*The fort was built to endure repeated attacks.*
1323	**évidemment**	**obviously**
	adv	Mon ami se sentait évidemment épuisé après le marathon.
	evidamɑ̃	*My friend was obviously exhausted after the marathon.*
1324	**image**	**picture, image**
	nf	Je ne peux voir cette image sans repenser à mon enfance.
	imaʒ	*I cannot see this picture without remembering my childhood.*
1325	**distance**	**distance**
	nf	Je ne suis pas habitué à marcher sur de longues distances.
	distɑ̃s	*I am not accustomed to walking long distances.*
1326	**commettre**	**to commit**

		verb	Ils ne montrent aucun regret pour leurs forfaits mais continuent de commettre crime sur crime.
		kɔmɛtʁ	*They show no remorse for their misdeeds, but continue to commit one crime after another.*
1327	**delà**		**beyond, above, over**
		adv	Ce qui est fait par amour a toujours lieu au-delà du bien et du mal.
		dəla	*What is done out of love always takes place beyond good and evil.*
1328	**laver**		**to wash, clean**
		verb	Lavez les endives et ôtez les feuilles qui pourraient être gâtées.
		lave	*Wash the chicory and remove the leaves which may spoil.*
1329	**somme**		**amount, sum; nap**
		nm, nf	Il a payé une somme impressionnante pour cette montre.
		sɔm	*He paid an enormous amount of money for this watch.*
1330	**affreux**		**dreadful, awful, horrible**
		noun, adj[pl]	Les natto sentent affreusement mauvais mais à manger le goût est délicieux.
		afʁø	*Natto smells awful but tastes delicious.*
1331	**ours**		**bear**
		adj(i), nm[pl]	Ne vends pas la peau de l'ours avant de l'avoir tué.
		uʁs	*Don't sell the bear's fur before hunting it.*
1332	**geste**		**gesture**
		nm	Les gestes sont très importants dans la communication entre humains.
		ʒɛst	*Gestures are very important in human communication.*
1333	**prisonnier**		**prisoner, captive**
		noun, adj	Ils ont tué Tom pour montrer l'exemple aux autres prisonniers.
		pʁizɔnje	*They killed Tom as an example to the other prisoners.*
1334	**directement**		**directly**
		adv	D'un point de vue théorique, l'argument de Peterson est en rapport direct avec notre discussion.
		diʁɛktəmã	*From a theoretical point of view, Peterson's argument is directly relevant to our discussion.*
1335	**tableau**		**frame, picture, painting, panel**
		nm	Il a pour passe-temps de peindre des tableaux de fleurs
		tablo	*His hobby is painting pictures of flowers.*
1336	**reconnaître**		**to recognize**
		verb	Un héros n'est souvent qu'une personne incapable de reconnaître un danger.
		ʁəkɔnɛtʁ	*A hero is often just a person who doesn't have the ability to recognise danger.*
1337	**demi**		**half**
		adj(i), adv, nm	Un demi-million d'enfants font encore face à la malnutrition au Niger.
		dəmi	*Half a million children still face malnutrition in Niger.*
1338	**commissaire**		**superintendent, commissioner**
		nm, nf	Un nouveau commissaire est chargé de l'enquête.
		kɔmisɛʁ	*A new commissioner is in charge of the investigation.*
1339	**alerte**		**agile, alert, warning**

	adj(f), nf	Les résultats de ces travaux de recherche seront intégrés dans de nouveaux programmes d'alerte rapide
	alɛʁt	*Research results will be integrated into new early warning programmes.*
1340	**plaisanter**	**to joke**
	verb	Dites-moi, je vous prie, que vous êtes en train de plaisanter !
	plɛzɑ̃te	*Please tell me you're joking.*
1341	**crier**	**to shout, scream, cry out**
	verb	On entend le cri des vendeurs en montant les escaliers : "Des hotdogs ! Par ici pour acheter des hotdogs !"
	kʁije	*As they walk up and down the rows they shout, "Get your hot dogs here! Get your hot dogs!"*
1342	**singe**	**monkey**
	nm	J'ai persuadé le policier de ne pas tirer sur le singe
	sɛ̃ʒ	*I persuaded the policeman not to shoot the monkey.*
1343	**prudent**	**prudent, careful, cautious**
	adj	Quelque chose pourrait te tomber dessus, alors sois prudente.
	pʁydɑ̃	*Something might fall on you, so be careful.*
1344	**ressentir**	**to feel**
	verb	Vous ne savez pas, jusqu'à ce que vous ayez un enfant, quelle douleur vous pouvez ressentir lorsque quelque chose leur arrive.
	ʁəsɑ̃tiʁ	*You don't know until you've had a child what pain you can feel when something happens to them.*
1345	**donne**	**given**
	adj	Faites ce que vous pouvez avec ce qui vous a été donné.
	dɔn	*Do what you can with what you have been given.*
1346	**convaincre**	**to convince**
	verb	Ce n'était pas facile de convaincre Tom de faire ça
	kɔ̃vɛ̃kʁ	*It wasn't easy to convince Tom to do that.*
1347	**aube**	**dawn, daybreak**
	nf	Elle a dit qu'elle devait être de retour avant l'aube.
	ob	*She said that she had to be back before dawn.*
1348	**propriétaire**	**owner**
	nm, nf	Ils pensent que le propriétaire de la maison étudie à l'étranger.
	pʁɔpʁijetɛʁ	*They think the owner of the house is studying abroad.*
1349	**laisse**	**leash, lead**
	nf	La première est de sortir votre chat en promenade chaque jour.
	lɛs	*One option is to walk your cat on a leash every day.*
1350	**coincer**	**to jam, hinder, get stuck**
	verb	Elles sont restées coincées dans l'ascenseur pendant quatre heures.
	kwɛ̃se	*They were stuck in the elevator for four hours.*
1351	**tenu**	**tenuous, slender, held**
	adj	Un lien ténu est néanmoins maintenu avec les dépenses agricoles
	təny	
		Nevertheless, a tenuous link is still maintained with agricultural expenditure

1352	**bite**	**cock**
	nf	Les garçons se demandaient qui avait la plus grosse bite
	bit	*The guys wondered who had the biggest cock.*
1353	**étoile**	**star**
	nf	Le ciel était trop nuageux pour voir les étoiles.
	etwal	*The sky was too cloudy to see the stars.*
1354	**frontière**	**border**
	nf	Il y a un point de contrôle à la frontière où ils vérifient le contenu de votre coffre.
	fʁɔ̃tjɛʁ	*There's a checkpoint at the border where they look in your trunk.*
1355	**remonter**	**to go back up**
	verb	Puis on remonte dans la voiture et on passe dans le tunnel.
	ʁəmɔ̃te	*Then we go back up in the car and we pass in the tunnel.*
1356	**sec**	**dry**
	adj, adv, nm	Les noix, les amandes, les noisettes, les pistaches et les pignons sont des fruits secs.
	sɛk	*Walnuts, almonds, hazelnuts, pistachios and pine nuts are dry fruits.*
1357	**diriger**	**to lead, direct**
	verb	Le compositeur du morceau a aussi dirigé l'orchestre.
	diʁiʒe	*The composer of the piece also directed the orchestra.*
1358	**soi**	**one, oneself, self**
	ni, pron	Il permet aussi d'apprendre la solidarité et le dépassement de soi.
	swa	*It is also a way of learning how to show solidarity and how to excel oneself.*
1359	**facilement**	**easily**
	adv	La confiture s'étend facilement sur le pain.
	fasilmɑ̃	*The jam spreads easily on the bread.*
1360	**porc**	**pig, pork**
	nm	En ce qui me concerne, je préfère le poulet au porc.
	pɔʁ	*As for me, I like chicken better than pork*
1361	**vierge**	**virgin**
	noun, adj(f)	Placez les pennette dans une grande assiette, assaisonnez avec une goutte d'huile d'olive vierge extra,
	vjɛʁʒ	*Place the pasta on a serving tray, season with a drop of extra virgin olive oil*
1362	**réserver**	**to book, to reserve**
	verb	S'il vous plait, réservez-moi une chambre dans un hôtel de première classe.
	ʁezɛʁve	*Please book me a room in a first-class hotel.*
1363	**haïr**	**to detest, hate, abhor**
	verb	Quand bien même Tom était mon meilleur ami, je commence à le haïr.
	aiʁ	*Even though Tom used to be my best friend, I'm beginning to hate him.*
1364	**suspect**	**suspicious, suspect**
	noun, adj	Le suspect s'était caché dans les montagnes pendant trois semaines.
	syspɛ	*The suspect was hiding out in the mountains for three weeks.*
1365	**station**	**station**
	nf	La station spatiale internationale est une étonnante prouesse technologique.
	stasjɔ̃	*The international space station is an amazing feat of engineering.*

1366	**tromper**	**to deceive**
	verb	Son apparence et son charme ont trompé beaucoup de gens
	tʀɔ̃pe	*His appearance and charm deceived many people.*
1367	**souffrir**	**to suffer**
	verb	J'ai une douleur au poignet et à l'avant-bras, je crois que je souffre peut-être du syndrome du canal carpien.
	sufʀiʀ	*My wrist and forearm hurt, I think I might be suffering from carpal tunnel syndrome.*
1368	**bagage**	**luggage, baggage**
	nm	N'oublie pas de donner un pourboire au porteur pour avoir porté tes bagages.
	bagaʒ	*Don't forget to tip the porter for carrying your luggage.*
1369	**protection**	**protection**
	nf	La fourrure fournit aux animaux une protection contre le froid.
	pʀɔtɛksjɔ̃	*Fur provides animals protection against the cold.*
1370	**tir**	**fire, shot, launch**
	nm	Finir n'importe quel niveau en explosant des bulles à chaque tir.
	tiʀ	*Clear a level by popping bubbles with every shot.*
1371	**dame**	**lady**
	int, nf	La vieille dame vivait seule dans un appartement de trois pièces.
	dam	*The old lady lived in a three-room apartment by herself.*
1372	**empereur**	**emperor**
	nm	Il était une fois un empereur qui était un grand conquérant et régnait sur davantage de pays que quiconque au monde.
	ɑ̃pʀœʀ	*Once upon a time there lived an emperor who was a great conqueror, and reigned over more countries than anyone in the world.*
1373	**océan**	**ocean**
	nm	Ce que nous savons est une goutte d'eau. Ce que nous ignorons est un océan.
	ɔseɑ̃	*What we know is a drop. What we don't know is an ocean.*
1374	**concert**	**concert**
	nm	Après le concert la foule se dirigea vers la porte la plus proche.
	kɔ̃sɛʀ	*After the concert, the crowd made for the nearest door.*
1375	**immeuble**	**building**
	noun, adj(f)	Ce n'est pas tous les jours qu'on a un immeuble à son nom.
	imœbl	*It's not every day you get a building named after you.*
1376	**virer**	**to turn, change, transfer, kick out**
	verb	La couleur de l'ongle peut virer au jaune-vert ou au marron.
	viʀe	*The color of the nail may change to yellow-green or brown.*
1377	**chaîne**	**chain, channel**
	nf	Cela ne vous dérange pas que je change de chaîne ?
	ʃɛn	*Do you mind if I change the channel?*
1378	**enfance**	**childhood**
	nf	Je ne suis pas né ici mais j'y ai passé toute ma prime enfance.
	ɑ̃fɑ̃s	*I wasn't born here, but I spent all of my early childhood here.*
1379	**maudire**	**to curse**

	verb	Mieux vaut allumer une bougie que de maudire l'obscurité.
	modiʁ	*It is better to light a candle than to curse the darkness.*
1380	**cauchemar**	**nightmare, bad dream**
	nm	On peut employer un capteur de rêves pour capturer ses cauchemars.
	koʃmaʁ	*You can use a dreamcatcher to catch your nightmares.*
1381	**amitié**	**friendship**
	nf	La bonne et vraie amitié ne doit être soupçonneuse en rien.
	amitje	*True and good friendship must not be suspicious of anything.*
1382	**partenaire**	**partner**
	nm, nf	Après dix ans comme partenaires en affaires, ils ont décidé de se séparer.
	paʁtənɛʁ	*After ten years as business partners, they decided to part ways.*
1383	**curieux**	**curious**
	noun, adj[pl]	En général, les Anglais ne sont pas curieux des autres.
	kyʁjø	*Generally speaking, Englishmen aren't curious about others.*
1384	**patte**	**paw, foot, leg**
	nf	La chambre était pleine d'insectes, des millions de petits insectes se tortillant avec plein de pattes.
	pat	*The room was full of bugs, millions of small, wriggling bugs with lots of legs.*
1385	**lendemain**	**next day**
	nm	J'ai acheté un appareil photo, mais je l'ai perdu le lendemain.
	lãdmɛ̃	*I bought a camera, but I lost it the next day.*
1386	**soupe**	**soup**
	nf	Cette soupe est trop chaude, je ne peux pas la manger.
	sup	*The soup's too hot, I can't eat it.*
1387	**uniforme**	**uniform, steady, regular**
	adj(f), nm	Les policiers de la ville de New York portent un uniforme bleu sombre.
	ynifɔʁm	*New York City policemen wear navy blue uniforms.*
1388	**marine**	**marine, navy**
	adj, nf	Qu'est-ce qu'une langue ? C'est un dialecte avec une armée et une marine.
	maʁin	*What is a language? It's a dialect with an army and a navy.*
1389	**reserve**	**reserve**
	nf	Certains scientifiques prévoient que les réserves mondiales de pétroles seront épuisées d'ici un siècle.
	ʁəzɛʁv	*Some scientists predict that the world oil reserves will be used up within a century.*
1390	**chine**	**China**
	nf	Trente-deux boursiers malgaches s'envolent pour la Chine.
	ʃin	*Thirty-two Madagascan scholars are flying to China.*
1391	**désir**	**desire**
	nm	La communauté a un désir sincère de nettoyer le fleuve
	deziʁ	*The community has a sincere desire to clean up the river.*
1392	**objet**	**objective; object**
	nm	Dans ce jeu, chacun doit toucher un objet et deviner ce que c'est.
	ɔbʒɛ	*In this game, you must feel an object and guess what it is.*
1393	**tracer**	**to draw, write, mark out**

	verb	J'ai tracé une ligne droite d'un point à l'autre.
	tʁase	*I drew a straight line from one dot to the other.*
1394	**recommencer**	**to resume, start again, start over**
	verb	Je pense que nous ferions mieux de recommencer du départ.
	ʁəkɔmãse	*I think we'd better start over again.*
1395	**traverser**	**to cross, traverse**
	verb	J'évite de traverser la rue ici si je suis pressé.
	tʁavɛʁse	*I avoid crossing the street here if I am in a hurry.*
1396	**humanité**	**humanity**
	nf	Les armes nucléaires sont une menace pour toute l'humanité.
	ymanite	*Nuclear weapons are a threat to all humanity.*
1397	**lapin**	**rabbit**
	nm	Deux petits lapins, un lapin blanc et un lapin noir, vivaient dans une grande forêt.
	lapɛ̃	*Two small rabbits, a white rabbit and a black rabbit, lived in a large forest.*
1398	**sonner**	**to ring**
	verb	
		Ce fait devrait certainement sonner l'alarme auprès des personnes qui se soucient de la justice
	sɔne	*This certainly has to ring alarm bells for people concerned with justice*
1399	**baguer**	**to ring, tag**
	verb	Les vols avaient pour objet de localiser et de baguer des cygnes trompettes.
	bage	*The purpose of the flights was to locate and tag Trumpeter swans.*
1400	**survivre**	**to survive**
	verb	Je me demande si cette phrase va survivre à la fin du monde.
	syʁvivʁ	*I ask myself if this sentence will survive till the end of the world.*
1401	**bâtiment**	**building**
	nm	Il y a un feu dans le bâtiment. Nous devons évacuer immédiatement.
	batimã	*There's a fire in the building. We have to evacuate immediately.*
1402	**chèque**	**check**
	nm	J'ai mille dollars en chèques de voyage et cinq cents dollars en liquide.
	ʃɛk	*I have one thousand dollars in travelers' checks and five hundred in cash.*
1403	**palais**	**palace, palate**
	nm[pl]	Nous avons assisté à la relève de la garde, au Palais de Buckingham.
	palɛ	*We watched the changing of the guard at Buckingham palace.*
1404	**valise**	**suitcase**
	nf	Je ne peux pas porter cette valise. C'est trop lourd.
	valiz	*I can't carry this suitcase. It's too heavy.*
1405	**charger**	**to load, charge**
	verb	Il est toutefois permis de charger des produits chimiques prémélangés dans le cas d'un produit en système fermé.
	ʃaʁʒe	*Loading of premixed chemicals with a closed system is permitted.*
1406	**haine**	**hatred, hate**
	nf	La haine n'existe pas sans raison, elle naît habituellement de l'envie ou de la peur.

εn

Hatred doesn't just appear out of thin air, it usually starts from envy or fear.

1407	**assurance**	**insurance, confidence**
	nf	Ma voiture est couverte par mon assurance en cas de vol
	asyʁɑ̃s	*My car is covered by my insurance in case of theft.*

1408	**navire**	**ship**
	nm	La coque du navire est divisée en compartiments étanches.
	naviʁ	*The ship hull is divided into watertight compartments.*

1409	**foyer**	**home, hearth**
	nm	En deux-mille-vingt-quatre, il y aura un robot dans chaque foyer.
	fwaje	*In 2024, there will be a robot in every home.*

1410	**printemps**	**spring**
	nm[pl]	Le printemps apporte un temps doux après l'hiver froid.
	pʁɛ̃tɑ̃	*Spring brings mild weather after the cold winter.*

1411	**voiler**	**to veil**
	verb	Les pouce et index toujours joints, couvrez le ciboire et voilez-le.
	vwale	*Still keeping the thumb and forefinger joined, cover and veil the ciborium.*

1412	**personnage**	**character, individual**
	nm	Le personnage principal est un homme dont on ne connaît pas le nom.
	pɛʁsɔnaʒ	*The main character is a man whose name we do not know.*

1413	**brave**	**brave, worthy, good, brave man**
	noun, adj	Tout le monde dit que j'étais brave, mais je n'ai fait que mon travail.
	bʁav	*Everyone says I was very brave, but I just did my work.*

1414	**évident**	**obviously, of course**
	adv	Il doit évidemment y avoir un rapport entre traduire et écrire soi-même des poèmes, mais lequel, je ne sais pas.
	evidɑ̃	*There must of course be a relationship between translating and making poems of your own, but what it is I just don't know.*

1415	**sale**	**dirty**
	noun, adj(f)	Marie ne supporte pas que Tom laisse ses vêtements sales sur le sol.
	sal	*Mary can't abide Tom leaving his dirty clothes on the floor.*

1416	**roule**	**rolled**
	adj	Vous avez probablement levé le nez sur le brocoli, picossé dans vos carottes et regardé vos pois rouler dans votre assiette
	ʁul	*You might have turned up your nose at the broccoli, nibbled away at the carrots and watched while the peas rolled around on your plate*

1417	**extraordinaire**	**extraordinary**
	adj(f)	L'honnête Benignus aimait extraordinairement la vie, mais il aimait l'or prodigieusement.
	ɛkstʁaɔʁdinɛʁ	*The honest Benignus loved life extraordinarily, but he loved gold prodigiously.*

1418	**explosion**	**explosion**
	nf	Il y a eu la nuit dernière une explosion dans une usine de feux d'artifice.
	ɛksplozjɔ̃	*Last night an explosion took place at a fireworks factory.*

1419	**sucre**	**sugar**
	nm	Il étendit la main pour attraper le sucre qui se trouvait sur l'autre table.

	sykʁ	*He reached out for the sugar that was on the other table.*
1420	**procureur**	**prosecutor**
	nm	Les procureurs au tribunal doivent étayer leurs affirmations pour prouver qu'un suspect est coupable.
	pʁɔkyʁœʁ	*Prosecutors in court have to substantiate their claims in order to prove a suspect is guilty.*
1421	**opinion**	**opinion**
	nf	Si j'avais voulu ton opinion, je te l'aurais demandée.
	ɔpinjɔ̃	*If I had wanted your opinion, I would have asked for it.*
1422	**davantage**	**more**
	adv	Davantage d'intérêt fut porté aux bons mots qu'aux problèmes réels.
	davɑ̃taʒ	*There has been more interest in clever words than in the real problems.*
1423	**gardé**	**guard**
	nm, nf	Il y a toujours un garde à l'entrée du château.
	gaʁde	*There is always a guard in front of the castle gate.*
1424	**net**	**clear; Internet, web**
	adj, nm	Elle passe carrément trop de temps à naviguer sur le Net.
	nɛt	*She spends way too much time surfing the web.*
1425	**vivant**	**alive, living**
	noun, adj	Les êtres humains sont les seules créatures vivantes qui emploient le feu.
	vivɑ̃	*Humans are the only living creatures that make use of fire.*
1426	**compliqué**	**complicated, complex**
	noun, adj	Ce formulaire a l'air bien compliqué. Aide-moi à le remplir.
	kɔ̃plike	*This form looks kind of complicated. Help me fill it out.*
1427	**fiancé**	**fiancé, engaged**
	noun, adj	La jeune fille qui est habillée en blanc est ma fiancée.
	fjɑ̃se	*The girl who is dressed in white is my fiancee.*
1428	**accuser**	**to accuse**
	verb	Socrate a été accusé d'athéisme parce qu'il ne croyait pas en Zeus.
	akyze	*Socrates was accused of atheism because he did not believe in Zeus.*
1429	**construire**	**to build, construct**
	verb	Ça m'a coûté beaucoup d'argent de construire une nouvelle maison.
	kɔ̃stʁɥiʁ	*It cost me a lot of money to build a new house.*
1430	**sombre**	**dark**
	adj(f)	Tout à coup, de grosses gouttes de pluie commencèrent à tomber du ciel sombre.
	sɔ̃bʁ	*All of a sudden, large drops of rain began falling from the dark sky.*
1431	**hâte**	**haste, impatience**
	nf	Comme il avait été publié à la hâte, le livre avait de nombreuses coquilles.
	at	*As it was printed in haste, the book has many misprints.*
1432	**voisin**	**neighbor**
	noun, adj	Je t'avais dit de ne pas jouer de violoncelle tard la nuit, mais tu l'as fait et maintenant les voisins se sont plaints.

		vwazɛ̃	*I told you not to play your cello late at night, but you did and now the neighbors have complained.*
1433	**lourd**		**heavy**
	adj		Cette caisse est très lourde de sorte que je ne peux pas la porter.
		luʁ	*This box is very heavy, so I can't carry it.*
1434	**retirer**		**to remove, withdraw**
	verb		Nous pouvons juste souhaiter que le gouvernement décide de retirer ses troupes.
		ʁətiʁe	*We can only hope that the government decides to withdraw its troops.*
1435	**comte**		**count**
	nm		Le comte italien Des Guidi, exilé politique en France, a découvert et étudié l'homéopathie en Italie
		kɔ̃t	*The Italian Count Des Guidi, a political exile in France, discovered and studied homeopathy in Italy.*
1436	**contrôler**		**to control, check, inspect, monitor**
	verb		De nouvelles technologies sont développées qui permettront de contrôler la manière dont les gènes s'expriment.
		kɔ̃tʁole	*New technologies are being developed that will be able to control how genes express themselves.*
1437	**réputation**		**reputation**
	nf		Il est très difficile d'être à la hauteur de votre réputation.
		ʁepytasjɔ̃	*It is very hard to live up to your reputation.*
1438	**exploser**		**to explode, blow up**
	verb		La colère du peuple explosa, entrainant une série d'émeutes.
		ɛksploze	*The anger of the people exploded, leading to a series of riots.*
1439	**créature**		**creature**
	nf		L'homme n'est pas tant la créature que le créateur des circonstances.
		kʁeatyʁ	*Man is not the creature, so much as he is the creator, of circumstances.*
1440	**étudier**		**to study**
	verb		Il a décidé d'aller à Paris dans le but d'étudier la peinture.
		etydje	*He decided to go to Paris for the purpose of studying painting.*
1441	**brûler**		**to burn**
	verb		Là où on brûle des livres, on finit par brûler des gens.
		bʁyle	*Where they burn books, they will in the end also burn people.*
1442	**soif**		**thirst**
	nf		L'appétit vient en mangeant, la soif s'en va en buvant.
		swaf	*Appetite comes with eating, but the thirst goes away with drinking.*
1443	**égal**		**equal**
	noun, adj		L'intervalle entre les poteaux de la clôture doit être égal.
		egal	*The spacing between the fence posts needs to be equal.*
1444	**sport**		**sport**
	adj(i), nm		Je n'aime pas les sports tel que le tennis et le golf.
		spɔʁ	*I don't like such sports as tennis and golf.*
1445	**résultat**		**result, follow-up**
	nm		Lorsque les résultats seront rendus publics, je te le ferai savoir.

	ʁezylta	*When the results are made public, I'll let you know.*
1446	**siège**	**seat, bench**
	nm	Le nombre de sièges de la minorité à la Chambre Basse s'érode rapidement.
	sjɛʒ	*The number of minority seats in the Lower House is rapidly eroding.*
1447	**adorable**	**adorable, sweet**
	adj	C'est difficile de résister à un adorable petit chiot.
	adɔʁabl	*It is hard to resist a sweet little puppy.*
1448	**cingler**	**to whip, to slash**
	verb	Le vent cingle la face
	sɛ̃gle	*The wind whips one's face*
1449	**canon**	**gun, cannon**
	nm	Les poèmes se font à peu près comme les canons : on prend un trou, et on met quelque chose autour.
	kanɔ̃	*Poems are made in about the same way that we make guns. We take a hole, and we put something around it.*
1450	**gardien**	**guardian, keeper**
	noun, adj	Une fois, Christophe Colomb a combattu Cerbère, le chien à trois têtes gardien des enfers, armé de son seul chapeau.
	gaʁdjɛ̃	*Christopher Columbus once fought Cerberus, the three-headed guardian of the underworld, with nothing but his hat.*
1451	**représenter**	**to represent**
	verb	Cette figurine est censée représenter Marilyn Monroe, mais je ne trouve pas qu'elle lui rende justice.
	ʁəpʁezɑ̃te	*This figure is supposed to represent Marilyn Monroe, but I don't think it does her justice.*
1452	**terme**	**term, deadline**
	nm	On a pris acte du besoin d'appui technique à long terme.
	tɛʁm	*The need for longer-term technical support was noted.*
1453	**troupe**	**troop**
	nf	Il en appela à la troupe pour mettre fin à la grève.
	tʁup	*He called on state troops to end the strike.*
1454	**théorie**	**theory**
	nf	Il existe de nombreuses théories sur l'origine de la vie.
	teɔʁi	*There are many theories about the origin of life.*
1455	**surveiller**	**to watch**
	verb	Je vais aller acheter un ticket, alors surveille mes sacs une minute, s'il te plaît.
	syʁveje	*I'm going to go buy a ticket, so please watch my bags for a minute.*
1456	**joueur**	**player**
	noun, adj	Pour devenir un joueur professionnel de banjo, il faut passer des milliers d'heures à pratiquer.
	ʒwœʁ	*To become a professional banjo player, you need to spend thousands of hours practicing.*
1457	**région**	**region**
	nf	Le récif corallien est la principale attraction de la région.

ʁeʒjɔ̃ | *The coral reef is the region's prime attraction.*

1458 commun **common**

noun, adj | Ne vous ont-ils pas enseigné le sens commun aussi bien que la dactylographie à l'école où tu as étudié ?

kɔmœ̃ | *Didn't they teach you common sense as well as typing at the school where you studied?*

1459 tien(s) **ah, well**

noun, adj[pl], int | Tiens, je ne savais pas.

tjɛ̃) | *Well, I didn't know.*

1460 médicament **drug, medication**

nm | Les scientifiques ont découvert de nouveaux médicaments, il y a donc toujours de l'espoir pour les personnes dans le coma.

medikamɑ̃ | *Scientists have been discovering new drugs, so there is always hope for the unconscious person.*

1461 crâne **skull**

adj(f), nm | Le mur autour de la hutte était fait d'os humains et sur son faîte, se trouvaient des crânes.

kʁan | *The wall around the hut was made of human bones and on its top were skulls.*

1462 traduction **translation**

nf | Ne modifiez pas des phrases sans fautes. Vous pouvez plutôt soumettre des traductions alternatives de la phrase originale.

tʁadyksjɔ̃ | *Don't change sentences that are correct. You can, instead, submit natural-sounding alternative translations.*

1463 studio **studio, studio apartment**

nm | Le studio est assez grand pour héberger deux étudiants.

stydjo | *The studio is large enough to accommodate two students.*

1464 libérer **to free, liberate, release**

verb | Lorsque la ville fut libérée, les gens encadrèrent les rues en jetant des confettis.

libeʁe | *When the city was liberated, people lined the streets throwing confetti.*

1465 responsabilité **responsibility**

nf | La responsabilité de ce choix incombe aux États membres

ʁɛspɔ̃sabilite | *Responsibility for this choice is a matter for the Member States.*

1466 délicieux **delicious**

adj | Je connais un super restaurant dans le coin. Ce n'est pas trop cher et la nourriture y est délicieuse.

delisjø | *I know a great restaurant in the area. It's not too pricey and the food is delicious.*

1467 quant **as for**

adv | Quant à mon expérience à bord du Buffalo, cela m'a permis d'apprendre que le vol aérien pouvait être amusant.

kɑ̃ | *As for my experience aboard the Buffalo, I learned that flying could be fun.*

1468 trace **trace, mark, track**

nf | L'auteur put presque faire disparaître complètement toutes ses traces

	tʁas	*The perpetrator could almost completely remove all traces.*
1469	**traiter**	**to treat, handle, deal with**
	verb	La Corée du Nord a été traitée comme un État paria le plus clair de son existence.
	tʁete	*North Korea has been treated as a pariah state for most of its existence.*
1470	**modèle**	**model**
	nm	Ce modèle peut être combiné avec n'importe quelle couleur de vêtement.
	mɔdɛl	*This model can be combined with any color.*
1471	**cellule**	**cell**
	nf	Pourquoi est-il si difficile d'établir que la cellule nerveuse constitue l'unité de base du tissu nerveux ?
	selyl	*Why is it so difficult to establish that the nervous cell is the basic unit for the nervous tissue?*
1472	**gêne**	**gene**
	nm	Je ne connais aucun gène qui se soit libéré de la sorte et se soit mis à voler dans les airs.
	ʒɛn	*I am not aware of any gene that has escaped in this way and flown out into the environment*
1473	**pêcher**	**to fish, go fishing; peach tree**
	nm, verb	J'aimerais savoir ce qui est arrivé à l'ami avec lequel j'avais coutume d'aller pêcher.
	peʃe	*I wonder what has become of the friend I used to go fishing with.*
1474	**poule**	**hen, chick**
	nf	Si une poule a dix poussins, combien de poules un poussin a-t-il ?
	pul	*If a hen has ten chicks, how many hens does a chick have?*
1475	**sénateur**	**senator**
	nm	Il semblait clair que le sénateur rejetterait le traité.
	senatœʁ	*It seemed clear the Senate would reject the treaty.*
1476	**péché**	**fishing; peach**
	nf	Il a été enregistré comme navire de marine marchande et a ensuite reçu sa licence de pêche.
	peʃe	*It was registered as a merchant marine vessel and then given a fishing licence.*
1477	**lentement**	**slowly**
	adv	Les scientifiques commencent lentement à assembler les mécanismes de la vieillesse.
	lãtmã	*Scientists are slowly piecing together the mechanism of aging.*
1478	**empire**	**empire**
	nm	Les romains ne voulaient pas que leur empire décline mais il a décliné.
	ãpiʁ	*Romans did not want their empire to decline; but it did.*
1479	**débile**	**debile, daft person**
	nm	Elle n'est que la mère d'un nain et d'une fille débile.
	debil	*She is just the mother of a dwarf and a daft girl.*
1480	**deviner**	**to guess, solve**
	verb	Tu ne devineras jamais ce qui m'est arrivé aujourd'hui.
	dəvine	*You'll never guess what happened to me today.*

1481	**imagination**	**imagination**
	nf	Mon monde est aussi grand ou aussi petit que mon imagination.
	imaʒinasjɔ̃	*My world is as big or as small as my imagination.*
1482	**liquide**	**liquid**
	noun, adj(f)	Il évacue le liquide de la pompe directement dans le ballon récepteur.
	likid	*At the same time it separates any liquid from the pump directly into the receiving flask.*
1483	**avancer**	**to advance, move forward**
	verb	Le programme Apollo a avancé grandement nos connaissances sur l'espace.
	avɑ̃se	*The Apollo program greatly advanced our knowledge of space.*
1484	**marin**	**sea, marine, sailor**
	noun, adj	Après avoir quitté le port, un marin a rarement le temps d'acquérir le pied marin avant qu'une bataille ne commence.
	maʁɛ̃	*A sailor frequently has no time to get his sea legs after leaving port before a battle starts.*
1485	**plaire**	**to please**
	verb	On n'est pas obligés d'adopter n'importe quoi pour leur plaire.
	plɛʁ	*We are not required to adopt any old thing just to please them.*
1486	**humeur**	**mood, temper**
	nf	Marie était dans une humeur triomphante après ses excellents résultats aux examens.
	ymœʁ	*Mary was in an exultant mood after her great exam results.*
1487	**auprès**	**nearby, close to, next to**
	adv	Elle s'assit auprès de lui et écouta tranquillement.
	opʁɛ	*She sat next to him and listened quietly.*
1488	**jaloux**	**jealous**
	noun, adj	Tu ne dois pas être jaloux du succès des autres.
	ʒalu	*You must not be jealous of others' success.*
1489	**temple**	**temple**
	nm	Tous les dimanches, je me rends en voiture au temple bouddhiste du coin.
	tɑ̃pl	*Every sunday, I drive to my local Buddhist temple.*
1490	**physique**	**physical, physics**
	noun, adj(f)	Nous nous référons au principe le plus général de la physique classique, à savoir la conservation de l'énergie.
	fizik	*We are referring to the most general principle in all classical physics, that of conservation of energy.*
1491	**bosser**	**to work, bash on**
	verb	« Ça ne me dérange pas de continuer à bosser après le mariage. » dit-elle.
	bɔse	*"I don't mind if I keep working even after we're married," she said.*
1492	**infirmier**	**nurse**
	noun, adj	Je prélevai mon échantillon d'urine dans un petit pot en plastique et le donnai à l'infirmier.
	ɛ̃fiʁmje	*I collected my urine sample in a small, plastic cup and gave it to the nurse.*
1493	**secteur**	**sector**

		nm	Il y a de nombreux emplois disponibles dans le secteur informatique.

	nm	Il y a de nombreux emplois disponibles dans le secteur informatique.
	sɛktœʁ	*There are many jobs available in the computer industry.*
1494	**tâcher**	**to endeavor, strive**
	verb	Les parents doivent tâcher de favoriser l'alphabétisme de leurs enfants.
	taʃe	*Parents should strive to nourish the literacy of their children.*
1495	**enfuir**	**to run away, flee**
	verb	Il ne peut s'enfuir ; il doit servir, affirme-t-il.
	ãfɥiʁ	*He cannot run away; he must serve, he declares*
1496	**cirque**	**circus; cirque**
	nm	Les éléphants sont l'attraction principale du cirque.
	siʁk	*The elephants are the chief attraction at the circus.*
1497	**particulier**	**particular, peculiar; person**
	noun, adj	Y a-t-il quelque chose de particulier que tu veuilles manger ?
	paʁtikylje	*Is there something in particular that you want to eat?*
1498	**engager**	**to hire, involve**
	verb	J'ai engagé un professeur particulier pour m'aider à pratiquer ma conversation allemande.
	ãgaʒe	*I've hired a private tutor to help me practice my German conversation.*
1499	**réaliser**	**to realize, achieve**
	verb	Je n'avais jamais réalisé que tu t'intéressais aux arts japonais.
	ʁealize	*I never realized you were interested in Japanese art.*
1500	**chut**	**hush**
	int	Oh ! chut, chut, mon enfant, fit Van Helsing.
	ʃy	*Oh, hush, hush, my child!" said Van Helsing.*
1501	**vision**	**vision, view**
	nf	Il prit part à cette organisation à but non lucratif pour contribuer à ce que sa vision du monde devienne réalité.
	vizjɔ̃	*He took part of this non-profit organisation to help make his vision of the world become reality.*
1502	**cloche**	**bell**
	nf	L'instituteur ajourna son cours lorsque la cloche retentit.
	klɔʃ	*The teacher dismissed his class when the bell rang.*
1503	**croix**	**cross**
	nf[pl]	Les églises sont représentées par une croix sur la carte.
	kʁwa	*Churches are designated on the map with crosses.*
1504	**vente**	**sale**
	nf	Il a fait de la publicité pour la vente de sa maison.
	vãt	*He advertised his house for sale.*
1505	**démon**	**demon, fiend, devil**
	nm	Si les hommes sont des loups alors les femmes sont des démones.
	demɔ̃	*If men are wolves then women are devils.*
1506	**barrer**	**to close, block, bar, cross**
	verb	Nous avons barré la porte et l'avons fermée à clé.
	baʁe	*We barred the door and locked it.*
1507	**aventure**	**adventure**

	nf	Bob a eu de nombreuses dangereuses aventures pendant la guerre.
	avɑ̃tyʁ	*Bob had had many dangerous adventures during the war.*
1508	**matériel**	**material, equipment**
	noun, adj	Les chromosomes de nos cellules contiennent l'ensemble de notre matériel génétique.
	mateʁjɛl	*The chromosomes in our cells contain the whole of our genetic material.*
1509	**surface**	**surface**
	nf	Un pic est un outil à long manche utilisé pour entamer les surfaces de sol dur.
	syʁfas	*A pick is a long handled tool used for breaking up hard ground surfaces.*
1510	**télévision**	**television, TV**
	nf	Certaines personnes lisent le journal et regardent la télévision en même temps.
	televizjɔ̃	*Some people read the newspaper and watch TV at the same time.*
1511	**jaune**	**yellow**
	adv, noun, adj(f)	Un paysage jaune, une multitude luxuriante de tournesols en fleur.
	ʒon	*The landscape of yellow, a mass of sunflowers flourishing beyond measure.*
1512	**veiller**	**to look after, stay up**
	verb	J'ai dormi trop longtemps parce que j'ai veillé tard.
	veje	*I overslept because I stayed up late.*
1513	**boutique**	**shop**
	nf	À la recherche du livre, je me suis rendue dans de nombreuses boutiques.
	butik	*I went to many shops to look for the book.*
1514	**rare**	**rare**
	adj(f)	Le sel était une denrée rare et chère dans les temps anciens.
	ʁaʁ	*Salt was a rare and costly commodity in ancient times.*
1515	**journaliste**	**journalist, reporter**
	nm, nf	Les journalistes exigèrent de savoir pourquoi le maire ne voulait pas leur parler.
	ʒuʁnalist	*The reporters demanded to know why the mayor wouldn't talk to them.*
1516	**magique**	**magic; magical**
	adj(f)	Le sorcier agita sa baguette magique et disparut dans le néant.
	maʒik	*The wizard waved his magic wand and disappeared into thin air.*
1517	**rat**	**rat**
	adj(f), nm	Une chauve-souris est autant un oiseau qu'un rat peut l'être.
	ʁa	*A bat is no more a bird than a rat is.*
1518	**cri**	**shout, cry**
	nm	Les résultats des élections sont en réalité le cri de la rue.
	kʁi	*The election results were a cry from the streets*
1519	**patience**	**patience**
	nf	Partout sur son chemin il enseignait l'amour, la patience, et par-dessus tout, la non-violence.
	pasjɑ̃s	*Everywhere he went, he taught love, patience, and most of all, non-violence.*
1520	**ménage**	**housekeeping, housework**

	nm	Il prit l'initiative d'aider sa maman à faire le ménage.
	menaʒ	*He takes the initiative in helping his mother do the housework.*
1521	**comité**	**committee**
	nm	Tous les membres du comité se haïssent l'un l'autre.
	kɔmite	*All the members of the committee hate one another.*
1522	**baisser**	**to lower, turn down, bend down**
	verb	Cela vous dérangerait-il que je baisse le son de la télévision ?
	bese	*Do you mind if I turn down the TV?*
1523	**combattre**	**to fight**
	verb	Il est nécessaire de combattre le SIDA quelles que soient les armes entre nos mains.
	kõbatʁ	*It is necessary to fight AIDS with whatever weapons are at hand.*
1524	**romantique**	**romantic**
	noun, adj(f)	Nous fuguâmes sous l'impulsion du moment. C'était tellement romantique !
	ʁomãtik	*We eloped on the spur of the moment. It was so romantic!*
1525	**port**	**harbor, port**
	nm	Vous tentez de vous connecter en utilisant un port hôte incorrect.
	pɔʁ	*You are trying to connect using the wrong host port.*
1526	**science**	**science**
	nf	La science se fonde sur une observation extrêmement soigneuse.
	sjãs	*Science is based on very careful observations.*
1527	**bouffe**	**food, grub**
	nf	La bouffe dans le nouveau restaurant n'a rien d'extraordinaire ; au mieux, moyenne.
	buf	*The food at the new restaurant is nothing special - average at best.*
1528	**crédit**	**credit**
	nm	Est-ce que je peux payer avec une carte de crédit ?
	kʁedi	*May I pay with a credit card?*
1529	**abrutir**	**stupefy, dumb down**
	verb	Lorsqu'on est jeune, on regarde la télévision et on pense qu'il y a une conspiration : Les réseaux ont conspiré pour nous abrutir
	abʁytiʁ	*When you're young, you look at television and think, there's a conspiracy. The networks have conspired to dumb us down.*
1530	**promesse**	**promise**
	nf	Il y a des conditions sous lesquelles rompre une promesse ou dire un mensonge sont acceptables.
	pʁɔmɛs	*There are conditions under which breaking a promise or telling a lie are acceptable.*
1531	**inconnu**	**unknown**
	noun, adj	Lorsque tu rencontres un mot inconnu, tu dois les chercher dans le dictionnaire.
	ɛ̃kɔny	*When you come across unknown words, you have to look them up in the dictionary.*
1532	**concourir**	**compete, participate**
	verb	Un professionnel de la vidéo ou du cinéma peut concourir au festival.

kɔ̃kuʁiʁ | *A video professional can participate in the festival.*

| 1533 | **ambulance** | **ambulance** |

nf — L'ambulance a perdu le contrôle et a failli écraser un piéton.

ãbylãs — *The ambulance went out of control and came close to running over a pedestrian.*

| 1534 | **cependant** | **however** |

adv, conj — Tom a de l'argent. Cependant, il n'est pas du tout heureux.

səpãdã — *Tom has money. However, he's not all that happy.*

| 1535 | **panique** | **panic** |

noun, adj(f) — La nouvelle a semé la panique parmi les actionnaires.

panik — *The news spread panic among the shareholders*

| 1536 | **criminel** | **criminal** |

noun, adj — La police demanda que le criminel leur remette le pistolet.

kʁiminɛl — *The police asked the criminal to give up his gun.*

| 1537 | **sauvage** | **savage, wild** |

noun, adj(f) — Il connaît beaucoup de choses sur les animaux sauvages.

sovaʒ — *He knows a lot about wild animals.*

| 1538 | **donnée** | **fact, datum** |

nf — Cette donnée confirme que le pilote a besoin d'une vitesse vers l'avant pour disposer de marges de contrôle franches.

dɔne — *This datum confirmed that the pilot requires forward speed to ensure positive control margins.*

| 1539 | **royaume** | **kingdom, state** |

nm — Il y a quelque chose de pourri au royaume du Danemark.

ʁwajom — *There is something rotten in the state of Denmark.*

| 1540 | **complet** | **full, complete, full** |

adj, nm — Je n'ai jamais imaginé un seul instant que je serais désigné pour une fouille au corps complète.

kɔ̃plɛ — *I never for a moment imagined that I'd be singled out for a full body search.*

| 1541 | **centaine** | **hundred** |

nf — Des centaines de champs ont été submergés par l'inondation.

sãtɛn — *Hundreds of fields were submerged in the flood.*

| 1542 | **scénario** | **scenario, script** |

nm — Le même scénario s'est répété à peu de chose près lors du second appel.

senaʁjo — *The same scenario was repeated with little change on the second call.*

| 1543 | **principal** | **principal** |

noun, adj — Son objectif fondamental consiste en la protection et l'amélioration des prestations des pensionné

pʁɛ̃sipal — *Its principal objective is to protect and enhance the benefits of pensioners*

| 1544 | **jus** | **juice, sauce** |

nm — Tom a versé du jus d'orange dans un verre.

ʒy — *Tom poured some orange juice into a glass.*

| 1545 | **pot** | **jar, pot** |

nm — Donc tout ce dont tu as besoin est de bon fromage et d'un pot de confiture de cerises noires.

		po	*So all you need is good cheese and a jar of black cherry jam.*
1546	**divorce**	**divorce**	
	nm	Dans certains cas, elle lui offre le choix entre le traitement ou le divorce.
	divɔʁs	*In some cases, she gives him the choice between getting help or getting a divorce.*
1547	**cochon**	**pig**	
	noun, adj	Un poulet dit à un cochon: «Formons une co-entreprise.
	kɔʃɔ̃	*A chicken said to a pig, Let us have a joint venture.*
1548	**cadavre**	**corpse**	
	nm	Le cadavre présente une blessure par balle à la poitrine.
	kadavʁ	*The corpse has a gunshot wound in the chest.*
1549	**révolution**	**revolution**	
	nf	Cette révolution des livres électroniques ne me plait pas du tout.
	ʁevɔlysjɔ̃	*I am not the least bit happy with this e-book revolution.*
1550	**existence**	**existence**	
	nf	Depuis que j'ai appris l'existence de l'université, j'ai toujours voulu y aller.
	ɛgzistɑ̃s	*Ever since I learned about the existence of the university, I wanted to go there.*
1551	**accompagner**	**to accompany**	
	verb	Si ce livre est utile et divertissant à lire allongé sur le canapé, il est destiné à accompagner le voyageur.
	akɔ̃paɲe	*While useful and entertaining to read on the couch, this is a book meant to accompany the traveler.*
1552	**lien**	**link, bond**	
	nm	Veuillez ne pas répondre à ce courriel frauduleux et ne cliquez en aucun cas sur les liens contenus dans le courriel.
	ljɛ̃	*Please do not answer this fraudulent e-mail and certainly do not click on the links in the e-mail.*
1553	**fromage**	**cheese**	
	nm	L'âge ne conduit pas à la maturité, à moins que vous ne soyez un fromage.
	fʁɔmaʒ	*Age doesn't lead to maturity, unless you're a cheese.*
1554	**période**	**period**	
	nm, nf	Tom a lutté contre la dépression durant plusieurs périodes de sa vie.
	peʁjɔd	*Tom has battled depression at various periods in his life.*
1555	**profond**	**deep**	
	adv, noun, adj	Lorsque j'inspire profondément, une douleur me lance le long du côté droit de mon dos.
	pʁɔfɔ̃	*When I take a deep breath, a pain runs down the right side of my back.*
1556	**malheureux**	**unhappy, miserable**	
	noun, adj[pl]	Je préfère rester seule que d'être malheureuse avec lui toute ma vie.
	maløʁø	*I would rather remain single than live an unhappy life with him.*
1557	**nommer**	**to call, name, appoint**	
	verb	Les chariots sont munis de quatre roues. Les engins à deux roues sont nommés des diables.
	nɔme	*Dollies have four wheels. The two-wheeled jobs are called hand trucks.*
1558	**roman**	**novel**	

	adj, nm	Les romans policiers sont appréciés par de nombreuses personnes.
	ʁɔmɑ̃	*Mystery novels are loved by a lot of people.*
1559	**poussière**	**dust**
	nf	Je vous montrerai la peur dans une poignée de poussière.
	pusjɛʁ	*I will show you fear in a handful of dust.*
1560	**passion**	**passion**
	nf	Ma passion pour la cuisine m'a amené à devenir chef.
	pasjɔ̃	*My passion for cooking led me to be a chef.*
1561	**récemment**	**recently**
	adv	As-tu récemment été en contact avec l'un de tes vieux amis d'école ?
	ʁesamɑ̃	*Have you been in contact with one of your old school friends recently?*
1562	**maitre**	**master**
	nm	Est-ce vrai que les Français sont des maîtres pour draguer ?
	mɛtʁ	*Is it true that the French are masters at flirting?*
1563	**lutte**	**struggle, fight, conflict**
	nf	L'histoire de toutes les sociétés existantes jusqu'à présent est l'histoire des luttes de classes.
	lyt	*The history of all hitherto existing societies is the history of class struggles.*
1564	**briser**	**to break**
	verb	Ah, j'oubliais. Si tu touches à Mayu, je te brise la colonne vertébrale.
	bʁize	*One more thing. If you try anything on Mayu I'll break your spine.*
1565	**quiconque**	**whoever, anyone who**
	pron	Je n'ai pas pensé que quiconque était chez lui.
	kikɔ̃k	*I didn't think anyone was home.*
1566	**cap**	**cape**
	nm	Un ensemble complet comprend une robe et un jupon, un bonnet et un manteau ou une cape.
	kap	*A complete ensemble might include a dress with a slip, a bonnet and a coat or cape.*
1567	**version**	**version**
	nf	La différence entre les deux versions n'est pas claire.
	vɛʁsjɔ̃	*The difference between the two versions isn't clear.*
1568	**entraînement**	**training**
	nm	Il fait preuve d'une grande discipline dans son entraînement
	ɑ̃tʁɛnmɑ̃	*He shows great discipline in his training.*
1569	**mardi**	**Tuesday**
	nm	Ils peuvent venir lundi ou mardi, mais pas mercredi ou jeudi.
	maʁdi	*They can come on Monday or Tuesday, but not on Wednesday or Thursday.*
1570	**indien**	**Indian**
	noun, adj	Avant l'avènement des jeux vidéo, les enfants jouaient aux cow-boys et aux indiens.
	ɛ̃djɛ̃	*Before the advent of video games children played cowboys and Indians.*
1571	**meurtrier**	**murderer, deadly, lethal**
	noun, adj	Il a fallu une enquête national pour trouver le meurtrier.
	mœʁtʁije	*It took a coast-to-coast investigation to find the murderer.*

1572	**examen**	**exam**
	nm	Je dois repasser un examen d'anglais la semaine prochaine.
	ɛgzamɛ̃	*I have to resit an English exam next week.*
1573	**septembre**	**September**
	nm	Je suis content, parce qu'à compter d'aujourd'hui, nous n'avons pas école jusqu'en septembre.
	sɛptɑ̃bʁ	*I'm happy because starting today, we don't have any school until September.*
1574	**élever**	**to grow, lift, raise**
	verb	Le gouvernement souhaite qu'il soit plus facile pour les gens d'avoir des enfants et de les élever.
	elve	*As a government we need to make it more affordable for people to have children and to raise them.*
1575	**profiter**	**to take advantage, profit**
	verb	Il profita du beau temps pour faire un peu de jardinage.
	pʁɔfite	*He took advantage of the good weather to do some gardening.*
1576	**serpent**	**snake**
	nm	Le serpent ne mord-il pas lorsqu'on le foule aux pieds ?
	sɛʁpɑ̃	*Does the snake not bite when we step on it?*
1577	**bouton**	**button, knob, spot**
	nm	Es-tu sûre d'avoir bien appuyé sur le dernier bouton ?
	butɔ̃	*Are you sure you pressed the last button?*
1578	**piscine**	**swimming pool**
	nf	Dans les piscines, l'eau est continuellement pompée à travers un filtre.
	pisin	*In swimming pools, water is continuously pumped through a filter.*
1579	**courrier**	**mail, post**
	nm	Tout ce que vous avez dit dans votre courrier électronique est juste excepté le prix.
	kuʁje	*Everything you said in your mail is just right - except the price.*
1580	**logique**	**logic, logical**
	noun, adj(f)	Il est capable de s'imposer par un raisonnement logique.
	lɔʒik	*He wins his arguments by logical reasoning.*
1581	**rythme**	**rhythm, rate**
	nm	Elle bouge comme une reine et démontre qu'elle a le rythme dans le sang.
	ʁitm	*She moves like a queen and shows that she has rhythm in her blood.*
1582	**cancer**	**cancer**
	nm	Cet article traite des progrès de la recherche contre le cancer.
	kɑ̃sɛʁ	*The essay treats of the progress of cancer research.*
1583	**proposer**	**to propose**
	verb	On a proposé que cette matière soit étudiée à la prochaine réunion.
	pʁɔpoze	*It was proposed that this matter be considered at the next meeting.*
1584	**peinture**	**painting, paint, picture**
	nf	Après sa mort ses peintures ont été exposés dans ce musée.
	pɛ̃tyʁ	*After his death, his paintings were hung in the museum.*
1585	**jeudi**	**Thursday**

	nm	Tout le monde sauf la famille Anderson viendra à la soirée jeudi prochain.
	ʒødi	*Everybody except the Anderson family is going to the party next Thursday evening.*
1586	**courageux**	**courageous**
	noun, adj[pl]	Le chien policier a été récompensé pour avoir été très courageux.
	kuʁaʒø	*The police dog was rewarded for being very courageous*
1587	**œuvrer**	**to work**
	verb	Je les invite donc à œuvrer de concert pour atteindre cet objectif commun.
	œvʁe	*I call on both neighbours to work together towards this shared goal.*
1588	**camarade**	**friend, comrade, pal, mate**
	nm, nf	Mon camarade semble oublier que nous parlons d'une institution publique qui investit les contributions publiques.
	kamaʁad	*My comrade seems to forget that we are talking about a public institution investing public contributions.*
1589	**hall**	**foyer, lobby**
	nm	Le hall de l'hôtel s'enorgueillit d'un beau chandelier en cristal des années dix-neuf-cent-vingts.
	ol	*The hotel lobby boasts a beautiful, crystal chandelier from the 1920s.*
1590	**figurer**	**to represent, appear**
	verb	Son nom complet figure sur son passeport.
	figyʁe	*His full name appears on his passport.*
1591	**ascenseur**	**elevator**
	nm	Après avoir demandé ma clé à la réception, j'ai pris l'ascenseur jusqu'à mon étage.
	asɑ̃sœʁ	*After asking for my key at the front desk, I took the elevator to my floor.*
1592	**garage**	**garage**
	nm	C'est assez courant en Amérique du Nord qu'une maison ait un garage pour une ou deux voitures.
	gaʁaʒ	*It is quite common in North America for homes to have a one or two-car garage.*
1593	**approcher**	**to approach**
	verb	Un homme approcha de Yoshi en dissimulant le bruit de ses pas.
	apʁɔʃe	*A man approached Yoko, concealing the sound of his footsteps.*
1594	**traitement**	**treatment, salary, wage**
	nm	Cette conséquence favorable est due à l'atmosphère décontractée qui règne pendant le traitement.
	tʁɛtmɑ̃	*This positive outcome can be ascribed to the informal atmosphere during the treatment.*
1595	**sein**	**breast, bosom**
	nm	Saviez-vous que les hommes pouvaient souffrir du cancer du sein ?
	sɛ̃	*Did you know that men can get breast cancer?*
1596	**nation**	**nation**
	nf	La grandeur d'une nation et ses progrès moraux peuvent être jugés par la manière dont ses animaux sont traités.
	nasjɔ̃	*The greatness of a nation and its moral progress can be judged by the way its animals are treated.*

1597	**propriété**	**property**
	nf	Dans certaines sociétés, les femmes sont encore considérées comme la propriété de leurs époux.
	pʀɔpʀijete	*In some societies, wives are still considered the property of their husbands.*
1598	**labo**	**lab**
	nm	Quand je ne suis pas au labo, je pense à mes travaux de recherche.
	labo	*When I am not in the lab, you can find me thinking about how I should be in the lab*
1599	**machine**	**machine**
	nf	Si tu disposais d'une machine à remonter le temps, quelle année irais-tu visiter ?
	maʃin	*If you had a time machine, which year would you visit?*
1600	**sable**	**sand**
	adj(i), nm	Les enfants construisirent un château de sable sur la plage.
	sabl	*The children built a sand castle on the beach.*
1601	**commission**	**commission**
	nf	J'ai une commission de trois pour cent sur tout ce que je vends.
	kɔmisjɔ̃	*I get a three percent commission on anything I sell.*
1602	**section**	**section**
	nf	Il y a sept hommes et quatre femmes dans ma section.
	sɛksjɔ̃	*There are seven men and four women in my section.*
1603	**nager**	**to swim**
	verb	En nageant, j'ai eu une crampe à la jambe.
	naʒe	*While I was swimming, I got a cramp in my leg.*
1604	**pratique**	**practice, practical**
	noun, adj(f)	Pour maîtriser une langue, il faut énormément de pratique.
	pʀatik	*It takes a great deal of practice to master a foreign language.*
1605	**écran**	**screen**
	nm	Peu importe le rôle qu'il joue à l'écran, Tom est magnifique.
	ekʀɑ̃	*No matter what he plays on the screen, Tom looks great.*
1606	**chuter**	**to fall**
	verb	Le prix de l'action de cette société a chuté hier.
	ʃyte	*That company's stock price fell yesterday.*
1607	**ceinture**	**belt, waist**
	nf	Veuillez boucler vos ceintures et vous tenir prêts au départ.
	sɛ̃tyʀ	*Please fasten your seat belts and prepare for departure.*
1608	**briller**	**to shine**
	verb	Aujourd'hui dans le ciel nocturne, les étoiles semblent très brillantes.
	bʀije	*Tonight in the night sky, the stars are shining very brightly.*
1609	**miel**	**honey**
	nm	Hawai est vraiment le pays où coule le lait et le miel.
	mjɛl	*Hawaii's really the land of milk and honey.*
1610	**crever**	**to burst, puncture**
	verb	Allez Aurel, c'est pas une raison pour crever les pneus de ta moto !
	kʀəve	*Come on Aurel, this is not a reason for puncturing your tyres!*
1611	**estomac**	**stomach**

	nm	Je veux voir un médecin à propos de mes maux d'estomac.
	ɛstɔma	*I want to see a doctor about my stomach-ache.*
1612	**salaire**	**salary, wage**
	nm	Ce que tu gagnes est de la roupie de sansonnet, comparé au salaire du patron.
	salɛʁ	*What you make is small potatoes compared to the boss's salary.*
1613	**inventer**	**to invent**
	verb	L'instrument de soin des cheveux le plus ancien est le peigne, inventé il y a plus de 5000 ans en Perse.
	ɛ̃vɑ̃te	*The oldest haircare tool is the comb, invented more than 5000 years ago in Persia.*
1614	**étonner**	**to astonish, amaze, surprise**
	verb	Je suis étonné que vous trouviez Tom inamical. Il a toujours été parfaitement amical avec moi.
	etɔne	*I'm surprised you find Tom unfriendly. He's always been perfectly friendly to me.*
1615	**nourrir**	**to feed, nourish**
	verb	Elle a travaillé sans repos pour nourrir ses enfants jusqu'à ce qu'ils se sont mariés.
	nuʁiʁ	*She worked without a break to feed her children until they got married.*
1616	**incendie**	**fire, blaze**
	nm	Un petit feu de forêt s'est rapidement étendu pour se transformer en un gros incendie.
	ɛ̃sɑ̃di	*A small forest fire quickly spread and became a huge conflagration.*
1617	**pur**	**pure; hard-liner**
	adj, nmf	Nous devons faire attention de ne boire que de l'eau pure.
	pyʁ	*We must be careful to drink only pure water.*
1618	**refaire**	**to redo, make again**
	verb	Certains de vous veulent venir ici et refaire ce que je viens de faire?
	ʁəfɛʁ	*Does one of you want to come here and redo what I just did?*
1619	**prénom**	**first name**
	nm	Je connais une femme qui a les mêmes nom et prénom que moi.
	pʁenɔ̃	*I know a woman whose first and last names are the same as mine.*
1620	**fuite**	**escape**
	nf	Les détenus devront faire l'objet de mesures spéciales en cas d'urgence pour prévenir toute tentative de fuite.
	fɥit	*Detainees must be subject to special emergency measures preventing their escape.*
1621	**invite**	**guest**
	nm	Sans plus attendre, laissez-moi vous présenter l'invité de ce soir.
	ɛ̃vit	*Without further ado, let me introduce tonight's guest.*
1622	**idéal**	**ideal**
	nm, adj	Ils leur manquent un idéal, une raison de se lever le matin.
	ideal	*They lack an ideal, a reason to get up in the morning.*
1623	**condition**	**condition**
	nf	Les conditions sanitaires dans les camps de réfugiés étaient terribles.

kɔ̃disjɔ̃ | *Sanitary conditions in the refugee camps were terrible.*

1624 élève — **high, heavy, tall**
adj — Ils espéraient vendre les actions à des prix encore plus élevés.
elɛv — *They hoped to sell the stocks at even higher prices.*

1625 douze — **twelve**
det, num — Mon fils de douze ans n'aime pas jouer au baseball.
duz — *My twelve year old boy doesn't like to play baseball.*

1626 virus — **virus**
nm[pl] — Le virus a causé la mort de plusieurs éléphants en Afrique.
viʁys — *The virus cut down many elephants in Africa.*

1627 poil — **hair, bristle**
nm — Alors tu as des poils sur le torse, après tout.
pwal — *So you've got hair on your chest after all.*

1628 jeunesse — **youth**
nf — Nous nous raccrochons encore aux rêves de notre jeunesse.
ʒœnɛs — *We are still clinging to the dreams of our youth.*

1629 ordinaire — **ordinary**
adv, nm, adj(f) — Je suis juste un mec ordinaire qui n'a rien à perdre.
ɔʁdinɛʁ — *I'm just an ordinary guy with nothing to loose.*

1630 agence — **agency**
nf — Afin de valoriser mon expérience dans les voyages, j'ai démarré une agence de voyages.
aʒɑ̃s — *Putting my traveling experience to good use, I started a travel agency.*

1631 loup — **wolf**
nm — Le loup changera de forme, mais continuera à manger du poulet.
lu — *The wolf will change shape, but will continue to eat chicken.*

1632 naturel — **naturalness, natural**
nm, adj — Tous les gens ont quelque talent naturel; la question est seulement de savoir s'ils peuvent également l'employer.
natyʁɛl — *All men have some natural talent, but the question is whether they can use it or not.*

1633 bombe — **bomb**
nf — La première bombe atomique a été larguée sur le Japon.
bɔ̃b — *The first atomic bomb was dropped on Japan.*

1634 autrefois — **in the past**
adv — Autrefois, les saucissons étaient suspendus sur de longs bâtons de bois.
otʁəfwa — *In the past, the sausages were arranged on long wooden sticks.*

1635 équipage — **crew, gear**
nm — Si vous ne faites pas ce que je dis, vous et votre équipage périrez.
ekipaʒ — *If you don't do as I say, you and your crew will perish.*

1636 tempête — **storm, gale, turmoil**
nf — Toute la compétence des marins céda sous la violence de la tempête.
tɑ̃pɛt — *All the skill of the sailors gave way to the violence of the storm.*

1637 central — **central; exchange**

	adj, nm	Lorsqu'on considère qu'il a trop augmenté, les banques centrales des principaux pays coopèrent pour intervenir.
	sãtʁal	*When it is seen to have risen too far, the central banks of major countries cooperate to intervene.*

1638 forcément — **without question, inevitably**

adv — L'investissement dans seulement un ou deux de ces domaines sera forcément vain et conduira à l'échec.

fɔʁsemã — *Investing in only one or two facets will inevitably lead to failure and waste of the investment.*

1639 acteur — **actor**

nm — Hier j'ai fait connaissance de l'un des acteurs les plus célèbres du monde.

aktœʁ — *Yesterday I met one of the most popular actors in the world.*

1640 calmer — **to calm down**

verb — Le garçon avait peur, mais son père l'a calmé.

kalme — *The boy was scared, but his father calmed him down.*

1641 miroir — **mirror**

nm — Un miroir est mieux que toute une série de portraits d'ancêtres.

miʁwaʁ — *A mirror is better than an entire row of ancestral portraits.*

1642 chic — **chic, luxurious**

adj — Dégustez une sélection de vins et de spiritueux raffinés dans un cadre digne des réceptions chic.

ʃik — *Warm up with a selection of fine wines and spirits in this chic reception-style setting.*

1643 jury — **jury, board of examiners**

nm — Dans le système judiciaire américain, il y a douze personnes dans un jury.

ʒyʁi — *In the justice system of the United States, there are twelve people on a jury.*

1644 pardonner — **to forgive, excuse**

verb — Je ne pense pas que je puisse me pardonner si je faisais cela.

paʁdɔne — *I don't think I could forgive myself if I did that.*

1645 affronter — **to confront, face**

verb — La plupart des gens craignent plus d'affronter leurs erreurs que de se tromper.

afʁõte — *Most people are rather afraid of facing their mistakes, than of making mistakes.*

1646 lâcher — **to let go, release**

verb — Le prix à payer pour trouver l'infini est de lâcher prise sur le fini.

laʃe — *The price of finding the Infinite is letting go of the finite.*

1647 cérémonie — **ceremony**

nf — Avez-vous regardé la cérémonie de clôture des Jeux olympiques?

seʁemɔni — *Did you watch the Olympics closing ceremony?*

1648 tasse — **cup**

nf — Ces tasses ne me plaisent pas, je préfère celles qui sont sur la table.

tas — *I don't like these cups; I prefer those on the table.*

1649 absence — **absence**

nf — En l'absence de sa mère, elle s'occupe de sa sœur.

apsãs — *In the absence of her mother, she looks after her sister.*

1650	**comportement**	**behavior**
	nm	Le comportement de Tom est imprévisible quand il est ivre.
	kɔ̃pɔʁtəmɑ̃	*Tom's behaviour is unpredictable when he's drunk.*
1651	**correct**	**correct**
	adj	Cette phrase n'est pas correcte. Elle comporte une faute d'orthographe.
	kɔʁɛkt	*This sentence is not correct. There is a spelling mistake.*
1652	**récompenser**	**to reward, recompense**
	verb	Tout le monde n'est pas adéquatement récompensé pour ses efforts.
	ʁekɔ̃pɑ̃se	*Not everyone is properly rewarded for his efforts.*
1653	**national**	**national; road, state highway**
	adj, nf	Je me demande comment un gouvernement s'y prendrait pour mesurer le bonheur national brut.
	nasjɔnal	*I wonder how a government would go about measuring gross national happiness.*
1654	**carte**	**card**
	nf	Veuillez me montrer votre carte d'identité ou votre passeport !
	kaʁt	*Please show me your identity card or passport!*
1655	**masque**	**mask**
	nm	L'homme commença par retirer son chapeau, ses lunettes et son masque.
	mask	*The man began to take off his hat, glasses and mask.*
1656	**raisonnable**	**reasonable, fair**
	adj(f)	Tom cherchait un endroit avec des prix raisonnables pour manger.
	ʁɛzɔnabl	*Tom was looking for place to eat that had reasonable prices.*
1657	**bijou**	**jewel**
	nm	Les bijoux sont disposés de manière aléatoire sur le stand
	biʒu	*The jewels are displayed in a haphazard manner on the stand*
1658	**mystère**	**mystery**
	nm	Aujourd'hui, nous allons percer le mystère du subjonctif anglais.
	misteʁ	*Today, we are going to unravel the mystery of the English subjunctive.*
1659	**cabine**	**hut, cubicle, booth, box, room, cabin**
	nf	Vous verrez que les cabines du bateau sont pourvues de tout le confort matériel d'une maison.
	kabin	*You will find that the ship's cabins have all the creature comforts of home.*
1660	**étudiant**	**student**
	nm/f, adj	Lorsque j'étais étudiant, j'écrivais un journal personnel en anglais.
	etydjɑ̃	*I used to keep a diary in English when I was a student.*
1661	**créme**	**cream**
	adj(i), nf	Les crèmes exfoliantes suppriment les cellules mortes ou endommagées de la peau.
	kʁem	*Exfoliating creams remove dead or damaged skin cells.*
1662	**parfum**	**perfume, scent, fragrance**
	nm	Les parfums sont souvent faits de la sueur de divers animaux mâles.
	paʁfœ̃	*Perfumes are often made from the sweat of various male animals.*
1663	**avouer**	**to admit**

	verb	C'est un défaut de la politique en générale mais surtout, il faut bien l'avouer, de la démocratie.
	avwe	*This is a flaw in politics in general but mostly, we have to admit, in democracy.*
1664	**vengeance**	**revenge**
	nf	Le suicide, c'est une vengeance personnelle, et moi, personnellement, je ne m'en veux pas.
	vãʒãs	*Suicide is an act of revenge against yourself, and I personally have nothing against myself.*
1665	**nu**	**naked, nude**
	nm, adj	La mère de Tom pourchassa Tom alors qu'il courait nu dans le hall.
	ny	*Tom's mother chased Tom as he ran naked around the lobby.*
1666	**presser**	**to squeeze, press**
	verb	Presser fermement 1 1/2 recette de mélange sur chaque plaque à biscuits; réfrigérer jusqu'à ce que la préparation soit ferme
	pʀese	*Firmly press 1 1/2 batches of the mixture onto each prepared baking sheet; chill sheets until firm.*
1667	**qualité**	**quality**
	nf	Tom fait tout ce qu'il peut pour améliorer la qualité de vie de ses patients.
	kalite	*Tom is doing everything within his power to improve the patients quality of life.*
1668	**couvert**	**covered, overcast; place, seat, cutlery**
	adj, nm	Le mur était couvert de photos de victimes de fusillades.
	kuvɛʀ	*The wall was covered with pictures of gunshot victims.*
1669	**couloir**	**corridor, aisle**
	nm	Le bureau du directeur est au fond du couloir.
	kulwaʀ	*The manager's office is at the end of the corridor.*
1670	**technique**	**technique, technics, technical**
	nf, adj(f)	Un bon diplomate est une personne qui a acquis la technique consistant à laisser à une autre le soin de révéler un secret.
	tɛknik	*A good diplomat is a person who practises the technique of letting someone else let the cat out of the bag.*
1671	**œuf**	**egg**
	nm	Il vaut mieux un œuf aujourd'hui qu'une poule demain.
	œf	*Better an egg today than a hen tomorrow.*
1672	**réaction**	**reaction**
	nf	Quelle a été la réaction lorsque nous avons placé les aimants sur la tête des pigeons ?
	ʀeaksjɔ̃	*When we put magnets on the pigeon's heads, what was the reaction?*
1673	**doué**	**gifted**
	adj	On n'a pas besoin d'être doué pour être quelqu'un de spécial.
	dwe	*You don't have to be gifted to be special.*
1674	**attente**	**wait**
	nf	Actuellement, les temps d'attente pour les services du programme constituent son plus grand défi.
	atãt	*The program's biggest challenge now is wait times for its services.*

1675	**nôtre**	**our**
	det	Cependant, notre système de suivi parlementaire est inapproprié.
	notʁ	*Our parliamentary monitoring system is inadequate, however.*
1676	**race**	**breed, race**
	nf	On se réfère parfois à New-York comme au creuset des races.
	ʁas	*New York is sometimes referred to as the melting pot of races.*
1677	**bêtise**	**foolishness, rubbish**
	nf	Chez les enfants, c'est plutôt de la bêtise, mais cela me touchait.
	betiz	*Coming from children, it might just seem like foolishness, but still it affected me.*
1678	**moquer**	**to mock, make fun of**
	verb	On devrait être respectueux des opinions d'autrui plutôt que de les moquer.
	mɔke	*One should be respectful of other's beliefs rather than mock them.*
1679	**colle**	**glue, adhesive**
	nf	J'ai réparé la chaise cassée à l'aide d'une colle forte.
	kɔl	*I fixed the broken chair using a strong glue.*
1680	**poitrine**	**chest, breast, breasts, bosom**
	nf	Elle posa sa tête sur ma poitrine pour écouter les battements de mon cœur.
	pwatʁin	*She lay her head on my chest so she could listen to my heartbeat.*
1681	**enterrement**	**burial, funeral**
	nm	On ne doit pas porter de minijupe rouge à un enterrement.
	ɑ̃tɛʁmɑ̃	*One does not wear a red mini skirt to a funeral.*
1682	**installer**	**to install**
	verb	J'ai installé un nouveau logiciel sur mon ordinateur, hier.
	ɛ̃stale	*I installed some new software yesterday on my computer.*
1683	**noble**	**noble, noble(wo)man**
	adj(f, nmf	Le noble chevalier retint son souffle tandis qu'il regardait fixement la belle princesse.
	nɔbl	*The noble knight held his breath as he gazed at the beautiful princess.*
1684	**large**	**wide, width**
	adj(f), adv, nm	La large gamme de produits proposés signifie que tout le monde trouve son compte.
	laʁʒ	*The wide range of products on offer really means that there is something for everyone.*
1685	**urgent**	**urgent**
	adj	Il faut de manière urgente que davantage de gens donnent leur temps et leur argent.
	yʁʒɑ̃	*There is an urgent need for more people to donate their time and money.*
1686	**digne**	**dignified, worthy**
	adj(f)	Vous devrez vous rendre digne de recevoir ces trésors spirituels.
	diɲ	*You will make yourself worthy in order to receive those spiritual treasures.*
1687	**être**	**human being**
	nm	Tous les êtres humains ont un droit fondamental à la vie.
	ɛtʁ	*All human beings have an inherent right to life.*

1688	**uniquement**	**only**
	adv	"As-tu des frères et sœurs ?" "Non, je suis fils unique."
	ynikmã	*"Do you have any siblings?" "No, I'm an only child."*
1689	**riz**	**rice**
	nm	Est-ce que les gens de ton pays mangent du riz?
	ʁi	*Do the people of your country eat rice?*
1690	**plaisant**	**pleasant**
	adj	Je sais que ce n'est pas plaisant, mais on n'y peut rien.
	plɛzã	*I know that this is not pleasant, but we cannot change the facts.*
1691	**condamner**	**to condemn**
	verb	Qui ne peut se souvenir de son passé est condamné à le revivre.
	kõdane	*Those who cannot remember the past are condemned to repeat it.*
1692	**puce**	**chip**
	nf	La puce de cette carte stocke les données personnelles du titulaire.
	pys	*The chip on this card stores the holder's personal data.*
1693	**ex**	**ex**
	nmfi	J'ai un nouveau petit ami mais mon ex ne le sait pas encore.
	ɛks	*I have a new boyfriend, but my ex-boyfriend doesn't know about it yet.*
1694	**origine**	**origin, source**
	nf	J'ai la nationalité française mais je suis d'origine vietnamienne.
	ɔʁiʒin	*I have French nationality but Vietnamese origins.*
1695	**attitude**	**attitude**
	nf	Vas-y, justifie ton attitude, justifie le fait que tu aies été là lorsque tout ça s'est passé.
	atityd	*Justify your attitude, come on, justify being there when it all happened.*
1696	**absurde**	**absurd**
	nm, adj(f)	On ne peut pas accomplir l'impossible sans tenter l'absurde.
	apsyʁd	*You cannot achieve the impossible without attempting the absurd.*
1697	**union**	**union**
	nf	Il n'y a pas de chance d'union entre ces deux pays.
	ynjõ	*There is no chance of a union between the two countries.*
1698	**bagnole**	**wagon, car**
	nf	J'adorerais me débarrasser de cette vieille bagnole.
	baɲɔl	*I'd love to get rid of this old car.*
1699	**maximum**	**maximum**
	nm, adj	Cette aide sera accordée pour (X) ans maximum, avec un plafond de (X) %
	maksimɔm	*This support will be granted for a maximum of (X) years, and with a ceiling of (X) %.*
1700	**effort**	**effort**
	nm	Personne ne peut accomplir quoi que ce soit sans effort.
	efɔʁ	*No one can achieve anything without effort.*
1701	**chambre**	**bedroom, chamber, room**
	nf	Quelqu'un a nettoyé ma chambre pendant que j'étais parti.
	ʃãbʁ	*Someone cleaned my room while I was gone.*
1702	**vélo**	**bike, bicycle**

	nm	Le vent froid de l'hiver n'incitait vraiment pas à faire du vélo.
	velo	*The cold winter wind was definitely a disincentive to cycling.*
1703	**esclave**	**slave**
	nmf	À une époque il y avait beaucoup d'esclaves en Amérique.
	ɛsklav	*At one time there were many slaves in America.*
1704	**éducation**	**education**
	nf	L'éducation de nos enfants nous a coûté beaucoup d'argent.
	edykasjɔ̃	*Our children's education set us back quite a lot.*
1705	**réellement**	**really**
	adv	C'était réellement prévenant à vous de me prêter 500 dollars quand j'avais des difficultés.
	ʁeɛlmɑ̃	*It was really considerate of you to lend me 500 dollars when I was in difficulty.*
1706	**pair**	**peer, pair, even**
	adj, nm	Je pense qu'il est temps pour moi d'acquérir une nouvelle paire de lunettes.
	pɛʁ	*I think it's time for me to get a new pair of glasses.*
1707	**moche**	**ugly**
	adj	Cette image ne me semble pas moche ; au contraire, je pense qu'elle est plutôt jolie.
	mɔʃ	*That picture doesn't seem ugly to me; on the contrary, I think it's rather beautiful.*
1708	**blond**	**blond, fair-haired**
	nmf, adj	Notre fille est rousse, bien que nous soyons tous les deux blonds comme les blés.
	blɔ̃	*Our daughter has red hair while both of us have blonde hair.*
1709	**boule**	**ball**
	nf	Formez des boules de 3 cm de diamètre et déposez-les sur une feuille de papier d'aluminium beurrée.
	bul	*Make balls 3 centimeters in diameter and place them on a sheet of buttered aluminum foil.*
1710	**ouah**	**wow!**
	int	Ouah ! Quelle grande horloge ! Oui, c'est une horloge comtoise.
	wa	*Wow, that's a big clock! Yes, it's a grandfather clock.*
1711	**déclaration**	**declaration**
	nf	Remplissez s'il vous plait le formulaire de déclaration à la douane.
	deklaʁasjɔ̃	*Please fill out the Customs Declaration Form.*
1712	**chasser**	**to hunt, chase away**
	verb	Une chauve-souris chasse et mange la nuit, mais dort la journée.
	ʃase	*A bat hunts food and eats at night, but sleeps during the day.*
1713	**site**	**site**
	nm	L'anthropologue rassemble les tessons de poterie qu'elle a déterrés sur le site de fouilles.
	sit	*The anthropologist is piecing together pottery shards she unearthed at the excavation site.*
1714	**scientifique**	**scientific; scientist**

	adj(f), nmf	La plupart des avancées scientifiques ne sont rien d'autre que la découverte d'une évidence.
	sjãtifik	*Most scientific breakthroughs are nothing else than the discovery of the obvious.*
1715	**traître**	**traitor, treacherous**
	nm, adj	Scandalisés, ils se demandèrent qui pourrait être ce traître.
	tʁɛtʁ	*They were appalled and asked who such a traitor could be.*
1716	**panne**	**breakdown, failure**
	nf	Le mode opératoire à respecter en cas d"incident ou de panne.
	pan	*The operating method to be followed in case of accident or breakdown.*
1717	**traîner**	**to drag, pull**
	verb	Persée vit ses enfants traînés en chaînes derrière le char du vainqueur.
	tʁene	*Perseus saw his children, one after the other, dragged behind the victor's chariot.*
1718	**cave**	**cellar, basement**
	adj(f), nm, nf	Je réalisai alors que cette horrible cave était le seul endroit qui pouvait sauver nos vies.
	kav	*I realized then that this awful cellar was the only place that could save our lives.*
1719	**cassette**	**cassette, tape**
	nf	Je vous enverrai une cassette avec un enregistrement de ma voix.
	kasɛt	*I will send you a tape of my voice.*
1720	**essai**	**attempt, try, test**
	nm	Je suppose que je ne comprends pas ce que vous essayez de dire.
	esɛ	*I guess I don't understand what you're trying to say.*
1721	**musée**	**museum**
	nf	Avant-hier, Tom a vu quelques épées intéressantes au musée.
	myze	*Tom saw some interesting swords at the museum the day before yesterday.*
1722	**minable**	**seedy, shabby**
	adj	Mes parents avaient l'habitude de camper avec nous dans une tente assez minable.
	minabl	*My parents used to take us camping in a shabby tent.*
1723	**sommet**	**summit**
	nm	Ils poursuivirent la conférence au sommet jusque tard dans la nuit.
	sɔmɛ	*They carried on the summit conference till late.*
1724	**blesser**	**to hurt**
	verb	Je sais que la dernière chose que tu veuilles faire est de me blesser.
	blese	*I know that the last thing you want to do is hurt me.*
1725	**aile**	**wing, sail, blade**
	nf	Pour conquérir le centre, il nous faudra nous aliéner l'aile gauche du parti.
	ɛl	*In order to conquer the centre, we'll have to alienate the left wing of the party.*
1726	**bagarre**	**fight**
	nf	Parfois, les joueurs de hockey se provoquent tellement les uns les autres que des bagarres éclatent.
	bagaʁ	*Sometimes hockey players get so competitive that fights break out.*

1727	**production**	**production**
	nf	La production de légumes est en croissance dans notre région.
	pʁɔdyksjɔ̃	*The production of vegetables is growing in our area.*
1728	**rang**	**rank, row**
	nm	Son salaire correspond à son rang dans la hiérarchie de l'entreprise.
	ʁɑ̃	*His salary corresponds with his rank in the company hierarchy.*
1729	**livrer**	**to deliver**
	verb	Dans ce cas, nous sommes généralement obligés de livrer.
	livʁe	*In such cases we are generally required to deliver.*
1730	**venger**	**to avenge, take revenge**
	verb	Je me vengerai de cet affront, tu peux en être sûr !
	vɑ̃ʒe	*I will get revenge for this insult, you can be sure of that!*
1731	**flotter**	**to float, hang, stream**
	verb	Une fille arrivait en courant, avec ses cheveux flottant au vent.
	flɔte	*A girl came running, with her hair streaming in the wind.*
1732	**humour**	**humor**
	nm	C'est souvent par l'humour que Tom désamorce les situations tendues.
	ymuʁ	*Tom often uses humor to defuse tense situations.*
1733	**naturellement**	**naturally**
	adv	Le livre le plus important pour apprendre une langue est, naturellement, un dictionnaire.
	natyʁɛlmɑ̃	*The most important book to learn a foreign language is, naturally, a dictionary.*
1734	**résoudre**	**to solve, resolve**
	verb	L'agent de service m'a aidé à résoudre mon problème.
	ʁezudʁ	*The service agent helped me solve my problem.*
1735	**commandement**	**command, order, commandment**
	nm	Cette autorisation porte notamment sur le pouvoir de modifier l'OPLAN et la chaîne de commandement.
	kɔmɑ̃dmɑ̃	*This authorisation shall include the power to amend the OPLAN and the chain of command.*
1736	**remplacer**	**to replace**
	verb	En politique, on succède à des imbéciles et on est remplacé par des incapables.
	ʁɑ̃plase	*In politics, one is preceded by imbeciles and replaced by morons.*
1737	**mandat**	**term, mandate**
	nm	L'église n'a pas le mandat de changer le monde.
	mɑ̃da	*The church does not have the mandate to change the world.*
1738	**milliard**	**billion, thousand million**
	nm	La Voie Lactée se compose d'environ cent milliards d'étoiles.
	miljaʁ	*The Milky Way consists of about a hundred billion stars.*
1739	**fruit**	**fruit**
	nm	Les fruits et les légumes sont essentiels à une alimentation équilibrée.
	fʁɥi	*Fruits and vegetables are essential to a balanced diet.*
1740	**plaindre**	**to pity, feel sorry for, complain**
	verb	Il est toujours en train de se plaindre à propos de son faible salaire.

		plɛ̃dʀ	*He is always complaining about his low salary.*
1741	**partage**		**division, cutting, sharing**
	nm		Pour les autres tests, REACH encourage le partage de données afin de réduire les coûts pour les entreprises
		paʀtaʒ	*For other tests, REACH encourages the sharing of data in order to reduce costs for companies*
1742	**bourse**		**purse, scholarship, grant**
	nf		Cette bourse d'études m'a été accordée par le Conseil Général (France).
		buʀs	*This study grant was given to me by the departmental council.*
1743	**jungle**		**jungle**
	nf		Il contracta la malaria, tandis qu'il vivait dans la jungle.
		ʒɶ̃gl	*He contracted malaria while living in the jungle.*
1744	**aimable**		**pleasant, kind, nice**
	adj(f)		Pendant ce voyage j'ai connu plusieurs individus intéressants et très aimables.
		ɛmabl	*During this trip I met several interesting and very kind individuals.*
1745	**guider**		**to guide**
	verb		Quelqu'un peut-il me guider dans l'utilisation de ce site ?
		gide	*Can someone guide me on how to use this site?*
1746	**gâcher**		**to waste, spoil**
	verb		Soudain, le moine bouddhiste éclata de rire, gâchant ainsi l'atmosphère solennelle.
		gaʃe	*All at once, the Buddhist priest burst into laughter, spoiling the solemn atmosphere.*
1747	**adulte**		**adult**
	nmf, adj(f)		Les livres de coloriage pour adultes sont populaires depuis peu.
		adylt	*Adult coloring books have become popular recently.*
1748	**pomme**		**apple**
	nf		Tu peux te servir de la tarte aux pommes. Je l'ai confectionnée pour toi.
		pɔm	*Please help yourself to some apple pie. I baked it for you.*
1749	**auteur**		**author**
	nm, nf		Comment cet auteur a pu se retrouver au programme est une énigme pour moi.
		otœʀ	*How this author ended up on the program is a mystery to me.*
1750	**jugement**		**judgement**
	nm		Vous n'avez aucun droit de porter un jugement sur ces gens.
		ʒyʒmɑ̃	*You have no right to pass judgement on these people.*
1751	**organisation**		**organization**
	nf		L'Arménie a rejoint l'Organisation mondiale du commerce en 2003.
		ɔʀganizasjɔ̃	*Armenia joined the World Trade Organization in 2003.*
1752	**vague**		**vague; wave**
	adj(f); nf		Une partie de l'île a été détruite par les vagues géantes.
		vag	*A portion of the island was destroyed by the massive waves.*
1753	**légende**		**legend, caption, key**
	nf		Une mystérieuse légende circule à propos de ce lac.
		leʒɑ̃d	*A mysterious legend has been handed down about this lake.*

1754	**botter**	**to kick**
	verb	Botter, puis suivre, pour atteindre le réceptionnaire en même temps que le ballon arrive sur lui.
	bɔte	*Kick, then chase, so as to reach the catcher at the same time as the ball.*
1755	**barbe**	**beard**
	nf	La barbe ne fait pas le philosophe, pas plus que de porter un manteau bon marché.
	baʁb	*A beard doesn't make a philosopher, nor does wearing a cheap coat.*
1756	**territoire**	**territory**
	nm	Quelle est la qualité de l'eau que boivent les Palestiniens dans les territoires occupés ?
	teʁitwaʁ	*What is the quality of the water that the Palestinians drink in the occupied territories?*
1757	**blessure**	**injury, wound**
	nf	Il ne s'est jamais pleinement remis de ses blessures.
	blesyʁ	*He never fully recovered from his injuries.*
1758	**géant**	**giant, gigantic**
	nmf, adj	C'est un petit pas pour l'homme, mais un bond de géant pour l'humanité.
	ʒeã	*That's one small step for man, one giant leap for mankind.*
1759	**moto**	**motorbike**
	nm	La moto de Tim est bien plus chère que la mienne.
	mɔto	*Tim's motorbike is far more expensive than mine is.*
1760	**communauté**	**community**
	nf	Le gouvernement a été encouragé par le manque de réaction de la communauté internationale.
	kɔmynote	*The government has been emboldened by the lack of response from the international community.*
1761	**cage**	**cage**
	nf	Pour peindre un oiseau, peindre d'abord une cage avec une porte ouverte.
	kaʒ	*To paint a bird, start by painting a cage with an open door.*
1762	**désirer**	**to desire, to want**
	verb	Je t'emmènerai où tu veux aller et t'achèterai ce que ton cœur désire.
	deziʁe	*I'll take you wherever you want to go and buy you whatever your heart desires.*
1763	**rayon**	**ray, beam, radius; department, section, shelf**
	nm	Un faisceau de lumière blanche est divisé par un prisme en rayons de différentes couleurs.
	ʁɛjõ	*A beam of white light is split by a prism into rays of various colors.*
1764	**sorcier**	**sorcerer, witch**
	nm	Un jour, une sorcière envoya le mauvais oeil à Christophe Colomb... et ne le vit jamais revenir.
	sɔʁsje	*A witch once gave Christopher Columbus an evil eye... and never got it back.*
1765	**pile**	**pile, stack, battery, tails**
	nf	L'horloge s'est arrêtée. Il y faut une nouvelle pile.
	pil	*The clock has stopped. It needs a new battery.*

1766	**kilo**	**kilo**
	nm	Il faut beaucoup plus de céréales pour obtenir un kilo de bœuf qu'un kilo de poulet.
	kilo	*it takes far more cereals to obtain a kilo of beef than it does to obtain the same quantity of chicken.*
1767	**écrivain**	**writer**
	nm	Les Voyages de Gulliver furent écrits par un célèbre écrivain anglais.
	ekʁivɛ̃	*Gulliver's Travels was written by a famous English writer.*
1768	**forcer**	**to force**
	verb	Personne ne peut te forcer à faire quelque chose contre ta volonté.
	fɔʁse	*No one can force you to do anything against your will.*
1769	**respecter**	**to respect**
	verb	Vous devriez respecter les règles que vos parents vous ont fixées.
	ʁɛspɛkte	*You should respect the rules your parents set for you.*
1770	**limite**	**limit**
	nf	L'intervention humaine sur la nature ne trouve pas ses limites.
	limit	*Human intervention in nature has no limits.*
1771	**orange**	**orange**
	adj(i), nf	Elle a apporté des pommes, des oranges, et ainsi de suite.
	ɔʁɑ̃ʒ	*She brought apples, oranges, and so on.*
1772	**associer**	**to associate**
	verb	Les gens associent souvent les chiens à la loyauté.
	asɔsje	*People often associate dogs with loyalty.*
1773	**bénir**	**to bless**
	verb	Le prêtre bénit la congrégation à la fin de la messe.
	beniʁ	*The priest blessed the congregation at the end of the mass.*
1774	**quinze**	**fifteen**
	det, num	Mon père a vécu à Nagoya pendant plus de quinze ans.
	kɛ̃z	*My father has lived in Nagoya for more than fifteen years.*
1775	**posséder**	**to possess, own, have**
	verb	L'Italie possède quelques-unes des meilleures galeries d'art du monde.
	pɔsede	*Italy has some of the best art galleries in the world.*
1776	**conseiller**	**adviser, to advise**
	nm, verb	Elle lui a conseillé d'aller à l'hôpital, mais il n'a pas suivi son conseil.
	kɔ̃seje	*She advised him to go to the hospital, but he didn't follow her advice.*
1777	**ligne**	**line**
	nf	Savez-vous comment utiliser ces outils en ligne de commande ?
	liɲ	*Do you know how to use these command line tools?*
1778	**escalier**	**stairs, staircase**
	nm	L'ascenseur est en panne alors nous devrons emprunter l'escalier. Au moins, il n'y a que deux étages !
	ɛskalje	*The elevator's out of order, so we'll have to take the stairs. At least it's only two floors!*
1779	**explication**	**explanation**
	nf	Tout le monde a compris l'explication claire du professeur.

ɛksplikasjɔ̃   *Everyone understood the teacher's clear explanation.*

1780 voyager   **to travel**

verb   Son salaire important lui permet de voyager à travers le monde à chaque année.

vwajaʒe   *His large income enables him to travel abroad every year.*

1781 attirer   **to attract**

verb   Vous pouvez utiliser ce matériel pour attirer de nouveaux membres.

atiʁe   *You can use these materials to attract new members.*

1782 poursuivre   **to pursue**

verb   Si j'étais en bonne santé, je pourrais poursuivre mes études.

puʁsɥivʁ   *If I were in good health, I could pursue my studies.*

1783 professionnel   **professional**

nmf, adj   Beaucoup, sinon la plupart des traducteurs professionnels traduisent seulement vers leur langue natale.

pʁofesjɔnɛl   *Many, if not most, professional translators only translate into their native language.*

1784 incident   **incident**

adj, nm   Ce qui me fait penser que ça fait plus de trente ans depuis cet incident.

ɛ̃sidɑ̃   *Which reminds me, it's been more than 30 years since that incident.*

1785 colline   **hill**

nf   La vieille église sur la colline date du douzième siècle.

kɔlin   *The old church on the hill dates back to the twelfth century.*

1786 autorisation   **authorization, permission, permit**

nf   Cette autorisation ne s'applique pas aux transmissions par voie électronique.

ɔtɔʁizasjɔ̃   *This permission does not extend to delivery by electronic means.*

1787 assassiner   **to murder, assassinate**

verb   Un citoyen canadien ait trempé dans un complot en vue d'assassiner un politicien.

asasine   *A Canadian citizen was involved in a conspiracy to assassinate a politician in a foreign country.*

1788 ministère   **minister**

nm, nf   Je cherche un poste au ministère français de la Culture.

ministɛʁ   *I am looking for a job with the Cultural Minister of France.*

1789 exprès   **deliberately, on purpose, intentionally**

adj[pl], adv   Jack cassa le vase précieux de sa mère, mais il ne l'avait pas fait exprès, elle ne fut donc pas en colère.

     Jack broke his mother's valuable vase, but he didn't do it on purpose, so she wasn't angry.

ɛkspʁɛs

1790 football   **football, soccer**

nm   Dans deux semaines l'équipe belge de football, les Diables Rouges, joue au Brésil.

futbol   *In two weeks the Belgian football team, the Red Devils, plays in Brazil.*

1791 rond   **round, circle, patrol,**

adj, nm, nf   Les plaques d'égout sont rondes afin qu'elles ne puissent pas tomber accidentellement dans leur trou.

ʁɔ̃

Manholes are round because that way they won't accidentally fall through the hole.

1792	**exercice**	**exercise,**
	nm	J'ai essayé de faire un petit peu d'exercice tous les jours.
	ɛgzɛʁsis	*I've been trying to get a little exercise every day.*
1793	**fichu**	**damn, rotten**
	adj	Cette fichue alarme ne cesse de se déclencher en pleine nuit.
	fiʃy	*That damn alarm keeps going off in the middle of the night.*
1794	**vote**	**vote**
	nm	En cas de partage des voix, celle du président est prépondérante.
	vɔt	*In the event of a tie, the President shall have the casting vote.*
1795	**domaine**	**domain, field**
	nm	Il vaudrait mieux que vous ne sortiez pas de votre domaine de compétence.
	dɔmɛn	*It is better not to go out of your field.*
1796	**retenir**	**to retain, hold back, remember**
	verb	Je trouve que les mots ayant des définitions précises sont les plus simples à retenir.
	ʁətəniʁ	*I find words with concise definitions to be the easiest to remember.*
1797	**religion**	**religion**
	nf	Peux-tu réciter les noms des sept péchés capitaux selon la religion chrétienne ?
	ʁəliʒjɔ̃	*Can you recite the names of the seven deadly sins according to the Christian religion?*
1798	**clairement**	**clearly**
	adv	Exprime-toi clairement et parle à voix haute afin que les autres t'entendent.
	klɛʁmã	*Speak clearly and make yourself heard.*
1799	**furieux**	**furious, raging, violent, mad**
	adj	Je sais que vous êtes probablement furieux à propos de ce que j'ai dit hier.
	fyʁjø	*I know you're probably mad about what I said yesterday.*
1800	**pisser**	**to piss**
	verb	Les chiens aiment pisser sur les bouches à incendie.
	pise	*Dogs like to piss on fire hydrants.*
1801	**circonstance**	**circumstance**
	nf	Le caractère de chaque action dépend des circonstances dans lesquelles elle est réalisée.
	siʁkɔ̃stãs	*The character of every act depends upon the circumstances in which it is done.*
1802	**excellence**	**excellence**
	nf	M. Després a également reçu de nombreux prix d'excellence de la part de ses pairs.
	ɛksɛlãs	*Mr. Després has also received numerous awards from his peers for excellence.*
1803	**cimetière**	**cemetary, graveyard**

nm	Au cimetière, se dresse une statue d'un serpent qui se mord la queue.
simtjɛʁ	*In the cemetery, there is a statue of a snake biting its own tail.*

1804 classique — **classic**

nm, adj(f)	Le qipao est un vêtement féminin classique dont l'origine remonte à la Chine du 17e siècle.
klasik	*The qipao is a classic female garment that originated in 17th century China.*

1805 arrestation — **arrest**

nf	Tom n'en est pas à sa première arrestation pour conduite en état d'ébriété.
aʁɛstasjɔ̃	*Tom has a history of arrests for drunken driving.*

1806 taper — **to beat, slam, bang, type, tap**

verb	Un étranger, derrière moi, m'a tapé sur l'épaule. Il m'a pris pour quelqu'un d'autre, c'est sûr.
tape	*A stranger tapped me on the shoulder from behind. He took me for some other person, I'm sure.*

1807 cabinet — **cabinet, agency, office**

nm	Je t'appellerai plus tard depuis le cabinet de travail.
kabinɛ	*I'll call you later from the office.*

1808 comédie — **comedy, playacting**

nf	La comédie est bien plus près de la vie réelle que le drame.
kɔmedi	*Comedy is much closer to real life than drama.*

1809 bond — **leap, rebound**

nm	Lorsqu'elle eut fini de chanter, je fus d'un bond près d'elle pour la remercier.
bɔ̃	*When her song was finished, I took one leap towards her in order to thank her.*

1810 tunnel — **tunnel**

nm	J'ai entendu dire qu'ils ont beaucoup de problèmes avec les tunnels en Nouvelle-Zélande.
tynɛl	*I hear they have a lot of problems with the tunnels in New Zealand.*

1811 amant — **lover**

nm	As-tu déjà eu une amante qui ne se trouvait jamais en travers du chemin ?
amɑ̃	*Have you ever had a lover who was never in the way?*

1812 tandis — *while*

adv	Ma sœur a l'habitude de souligner les mots qu'elle ignore tandis qu'elle lit.
tɑ̃di	*My sister has the habit of underlining words she doesn't know while reading.*

1813 incapable — **incapable, incompetent**

adj	Elle est incapable de faire quoi que ce soit seule.
ɛ̃kapabl	*She is incapable of doing anything alone.*

1814 drapeau — **flag**

nm	Les Chinois ont un grand drapeau et un petit livre rouges.
dʁapo	*Chinese people have a big red flag and a little red book.*

1815 échouer — **to fail**

verb	Je croyais qu'il allait échouer à l'examen, mais au final il l'a réussi.
eʃwe	*I thought he was going to fail the exam, but he passed after all.*

1816	**auparavant**	**beforehand**
	adv	Auparavant, beaucoup d'Autrichiens pensaient que le parti de M. Kreisky perdrait la majorité absolue.
	opaʁavɑ̃	*Many Austrians had thought beforehand that Mr. Kreisky's party would lose its absolute majority.*
1817	**risquer**	**to risk**
	verb	Il a risqué sa vie pour sauver sa famille de l'incendie.
	ʁiske	*He risked his life to save his family from the fire.*
1818	**magazine**	**magazine**
	nm	Le magazine recherche les insectes les plus dégoûtants de la planète.
	magazin	*The magazine is researching the most disgusting insects on the planet.*
1819	**remplir**	**to fill, fulfill, fill out**
	verb	Les nouvelles procédures comptables exigent que nous remplissions différents formulaires pour rendre compte des dépenses.
	ʁɑ̃pliʁ	*The new accounting procedures require us to fill out different forms for reporting expenses.*
1820	**véhiculer**	**to transport, convey**
	verb	Le langage a été inventé pour véhiculer du sens. C'est sans doute la forme de communication humaine la plus directe.
	veikyle	*Language was invented to convey meaning. It's arguably the most direct form of human communication.*
1821	**précieux**	**precious**
	adj [pl]	On dit qu'il n'est rien de plus précieux que le temps.
	pʁesjø	*It's said that nothing is more precious than time.*
1822	**éternité**	**eternity, lifetime**
	nf	Il y aura toujours des choses que je n'apprendrai jamais, je n'ai pas l'éternité devant moi !
	etɛʁnite	*There will always be things I will never learn, I don't have eternity before me!*
1823	**citer**	**to quote**
	verb	Je vais vous citer quelques phrases d'une de ces lettres.
	site	*I will quote you a passage from one of those letters.*
1824	**huile**	**oil**
	nf	En novembre, on récolte les olives sur les arbres pour produire de l'huile.
	ɥil	*In November, olives are harvested from the trees to make oil.*
1825	**proposition**	**proposition, proposal**
	nf	Je ne vois pas d'autres moyens de lui faire accepter notre proposition.
	pʁɔpozisjɔ̃	*I can't think of any other way of getting him to accept our proposal.*
1826	**soutien**	**support**
	nm	Je suis le meilleur ami, le meilleur soutien, le meilleur partenaire que tu auras jamais.
	sutjɛ̃	*I am the best friend, the best support, the best partner you will ever have.*
1827	**hauteur**	**height**
	nf	Vous allez devoir modifier la hauteur de la table pour la faire rentrer.
	otœʁ	*You'll have to modify the height of the table to make it fit.*

1828	**échec**	**failure**
	adj(i), nm	Il n'est pas juste de rejeter la faute de ses échecs sur ses parents.
	eʃɛk	*It's not fair to attribute your failure to your parents.*
1829	**fâcher**	**to anger, make angry, get angry**
	verb	Dan se fâcha et a claqué la porte de la salle à manger.
	faʃe	*Dan got angry and stormed out of the dining hall.*
1830	**culture**	**culture**
	nf	Il est important de comprendre que chaque pays a sa propre culture.
	kyltyʁ	*It is important to understand that each country has its own culture.*
1831	**précis**	**precise; noun**
	adj[pl, noun	Les plans doivent être détaillés et précis, et fournir des orientations aux acteurs concernés.
	pʁesi	*The plans should be concrete and precise, and should provide guidance to all stakeholders.*
1832	**langage**	**language**
	nm	Ma connaissance de l'espéranto m'a permis de considérer plus profondément la structure et la fonction du langage.
	lɑ̃gaʒ	*My acquaintance with Esperanto enabled me to look deeper into the make-up and function of language.*
1833	**objectif**	**objective, aim, goal; lens**
	adj, nm	Efforce-toi d'atteindre tes objectifs et ne cède pas face aux échecs.
	ɔbʒɛktif	*Try to reach your goals and don't give in to failures.*
1834	**profondément**	**profoundly, deeply**
	adv	Je n'ose pas enquêter trop profondément, de peur de découvrir l'horrible vérité !
	pʁɔfɔ̃demɑ̃	*I dare not probe too deeply, lest I uncover the awful truth!*
1835	**souffrance**	**suffering**
	nf	L'amour est une dragée composée des souffrances de nombreux hommes.
	sufʁɑ̃s	*Love is a pill made from a great many people's sufferings.*
1836	**pétrole**	**crude oil, petroleum**
	nm	Ce produit contient un distillat de pétrole qui est modérément ou hautement toxique pour les organismes aquatiques.
	petʁɔl	*This product contains a petroleum distillate which is moderately to highly toxic to aquatic organisms.*
1837	**entièrement**	**entirely, completely**
	adv	Le Japon est un pays qui est entièrement entouré par les mers.
	ɑ̃tjɛʁmɑ̃	*Japan is a country that is completely surrounded by oceans.*
1838	**épreuve**	**test, ordeal, trial**
	nf	Une pièce comportant de nombreux changements de décors peut être une épreuve pour la troupe ou pour le public.
	epʁœv	*A play with many scene changes may be a trial for the crew or a trial for the audience.*
1839	**copier**	**to copy, reproduce**
	verb	Tous les enfants ont besoin d'admirer et de copier quelqu'un.
	kɔpje	*Every child needs someone to look up to and copy.*

1840	**bibliothèque**	**library**
	nf	Veuillez ne pas écrire dans ce livre de la bibliothèque.
	biblijɔtɛk	*Please do not write in this library book.*
1841	**énerver**	**to annoy, get on someone nerves**
	verb	Tu es ici depuis quelques minutes à peine et tu commences déjà à m'énerver
	enɛʁve	*You've only been here a few moments, and you are already getting on my nerves.*
1842	**trente**	**thirty**
	det, num	En trente minutes seulement, nous n'avons pas pu répondre à toutes les questions.
	tʁɑ̃t	*Given only thirty minutes, we couldn't answer all the questions.*
1843	**électrique**	**electric**
	adj(f)	L'appareil électrique a dû être endommagé durant le transport.
	elɛktʁik	*The electrical appliance must have been damaged in transit.*
1844	**ranger**	**to tidy up, put away**
	nm, verb	Ranger est bien beau mais ça a le désavantage fatal que l'on ne retrouve plus rien par la suite !
	ʁɑ̃ʒe	*Tidying up is great, but it has the downside that one can never find anything afterwards!*
1845	**enterrer**	**to bury, lay aside**
	verb	Amis, Romains, compatriotes, prêtez-moi l'oreille: je viens pour enterrer César et non pas pour le louer
	ɑ̃teʁe	*Friends, Romans, countrymen, lend me your ears; I come to bury Caesar, not to praise him.*
1846	**assister**	**to attend; assist, help**
	verb	N'importe qui peut assister à mes cours, mais il n'est pas donné à tout le monde de les comprendre.
	asiste	*Anyone can attend my lectures, but not everyone can understand them.*
1847	**vallée**	**valley**
	nf	Le scientifique cherchait dans la vallée pour des os de dinosaures.
	vale	*The scientist searched for the bones of the dinosaurs in the valley.*
1848	**golf**	**golf, golf course**
	nm	Robert était tellement occupé qu'il a dû refuser une invitation de jouer au golf.
	gɔlf	*Robert was so busy he had to turn down an invitation to play golf.*
1849	**las**	**tired, weary**
	adj	J'espère qu'Emi ne va plus tarder. Je suis las de l'attendre.
	la	*I hope that Emi will appear soon. I'm tired of waiting for her.*
1850	**soigner**	**to treat, look after, take care for**
	verb	La poupée vécut très longtemps bien soignée, bien aimée ; mais petit à petit elle perdit ses charmes.
	swaɲe	*The doll lived for a very long time, being well cared for and loved, but bit by bit, it lost its charm.*
1851	**loyer**	**rent**
	nm	Il n'a pas payé le loyer depuis un temps considérable.

lwaʒe   *He is way behind on his rent.*

1852 producteur   **producer**

nm/f, adj   Elle crée un désavantage concurrentiel qu'aucun producteur de l'hémisphère nord ne peut égaler.

pʀɔdyktœʀ   *It has opened up a competitive gap no producer in the northern hemisphere can match.*

1853 quart   **quarter**

nm   Comme à son habitude, il arriva un quart d'heure en retard.

kaʀ   *As is usual with him, he arrived a quarter of an hour late.*

1854 critique   **criticism, critical, critic**

adj(f), nmf   Je ne peux pas comprendre pourquoi tu es si critique à son égard.

kʀitik   *I can't understand why you are so critical of him.*

1855 acte   **act**

nm   Cet article de magazine exposa en plein jour ses actes démoniaques.

akt   *That magazine article exposed his devilish acts to the full light of day.*

1856 plateau   **plateau, tray, set, stage**

nm   Les serveurs se sont téléscopés et ont fait tomber leurs plateaux.

plato   *The waiters bumped into each other and dropped their trays.*

1857 auto   **car**

nm, nf   Dix minutes après qu'ils aient passé Nara, l'auto s'est retrouvée sans essence.

oto   *Ten minutes after they had passed Nara, the car ran out of gas.*

1858 concernant   **concerning**

adv, prep   Le professeur a répondu à des questions concernant l'examen.

kɔ̃sɛʀnɑ̃   *The teacher answered questions concerning the exam*

1859 conférence   **conference**

nf   Il refusa notre proposition d'organiser une conférence de presse.

kɔ̃feʀɑ̃s   *He refused our offer to arrange a press conference.*

1860 charme   **charm**

nm   Il use de son charme pour attirer les jeunes filles et gagner leur confiance.

ʃaʀm   *He uses his charm to attract the girls to gain their trust*

1861 fièvre   **fever**

nf   La pauvre petite avait régulièrement la fièvre, et ses douleurs à la tête devinrent intolérables.

fjɛvʀ   *The poor girl regularly had bouts of fever, and her headaches became unbearable.*

1862 réception   **reception**

nf   Je prévois des réceptions de mariage dans un manoir historique avec la cuisine gastronomique.

ʀesɛpsjɔ̃   *I plan wedding receptions in a historic mansion with gourmet cuisine.*

1863 duc   **duke**

nm   Le duc et la duchesse sont arrivés en retard à la cérémonie.

dyk   *The duke and the duchess arrived late to the ceremony.*

1864 italien   **Italian**

nm/f, adj   Je parle espagnol à Dieu, italien aux femmes, français aux hommes et allemand à mon cheval.

	italjɛ̃	*I speak Spanish to God, Italian to women, French to men, and German to my horse.*
1865	**fenêtre**	**window**
	nf	Il y a de jolis volets des deux côtés des fenêtres de devant.
	fənɛtʁ	*There are pretty shutters on either side of the front windows.*
1866	**couvrir**	**to cover**
	verb	N'essayez pas de couvrir le ciel entier de la paume de votre main.
	kuvʁiʁ	*Don't try to cover the whole sky with the palm of your hand.*
1867	**cervelle**	**brain, brains**
	nf	J'espère que vous avez assez de cervelle pour voir la différence.
	sɛʁvɛl	*I hope you have brains enough to see the difference.*
1868	**moral**	**moral, morale**
	adj, nm	La justice morale ne saurait prendre l'innocent pour le coupable, dût l'innocent s'offrir.
	mɔʁal	*Moral justice cannot take the innocent for the guilty even if the innocent would offer itself.*
1869	**supérieur**	**superior**
	adj, nmf	Les personnes vaniteuses considèrent comme normal de se sentir supérieures aux autres.
	sypeʁjœʁ	*Conceited people take it for granted that they are superior to others.*
1870	**personnellement**	**personally**
	adv	Elle a dit que ça ne lui plaisait, mais personnellement je pense que c'est très bien.
	pɛʁsɔnɛlmɑ̃	*She said she didn't like it, but I thought, personally, it was very good.*
1871	**tendre**	**tender, soft**
	adj(f)	Cette viande de bœuf est super tendre. Elle fond littéralement dans la bouche.
	tɑ̃dʁ	*That beef is very tender. It just melts in your mouth.*
1872	**discussion**	**discussion**
	nf	Pourquoi vous et moi ne continuons pas cette discussion en privé ?
	diskysjɔ̃	*Why don't you and I continue this discussion in private?*
1873	**alarmer**	**to alarm**
	verb	Tout allait bien jusqu'à présent et on ne voulait pas alarmer les passagers.
	alaʁme	*Everything was going well to this point, and they did not want to alarm the passengers.*
1874	**ivre**	**drunk, intoxicated**
	adj	Je ne bois pas, mais je suis ivre à cause de toi.
	ivʁ	*I don't drink, but I'm drunk because of you.*
1875	**héler**	**to hail, call out**
	verb	Héler un taxi à Manhattan à cinq heures de l'après-midi est presque impossible.
	ele	*Hailing a cab in Manhattan at 5:00 p.m. is nearly impossible.*
1876	**gagnant**	**winner, winning**
	nmf, adj	Le gagnant de chaque échange marque un point et devient le serveur du prochain échange.

	gaɲɑ̃	*The winner of each rally scores a point, with the winner of the rally serving to start the next rally.*
1877	**beurre**	**butter**
	nm	Pan est un singe capable d'étaler du beurre sur son pain.
	bœʁ	*Pan is a monkey that can spread butter on bread.*
1878	**commerce**	**trade, commerce**
	nm	Il a investi son capital dans le commerce de l'acier.
	kɔmɛʁs	*He invested his capital in the steel trade.*
1879	**fleuve**	**river**
	nm	Il n'y a pas deux fleuves au monde qui soient parfaitement semblables.
	flœv	*No two rivers in the world are completely the same.*
1880	**nerf**	**nerve**
	nm	La façon de parler de Sakura me tape sur les nerfs.
	nɛʁ	*Sakura's way of speaking gets on my nerves.*
1881	**séparer**	**to separate**
	verb	Tu ne peux plus séparer le lait du café une fois que tu l'as versé dedans.
	sepaʁe	*You cannot separate the milk from the coffee once you put it in.*
1882	**pédé**	**homosexual, queer**
	nf	Il me demanda si j'étais un pédé, et je lui répondis : «Oui, ça vous gêne ?
	pede	*He asked me if I was queer and I said "Yes, do you have a problem with that?*
1883	**assis**	**seated**
	adj	Il se lève souvent en classe ou n'arrive pas à rester assis.
	asi	*Gets up often in class or cannot stay seated.*
1884	**employer**	**to use, employ**
	verb	Les utilisateurs en aval ne peuvent employer ces substances que pour les utilisations qui ont été autorisées.
	ɑ̃plwaje	*Downstream users may only use such substances for uses which have been authorised.*
1885	**liaison**	**liaison, connection**
	nf	Il est particulièrement fier de son travail d'agent de liaison.
	ljɛzɔ̃	*He takes greatest pride in his work as a liaison officer.*
1886	**document**	**document**
	nm	Veuillez transmettre le document à l'administration, pour vérification.
	dɔkymɑ̃	*Please forward the document to the administrative office for review.*
1887	**salopard**	**bastard**
	nm	Aucun pauvre salopard n'a jamais gagné une guerre en mourant pour son pays.
	salɔpaʁ	*No poor bastard ever won a war by dying for his country.*
1888	**place**	**room, space, seat, square, place**
	nf	En parfait gentleman, il s'est levé et lui a offert sa place.
	plas	*Like a gentleman, he rose and offered her his seat.*
1889	**nuage**	**cloud**
	nm	Voyez-vous ce nuage, qui a presque la forme d'un chameau?
	nyaʒ	*Do you see that cloud that almost looks like a camel?*
1890	**fiancer**	**to get engaged, to betroth**

	fiance	Monsieur Westcott insista pour que le jeune couple attende quatre ou cinq ans avant de se fiancer.
	fijãse	*Mr. Westcott insisted that they wait four or five years to become engaged.*
1891	**avenue**	**avenue**
	nf	La cinquième avenue de New-York est comparable au quartier de Ginza.
	avəny	*New York's Fifth Avenue is comparable to Ginza.*
1892	**guitare**	**guitar**
	nf	Je joue de la guitare dans un groupe qui chante des vieux tubes.
	gitaʀ	*I play guitar in an oldies band.*
1893	**portraire**	**to portray**
	verb	Je ne me suis jamais senti grand goût pour portraire les triomphants et les glorieux de ce monde.
	pɔʀtʀɛʀ	*I never felt great fondness for portraying the triumphant and glorious in the world.*
1894	**final**	**final**
	nm, adj	Un rapport final est également présenté dans les trois mois suivant la réalisation de l'action
	final	*A final report shall also be submitted within three months of the completion of the action.*
1895	**brise**	**breeze, air**
	nf	A cette période de l'année, il y a habituellement une petite brise matinale.
	bʀiz	*At this time of the year there is usually a bit of a morning breeze.*
1896	**réseau**	**network**
	nm	Avec le développement des réseaux, une quantité énorme et sans précédent de messages vole autour de la planète.
	ʀezo	*With the development of networks a huge and unprecedented volume of messages flies around the world.*
1897	**prière**	**prayer**
	nf	La prière est une façon de s'adresser à une divinité.
	pʀijɛʀ	*Prayer is a means of turning oneself towards a Deity.*
1898	**réalisateur**	**director**
	nmf	Le réalisateur a recréé la scène la plus célèbre du roman.
	ʀealizatœʀ	*The director recreated the novel's most famous scene.*
1899	**surveillance**	**surveillance, monitoring**
	nf	Finalement, il fut décidé que les magasins seraient équipés de caméras de surveillance.
	syʀvɛjãs	*Eventually it was decided that the stores be equipped with surveillance cameras.*
1900	**épaule**	**shoulder**
	nf	J'ai très mal à l'épaule, et je ne sais que faire.
	epol	*My shoulder hurts so much, I don't know what to do.*
1901	**placard**	**cupboard, locker**
	nm	La veille, portez la bouteille délicatement dans un placard de la cuisine ou du salon ; laissez-la verticale.
	plakaʀ	*The day before, place the bottle delicately in a cupboard in the kitchen or living room; leave it upright.*

1902	**mercredi**	**Wednesday**
	nm	Chaque semaine, j'étudie le piano le lundi, et la danse le mercredi et le vendredi.
	mɛʁkʁədi	*Every week I study piano on Monday and Tuesday, and dancing on Wednesday and Friday.*
1903	**chiffre**	**figure, number**
	nm	Tom et Marie ont une vingtaine d'enfants, mais ils ne sont pas certains du chiffre exact.
	ʃifʁ	*Tom and Mary have about 20 children, but they're not quite sure of the exact number.*
1904	**lampe**	**lamp, light**
	nf	La lampe était suspendue à la branche d'un arbre.
	lɑ̃p	*The lamp was suspended from the branch of a tree.*
1905	**expert**	**expert**
	nm, adj	En amour, les femmes sont expertes et les hommes sont d'éternels novices.
	ɛkspɛʁ	*When it comes to love, women are experts and men eternal novices.*
1906	**autorité**	**authority**
	nf	En raison de l'arrivée précoce de l'hiver, cette année, les autorités prévoient des pénuries de mazout.
	ɔtɔʁite	*Due to the early onset of winter this year, authorities are forecasting shortages of heating oil.*
1907	**destruction**	**destruction**
	nf	Une guerre nucléaire provoquerait la destruction de l'humanité.
	dɛstʁyksjɔ̃	*A nuclear war will bring about the destruction of mankind.*
1908	**congrès**	**congres, convention, conference**
	nm	Le président a opposé son veto à la loi après que le Congrès l'ait adoptée.
	kɔ̃gʁɛ	*The President vetoed the law after Congress passed it.*
1909	**poudre**	**powder, dust**
	nf	Tu dois prendre cette poudre à l'issue de chaque repas.
	pudʁ	*You have to take this powder after each meal.*
1910	**juillet**	**July**
	nm	La société a rappelé toute sa nourriture pour bébé qui avait été produite au mois de juillet.
	ʒɥijɛ	*The company called in all the baby food made in July.*
1911	**moderne**	**modern**
	adj	Il a des connaissances en histoire moderne de la France.
	mɔdɛʁn	*He knows about the modern history of France.*
1912	**stade**	**stadium, stage**
	nm	Les nations sont-elles le dernier stade de l'évolution de la société humaine ?
	stad	*Are nations the last stage of evolution in human society?*
1913	**serment**	**oath, vow**
	nm	Avec chaque serment rompu, tu rapproches un peu plus notre idéal de la destruction.
	sɛʁmɑ̃	*With every broken vow, you bring our ideal closer to destruction.*

1914	**dette**	**debt**
	nf	Quand j'aurai remboursé toutes mes dettes, il ne me restera plus d'argent.
	dɛt	*When I pay all my debts, I'll have no money left.*
1915	**entraîner**	**to train**
	verb	Le coach entraîne les joueurs de baseball.
	ɑ̃tʁene	*The coach trains the baseball players.*
1916	**sensible**	**sensitive**
	adj(f)	En tant qu'Anglais, il est particulièrement sensible aux différences entre les usages anglais et étasunien.
	sɑ̃sibl	*As an Englishman, he is particularly sensitive to the differences between English and American usage.*
1917	**ajouter**	**to add**
	verb	Nous devons ajouter quelques statistiques à la présentation Powerpoint.
	aʒute	*We need to add some statistics to the PowerPoint.*
1918	**expression**	**expression**
	nf	Le professeur a dit que nous devions apprendre toutes ces expressions par cœur.
	ɛkspʁesjɔ̃	*The teacher said we had to learn all these expressions by heart.*
1919	**métro**	**metro, subway**
	nm	Excusez-moi. Pourriez-vous m'indiquer la station de métro la plus proche ?
	metʁo	*Excuse me. Can you direct me to the nearest subway station?*
1920	**fonce**	**dark**
	adj	Elle a le teint clair alors que son frère a la peau foncée.
	fɔ̃s	*She's got a fair complexion while her brother is very dark.*
1921	**chat**	**cat; chat**
	nm	Pour son anniversaire, Dan a reçu un chat porte-bonheur de la part de ses collègues.
	ʃa	*Dan got a lucky cat figurine from a co-worker for his birthday.*
1922	**durer**	**to last**
	verb	Les négociations pour le nouveau contrat ont duré toute la journée.
	dyʁe	*Negotiations for the new contract lasted all day.*
1923	**balance**	**scales, balance**
	nf	La balance ne doit pas pencher dans un sens, ni dans l'autre.
	balɑ̃s	*It should not tip the scales in favour of either one.*
1924	**extrêmement**	**extremely**
	adv	Faire en sorte que les gens changent est extrêmement difficile.
	ɛkstʁɛmmɑ̃	*Getting people to change is extremely difficult.*
1925	**séance**	**meeting**
	nf	Il est erroné de croire que les délégations diront en séance informelle ce qu'elles ne diraient pas en séance officielle.
	seɑ̃s	*It is not correct to assume that delegations will be able to say in an informal setting what they will not say in formal meetings.*
1926	**collier**	**necklace**
	nm	J'ai donné un collier de perles à ma sœur pour son anniversaire.
	kɔlje	*I gave my sister a pearl necklace on her birthday.*

1927	**alliance**	**alliance**
	nf	Le Japon a conclu une alliance avec la France juste avant la guerre.
	aljɑ̃s	*Japan entered into an alliance with France just before the war.*
1928	**congé**	**time off, leave**
	nm	Il envisage de rentrer à la maison pendant ses congés.
	kɔ̃ʒe	*He is planning to go home on leave.*
1929	**portefeuille**	**wallet**
	nm	Il remarqua tout à coup que son portefeuille était manquant.
	pɔʁtəfœj	*He suddenly noticed his wallet was missing.*
1930	**trahir**	**to betray, give away**
	verb	Vous pouvez lui faire confiance. Il ne vous trahira jamais.
	tʁaiʁ	*You can trust him. He'll never betray you.*
1931	**repartir**	**to distribute, spread out, share out, divide**
	verb	Les biens furent repartis équitablement entre les héritiers.
	ʁəpaʁtiʁ	*The property was divided equally among the heirs.*
1932	**terroriste**	**terrorist**
	nm, nf	Le terroriste pour l'un est un combattant de la liberté pour un autre.
	teʁɔʁist	*One man's terrorist is another man's freedom fighter.*
1933	**clan**	**clan**
	nm	L'industrie locale était florissante par tout le pays pendant la période Edo grâce à l'effort de promotion de chaque clan.
	klɑ̃	*Local industry flourished throughout the land in the Edo period thanks to the promotional efforts by each clan.*
1934	**exécution**	**execution**
	nf	Le jour fixé pour leur exécution, elle se coupa les cheveux et se vêtit comme pour se rendre à une fête.
	ɛgzekysjɔ̃	*Upon the day appointed for their execution she cut off her hair and dressed herself as if going to a fete.*
1935	**convenir**	**to suit, to agree on**
	verb	Il est parfois très difficile de convenir d'une approche statistique uniforme.
	kɔ̃vəniʁ	*it is often very hard to agree on the method of counting.*
1936	**pourrir**	**to rot**
	verb	Il ne faut pas non plus laisser le cadavre pourrir quelque part.
	puʁiʁ	*Neither should you leave the body somewhere to rot.*
1937	**juger**	**to judge**
	verb	On ne peut pas juger un livre sur sa couverture.
	ʒyʒe	*You can't judge a book by its cover.*
1938	**invitation**	**invitation**
	nf	Nous avons envoyé les invitations quatre mois avant le mariage.
	ɛ̃vitasjɔ̃	*We sent the invitations four months before the wedding.*
1939	**électricité**	**electricity**
	nf	Nous utilisons de l'électricité pour chauffer l'eau dans notre maison.
	elɛktʁisite	*We use electricity to heat the water in our house.*
1940	**admettre**	**to admit**
	verb	Il n'eut pas la décence d'admettre qu'il avait tort.

admɛtʁ | *He didn't have the decency to admit that he was wrong.*

1941 avril — **April**

nm — Si vos sentiments sont toujours tels qu'ils étaient en avril, dites-le-moi tout de suite.

avʁil — *If your feelings are still what they were last April, tell me so at once.*

1942 convier — **to invite**

verb — Je ne peux pas assister à la fête mais je vous remercie de m'y avoir conviée.

kɔ̃vje — *I cannot go to the party, but thank you for inviting me all the same.*

1943 acier — **steel**

nm — Le béton sera renforcé par la pose de barres d'acier.

asje — *Concrete can be reinforced by putting steel bars inside it.*

1944 promener — **to take for a walk, go for a walk**

verb — S'il y a une éclaircie, nous irons nous promener en forêt.

pʁɔmne — *If the weather clears up, we'll go for a walk in the forest.*

1945 sourd — **deaf, deaf person**

adj, nmf — Il n'est pas de pire sourd que celui qui ne veut écouter.

suʁ — *There's no one more deaf than he who does not want to listen.*

1946 degré — **degree**

nm — Pendant l'été, la température oscille entre trente et quarante degrés Celsius.

dəgʁe — *In the summer, the temperature ranges from thirty to forty degrees Celsius.*

1947 instruction — **instruction, direction**

nf — De la lecture de bons livres on peut tirer du plaisir, de l'amitié, de l'expérience et de l'instruction.

ɛ̃stʁyksjɔ̃ — *From reading good books we can derive pleasure, friendship, experience and instruction.*

1948 injuste — **unfair, unjust**

adj(f) — Le gouvernement doit agir pour remédier à cette situation injuste.

ɛ̃ʒyst — *The government must act to rectify this unjust situation.*

1949 division — **division**

nf — La division est un terme qui doit appartenir au passé de l'Europe.

divizjɔ̃ — *Division is a word which must belong to Europe's past.*

1950 fierté — **pride**

nf — Et le Diable ricana car son péché mignon est la fierté déguisée en humilité.

fjɛʁte — *And the Devil did grin, for his darling sin is pride that apes humility.*

1951 exprimer — **to express**

verb — Étant profondément reconnaissant, il tenta d'exprimer ses remerciements.

ɛkspʁime — *Being deeply thankful, he tried to express his thanks.*

1952 fidèle — **faithful**

adj — Je serai ton fidèle partenaire jusqu'à la fermeture de mon cercueil.

fidɛl — *Until my coffin closes I will be your faithful spouse.*

1953 causer — **to cause; to chat**

verb — Savez-vous quelle est la première cause de discrimination en Italie ?

koze — *Do you know what is the first cause of discrimination in Italy?*

1954 couler — **to flow, run, sink**

	verb	Il lut la lettre, les larmes lui coulant le long des joues.
	kule	*He read the letter with tears running down his cheeks.*
1955	**renseignement**	**information**
	nm	Même un renseignement en apparence anodin peut s'avérer important pour un client.
	ʁɑ̃sɛɲmɑ̃	*Even seemingly trivial information like this may be important to a customer.*
1956	**total**	**total**
	adj, nm	Tout est compris dans le coût total de 200 dollars.
	tɔtal	*Everything is included in the total cost of 200 dollars.*
1957	**réservé**	**reserved**
	adj	Il était entouré de lignes blanches et une notice précisait "Réservé au directeur".
	ʁezɛʁve	*There were white lines around it, and it had a notice saying, "Reserved for Head of College."*
1958	**tare**	**defect**
	nf	Le défaut technique a été corrigé par l'ingénieur.
	taʁ	*The technical defect has been fixed by the engineer.*
1959	**espagnol**	**Spanish**
	nm, adj	Les soldats espagnols utilisaient de la poudre à canon qui ne produit pas de fumée.
	ɛspaɲɔl	*The Spanish soldiers used smokeless gunpowder.*
1960	**solide**	**solid**
	nm, adj(f)	Tom n'a pas pu manger des aliments solides durant une semaine.
	sɔlid	*Tom couldn't eat solid food for a week.*
1961	**avantage**	**advantage**
	nm	Sa maîtrise du chinois est un avantage notable dans sa recherche d'emploi.
	avɑ̃taʒ	*His knowledge of Chinese is a significant advantage in his job search.*
1962	**habitant**	**inhabitant**
	nm	Les pompiers et les habitants ont travaillé main dans la main pour éteindre le feu.
	abitɑ̃	*The firefighters and inhabitants worked side by side to put out the fire.*
1963	**rage**	**rage, fury, rabies**
	nf	La rage est une maladie d'origine virale que l'on trouve chez les animaux domestiques et sauvages.
	ʁaʒ	*Rabies is a disease of viral origin that affects both wild and domestic animals.*
1964	**normalement**	**normally**
	adv	Le taux d'intérêt de la facilité de dépôt constitue normalement un plancher pour le taux du marché au jour le jour.
	nɔʁmalmɑ̃	*The interest rate on the deposit facility normally provides a floor for the overnight market interest rate.*
1965	**cesser**	**to cease, stop**
	verb	Si vous vous trouvez dans un trou, cessez de creuser.
	sese	*If you find yourself in a hole, stop digging.*
1966	**neveu**	**nephew**

	nm	Comme mon neveu était encore jeune, il a été épargné.
	nəvø	*Since my nephew was still young, he was let off the hook.*
1967	**emprunter**	**to borrow**
	verb	Il demanda à sa petite copine d'emprunter le parapluie de sa mère.
	ɑ̃pʁœ̃te	*He asked his girlfriend to borrow her mother's umbrella.*
1968	**ouverture**	**opening**
	nf	Je compte sur vous pour prononcer le discours d'ouverture.
	uvɛʁtyʁ	*I am counting on you to deliver the opening address.*
1969	**habiller**	**to dress, get dressed**
	verb	Si tu t'habilles comme ça à ton âge, tu vas te ridiculiser.
	abije	*If you dress like that at your age, you'll make a fool of yourself.*
1970	**veuf**	**widow, widowed, widower**
	nmf, adj	C'est un veuf avec trois jeunes enfants dont il doit s'occuper.
	vœf	*He's a widower with three small children to take care of.*
1971	**munition**	**ammunition, supplies**
	nf	35 mètres représentent de toute façon la distance de tir maximum, indépendamment du type de munition utilisé.
	mynisjɔ̃	*35 meters is the maximum shooting distance anyway, regardless of the type of ammunition.*
1972	**écraser**	**to crush**
	verb	J'ai écrasé de l'ail et l'ai fait frire dans une poêle.
	ekʁaze	*I crushed some garlic and fried it in a pan.*
1973	**juin**	**June**
	nm	Au fait, c'est aujourd'hui le 8 juin - l'anniversaire de ma femme.
	ʒɥɛ̃	*By the way, today is the 8th of June — my wife's birthday.*
1974	**dégoûter**	**to disgust**
	verb	Je suis capable de manger une plaque de chocolat d'un coup mais après, je me sens si mal que je me dégoûte.
	degute	*I can down a whole chocolate bar at a time, but afterwards I feel so sick that I disgust myself.*
1975	**démarrer**	**to start**
	verb	Il avait besoin de fonds pour démarrer sa nouvelle entreprise.
	demaʁe	*He needed capital to start a new business.*
1976	**louer**	**to rent, praise**
	verb	J'ai écrit un courriel à mon ami et il m'a loué pour mon écriture.
	lwe	*I wrote an email to my friend and he praised me for my writing skills.*
1977	**bâton**	**stick, rod**
	nm	Il tailla le bâton en une pointe acérée, à l'aide de son couteau de chasse.
	batɔ̃	*He whittled the stick to a sharp point with his hunting knife.*
1978	**timide**	**timid, shy, bashful**
	adj(f)	Elle était plutôt timide mais depuis qu'elle est allée en Fac elle s'est vraiment épanouie.
	timid	*She used to be rather shy but since she went to University she has really blossomed.*
1979	**fermé**	**shut, closed, locked**

	adj	Nous ne pouvions ouvrir la porte, car elle était fermée à clé de l'intérieur.
	fɛʁme	*We couldn't open the door because it was locked from the inside.*
1980	**caractère**	**nature, character**
	nm	Attention: les caractères non supportés sont affichés avec le caractère '_'.
	kaʁaktɛʁ	*Warning: unsupported characters are displayed using the '_' character.*
1981	**dépêcher**	**to hurry, to dispatch**
	verb	Avant de dépêcher une véritable mission, l'UA doit envoyer une mission d'évaluation.
	depeʃe	*Prior to sending a full-fledged mission, the AU dispatches an assessment team.*
1982	**célibataire**	**single**
	adj, nf, nm	Bill était célibataire jusqu'à ce qu'il se marie la semaine dernière.
	selibatɛʁ	*Bill was single until he tied the knot last week.*
1983	**pasteur**	**minister, clergyman, pastor**
	nm	Le pasteur délivra un sermon enflammé qui laissa les pécheurs parmi eux trembler dans leurs bottes.
	pastœʁ	*The pastor gave a fiery sermon that left the sinners among them shaking in their boots.*
1984	**progrès**	**progress**
	nm	Il fait des progrès remarquables en anglais ces derniers temps.
	pʁɔgʁɛ	*He has recently made remarkable progress in English.*
1985	**ordure**	**filth**
	nf	Je ne peux me tenir avec eux et supporter et renforcir une église qui est remplis d'ordure.
	ɔʁdyʁ	*I cannot stand by and support and empower a church that is filled with filth.*
1986	**matière**	**matter**
	nf	Pourquoi la forme ne peut-elle être un attribut intime de la matière ?
	matjɛʁ	*Why can't shape be an intimate attribute of matter?*
1987	**puits**	**well, shaft, pit**
	nm[pl]	L'hiver passé, il faisait si froid que l'eau avait gelé dans les puits.
	pɥi	*Last winter, it was so cold that water froze in the wells.*
1988	**bonté**	**kindness**
	nf	Aucun acte de bonté, peu importe à quel point il est petit, n'est jamais gaspillé.
	bõte	*No act of kindness, no matter how small, is ever wasted.*
1989	**déposer**	**to deposit, to leave, to put down**
	verb	Il y a des gens qui n'aiment pas déposer l'argent dans la banque.
	depoze	*Some people do not like to deposit their money in banks.*
1990	**mondial**	**world, global**
	adj	L'OCDE a présenté son nouveau classement mondial sur l'éducation.
	mõdjal	*The OECD presented its new global education ranking.*
1991	**intelligence**	**intelligence**
	nf	Axiome de Cole : La somme de l'intelligence répartie sur la planète est une constante ; la population augmente.

	ɛ̃teliʒɑ̃s	*Cole's Axiom: The sum of the intelligence on the planet is a constant; the population is growing.*
1992	**généreux**	**generous**
	adj	C'est pourquoi je suis enclin à penser que l'on devrait se montrer plus généreux avec ce rapport.
	ʒeneʁø	*It is for this reason that I can well imagine that we could adopt a much more generous approach in this area.*
1993	**gérer**	**to manage**
	verb	Je doute qu'il soit assez qualifié pour gérer une telle équipe!
	ʒeʁe	*I doubt he is qualified enough to manage such a team!*
1994	**température**	**temperature**
	nf	Mais c'est un pays de savane typique, et nous apprécions des températures plus fraîches.
	tɑ̃peʁatyʁ	*But it's a typical savannah country, and we enjoy cooler temperatures.*
1995	**fête**	**party**
	nf	Je sais que vous ne venez pas à ma fête mais j'aimerais que vous y veniez.
	fɛt	*I know you're not coming to my party, but I wish you were.*
1996	**saloperie**	**trash, junk, filth**
	nf	Les mêmes saloperies qui étaient patentes par le passé sont un peu mieux cachées, mais toujours là.
	salɔpʁi	*The same shit that was blatant in the past is now a little more hidden but is still here.*
1997	**rapporter**	**to bring back, report**
	verb	Le témoin a rapporté ce qu'il avait vu à la police.
	ʁapɔʁte	*The witness reported what he had seen to the police.*
1998	**filmer**	**to film, shoot**
	verb	En revenant, le journaliste et les cameramen sont repassés par le même poste de contrôle tout en continuant à filmer.
	filme	*On their way back, the journalist and the camera crew passed through the same check post, where they continued to film.*
1999	**tension**	**tension**
	nf	Il y a des signes de tension grandissante entre les deux pays.
	tɑ̃sjɔ̃	*There are signs of growing tensions between the two countries.*
2000	**serviette**	**towel, napkin**
	nf	J'ai pensé que nous pourrions utiliser les serviettes en tissu.
	sɛʁvjɛt	*I thought we could use the cloth napkins.*
2001	**guérir**	**to cure**
	verb	Les médecins ont pu le guérir avec un nouveau médicament.
	geʁiʁ	*The doctors were able to cure him with a new medication.*
2002	**rouler**	**to roll**
	verb	Une histoire raconte que si la pièce de monnaie est ronde c'est pour lui permettre de rouler d'un endroit à l'autre.
	ʁule	*According to one story, the money was round so that it could roll from place to place.*
2003	**passeport**	**passport**

		nm	Pour voyager à l'étranger, on a habituellement besoin d'un passeport.

nm

Pour voyager à l'étranger, on a habituellement besoin d'un passeport.

paspɔʁ

When you travel abroad, you usually need a passport.

2004 suffisamment — **sufficiently**

adv

Pour chaque demande de confidentialité, des motifs suffisamment détaillés sont exigés.

syfizamã

For every confidentiality request sufficiently detailed reasons are required.

2005 échelle — **ladder**

nf

Ne grimpez pas à cette échelle, elle n'est pas sûre.

eʃɛl

Don't climb that ladder - it's not secure.

2006 cercle — **circle, cycle**

nm

Notre professeur de mathématiques traça un cercle au tableau.

sɛʁkl

Our math teacher drew a circle on the blackboard.

2007 exiger — **to require, demand**

verb

L'employé refusa de me rembourser, sur quoi j'exigeai de voir le patron.

ɛgziʒe

The clerk refused to give me a refund at which point I demanded to see the manager.

2008 citoyen — **citizen**

nmf

Les cultivateurs de la terre sont les citoyens les plus précieux.

sitwajɛ̃

Cultivators of the earth are the most valuable citizens.

2009 pervers — **pervert; perverse, perverted**

nmf; adj[pl]

C'est un effet pervers du droit du travail moderne.

pɛʁvɛʁ

This is a perverse effect of modern labour law.

2010 tentative — **attempt**

nf

Elle n'a pas réussi, mais c'était sa première tentative après tout.

tãtativ

She did not succeed, but after all that was her first attempt.

2011 règlement — **settlement, solution**

nm

Votre responsabilité consiste à procéder au règlement de la succession du défunt.

ʁɛgləmã

Your responsibility will include the settlement of the deceased's succession.

2012 immense — **immense**

adj(f)

Pas un accord, pas une entente pour sauver de la faillite l'immense majorité de la paysannerie.

Not a single agreement, no common ground to save the immense majority of farmers from bankruptcy.

imãs

2013 comté — **count**

nm

La Commission a été appelée comme son président, Comte Maurice Lippens.

kɔ̃te

The commission was named after its chairman, Count Maurice Lippens.

2014 crainte — **fear**

nf

Que ce soit par crainte ou par fierté, il ne répondit pas.

kʁɛ̃t

Whether by fear or by pride, he didn't respond.

2015 plaquer — **to tackle, drop, ditch, dump**

verb

Elle a plaqué son petit ami parce qu'elle voulait être seule.

plake

She dumped her boyfriend because she wanted to be alone.

2016 réunir — **to reunite**

	verb	Leur décision de se focaliser exclusivement sur l'élargissement a joliment porté ses fruits : l'Europe peut désormais se réunifier.
	ʁeyniʁ	*Their decision to focus single-mindedly on enlargement paid off handsomely: Europe can now reunite.*
2017	**manuel**	**manual**
	adj, nm	Il y a deux sortes de travail dans le monde : celui de la tête et celui des mains ; intellectuel et manuel.
	manɥɛl	*There are two kinds of work in the world--head work and hand work; mental and manual.*
2018	**cruel**	**cruel, ferocious, bitter**
	adj	S'il fallait absolument choisir, j'aimerais mieux faire une chose immorale qu'une chose cruelle.
	kʁyɛl	*If it were absolutely necessary to choose, I would rather be guilty of an immoral act than of a cruel one.*
2019	**octobre**	**October**
	nm	Le crash du marché boursier de New-York d'octobre 1987 est toujours bien vivant dans les mémoires.
	ɔktɔbʁ	*The stock market crash of October 1987 in New York is still vividly remembered.*
2020	**méchant**	**bad, mean**
	adj	Le méchant loup est un personnage courant des contes de fées.
	meʃɑ̃	*The bad wolf is a popular figure in fairy tales.*
2021	**dessin**	**drawing, pattern, design**
	nm	Ensuite, dans le carré de droite, définir l'objectif visé en quelques mots, au moyen d'un dessin.
	desɛ̃	*Then, in the right-hand box, define the desired goal either in words or with a drawing.*
2022	**inde**	**India**
	nf	Les populations de la Chine et de l'Inde font paraître les autres états comme des nains.
	ɛ̃d	*The populations of China and India dwarf those of every other nation.*
2023	**demeurer**	**to remain, live**
	verb	Plusieurs facteurs nous incitent cependant à demeurer prudents.
	dəmœʁe	*At the same time, a number of factors tell us that we must remain vigilant.*
2024	**léger**	**light, slight, thin**
	adj	Si tu sautes le petit déjeuner et que tu prends un repas de midi léger, alors tu peux manger ce que tu veux le soir.
	leʒe	*If you skip breakfast and keep lunch light, then in the evening you can have whatever you want.*
2025	**diamant**	**diamond**
	nm	Mieux vaut un vieux diamant d'occasion que pas de diamant du tout.
	djamɑ̃	*It is better to have old second-hand diamonds than none at all.*
2026	**publique**	**public**
	adj, nf	La plupart des endroits publiques ne sont tout simplement pas adaptés au personnes handicapées.

	pyblik	*Most public places are simply not geared to people with disabilities.*
2027	**emporter**	**to take, remove**
	verb	Vous pourrez alors les imprimer et les emporter avec vous.
	ãpɔʁte	*This can then be printed out and taken with you wherever you go.*
2028	**asile**	**shelter, asylum, hospital**
	nm	Un dangereux criminel s'est échappé de l'asile de fous
	azil	*A dangerous criminal has escaped from the insane asylum.*
2029	**organiser**	**to organise, throw**
	verb	Ma femme organise une célébration de naissance pour sa meilleure amie.
	ɔʁganize	*My wife is throwing a baby shower for her best friend.*
2030	**sou**	**penny**
	nm	Ses idées ne lui rapportèrent jamais même un sou.
	su	*His ideas never earned him even one penny.*
2031	**oser**	**to dare**
	verb	Nous devons oser ouvrir nos oreilles au Seigneur qui nous appelle, et aux personnes qui nous entourent.
	oze	*So we must dare to open our ears to the Lord who calls us, and to the people around us.*
2032	**tournage**	**shooting**
	nm	ous les supports de tournage sont acceptés (vidéo et pellicule)
	tuʁnaʒ	*All shooting formats (video or film) are accepted*
2033	**nucléaire**	**nuclear, nuclear power**
	adj, nm	L'humanité parviendra à utiliser pacifiquement l'énergie nucléaire.
	nykleɛʁ	*Mankind will succeed in using nuclear energy peacefully.*
2034	**populaire**	**popular**
	adj(f)	Est-ce vrai que Boston est une destination touristique populaire ?
	pɔpylɛʁ	*Is it true that Boston is a popular destination for tourists?*
2035	**orchestrer**	**to orchestrate**
	verb	Un maquillage de grande ampleur a été orchestré aux plus hauts niveaux du gouvernement.
	ɔʁkɛstʁe	*A massive coverup was orchestrated at the highest levels of government.*
2036	**couronne**	**crown, wreath**
	nf	La fille sur cette image porte une couronne non pas d'or mais de fleurs.
	kuʁɔn	*The girl in the picture is wearing a crown not of gold but of flowers.*
2037	**nue**	**naked**
	adj	Elle était aussi nue que le jour de sa naissance.
	ny	*She was as naked as the day she was born.*
2038	**vedette**	**star, patrol boat**
	nf	Les acteurs et les vedettes sportives monnaient souvent leur célébrité en contrats publicitaires.
	vədɛt	*Actors and sports stars often parlay their celebrity into endorsement deals.*
2039	**renvoyer**	**to send back, dismiss**
	verb	Jason, qui était en charge du projet, a été renvoyé pour cause de corruption.
	ʁãvwaje	*Jason, who was in charge of the project, was dismissed for corruption.*

2040	**garce**	**bitch**
	nf	Cette garce m'a volé mon idée et en a reçu tout le mérite.
	gaʁs	*That bitch stole my idea and got all the credit.*
2041	**formation**	**training**
	nf	L'idée de proposer aux salariés des formations sur ordinateur fait son chemin dans les entreprises.
	fɔʁmasjɔ̃	*The idea to propose computer-based training to salaried employees is maturing in businesses.*
2042	**audience**	**audience, hearing**
	nf	La totalité de l'audience se leva et commença à applaudir.
	odjãs	*The whole audience got up and started to applaud.*
2043	**participer**	**to participate**
	verb	J'ai participé principalement au groupe de travail « Protection de l'environnement et agriculture durable ».
	paʁtisipe	*I mainly participated in the working group "environmental protection and sustainable agriculture".*
2044	**issu**	**descended from, come from**
	adj	Issu d'immigrants Irlandais pauvres, mon père fit toujours preuve d'un grand intérêt pour les pauvres et moins fortunés.
	isy	*Coming from poor Irish immigrant parents, he always demonstrated great concern for the poor and less fortunate.*
2045	**procédure**	**procedure**
	nf	Vous gagnerez du temps si vous adoptez cette nouvelle procédure.
	pʁɔsedyʁ	*You will save time if you adopt this new procedure.*
2046	**brancher**	**to plug in, connect**
	verb	Je branche mon ordinateur portable sur la prise de courant pour le charger.
	bʁãʃe	*I plug my laptop into the outlet to charge it.*
2047	**influencer**	**to influence**
	verb	La violence au petit écran est présente au point d'influencer le comportement de nos jeunes.
	ɛ̃flyãse	*There is enough violence on television to influence the behaviour of our young people.*
2048	**mouche**	**fly**
	nf	Larvicide biologique très sélectif qui lutte contre les larves de moustique et de mouche noire.
	muʃ	*A highly selective biological larvicide used to control mosquito and black fly larvae.*
2049	**conséquence**	**result, consequence**
	nf	La décision de la direction a eu des conséquences importantes.
	kɔ̃sekãs	*The management's decision had serious consequences.*
2050	**groupe**	**group**
	nm	Un ménage est un groupe qui partage le même espace de vie et les mêmes finances.
	gʁup	*A household is a group that shares the same living space and finances.*
2051	**mortel**	**mortal, deadly, lethal**

	nmf, adj	La pointe de la lance avait été trempée dans un poison mortel.
	mɔʁtɛl	*The tip of the spear was dipped in a deadly poison.*
2052	**collègue**	**colleague**
	nm, nf	Le travail du professeur Wilson n'a pas toujours rencontré l'approbation de ses collègues collet montés.
	kɔlɛg	*Prof. Wilson's work has not always met the approval of her straight-laced colleagues.*
2053	**objection**	**objection**
	nf	
		The most important objection is that it would not ensure consumers' ability to make an informed choice.
	ɔbʒɛksjɔ̃	*La principale objection est qu'elle ne devrait pas permettre aux consommateurs de faire un choix informé.*
2054	**éteindre**	**to switch off, to turn off, to extinguish**
	verb	Nous tentâmes d'éteindre le feu mais sans succès. Nous dûmes appeler la brigade des pompiers.
	etɛ̃dʁ	*We tried to put out the fire but we were unsuccessful. We had to call the fire brigade.*
2055	**allumer**	**to switch on, light up, turn on**
	verb	Voyez-vous un inconvénient à ce que j'allume la radio ?
	alyme	*Do you mind if I turn on the radio?*
2056	**obéir**	**to obey**
	verb	On joue au cowboy et à l'Indien ? Je m'autoproclame shérif et vous devez tous m'obéir.
	ɔbeiʁ	*Shall we play cowboy and Indians? I declare myself a sheriff, and you all must obey me.*
2057	**sabrer**	**to cut**
	verb	La recette bien connue des politiciens, ceux d'alors comme ceux d'aujourd'hui, est de sabrer dans la défense.
	sabʁe	*The politicians' time-honoured solution, then as now, was to cut the defence budget.*
2058	**sain**	**healthy, sane**
	adj	Dans les années 50, on citait les Finnois comme ayant les régimes alimentaires les moins sains du monde.
	sɛ̃	*In the 1950's, the Finns were cited as having one of the least healthy diets in the world.*
2059	**tradition**	**tradition**
	nf	Ensemble, vous représentez l'harmonie entre la tradition et le progrès.
	tʁadisjɔ̃	*Together, you represent the harmony between tradition and progress.*
2060	**décevoir**	**to dissapoint**
	verb	Je sais qu'il continuera juste à me décevoir, mais je ne peux m'empêcher de l'aimer.
	desəvwaʁ	*I know he will only continue disappointing me, but I can't help loving him.*
2061	**département**	**department**
	nm	J'ai manqué la réunion du département parce que j'étais malade.

		depaʁtəmɑ̃	*I missed the department meeting because I was sick.*
2062	**résister**		**to resist**
	verb	On résiste à l'invasion des armées; on ne résiste pas à l'invasion des idées.
	ʁeziste	*One resists the invasion of armies; one does not resist the invasion of ideas*
2063	**impressionnant**		**impressive, upsetting**
	adj	Je pense qu'il s'agit du bâtiment le plus impressionnant sur la rue Park.
	ɛ̃pʁesjɔnɑ̃	*I think this is the most impressive building on Park Street.*
2064	**accusation**		**accusation, indictment**
	nf	Il y a toute une panoplie d'outils conduisant à la mise en accusation d'un individu
	akyzasjɔ̃	*There is a whole range of tools that can be used in making an accusation against an individual.*
2065	**disque**		**disc, disk**
	nm	As-tu remis une copie du disque à qui que ce soit ?
	disk	*Did you give a copy of the disk to anyone?*
2066	**piquer**		**to sting, bite, prick, be hot; to steal**
	verb	Couper l'excédent de pâte au rouleau et piquer le fond de la tarte à la fourchette.
	pike	*Cut off the excess paste with the rolling pin and prick the base with a fork.*
2067	**entretien**		**interview, discussion, maintenance**
	nm	Une cravate classique est préférable à une cravate criarde pour un entretien d'embauche.
	ɑ̃tʁətjɛ̃	*A conservative tie is preferable to a loud one for a job interview.*
2068	**accueillir**		**to welcome, greet, accommodate**
	verb	Qu'apprendre d'un chien ? Que lorsque les êtres aimés arrivent à la maison, il faut toujours courir les accueillir.
	akœjiʁ	*What can we learn from a dog? When loved ones come home, always run to greet them.*
2069	**chasseur**		**hunter, fighter, page, messenger**
	nm	L'un des chasseurs a été touché par une balle et a dû être amené à l'hôpital où il se remet maintenant rapidement.
	ʃasœʁ	*One of the hunters was shot and had to be taken to hospital, where he is now making a speedy recovery.*
2070	**examiner**		**to examine**
	verb	Tu ferais mieux d'examiner attentivement le contrat avant de signer.
	ɛgzamine	*You'd better examine the contract carefully before signing.*
2071	**solitaire**		**solitary, lone, lonely, loner**
	adj(f, nmf	Juste parce que je suis seul ne signifie pas que je sois solitaire.
	sɔlitɛʁ	*Just because I'm alone doesn't mean I'm lonely.*
2072	**goutter**		**to drip**
	verb	Empêcher les robinets de goutter en veillant à ce qu'ils soient toujours bien fermés.
	gute	*Ensure that taps are turned off tightly to avoid dripping.*
2073	**micro**		**mike, micro, microphone**
	nm	Pour l'utiliser, vous avez besoin d'écouteurs et d'un micro.
	mikʁo	*To use it you will need a headset with microphone.*

2074 technologie — technology

nf

La formation et le mouvement des ouragans sont capricieux, même avec notre technologie contemporaine.

tɛknɔlɔʒi

The formation and movement of hurricanes are capricious, even with our present-day technology.

2075 original — original

nm, adj

Pour éviter que son idée originale soit copiée, Henry se fit silencieux.

ɔʁiʒinal

In order to keep his original idea from being copied, Henry kept quiet.

2076 trompe — horn, trunk

adj

La trompe d'un éléphant peut peser plus de 100 kilos.

tʁɔ̃p

The trunk of an elephant can weigh over 100 pounds.

2077 dépasser — to exceed, to overtake

verb

Le nombre de personnes travaillant dans cette ville dépassera le millier d'ici la fin du mois.

depase

The number of the people working in this city will be more than one thousand by the end of this month.

2078 patrie — homeland, home country

nf

On n'habite pas un pays, on habite une langue. Une patrie, c'est cela et rien d'autre.

patʁi

You don't live in a country; you live in a language. Your homeland, that's that and nothing else.

2079 tuyau — pipe, tube

nm

Le plombier pompa l'eau pour la faire sortir du tuyau.

tɥijo

The plumber pumped the water out of the pipe.

2080 clinique — clinical, private hospital

adj(f), nf

Elles l'ont mis dans cette clinique après qu'il a dit qu'il entendait des voix.

klinik

They put him in this clinic after he said he was hearing voices.

2081 régime — diet, regime

nf

Nous savons tous qu'avoir un régime équilibré est bon pour nous.

ʁeʒim

We all know that eating a balanced diet is good for you.

2082 album — album

nm

Ils ouvrirent leur album de mariage et firent une petite promenade dans le temps.

albɔm

They opened up their wedding album and had a little stroll down memory lane.

2083 suprême — supreme

adj

La crainte de quelques pouvoirs suprêmes et divins conservent les hommes dans l'obéissance.

sypʁɛm

The fear of some divine and supreme powers keeps men in obedience.

2084 sincère — sincere

adj

La communauté a un désir sincère de nettoyer le fleuve.

sɛ̃sɛʁ

The community has a sincere desire to clean up the river.

2085 pipe — pipe

nf

Au Palatinat, le pasteur entre au temple avec une pipe.

pip

In the Palatinate the pastor goes to church with a pipe.

2086 violent — violent

adj		Toute l'après-midi, une violente tempête doucha les rues de la bourgade.
vjɔlɑ̃		*All afternoon a violent storm scoured the little town's streets.*

2087 émotion — **emotion**

nm — Il a caché ses émotions et a prétendu être enthousiaste.

emɔsjɔ̃ — *He hid his emotions and pretended to be enthusiastic.*

2088 coucou — **hello**

int — Le Musicserver démarre et lance une diffusion (« Coucou, je suis un serveur multimédia et vous pouvez me joindre ici!)

kuku — *The music server starts and sends a broadcast ("Hello, I'm a music server and this is my address!)*

2089 franc — **frank; franc**

adj, adv, adj, nm — Le franc français participe au Mécanisme de change européen depuis bien plus de deux ans.

fʁɑ̃ — *The French franc has been participating in the ERM for much longer than two years.*

2090 remarque — **remark**

nf — Avant que nous commencions, un certain nombre de remarques préliminaires sont nécessaires.

ʁəmaʁk — *Before we begin, a number of preliminary remarks are in order.*

2091 excitant — **exciting**

adj — C'est très excitant et un peu intense, mais j'adore ça.

ɛksitɑ̃ — *It's very exciting and a bit hectic, but I love it.*

2092 guère — **hardly**

adv — Il n'en reste pas moins qu'une stabilité de ce type ne peut guère être considérée comme un atout.

gɛʁ — *This kind of stability, however, can hardly be regarded as positive.*

2093 sel — **salt**

nm — En ce temps-là, le sucre avait moins de valeur que le sel.

sɛl — *In those days, sugar was less valuable than salt.*

2094 canapé — **couch, sofa**

nf — Elle m'a dit que je pouvais dormir sur le canapé.

kanape — *She told me that I could sleep on the sofa.*

2095 abattre — **to pull down, kill, beat, cut down**

verb — Si vous êtes dans l'obligation d'abattre un frêne, les périodes recommandées sont les mois d'octobre à décembre

abatʁ — *If you must cut down an ash tree, it is recommended that you do so between October and December.*

2096 déclarer — **to declare, disclose**

verb — Les candidats à l'élection sont tenus de déclarer leurs avoirs.

deklaʁe — *Candidates in the election are required to disclose their assets.*

2097 splendide — **magnificent, wonderful**

adj — Je n'avais jamais vu un aussi splendide coucher de soleil.

splɑ̃did — *I've never seen such a wonderful sunset.*

2098 promotion — **promotion, advertising**

	nf	Il est heureux. Pour une chose il a eu une promotion et de l'autre il vient juste de se marier.
	pʀɔmɔsjɔ̃	*He is happy. For one thing he's got a promotion and for another he has just got married.*
2099	**scandale**	**scandal, uproar**
	nm	Les récents scandales impliquant des chefs religieux et des enfants de chœur ont sérieusement entamé la foi des gens dans les églises.
	skɑ̃dal	*The recent scandals involving altar boys and religious leaders have undermined the faith people have in the Church.*
2100	**cran**	**guts, notch**
	nm	Ma ceinture est trop longue, je dois rajouter des crans.
	kʀɑ̃	*My belt is too long, I must add some notches.*
2101	**mêler**	**to mix, get mixed up with**
	verb	Il s'est trouvé mêlé aux affaires de son ami.
	mele	*He got mixed up in his friend's affair.*
2102	**élément**	**element**
	nm	La pertinence est un élément clé dans la communication.
	elemɑ̃	*Relevance is a key element in communication.*
2103	**arracher**	**to pull up, tear up**
	verb	Arracher les mauvaises herbes dans le jardin est sa tâche.
	aʀaʃe	*It's his job to pull up the weeds in the garden.*
2104	**interroger**	**to question, interrogate**
	verb	La police a interrogé de nombreuses personnes qui travaillaient près de la scène de crime.
	ɛ̃teʀɔʒe	*Police questioned many persons who worked near the crime scene.*
2105	**efficace**	**efficient, effective**
	adj(f)	L'homéopathie est considérée comme une pseudo-science et n'est pas plus efficace que les placebos.
	efikas	*Homeopathy is considered a pseudoscience and is no more effective than placebos.*
2106	**événement**	**event**
	nm	Selon l'enquête de police, Tom était sur les lieux du crime au moment de l'événement.
	evɛnmɑ̃	*According to the police investigation, Tom was at the scene of the crime at the time of the event.*
2107	**personnalité**	**personality**
	nf	Il y a beaucoup de choses que tu ne sais pas sur ma personnalité.
	pɛʀsɔnalite	*There are a lot of things you don't know about my personality.*
2108	**buter**	**to stumble, trip, run into, prop up, score**
	verb	Il ne faut rien mettre devant votre frère qui le fasse buter ou tomber.
	byte	*You should not put anything before your brother or sister to make them stumble or fall.*
2109	**rumeur**	**rumor**

	nf	Il y a une rumeur dans le village de ma mère selon laquelle il y aurait des ancêtres japonais.
	ʁymœʁ	*There's a rumor in my mother's village that we have Japanese ancestors.*
2110	**divin**	**divine, heavenly**
	adj, nm	Et la douleur corporelle qui accompagne tout excès n'est-elle pas un signe de la volonté divine ?
	divɛ̃	*And is not the bodily pain which follows every excess a manifest declaration of the divine will?*
2111	**dégât**	**damage**
	pl, nm	Cet essai ne doit pas provoquer l'ouverture des dispositifs, ni causer aucun dégât.
	dega	*The test shall not cause the closure to open and it shall not cause any damage.*
2112	**négatif**	**negative**
	adj, nm	La fonction d'initialisation est supposée retourner une valeur non négative si tout est OK.
	negatif	*The init function is expected to return a non-negative value if everything is OK.*
2113	**éclater**	**to burst, to shatter**
	verb	Le clown a éclaté le ballon avec une épingle
	eklate	*The clown burst the balloon with a pin.*
2114	**viser**	**to aim**
	verb	Il a soigneusement visé la cible avant de tirer.
	vize	*He carefully aimed at the target before shooting.*
2115	**invisible**	**invisible**
	adj(f)	On ne voit bien qu'avec le cœur. L'essentiel est invisible aux yeux.
	ɛ̃vizibl	*One sees clearly only with the heart. What is essential is invisible to the eye.*
2116	**signature**	**signature**
	nf	Il a fait le tour du quartier en récupérant des signatures.
	siɲatyʁ	*He went around the neighborhood collecting signatures.*
2117	**user**	**to wear out, wear away, use up**
	verb	Certaines femmes aiment tellement leur mari que, pour ne pas l'user, elles prennent ceux de leurs amies.
	yze	*Some women love their husband so much, that, in order not to wear him out too much, they borrow their friends' husbands.*
2118	**insister**	**to insist**
	verb	Il fut embarrassé, comme j'insistai pour lui lire les critiques de son nouveau livre.
	ɛ̃siste	*He was embarrassed when I insisted on reading the criticism of his new book.*
2119	**autoriser**	**to authorize, allow**
	verb	Ma mère m'autorisa à aller à l'étranger.
	ɔtɔʁize	*My mother allowed me to go abroad.*
2120	**canard**	**duck**
	nm	Il a préparé une sauce aux airelles pour accompagner le canard.

		kanaʁ	*He made a cranberry sauce to accompany duck.*
2121	**stylo**	**pen**
	nm	Je dois rassembler mes idées avant de prendre le stylo.
	stilo	*I must put my ideas together before I take up a pen.*
2122	**possibilité**	**possibility**
	nf	Nous ne pouvons pas écarter la possibilité qu'une guerre civile éclate dans ce pays
	pɔsibilite	*We cannot rule out the possibility that civil war will break out in that country.*
2123	**réveil**	**the waking up, alarm clock**
	nm	Vous devez lui expliquer comment utiliser le réveil.
	ʁevɛj	*You should explain to her how to set the alarm clock.*
2124	**pleuvoir**	**to rain**
	verb	Nous commencerons à quatorze heures, si il a cessé de pleuvoir d'ici là.
	pløvwaʁ	*We will start at two o'clock if it has stopped raining by that time.*
2125	**ère**	**era**
	nf	Après la guerre, une nouvelle ère de paix a commencé.
	ɛʁ	*After the war, a new era of peace began.*
2126	**conclure**	**to conclude**
	verb	De cela, on peut conclure que le féminisme est encore nécessaire.
	kõklyʁ	*From this you can conclude that feminism is still necessary.*
2127	**étape**	**stage, step, phase**
	nf	L'observation d'ondes gravitationnelles inaugurera une nouvelle étape dans l'étude de l'univers.
	etap	*The observation of gravitational waves will start a new phase in the study of the universe.*
2128	**contacter**	**to contact, get in touch with**
	verb	Elle se débrouilla finalement pour entrer en contact avec son vieil ami.
	kõtakte	*She finally managed to get in touch with her old friend.*
2129	**identifier**	**to identify**
	verb	Ils réussirent à l'identifier grâce à son bracelet-montre.
	idãtifje	*They were able to identify him by his wrist watch.*
2130	**attacher**	**to attach**
	verb	Le chauffeur est profondément attaché à sa vieille voiture.
	ataʃe	*The driver is deeply attached to his old car.*
2131	**prime**	**free gift, premium, bonus**
	noun, adj(f), nf	Lorsque vous volez une banque, vous allez en prison. Lorsqu'une banque vous vole, elle distribue des primes.
	pʁim	*When you rob a bank, you go to jail. When a bank robs you, they hand out bonuses.*
2132	**renfort**	**help, back-up, support**
	nm	Il a occupé les assaillants suffisamment longtemps pour que les renforts arrivent.
	ʁãfɔʁ	*He held off the attackers long enough for back-up to arrive.*
2133	**publicité**	**publicity**
	nf	Il ne faut pas vous en faire pour la publicité.

		pyblisite	*You don't have to worry about publicity.*
2134	**zut**		**heck**
	int		«Zut ! J'ai oublié le parapluie dans le train !» «Écervelé !»
	zy		*"Oh heck! I left my umbrella on the train." "You are a scatterbrain!"*
2135	**séjour**		**stay**
	nm		C'est pourquoi j'ai besoin d'un long séjour en France et de fonds pour financer mon séjour.
	seʒuʁ		*This is why I would like an extended visa as well as as funds for my stay.*
2136	**tabac**		**tobacco**
	nm		Ni le vin, ni l'opium, ni le tabac ne sont nécessaires à la vie humaine.
	taba		*Neither wine, nor opium, nor tobacco are necessary for people's lives.*
2137	**chaos**		**chaos**
	nm[pl]		Le chaos de l'hiver me rend fou, mais bientôt viendront les vacances.
	kao		*The winter chaos is driving me crazy, but soon the holidays will come.*
2138	**enfermer**		**to shut, lock in**
	verb		Elle s'enferma dans la salle de bains pour pleurer.
	ɑ̃fɛʁme		*She locked herself in the bathroom and howled.*
2139	**tarte**		**pie**
	nf		Si tu veux faire une tarte aux pommes à partir de rien, tu dois d'abord inventer l'univers.
	taʁt		*If you wish to make an apple pie from scratch, you must first invent the universe.*
2140	**cravete**		**necktie**
	nf		Je dois toujours porter une cravate à cause de mon travail.
	kʁavɛt		*I always have to wear a tie because of my job.*
2141	**frigo**		**fridge**
	nm		Y a-t-il quoi que ce soit à boire dans le frigo ?
	fʁigo		*Is there anything to drink in the fridge?*
2142	**traîne**		**train**
	nf		Étendez la traîne de l'autre côté, de manière à sortir la première, suivie de la traîne.
	tʁɛn		*Spread the train out on the other side, so that when you get out it will be you first and then the train.*
2143	**câble**		**cable**
	nm		Tom garde toujours des câbles de démarrage dans le coffre de sa voiture.
	kabl		*Tom always keeps a set of jumper cables in the trunk of his car.*
2144	**rarement**		**rarely, seldom**
	adv		Cette araignée ne mord que très rarement les hommes.
	ʁaʁmɑ̃		*This spider rarely bites humans.*
2145	**goûter**		**to taste**
	verb		C'est la dinde la plus délicieuse que j'ai jamais goûtée.
	gute		*It's the best turkey I've ever tasted.*
2146	**disputer**		**to dispute, contest**
	verb		De plus, la partie requérante n'a pas contesté les faits établis dans la communication des griefs

	dispyte	*Moreover, the applicant did not contest the facts found in the statement of objections*
2147	**impliquer**	**to imply, implicate**
	verb	Cela implique une résidence suivie et non pas un simple séjour.
	ε̃plike	*This implies continued residence and not a mere visit.*
2148	**remarquable**	**remarkable, outstanding**
	adj(f)	Dans les dernières années, la science a fait des progrès remarquables.
	ʁəmaʁkabl	*In recent years, science has made remarkable progress.*
2149	**exception**	**exception**
	nf	Le jeune homme connaît les règles, mais le vieillard connait les exceptions.
	ɛksɛpsjɔ̃	*The young man knows the rules, but the old man knows the exceptions.*
2150	**gant**	**glove**
	nm	J'ai trouvé une paire de gants sous la chaise.
	gɑ̃	*I found a pair of gloves under the chair.*
2151	**ennuyeux**	**boring, annoying, dull**
	adj	Par peur des journaux, les politiciens sont ennuyeux, et à la fin ils sont trop ennuyeux même pour les journaux.
	ɑ̃nɥijø	*For fear of the newspapers politicians are dull, and at last they are too dull even for the newspapers.*
2152	**ouvrier**	**worker, working-class**
	nmf, adj	Sa mère et sa sœur venaient visiter la jeune ouvrière, et passer parfois une journée avec elle.
	uvʁije	*Her mother and her sister came to visit the young worker, and sometimes they spent a day with her.*
2153	**record**	**record**
	nm	La production d'automobiles a cette année atteint le chiffre record de dix millions de véhicules.
	ʁəkɔʁ	*Car production in that year reached a record 10 million vehicles.*
2154	**délirer**	**to rave, to be delirious**
	verb	À 20 heures ce soir-là, il a commencé à délirer et à être confus.
	deliʁe	*At 8:00 P.M. that night he became delirious and confused.*
2155	**enseigne**	**sign**
	nf	Il y a aussi la croix de la pharmacie et l'enseigne en forme de serpent.
	ɑ̃sɛɲ	*There is also the cross and the sign in the form of a snake.*
2156	**angle**	**angle, point of view**
	nm	Si un triangle a deux angles droits, c'est un carré avec un côté en moins.
	ɑ̃gl	*If a triangle has two right angles, it's a square missing one side.*
2157	**instinct**	**instinct**
	nm	Les réseaux sociaux permettent aux hommes de retrouver leur instinct de prédation en meute.
	ε̃stε̃	*Social networks enable men to revive their instinct of pack hunters.*
2158	**impôt**	**tax**
	nm	La loi contraint tous les citoyens à payer des impôts.
	ε̃po	*The laws oblige all citizens to pay taxes.*
2159	**rompre**	**to break, to break up**

	verb	Si je t'ai bien compris, tu veux rompre avec moi !
	ʁɔ̃pʁ	*If I understood you right you want to break up with me!*
2160	**rattraper**	**to recapture, recover, catch up, make up for**
	verb	Il courait si vite que nous ne pouvions le rattraper.
	ʁatʁape	*He ran too fast for us to catch up with.*
2161	**complexe**	**complex**
	nm, adj(f)	Mozart a écrit de brillantes et complexes compositions musicales aussi facilement que toi ou moi écririons une lettre.
	kɔ̃plɛks	*Mozart wrote brilliant, complex musical compositions as easily as you or I would write a letter.*
2162	**méthode**	**method**
	nf	La méthode proposée est appliquée à trois études de cas basées sur des simulations.
	metɔd	*The proposed method is applied to three simulated case studies.*
2163	**suggérer**	**to suggest**
	verb	Es-tu en train de suggérer que nous nous fassions passer pour des agents de police ?
	sygʒeʁe	*Are you suggesting that we impersonate policemen?*
2164	**tigre**	**tiger**
	nm	"C'est un tigre quand il se met en colère" est un exemple de métaphore.
	tigʁ	*"He's a tiger when he's angry" is an example of metaphor.*
2165	**tragédie**	**tragedy**
	nf	C'était une grande tragédie pour eux d'avoir perdu leur fils unique.
	tʁaʒedi	*It was a great tragedy for them to lose their only son.*
2166	**torture**	**torture**
	nf	Il a été sujet à des tortures de la part de la police.
	tɔʁtyʁ	*He was subjected to torture by the police.*
2167	**industrie**	**industry**
	nf	Le Japon est en tête de l'industrie mondiale des hautes technologies.
	ɛ̃dystʁi	*Japan is a leader in the world's high-tech industry.*
2168	**population**	**population**
	nf	La population du Japon est plus importante que celle de la Grande-Bretagne.
	pɔpylasjɔ̃	*The population of Japan is larger than that of Britain.*
2169	**adaptation**	**adaptation**
	nf	Enfin, d'autres domaines susceptibles de requérir des adaptations des statuts d'une BCN sont mentionnés.
	adaptasjɔ̃	*Finally, other areas where an NCB's statutes may require adaptation are mentioned.*
2170	**admirer**	**to admire**
	verb	Tout le monde admire les tableaux qu'il a peints.
	admiʁe	*Everyone admires the pictures painted by him.*
2171	**autoroute**	**motorway, highway, freeway**
	nf	Il vous faut la monnaie exacte pour payer le péage de l'autoroute.
	otoʁut	*You need to have exact change to pay the toll of the expressway.*

2172	**obscurité**	**darkness, obscurity**
	nf	Mieux vaut allumer une bougie que de maudire l'obscurité.
	ɔpskyʁite	*It is better to light a candle than to curse the darkness.*
2173	**fabuleux**	**fabulous**
	adj	Ce fut un spectacle fabuleux qui nous procura un plaisir sans fin.
	fabylø	*It was a fabulous show which brought us an endless delight.*
2174	**linge**	**linen, cloth**
	nf	Vérifiez le linge de maison, la vaisselle et les plats et remplacez ou empruntez les pièces manquantes.
	lɛ̃ʒ	*Check your linens, tableware and serving dishes and replace or borrow missing pieces.*
2175	**illégal**	**illegal**
	adj	Il y a plus d'un siècle que l'esclavage a été rendu illégal.
	ilegal	*It is over a century since slavery was made illegal.*
2176	**rigole**	**laugh**
	nf	On cueille, on chasse, on fabrique tout à partir de presque rien, on danse, on rigole.
	ʁigɔl	*They pick fruits, they hunt, they build from almost nothing, they danse, they laugh.*
2177	**opérer**	**to operate**
	verb	Le chirurgien qui a opéré Tom est très expérimenté et hautement réputé.
	ɔpeʁe	*The surgeon who operated on Tom is very experienced and highly regarded.*
2178	**fauteuil**	**armchair, seat**
	nm	En entendant les nouvelles, il bondit hors de son fauteuil.
	fotœj	*Hearing the news, he jumped out of his chair.*
2179	**vendeur**	**salesman, seller**
	nm	Le vendeur a fait la démonstration de l'utilisation de la machine.
	vɑ̃dœʁ	*The salesman demonstrated how to use the machine.*
2180	**novembre**	**November**
	nm	En Chine le 11 novembre c'est la fête des célibataires.
	nɔvɑ̃bʁ	*In China, the 11th of November is Singles Day.*
2181	**collection**	**collection, series**
	nf	Mais une collection de faits n'est pas plus de la science qu'un dictionnaire n'est de la poésie
	kɔlɛksjɔ̃	*But a collection of facts is not science any more than a dictionary is poetry.*
2182	**tonne**	**metric ton, tonne**
	nf	Chacun de ces phoques consomme environ une tonne de poisson par année.
	tɔn	*Each of these seals eat about a tonne of fish per year.*
2183	**accent**	**accent**
	nm	Dans la discussion, l'accent était mis sur le chômage.
	aksɑ̃	*In the discussion the accent was on unemployment.*
2184	**déplacer**	**to move, to put off, to displace**
	verb	L'homme était trop gros pour se déplacer par lui-même.
	deplase	*The man was too fat to move by himself.*

2185	**serrer**	**to tighten, squeeze**
	verb	Le bébé m'a attrapé la main et l'a serrée.
	seʁe	*The baby grabbed my hand and squeezed it.*
2186	**plastique**	**plastic**
	nm, adj(f)	La mer est polluée par de minuscules particules de plastique qui affectent les animaux marins.
	plastik	*The sea is polluted by tiny plastic particles that are harmful to marine animals.*
2187	**marche**	**walk, step, march**
	nf	Cet escalier a cinquante marches.
	maʁʃ	*These stairs have fifty steps.*
2188	**commande**	**order, control**
	nf	Il passa la commande par téléphone une fois arrivé à son travail.
	kɔmɑ̃d	*He placed the order over the phone after he got to his workplace.*
2189	**lot**	**share, prize, lot**
	nm	Les lots seront attribués à la fin du concours.
	lo	*Prizes will be awarded at the end of the contest.*
2190	**trahison**	**betrayal, treachery, treason**
	nf	Il fut exilé sur une île pour le crime de haute trahison.
	tʁaizɔ̃	*He was exiled to an island for the crime of high treason.*
2191	**sensation**	**sensation**
	nf	J'avais la sensation persistante de l'avoir vu quelque part auparavant.
	sɑ̃sasjɔ̃	*I had a nagging sensation that I'd seen him somewhere before.*
2192	**mesure**	**measure**
	nf	Le gouvernement a pris des mesures pour améliorer la sécurité routière.
	məzyʁ	*The government has taken measures to improve road safety.*
2193	**chanceux**	**fortunate, lucky**
	adj	Tout le monde ne fut pas aussi chanceux que nous le fûmes.
	ʃɑ̃sø	*Not everybody was as lucky as we were.*
2194	**boue**	**mud**
	nf	L'analyse médico-légale n'a pas pu déterminer d'où venait la boue.
	bu	*The forensic analysis couldn't determine where the mud had come from.*
2195	**cabane**	**hut, cabine**
	nf	La neige profonde empêcha l'équipe d'atteindre la cabane.
	kaban	*The deep snow prevented the party from getting to the hut.*
2196	**merveille**	**marvel, wonder**
	nf	Quand j'étais petit, je voulais découvrir toutes les merveilles de l'univers.
	mɛʁvɛj	*As a child, I wanted to discover all the wonders of the universe.*
2197	**poing**	**fist, punch**
	nm	Je veux vous mettre mon poing à la figure.
	pwɛ̃	*I want to punch you in your face.*
2198	**sacrifice**	**sacrifice**
	nm	Ils ont tué la chèvre en sacrifice à Dieu.
	sakʁifis	*They killed a goat as a sacrifice to God.*
2199	**communication**	**communication**

	nf	Le courrier électronique est un moyen de communication essentiel
	kɔmynikasjɔ̃	*Email is an essential channel of communication.*
2200	**appuyer**	**to lean, support**
	verb	J'espère que tu détiens des preuves pour appuyer tes dires.
	apɥije	*I hope you've got some proof to back up your allegations.*
2201	**chagrin**	**grief, sorrow**
	adj, nm	Entre stupéfaction et chagrin, elle ne pouvait prononcer un mot.
	ʃagʁɛ̃	*Between astonishment and sorrow, she could not speak a word.*
2202	**concentrer**	**to concentrate**
	verb	La télé était tellement bruyante que je n'arrivais pas à me concentrer sur ma lecture.
	kɔ̃sɑ̃tʁe	*The TV was so noisy that I couldn't concentrate on my reading.*
2203	**drogue**	**drug**
	nf	Elle a passé la majeure partie de sa dernière année au lycée accrochée à la drogue.
	dʁɔg	*She spent most of her senior year in high school strung out on drugs.*
2204	**gratuit**	**free, gratuitous, unwarranted**
	adj	Ce parc est ouvert au public et il est gratuit.
	gʁatɥi	*This garden is open to the public and it's free.*
2205	**britannique**	**British**
	adj(f)	Soixante-dix pour cent du peuple britannique ne parle pas de seconde langue.
	bʁitanik	*Seventy percent of the British people don't speak a second language.*
2206	**social**	**social**
	adj	La nouvelle loi garantit les mêmes droits judiciaires et sociaux aux couples homosexuels.
	sɔsjal	*The new law guarantees the same judicial and social rights to homosexual couples.*
2207	**coïncidence**	**coincidence**
	nf	Tiens, quelle coïncidence incroyable ! Tom a les mêmes empreintes digitales que moi.
	kɔɛ̃sidɑ̃s	*Look, what an incredible coincidence! Tom has the same fingerprints as me.*
2208	**viré**	**fired**
	adj	De toute façon, il n'aurait jamais viré quiconque !
	viʁ	*In any case, he would never have actually fired anybody!*
2209	**août**	**August**
	nm	Beaucoup de magasins proposent des rabais au mois d'août.
	ut	*Many stores offer discounts in the month of August.*
2210	**malédiction**	**curse**
	nf	Un guérisseur qui a de l'expérience peut lever les malédictions et dissiper le mauvais œil.
	malediksjɔ̃	*An experienced healer can lift curses and dispel evil eyes.*
2211	**pension**	**pension; room and board, boarding school**
	nf	La pension de ma grand-mère est suffisante pour qu'elle vive confortablement.
	pɑ̃sjɔ̃	*My grandmother's pension is enough for her to live comfortably.*

2212	ténèbre	darkness
	nf	Vite soufflons la lampe, afin de nous cacher dans les ténèbres!
	tenɛbʁ	*Quick, turn off the lamp, I want to hide in the darkness.*
2213	phase	phase, round
	nf	Les participants s'échauffent pour la phase finale de la compétition.
	faz	*The contestants are gearing up for the final round of competition.*
2214	noix	nuts
	nf	Les noix, les amandes, les noisettes, les pistaches et les pignons sont des fruits secs.
	nwa	*Walnuts, almonds, hazelnuts, pistachios and pine nuts are dry fruits.*
2215	boum	bang
	nm	Les membres de groupes nihiliste préfèrent partir dans un gros boum.
	bum	*Members of nihilist groups like to go out in a big bang.*
2216	sexuel	sexual
	adj	Dans une relation sexuelle, tromper quelqu'un consiste à avoir une relation sexuelle avec quelqu'un d'autre.
	sɛksɥɛl	*In a sexual relationship cheating on someone is if the person has sex with someone else.*
2217	honnêtement	honestly
	adv	Honnêtement, je ne pense pas que tu aies l'étoffe pour devenir enseignante.
	ɔnɛtmã	*Honestly, I don't think you have what it takes to become a teacher.*
2218	défi	challenge
	nm	La recherche de vie extra-terrestre est l'un des défis technologiques majeurs de l'humanité.
	defi	*The search for alien life is one of humankind's greatest technological challenges.*
2219	estimer	to estimate; to consider, deem
	verb	J'ai demandé à un expert d'estimer le coût des travaux.
	ɛstime	*I asked an expert to estimate the cost of the work.*
2220	désastre	disaster
	nm	L'inondation était le plus grand désastre qu'ils ont jamais eu.
	dezastʁ	*The flood was the greatest disaster they had ever had.*
2221	feuille	leaf, sheet
	nf	Ma poitrine était devenue plus vulnérable que le fruit du figuier et mon cœur plus fragile que ses feuilles.
	fœj	*My chest had become softer than the fig tree's fruit and my heart had become more fragile than the fig tree's leaves.*
2222	éliminer	to eliminate
	verb	Lorsque l'on a éliminé l'impossible, tout ce qui reste, quoiqu'improbable, doit être la vérité
	elimine	*When you have eliminated the impossible, whatever remains, however improbable, must be the truth.*
2223	reconnaissant	grateful
	adj	Je te serais reconnaissant si tu peux faire ça pour moi.
	ʁəkɔnɛsã	*I'll be grateful to you if you can do that for me.*

2224	**particulièrement**	**particulary**
	adv	Le plancher est particulièrement glissant.
	paʁtikyljɛʁmɑ̃	*The floor is very slippery.*
2225	**solitude**	**solitude, loneliness**
	nf	De nombreuses craintes naissent de l'épuisement et de la solitude.
	sɔlityd	*Many fears are born of fatigue and loneliness.*
2226	**débrouiller**	**to untangle, to sort out**
	verb	Je vous laisserai vous en débrouiller.
	debʁuje	*I'll leave you to sort this out.*
2227	**jouet**	**toy**
	nm	Je ne pense pas que ce soit la bonne boite pour ce jouet ; il n'y rentrera pas.
	ʒwɛ	*I don't think this is the box that this toy came in; it won't fit in.*
2228	**tarder**	**to delay**
	verb	C'est maintenant à la Commission de se mettre au travail sans tarder pour mettre en œuvre cette directive.
	taʁde	*It is now up to the Commission to get down to work without delay and to implement the directive.*
2229	**ingénieur**	**engineer**
	nm	Les sept questions que doit se poser un ingénieur sont : qui, quoi, quand, où, pourquoi, comment et combien.
	ɛ̃ʒenjœʁ	*The seven questions that an engineer has to ask himself are: who, what, when, where, why, how and how much.*
2230	**chant**	**song**
	nm	
		Mettons-nous debout pour le louer et exprimer notre joie par le chant et la danse
	ʃɑ̃	*Let us now stand to give praise to him and express our joy in song and dance.*
2231	**ongle**	**nail, fingernail**
	nf	Lorsque la mort approche, tout ce qu'on peut faire est de lentement ronger ses ongles.
	ɔ̃gl	*When death approaches, all you can do is slowly chew your fingernails.*
2232	**trafic**	**traffic, circulation**
	nm	Nous empruntâmes une rue parallèle afin d'éviter le trafic intense.
	tʁafik	*We took a back road to avoid the heavy traffic.*
2233	**activité**	**activity**
	nf	À quelle activité t'adonnes-tu la plupart du temps ?
	aktivite	*What activity do you spend most of your time doing?*
2234	**reconnaissance**	**recognition, gratitude**
	nf	Lorsqu'un fonds d'investissement privé acquiert une entreprise, il doit maintenir la reconnaissance syndicale en vigueur.
	ʁəkɔnɛsɑ̃s	*Where a private equity firm is buying a company, existing union recognition must continue.*
2235	**foie**	**liver**

	nm	Un cœur, des reins et un foie surmenés sont les conséquences inévitables d'une nourriture trop abondante.
	fwa	*Overtaxed heart, kidneys and liver are inevitable results of too much food.*
2236	**jusque**	**to, up to, until, till**
	adv, prep	Nous pouvons tout aussi bien rester ici jusqu'à ce que le temps s'améliore.
	ʒysk	*We may as well stay here till the weather improves.*
2237	**cercueil**	**coffin**
	nm	Des photos de cercueils recouverts de drapeaux s'éparpillèrent au-dessus des papiers.
	sɛʁkœj	*Pictures of coffins covered with flags went all over the papers.*
2238	**gris**	**gray**
	nm, adj[pl]	J'ai remarqué qu'un petit animal gris nous regardait.
	gʁi	*I noticed that a small gray animal was looking toward us.*
2239	**livraison**	**delivery**
	nf	La livraison des marchandises a été retardée à cause de la tempête.
	livʁɛzɔ̃	*The delivery of the goods was delayed due to the storm.*
2240	**pilule**	**pill**
	nf	Si tu oublies un jour de prendre ta pilule, prends-en deux le jour suivant.
	pilyl	*If you forget to take your pills for one day, take two pills the following day.*
2241	**pratiquement**	**practically**
	adv	Cette combinaison permet aux utilisateurs de se joindre à tout moment, et pratiquement n'importe où.
	pʁatikmã	*This combination allows users to reach one another at any time, and practically anywhere.*
2242	**diplômer**	**to graduate**
	verb	L'important, ce n'est pas l'université où tu as obtenu ton diplôme, mais ce que tu as appris lorsque tu y étais.
	diplome	*What's important isn't which university you've graduated from, but what you learned while you were there.*
2243	**cinquante**	**fifty**
	det, num	Les prix du café ont bondi de presque cinquante pour cent en six mois.
	sɛ̃kãt	*Coffee prices have jumped almost fifty per cent in six months.*
2244	**armé**	**armed**
	adj	Le détective Dan Anderson est retourné à la maison de Linda armé d'un mandat de perquisition.
	aʁme	*Detective Dan Anderson returned to Linda's house armed with a search warrant.*
2245	**chapitre**	**chapter**
	nm	Hier, les élèves ont terminé le premier chapitre, par conséquent, ils vont maintenant continuer avec le deuxième.
	ʃapitʁ	*Yesterday the students finished Chapter 1 so now they'll move on to Chapter 2.*
2246	**communiste**	**communist**
	adj(f, nmf	Aucun système politique viable n'a remplacé le système communiste en Russie.

| | | kɔmynist | *Since the collapse of the communist system, Russia has had no viable political system.* |

2247 commissariat — **police station**
nm
Comment puis-je me rendre au commissariat de police ?
kɔmisaʁja
How can I get to the police station?

2248 trouille — **(avoir la) trouille: to be scared stiff**
nf
Moi petite crevette plutôt brune et morte de trouille à l'idée d'être sur les planches pour la première fois
tʁuj
There I was, teeny brunette, scared stiff at the meer idea of being on stage professionally for the first time

2249 analyser — **to analyse**
verb
Tu ne peux pas analyser les données efficacement avant d'avoir tracé un graphique.
analize
You cannot analyse the data efficiently unless you draw a plot.

2250 pisse — **piss**
nf
Les bouteilles volaient, les crachats étaient de sortie, Mike Patton buvait sa pisse : bref c'était le bon vieux temps.
pis
Bottles would fly, spit was everywhere, Mike Patton was drinking his piss: basically, the good old days.

2251 essentiel — **essential**
nm, adj
La mémoire est une fonction essentielle de notre cerveau.
esãsjɛl
Memory is an essential function of our brain.

2252 génération — **generation**
nm
Il y a eu un avocat dans la famille depuis des générations.
ʒeneʁasjõ
There's been a lawyer in the family for generations.

2253 adjoindre — **to add sth to, to appoint**
verb
Monsieur le Président, adjoindre un institut de technologie aux universités existantes semble être une bonne idée.
adʒwɛ̃dʁ
Mr President, adding an institute of technology to stand with the existing universities sounds a good idea

2254 écriture — **writing, entry**
nf
Ce qui est difficile en japonais, c'est la façon dont les caractères sont utilisés dans le système d'écriture.
ekʁityʁ
What is difficult about Japanese is how characters are used in its writing system.

2255 annuler — **to cancel**
verb
J'ai annulé la réservation à l'hôtel et je suis resté chez des amis.
anyle
I canceled my hotel reservations and stayed with friends.

2256 massacre — **massacre, slaughter**
nm
Le général ordonna le massacre de tous les prisonniers de guerre.
masakʁ
The general ordered the massacre of all war prisoners.

2257 volontiers — **with pleasure, willingly, gladly**
adv
Tom a volontiers fait tout ce que nous lui avons demandé de faire.
vɔlõtje
Tom has willingly done everything we've asked him to do.

2258 phrase — **sentence, phrase**

	nf	Pourriez-vous mettre un point à la fin de votre phrase, s'il vous plait?
	fʁaz	*Could you put a period at the end of your sentence, please?*
2259	**poème**	**poem**
	nm	Elle n'a pas eu de mal à apprendre le poème par cœur.
	pɔɛm	*She had no difficulty in learning the poem by heart.*
2260	**pénis**	**penis**
	nm	Elle a reçu une publicité pour l'agrandissement du pénis dans sa boîte de réception.
	penis	*She received an ad for penis enlargement in her inbox.*
2261	**singe**	**monkey**
	nm	Les singes tuent des gens aussi, mais seulement s'ils ont des pistolets.
	sɛ̃ʒ	*Monkeys kill people too, but only if they have guns.*
2262	**statuer**	**to rule**
	verb	Le juge a statué que le prisonnier devait être libéré.
	statɥe	*The judge ruled that the prisoner should be released.*
2263	**époux**	**husband**
	nm	Le traitement du médecin n'a fait qu'aggraver la condition de mon époux.
	epu	*The doctor's treatment has only aggravated my husband's condition.*
2264	**automne**	**fall, autumn**
	nm	Avec ce vent d'automne frais, on ressent vraiment le changement de saison.
	ɔtɔn	*With this cool autumn wind blowing, we can feel the change of season.*
2265	**brigade**	**team, squad, brigade**
	nf	Cet homme est un policier de la brigade criminelle, et non pas un criminel.
	bʁigad	*This man is a police officer in the crime squad, not a criminal.*
2266	**éloigner**	**to remove**
	verb	Aucune difficulté ne devrait éloigner les personnes consacrées de l'école et de l'éducation en général.
	elwaɲe	*No difficulty should remove consecrated men and women from schools and from education in general*
2267	**survie**	**survival**
	nf	Nous avons une meilleure chance de survie si nous restons calmes
	syʁvi	*We'll have a better chance of survival if we stay calm.*
2268	**batterie**	**battery; drum set**
	nf	La batterie de mon téléphone portable ne fonctionne plus très bien.
	batʁi	*The battery of my cellphone doesn't function anymore.*
2269	**ordonner**	**to ordain, organize, order**
	verb	En une occasion, Christophe Colomb a aperçu un OVNI et a ordonné à ses hommes de l'abattre avec les canons du vaisseau.
	ɔʁdɔne	*Christopher Columbus once saw a UFO, and ordered his men to fire his ship's cannons at it.*
2270	**manche**	**handle, sleeve**
	nm, nf	Papa s'est fait une longue déchirure à la manche.
	mɑ̃ʃ	*Father made a long tear in his sleeve.*
2271	**creuser**	**to dig**

	verb	L'enfant creusa une tombe pour son chien qui venait de mourir.
	kʁøze	*The boy dug a grave for his dog that had died.*
2272	**pourvu**	**equiped with; so long as, provided**
	adj; adv	N'importe quel livre fera l'affaire pourvu qu'il soit intéressant.
	puʁvy	*Any book will do provided it is interesting.*
2273	**mordre**	**to bite, overlap into**
	verb	Dis-lui que tu l'aimes. N'aie pas peur. Elle ne va pas te mordre.
	mɔʁdʁ	*Tell her you like her. Don't be afraid. She won't bite you.*
2274	**contenir**	**to contain**
	verb	En plus d'environ 30.000 yens, son portefeuille contenait son permis de conduire.
	kõtniʁ	*In addition, to about 30,000 yen, the wallet contained his driver's license.*
2275	**principe**	**principle**
	nm	Nous nous référons au principe le plus général de toute la physique classique, celui de la conservation de l'énergie.
	pʁɛ̃sip	*We are referring to the most general principle in all classical physics, that of conservation of energy.*
2276	**bourrer**	**to stuff**
	verb	Nous avions ainsi l'assurance que les autorités ne profiteraient pas de son absence, toute brève fut-elle, pour bourrer les urnes
	buʁe	*This way we made sure that authorities were not stuffing ballot boxes during the observer's brief absence.*
2277	**rembourser**	**to reimburse, pay back, pay off, repay**
	verb	La famille est trop pauvre pour rembourser les dettes.
	ʁɑ̃buʁse	*The family is too poor to pay back the debts.*
2278	**masse**	**mass**
	nf	Cette application vous permet de calculer rapidement l'indice de masse corporelle - IMC.
	mas	*The application allows you to quickly calculate the ratio of body mass index - BMI.*
2279	**luxe**	**luxury**
	nm	Notre voisine a touché le gros lot et elle est partie aux Bahamas en croisière de luxe.
	lyks	*Our neighbor won the lottery, and she's gone to the Bahamas on a luxury cruise.*
2280	**terreur**	**terror, dread**
	nf	La véritable terreur est de se réveiller un matin et de découvrir que votre classe de lycée dirige le pays.
	teʁœʁ	*True terror is to wake up one morning and discover that your high school class is running the country.*
2281	**mobile**	**mobile, portable; motive**
	adj(f), nm	J'ai un forfait pour les réseaux fixes mais pas pour les réseaux mobiles.
	mɔbil	*My plan covers unlimited calls to landlines, but not mobiles.*
2282	**sagesse**	**wisdom, moderation**
	nf	Il faut de la sagesse pour comprendre la sagesse : la musique n'est rien si le public est sourd.

saʒɛs | *It requires wisdom to understand wisdom: the music is nothing if the audience is deaf.*

2283 **rigoler** — **to laugh,**
verb
Ils vont bien rigoler, lorsqu'ils te verront ainsi.
ʁigɔle | *They will have a good laugh when they see you like this.*

2284 **informer** — **to inform, notify**
verb
J'ai informé ma banque de mon changement de domicile.
ɛ̃fɔʁme | *I notified my bank of my change of address.*

2285 **saluer** — **to greet, salute**
verb
Il était au courant de ma présence mais il ne m'a pas salué.
salɥe | *He was aware of my presence but he did not greet me.*

2286 **terriblement** — **terribly, awfully**
adv
Je ne peux pas dire que je sois terriblement fière de ce que j'ai fait.
teʁibləmã | *I can't say I'm terribly proud of what I did.*

2287 **satisfaire** — **to satisfy**
verb
L'art d'enseigner n'est que l'art d'éveiller la curiosité des jeunes âmes pour la satisfaire ensuite.
satisfɛʁ | *The art of teaching is only the art of awakening the natural curiosity of young minds to satisfy it afterwards.*

2288 **avaler** — **to swallow**
verb
Je ne peux pas avaler ces cachets sans un verre d'eau.
avale | *I can't swallow these tablets without a drink of water.*

2289 **décembre** — **December**
nm
Le Japon déclara la guerre aux États-Unis en décembre 1941.
desãbʁ | *Japan declared war on the United States in December, 1941.*

2290 **planter** — **to plant, pitch**
verb
Le jardinier planta un rosier au milieu du jardin.
plãte | *The gardener planted a rose tree in the middle of the garden.*

2291 **usage** — **use, usage**
nm
Même l'usage correct des participes ne te garantit pas qu'on te comprenne.
yzaʒ | *Even the correct use of participles doesn't guarantee you that you'll be understood.*

2292 **collège** — **secondary school, body**
nm
L'anglais est généralement enseigné dès le collège en France.
kɔlɛʒ | *English is usually taught in France from the junior high school.*

2293 **symbole** — **symbol**
nm
Nous utilisons le symbole ⊂ pour noter l'inclusion stricte.
sɛ̃bɔl | *We use the symbol "⊂" to denote proper inclusion.*

2294 **aile** — **wing, fender**
nf
L'autruche a des ailes mais ne peut pas voler.
ɛl | *The ostrich has wings, but it cannot fly.*

2295 **flamme** — **flame, fire, fervor, brilliance**
nf
Les hommes étaient attirés par elle comme les papillons de nuit par une flamme.
flam | *Men were attracted to her like moths to a flame.*

2296	**bloc**	**block**
	nm	Tous dans le bloc d'appartements partagent la cuisine.
	blɔk	*Everyone in the apartment block shares a kitchen.*
2297	**règne**	**reign**
	nm	En effet, le Royaume de Dieu est Dieu lui-même, qui se rend présent parmi nous et qui règne à travers nous.
	ʁɛɲ	*The Kingdom of God is really God himself, who makes himself present in our midst and reigns through us.*
2298	**orage**	**storm, thunderstorm**
	nm	Les horaires de trains furent bouleversés à cause de l'orage.
	ɔʁaʒ	*Trains were disrupted due to a thunderstorm.*
2299	**poste**	**post, position; post office**
	nm, nf	Il supposait qu'il pouvait toujours quitter le poste à la dernière extrémité.
	pɔst	*He supposed he could always quit the position in the last resort.*
2300	**destiner**	**to intend, be used**
	verb	Nous avions destiné la cave à un labo photo.
	dɛstine	*We had intended to use the cellar as a photographic lab.*
2301	**renoncer**	**to give up, renounce**
	verb	Vous ne devez pas renoncer simplement parce que vous n'avez aucun talent.
	ʁənɔ̃se	*You shouldn't give up just because you have no talent.*
2302	**grever**	**to put strain on, encumber**
	verb	Aucun membre n'a le droit de céder, d'aliéner, de grever d'une charge ou de racheter une prestation de revenu mensuelle.
	gʁeve	*No member has the right to assign, alienate, encumber, or commute any monthly income benefit.*
2303	**royal**	**royal**
	adj	La Royal Shakespeare Company donne une représentation du Marchand de Venise la semaine prochaine.
	ʁwajal	*The Royal Shakespeare Company is presenting The Merchant of Venice next week.*
2304	**texte**	**text**
	nm	Veuillez ouvrir le fichier entouré de rouge avec un éditeur de texte.
	tɛkst	*Please open the file circled in red with a text editor.*
2305	**officiel**	**official**
	adj, nmf	As-tu une fois comparé les assertions de la propagande officielle avec la réalité ?
	ɔfisjɛl	*Have you ever compared the assertions of official propaganda to reality?*
2306	**pompe**	**pump**
	nf	Pouvez-vous me montrer comment utiliser cette pompe ?
	pɔ̃p	*Could you show me how to use this pump?*
2307	**poubelle**	**trash can, garbage**
	nf	J'ai vu un homme hier, manger dans une poubelle.
	pubɛl	*I saw a man yesterday eating from a garbage can.*
2308	**patrouille**	**patrol**
	nf	On a vu une voiture de patrouille foncer à toute vitesse.

	patʁuj	*We saw a patrol car running at full speed.*
2309	**équippement**	**equipment**
	nm	Bientôt, il y aura un nouveau centre aquatique à Sollefteå et nous livrons les équippement.
	ekipmã	*Shortly, there will be a new aquatic centre in Sollefteå and we will deliver the equipment.*
2310	**taux**	**rate**
	nm	Les taux de change sont affichés quotidiennement à l'extérieur de la caisse.
	to	*The exchange rates are posted daily outside the cashier's office.*
2311	**taudis**	**slum**
	nm	Le film est une peinture déchirante de la vie dans un taudis urbain.
	todi	*The movie is a harrowing depiction of life in an urban slum.*
2312	**métal**	**metal**
	nm	La pierre philosophale aurait le pouvoir de transformer n'importe quel métal en or.
	metal	*The philosopher's stone could transmute every precious metal into gold.*
2313	**destination**	**destination**
	nf	Notre destination n'est jamais un lieu, mais une nouvelle façon de voir les choses.
	dɛstinasjõ	*One's destination is never a place but rather a new way of looking at things.*
2314	**accomplir**	**to accomplish**
	verb	Qui sait ce qu'il accomplira si une chance lui est accordée ?
	akõpliʁ	*Who knows what he'll accomplish if given the chance?*
2315	**pique**	**pike, critique; spade**
	nf;nm	La première carte tirée était le valet de pique.
	pik	*The first card drawn was the jack of spades.*
2316	**accueil**	**welcome, reception**
	nm	L'orateur a reçu un accueil chaleureux.
	akœj	*The speaker received a hearty welcome.*
2317	**roue**	**wheel**
	nf	Télègue, voiture russe à quatre roues, quand elle part, — et à deux roues, quand elle arrive.
	ʁu	*The Telega, a Russian four-wheel car when it leaves, and a two-wheeled car when it arrives.*
2318	**économie**	**economy**
	nf	Un régime fiscal concurrentiel constitue l'une des pierres angulaires d'une économie dynamique et productive.
	ekɔnɔmi	*A competitive tax regime is one of the building blocks of a vibrant, productive economy.*
2319	**tombe**	**grave, tomb**
	nf	Je pris place au pied de ma propre tombe et me regardai.
	tõb	*I sat down on the edge of my own grave and looked at myself.*
2320	**charité**	**charity**
	nf	Il donna tout son argent aux œuvres de charité.

ʃaʁite | *He gave away all his money to charity.*

2321 mélanger — **to mix, mix up, confuse**
verb
Je suis désolée. Je vous ai mélangées toutes les deux.
melɑ̃ʒe | *I'm sorry. I got you two mixed up.*

2322 endormir — **to put to sleep, fall asleep**
verb
J'étais très fatigué alors je me suis immédiatement endormi.
ɑ̃dɔʁmiʁ | *I was very tired, so I fell asleep right away.*

2323 cuisine — **cooking, kitchen**
nf
Il se leva pour s'assurer qu'il avait éteint la lumière dans la cuisine.
kɥizin | *He got up to see if he had turned off the light in the kitchen.*

2324 laboratoire — **laboratory**
nm
Dans son laboratoire plus de mille cahiers sont archivés.
labɔʁatwaʁ | *Preserved in his laboratory were more than a thousand notebooks.*

2325 déconner — **to talk crap, to screw around, mess around**
nm
Nous à l'évolution ont été déconner avec 3D depuis environ cinq ans.
dekɔne | *We at Evolution have been messing around with 3D for about five years.*

2326 plaisanterie — **joke**
nf
Il a besoin de quelques plaisanteries pour alléger son discours.
plɛzɑ̃tʁi | *He needs a few jokes to lighten up his talk.*

2327 quitte — **to be clear off, quits**
adj
C'est quitte ou double
kit | *Double or quits*

2328 culotte — **pants, panties**
nf
On a dit aux gens de se mettre en ligne et de baisser leur culotte, et on leur a administré un vaccin dans la fesse droite
kylɔt | *People were told to stand in line and pull down their pants, and they were given a shot in the right buttock.*

2329 boisson — **drink, beverage**
nf
Le goût de cette boisson est clairement celui du thé.
bwasɔ̃ | *This drink clearly has the same flavor as tea.*

2330 saut — **jump, leap**
nm
Elle a établi le record du monde de saut en hauteur.
so | *She set the world record for the high jump.*

2331 matinée — **morning**
nf
Nous consacrons chacun une matinée par semaine à cette activité.
matine | *We each give one morning per week of our time to this activity.*

2332 relever — **to raise , lift**
verb
Mon frère a relevé sa chemise pour me montrer son tatouage.
ʁələve | *My brother lifted his shirt to show me his tattoo.*

2333 otage — **hostage**
nm
Le destin des otages dépend du résultat de la négociation.
ɔtaʒ | *The fate of the hostages depends on the result of the negotiation.*

2334 ravissant — **delightful, ravishing**
adj
Is conjuguent le bleu et le gris avec subtilité pour donner un effet absolument ravissant.

	ʁavisɑ̃	*When they're snuggled next to blue and grey, the results are absolutely ravishing.*
2335	**fabriquer**	**to manufacture, invent, make**
	verb	On demanda au technicien de fabriquer une boîte imperméable à la lumière.
	fabʁike	*The tech was asked to make a light-tight box.*
2336	**tireur**	**shooter**
	nm	Cela contredisait son témoignage initial, où elle affirmait avoir vu le tireur s'enfuir en courant.
	tiʁœʁ	*This contradicted her initial witness statement that she saw the shooter running from the scene.*
2337	**lave**	**washed**
	adj	Le retrait du mucilage est généralement suivi par le séchage et l'écalage pour produire du café vert "lavé".
	lav	*Removal of the mucilage is usually followed by drying and hulling to produce "washed" green coffee.*
2338	**ambassadeur**	**ambassador**
	nm	Un ambassadeur est un homme honnête envoyé mentir à l'étranger pour le bien de son pays.
	ɑ̃basadœʁ	*An ambassador is an honest man sent to lie abroad for the good of his country.*
2339	**atmosphère**	**atmosphere**
	nf	Selon les scientifiques, l'atmosphère se réchauffe d'année en année.
	atmɔsfɛʁ	*According to scientists, the atmosphere is getting warmer year after year.*
2340	**menacer**	**to threaten**
	verb	Son père atrabilaire menaçait de lui donner une fessée s'il ne se comportait pas bien.
	mənase	*His splenetic father threatened to spank him if he didn't behave himself.*
2341	**casier**	**locker**
	nm	Elle a perdu la clé de son casier alors qu'elle nageait dans la piscine.
	kazje	*While swimming in the pool, she lost her locker key.*
2342	**capital**	**major, chief, principal; capital, assets**
	nm, nf, adj	Ils disposent de suffisamment de capital pour bâtir une seconde usine.
	kapital	*They have enough capital to build a second factory.*
2343	**cendre**	**ash**
	nf	Les cendres de ma grand-mère sont dans une urne au temple.
	sɑ̃dʁ	*Grandmother's ashes are in an urn at the temple.*
2344	**syndicat**	**union**
	nm	Le syndicat exerce une influence prépondérante sur le parti conservateur.
	sɛ̃dika	*The union exerts a dominant influence on the conservative party.*
2345	**suisse**	**Swiss**
	adj(f)	La Commission a récemment publié une étude menée en son nom par l'Institut suisse de droit comparé.
	sɥis	*The Commission recently published a study carried out on its behalf by the Swiss Institute of Comparative Law.*

2346	**énormément**	**enormously**
	adv	Les rendements peuvent varier énormément, même au cours de la même année etdans la même zone.
	enɔʁmemɑ̃	*Yields may vary enormously even in the same year and within the same zone.*
2347	**outil**	**tool**
	nm	Une langue acérée est le seul outil tranchant qui s'aiguise à l'usage.
	uti	*A sharp tongue is the only edged tool that grows keener with constant use.*
2348	**testament**	**will**
	nm	Les héritiers ont lu le testament de la femme décédée.
	tɛstamɑ̃	*The heirs read the deceased woman's will.*
2349	**poète**	**poet**
	nm	Ce poète tenta de se suicider dans leur bibliothèque.
	pɔɛt	*That poet attempted suicide in their library.*
2350	**combinaison**	**combination**
	nf	La musique peut se définir l'art d'émouvoir par la combinaison des sons.
	kɔ̃binɛzɔ̃	*Music can be defined as the art of producing emotion by the combination of sounds.*
2351	**transformer**	**to transform**
	verb	Le couple a transformé la chimie en une science moderne.
	tʁɑ̃sfɔʁme	*The two of them transformed chemistry into a modern science.*
2352	**ramasser**	**to pick up, collect, gather**
	verb	C'est très amusant de ramasser différents coquillages sur les plages.
	ʁamase	*It is a lot of fun picking various shells on the sands.*
2353	**avertir**	**to warn**
	verb	Les médecins nous ont avertis d'un probable danger.
	avɛʁtiʁ	*Doctors warn us of a possible danger.*
2354	**lecture**	**reading**
	nf	Je ne sais pas de lecture plus facile, plus attrayante, plus douce que celle d'un catalogue.
	lɛktyʁ	*I do not know any reading more easy, more fascinating, more delightful than a catalogue.*
2355	**processus**	**process**
	nm[pl]	Ça devrait être examiné au travers d'un processus de test soigneusement conçu.
	pʁɔsesys	*It should be vetted through a well-designed testing process.*
2356	**vaincre**	**to beat, defeat, overcome, conquer**
	verb	Il ne suffit pas de vaincre les ennemis du dehors, il faut encore exterminer les ennemis du dedans.
	vɛ̃kʁ	*It is not enough to defeat our external enemies, it is also necessary to exterminate our internal enemies.*
2357	**médical**	**medical**
	adj	J'avais l'intention d'étudier la science médicale aux États-Unis de l'Amérique du Nord.
	medikal	*I intended to study medical science in America.*
2358	**atelier**	**workshop, studio**

	nm	Pendant le sommeil notre système immunitaire ouvre son atelier de réparation.
	atəlje	*While we're sleeping the immune system opens its repair workshop.*
2359	**guerrier**	**warrior; warlike**
	nmf, adj	La force irradie d'un grand guerrier. Il n'a pas besoin de combattre à mort.
	gɛʁje	*A great warrior radiates strength. He doesn't have to fight to the death.*
2360	**pouce**	**thumb, inch**
	nm	Entre quinze et seize ans, il a grandi de trois pouces entiers.
	pus	*Between the ages of 15 and 16, he grew three whole inches.*
2361	**entraîneur**	**coach, trainer**
	nm	L'entraîneur de l'équipe de basket est à la recherche de l'étudiant le plus grand.
	ɑ̃tʁɛnœʁ	*The coach of the basketball team is looking for the tallest student.*
2362	**peindre**	**to paint, depict, portray**
	verb	Dès que je peux en avoir l'occasion, j'aiderai votre mère à peindre la clôture.
	pɛ̃dʁ	*As soon as I can get the chance, I'll help your mother paint the fence.*
2363	**panier**	**basket**
	nm	Il y avait beaucoup de pommes pourries dans le panier.
	panje	*Quite a lot of rotten apples were in the basket.*
2364	**pétrin**	**mess, spot, pickle**
	nm	Si tu avais suivi mon conseil, tu ne serais pas dans un tel pétrin, maintenant.
	petʁɛ̃	*If you had followed my advice, you wouldn't be in such a fix now.*
2365	**carrément**	**completely, directly, straight out**
	adv	Toutes ces constatations nous amènent à l'évidence que les plus démunis sont carrément mis à l'écart par ce gouvernement.
	kaʁemɑ̃	*All the signs provide evidence that the most unfortunate have been completely cast aside by this government.*
2366	**tonnerre**	**thunder**
	nf	Il y eut le bruit d'un claquement de tonnerre à mes oreilles.
	tɔnɛʁ	*There was the sound of a clap of thunder in my ears.*
2367	**témoignage**	**testimoney, evidence, witness**
	nm	Les témoins ont pu réfuter le faux témoignage du suspect.
	temwaɲaʒ	*The witnesses were able to refute the false testimony of the suspect.*
2368	**douter**	**to doubt**
	verb	Je doute que ce soit quoi que ce soit qui vous intéresserait.
	dute	*I doubt this is anything you'd be interested in.*
2369	**indice**	**indication, sign, clue, hint**
	nm	Au moment où je ne savais pas répondre à la question, il m'a donné un indice.
	ɛ̃dis	*When I didn't know how to answer the question, he gave me a hint.*
2370	**création**	**creation**
	nf	La vérité scientifique est une création de l'esprit humain.
	kʁeasjɔ̃	*Scientific truth is a creation of the human mind.*
2371	**environnement**	**environment**

	nm	L'humanité est en train de rapidement détruire l'environnement de la Terre.
	ãviʁɔnmã	*umanity is rapidly destroying the Earth's environment.*
2372	**certes**	**indeed, certainly, of course**
	adv	Certes il souhaita son succès, mais en réalité il n'en eut aucun.
	sɛʁt	*Of course he hoped for success. But in reality it turned out to be no good at all.*
2373	**dégueulasse**	**disgusting, filthy**
	adj	C'est un boulot dégueulasse et je ne veux pas le faire.
	degœlas	*That's a filthy job and I don't want to do it.*
2374	**enseigner**	**to teach**
	verb	Le plaisir d'enseigner n'est pas inférieur à celui d'apprendre.
	ãseɲe	*The pleasure of teaching is not smaller than the pleasure of learning.*
2375	**dose**	**dose, amount**
	nf	Les médecins ont diminué la dose du médicament.
	doz	*The doctors reduced the dose of the medication.*
2376	**effrayer**	**to frighten, scare**
	verb	Elle n'avait jamais été aussi effrayée auparavant.
	efʁeje	*She'd never been this frightened before.*
2377	**môme**	**kid**
	nm, nf	J'ai ici la fille de mon frère avec ses mômes.
	mom	*I have here my brother's daughter with her kids.*
2378	**curiosité**	**curiosity**
	nf	Juste par curiosité, qu'attendez-vous qu'il se passe ?
	kyʁjozite	*Just out of curiosity, what do you expect to happen?*
2379	**administration**	**administration**
	nf	Si l'université ne dispose pas de suffisamment d'étudiants, l'administration annulera le cours.
	administʁasjõ	*If the university doesn't have enough students, the administration will cancel the class.*
2380	**misère**	**misery, poverty**
	nf	La misère est la mère de tous les vices.
	mizɛʁ	*Poverty is the mother of all vices.*
2381	**cuir**	**leather**
	nm	Dan a été vu pour la dernière fois avec un jean bleu et une veste en cuir noir.
	kɥiʁ	*Dan was last seen wearing blue jeans and a black leather jacket.*
2382	**transport**	**transportation**
	nm	Ce bus assure le transport entre Paris et Amsterdam.
	tʁãspɔʁ	*This bus provides transportation between Paris and Amsterdam.*
2383	**prêter**	**to lend**
	verb	Je te prêterai tous les livres dont je dispose, pourvu que tu les gardes propres.
	pʁete	*I'll lend you any book that I have, as long as you keep it clean.*
2384	**savon**	**soap**
	nm	J'utilise un savon doux pour me nettoyer le visage.

		savɔ̃	*I use a gentle soap to cleanse my face.*
2385	**pipi**		**pee, wee**
	nm		Ma fille utilise le petit pot depuis maintenant deux semaines pour faire son pipi.
		pipi	*My toddler has been going to the potty for two weeks to pee.*
2386	**fouiller**		**to search, frisk, go through, rummage through**
	verb		En fouillant dans des cartons, je suis tombée sur une vieille photo de famille.
		fuje	*Rummaging around in boxes, I stumbled upon an old family photo.*
2387	**plante**		**plant**
	nf		Une absence de pluie a entraîné la mort des plantes sauvages.
		plɑ̃t	*An absence of rain caused wild plants to die.*
2388	**viol**		**rape**
	nm		Linda a identifié Dan comme l'homme de son viol.
		vjɔl	*Linda identified Dan as the man who had raped her.*
2389	**douceur**		**softness, smoothness, mildness, gentleness, sweetness**
	nf		Il parlait avec une douceur caractéristique des gens du Sud.
		dusœʁ	*He spoke with a softness characteristic of southerners.*
2390	**vain**		**vain**
	adj		Nous avons cherché le chiot, mais ce fut en vain.
		vɛ̃	*We looked for the puppy, but it was in vain.*
2391	**détendre**		**to loosen, to relax**
	verb		Je vais m'en occuper. Tu peux te détendre et compter sur moi.
		detɑ̃dʁ	*I'm taking care of it. You can relax, you can rely on me.*
2392	**parent**		**parent**
	nmf, adj		Non seulement elle mais aussi ses parents ont été invité à la fête.
		paʁɑ̃	*Not only she but also her parents were invited to the party.*
2393	**interrompre**		**to interrupt**
	verb		Je suis désolé de vous interrompre, mais il y a quelque chose que vous devriez voir.
		ɛ̃tɛʁɔ̃pʁ	*I'm sorry to interrupt you, but there's something you should see.*
2394	**etc**		**et cetera , etc.**
	adv		Les permaliens sont essentiellement des liens vers des choses comme les messages, les commentaires, etc.
		ɛtseteʁa	*Permalinks are basically links to items like posts, comments, etc.*
2395	**écart**		**space, gap**
	nm		l y a un écart entre le lit et le mur de la chambre.
		ekaʁ	*There is a gap between the bed and the bedroom wall.*
2396	**pester**		**pester contre: to curse**
	verb		Le mauvais état des routes a fait pester les hommes depuis les premiers va-et-vient d'un village à un autre.
		pɛste	*People have been grumbling about roads ever since they started travelling from village to village.*
2397	**fonction**		**function**
	nf		L'actualisation du logiciel a ajouté plusieurs fonctions.
		fɔ̃ksjɔ̃	*The software update added several functions.*

2398	**élire**	**to elect**
	verb	Quel critère avez-vous utilisé pour élire cet essai en tant que gagnant ?
	eliʁ	*What criterion did you use when you elected this essay as the winner?*
2399	**machin**	**thingy**
	nm	Quoi qu'il en soit, le nouvel éditeur supporte ce machin à défiler qui se trouve sur votre souris.
	maʃɛ̃	*But the new editor still supports that scroll thingy that is located on your mouse*
2400	**fameux**	**famous**
	adj[pl]	Il a légué à ses étudiants ces fameuses paroles.
	famø	*He left his students these famous words.*
2401	**talent**	**talent**
	nm	Vous devriez choisir un emploi en rapport avec vos talents et vos intérêts.
	talɑ̃	*You should choose a job in relation to your talents and interests.*
2402	**nègre**	**negro**
	nm, adj	Mais ce nègre-là n'était pas né dans les champs de coton du Mississipi.
	nɛgʁ	*But this black man wasn't born in the Mississipi cotton fields.*
2403	**catholique**	**catholic**
	nmf, adj(f)	L'Église catholique n'approuve pas l'utilisation du préservatif.
	katɔlik	*The Catholic Church doesn't condone the use of condoms.*
2404	**indiquer**	**to indicate, signal**
	verb	Mon bulletin de paie indique mon salaire brut et net.
	ɛ̃dike	*My payslip indicates my gross and net salary.*
2405	**misérable**	**miserable, wretched**
	nmf, adj	Il dût passer une vie misérable durant de nombreuses années.
	mizeʁabl	*He had to lead a miserable life for many years.*
2406	**requin**	**shark**
	nm	Le requin blanc atteint souvent, dans les mers tropicales, une taille de plus de 9 mètres.
	ʁəkɛ̃	*The white shark frequently attains, in the tropical seas, the length of more than 30 feet.*
2407	**sincèrement**	**truly, sincerely**
	adv	J'espère sincèrement que tu te remettras bientôt de ta maladie.
	sɛ̃sɛʁmɑ̃	*I sincerely hope that you will soon recover from your illness.*
2408	**affection**	**affection, ailment**
	nf	Elle montre son affection en achetant des cadeaux à ses amis
	afɛksjɔ̃	*She shows her affection by buying gifts for her friends.*
2409	**adversaire**	**opponent, adversary**
	nm, nf	L'équipe locale a toujours un avantage sur son adversaire.
	advɛʁsɛʁ	*The home team always have an advantage over their opponents.*
2410	**actuellement**	**at present, at the moment**
	adv	Je suis né en Italie, mais je vis actuellement en Chine.
	aktɥɛlmɑ̃	*I was born in Italy, but I currently live in China.*
2411	**meuble**	**piece of furniture**
	nm, adj(f)	Il n'y a pas beaucoup de meubles dans ma maison.

	mœbl	*There isn't much furniture in my house.*
2412	**foutu**	**fucking, damned**
	adj	Je ne pense pas que ces foutues piles soient dans ce foutu tiroir.
	futy	*I don't think that those damn batteries are in this damn drawer.*
2413	**dignité**	**dignity**
	nf	La dignité de l'homme est intangible. La respecter et la protéger est le devoir de toute autorité étatique.
	diɲite	*The dignity of man is inviolable. To respect and protect it is the duty of all state authority.*
2414	**ramer**	**to row**
	verb	La fille qui rame pour faire avancer ce bateau est ma cousine.
	ʁame	*The girl rowing a boat is my cousin.*
2415	**rat**	**rat**
	nf	Les rats ont appris à réagir à un certain stimulus
	ʁa	*The rats learned to react to a certain stimulus.*
2416	**patienter**	**to wait**
	verb	Tom attendit patiemment trois heures durant, puis renonça.
	pasjɑ̃te	*Tom waited patiently for three hours, then left.*
2417	**vomir**	**to throw up, to vomit**
	verb	En deux jours, deux filles ont vomi dans l'autobus.
	vɔmiʁ	*Two girls threw up on the bus in two days.*
2418	**dépression**	**depression**
	nm	Il se peut que votre chien soit en dépression.
	depʁesjɔ̃	*Your dog could be suffering from depression.*
2419	**précisément**	**precisely**
	adv	Il vaut mieux avoir approximativement raison que précisément tort.
	pʁesizemɑ̃	*It is better to be approximately right than precisely wrong.*
2420	**circuit**	**circuit**
	nm	Tu dois couper le courant avant de vérifier le circuit.
	siʁkɥi	*You must switch off the power before checking the circuit.*
2421	**voile**	**veil, sail**
	nm, nf	Le coup de vent soudain gonfla les voiles et poussa le bateau en avant dans une embardée.
	vwal	*The sudden gust of wind filled the sails and lurched the boat forward.*
2422	**correctement**	**properly**
	adv	Si on nourrit son chien correctement, on peut accroître sa durée de vie.
	kɔʁɛktəmɑ̃	*If you feed your dog properly, you can increase his lifespan.*
2423	**fringuer**	**to dress**
	verb	Il est bien fringué.
	fʁɛ̃ge	*He's well dressed.*
2424	**améliorer**	**to improve**
	verb	En nous corrigeant l'un l'autre, nous nous améliorerons tous en espéranto.
	ameljɔʁe	*Correcting one another, we will all improve our Esperanto.*
2425	**observer**	**to observe, watch**
	verb	Nous avons observé cette plante de près pendant quelques semaines.

ɔpsɛʁve | *We observed this plant closely for a few weeks.*

2426 volontaire — **volunteer; voluntary**

nmf, adj(f) — Cette entreprise cherche à réduire le nombre de ses employés en mettant à disposition beaucoup d'argent pour les départs volontaires.

vɔlɔ̃tɛʁ — *That company aims to reduce employee numbers by arranging a lot of retirement money for voluntary redundancies.*

2427 fumier — **manure**

nm — « Que fais-tu avec le fumier ? » « Je le dispense sur les fraises. »

fymje — *"What are you doing with the manure? "I'm putting it on the strawberries."*

2428 égoïste — **selfish, egoist**

adj, nm, nf — Un homme égoïste ne pense à rien sauf à ses propres sentiments.

egɔist — *A selfish man thinks of nothing but his own feelings.*

2429 brouillard — **fog, mist, haze**

nm — Le vol a été annulé en raison d'un épais brouillard.

bʁujaʁ — *The flight was cancelled because of the thick fog.*

2430 construction — **construction, building**

nf — Les matériaux de construction coûtent très cher actuellement.

kɔ̃stʁyksjɔ̃ — *Construction materials are very expensive at this time.*

2431 météo — **weather forecast, weather report**

nf — Le bulletin météo a dit que demain soir il y aurait de l'orage.

meteo — *The weather report said that there will be thunderstorms tomorrow evening.*

2432 fillette — **little girl, girl**

nf — La fillette remporta le prix pour sa magnifique danse au récital.

fijɛt — *The girl won the prize for her wonderful dancing at the recital.*

2433 motif — **motive, purpose**

nm — Ces jours-ci, les motifs derrière le mariage ne sont pas nécessairement purs.

mɔtif — *These days, the motives for marriage are not necessarily pure.*

2434 sien — **his, hers**

pron — Y a-t-il la moindre différence entre votre idée et la sienne ?

sjɛ̃ — *Is there any difference between your idea and hers?*

2435 loyauté — **loyalty**

nf — Le chemin vers le mal peut apporter un grand pouvoir, mais pas la loyauté.

lwajote — *The path to evil may bring great power, but not loyalty.*

2436 évidence — **evidence**

nf — On ne pourra pourtant pas nier l'évidence indéfiniment.

evidɑ̃s — *However, the evidence cannot be denied forever.*

2437 mouton — **sheep**

nm — Tous les moutons étaient entassés à l'ombre du seul arbre de l'enclos.

mutɔ̃ — *All the sheep were huddled together in the shade of the only tree in the paddock.*

2438 commercial — **commercial, marketeer**

adj, nm — Il y a de nombreuses sociétés commerciales à New-York.

kɔmɛʁsjal — *There are many commercial firms in New York.*

2439 lier — **to link, join, tie to**

		verb	Les villageois étaient convaincus que la série de meurtres était liée à un culte satanique.

lje — *The townsfolk were convinced that the string of murders was tied to a satanic cult.*

2440	**remède**		**remedy**
	nf		Presque tous les hommes meurent de leurs remèdes, et non pas de leurs maladies.

ʁəmɛd — *Nearly all men die of their remedies, and not of their illnesses*

2441	**maintenir**		**to maintain**
	verb		S'il maintient cette cadence, il gagnera la course.

mɛ̃tniʁ — *If he maintains this pace, he will win the race.*

2442	**catastrophe**		**catastrophe, disaster**
	nf		Si l'accident s'était produit en ville, il aurait conduit à une catastrophe.

katastʁof — *If that accident had happened in a city, it would have caused a disaster.*

2443	**disparition**		**disappearance**
	nf		Les disparitions qui ont eu lieu dans le triangle des Bermudes sont inexplicables.

dispaʁisjɔ̃ — *The disappearances in the Bermuda Triangle are inexplicable.*

2444	**éternel**		**eternal**
	adj		Le Père est la source du Paradis comme il est le Père du Fils Éternel.

etɛʁnɛl — *The Father is the source of Paradise as he is Father of the Eternal Son.*

2445	**drap**		**sheet**
	nm		J'ai mis une pierre sur le bord du drap pour empêcher que le vent ne l'emporte.

dʁa — *I put a stone at the edge of the sheet so that it won't get blown away by the wind.*

2446	**envelopper**		**to wrap, surround, veil**
	verb		La Russie est un rébus enveloppé de mystère au sein d'une énigme.

ãvlɔpe — *Russia is a riddle wrapped in a mystery inside an enigma.*

2447	**coco**		**mate, coconut**
	nm		En Thaïlande, on utilise la noix de coco pour la cuisine, les boissons et les jouets.

koko — *In Thailand, people use coconuts for food, drink and toys.*

2448	**éclair**		**flash, spark**
	nm		Le point éclair du liquide inflammable était assez élevé.

eklɛʁ — *The flash point of the flammable liquid was quite high.*

2449	**témoigner**		**to bear witness, to testify**
	verb		On ne peut vous forcer à témoigner contre votre mari.

temwaɲe — *You can't be forced to testify against your husband.*

2450	**onze**		**eleven**
	det, num		Je vais me coucher à onze heures du soir.

ɔ̃z — *I go to bed at eleven.*

2451	**feuille**		**leaf, sheet, slip**
	nf		Il vit des oiseaux, des fleurs et des feuilles, tous de vives couleurs.

fœj — *He saw brightly-colored birds, flowers and leaves.*

2452	**embêter**		**to bother**

	verb	Je ne sais pas pourquoi je m'embête à me répéter.
	ãbete	*I don't know why I bother repeating myself.*
2453	**nichon**	**boob, tit, breast**
	nm	Ça ne dérangeait pas Tom que Marie ait de petits nichons.
	niʃɔ̃	*Tom didn't mind that Mary had small breasts.*
2454	**interview**	**interview**
	nf	Dans cette interview, Antonio parle de son fils qui est mort il y a de ça quelques années.
	ɛ̃tɛʁvju	*In that interview, Antonio talks about his son that died a few years ago.*
2455	**partant**	**thus, consequencly, therefore**
	adv	L'accroissement de la dette serait stable et, partant, défendable à long terme
	paʁtã	*The increase in debt would be stable and therefore defensible in the long term.*
2456	**promenade**	**walk, stroll**
	nf	La vie est une courte promenade avant le sommeil éternel.
	pʁɔmnad	*Life is a short walk before eternal sleep.*
2457	**association**	**association**
	nf	J'ai soumis ma candidature pour devenir membre de l'association.
	asɔsjasjɔ̃	*I applied for membership in the association.*
2458	**leader**	**leader**
	nm, nf	Le peuple britannique se tourna vers un nouveau leader : Winston Churchill.
	lidœʁ	*The British people turned to a new leader, Winston Churchill.*
2459	**discipline**	**discipline**
	nf	Au-delà d'une saine discipline, ménagez-vous.
	disiplin	*Beyond a wholesome discipline, be gentle with yourself.*
2460	**civil**	**civil; civilian**
	f	La population civile a versé un lourd tribut à la guerre.
	sivil	*The war has taken a terrible toll on the civilian population.*
2461	**lancement**	**launch**
	nm	Le lancement de produit s'est déroulé la semaine dernière.
	lãsmã	*The product launch happened last week.*
2462	**gras**	**fatty, fat, greasy**
	adj[pl], adv, nm[pl]	Nous appelons notre professeur «Doraemon» parce qu'il est gras.
	gʁa	*We call our teacher "Doraemon" because he's fat.*
2463	**transfert**	**transfer**
	nm	Le joueur a demandé un transfert d'un club à l'autre.
	tʁãsfɛʁ	*The player requested a transfer from one club to the other.*
2464	**satellite**	**satellite**
	nm	Des milliers de satellites orbitent autour de la Terre.
	satelit	*Thousands of satellites orbit around the earth.*
2465	**pompier**	**fireman, firefighter**
	adj, nm	L'incendie était tel que les pompiers n'ont pas pu rentrer à l'intérieur de la maison.

pɔ̃pje

The fire was so intense that the firemen couldn't get into the house.

2466 tennis — **tennis**

nf

Le tennis est difficile. Je ne sais jamais où la balle va voler.

tenis

Tennis is difficult. I never know which way the ball is going to fly.

2467 tragique — **tragic, tragedy**

adj(f), nm

La mort tragique de la princesse Diana a choqué le monde.

tʁaʒik

Princess Diana's tragic death shocked the world.

2468 enregistrement — **recording, registration, check-in, logging**

nm

Le temps d'enregistrement actuel est également affiché

ɑ̃ʁəʒistʁəmɑ̃

The current recording time is also displayed in the same way.

2469 circulation — **circulation, traffic**

nf

Le centre-ville devrait être fermé à toute circulation non piétonne.

siʁkylasjɔ̃

The city center should be closed to all but pedestrian traffic.

2470 casque — **helmet**

nf

Tu joues avec le feu à rouler constamment à moto sans casque.

kask

You're playing with fire if you insist on riding your motorcycle without a helmet on.

2471 compétition — **competition**

nm

J'aime faire du sport pour le plaisir et non pour la compétition.

kɔ̃petisjɔ̃

I like to play sport for fun not for competition.

2472 caution — **deposit, guarantee, bail**

nf

Je ne veux pas perdre ma caution.

kosjɔ̃

I don't want to lose my deposit.

2473 adn — **DNA**

nm

L'enquêteur de police a soigneusement collecté des échantillons pour un test ADN.

adn

The police detective carefully collected samples for DNA testing.

2474 opportunité — **opportunity, appropriateness**

nf

Il a profité de cette opportunité pour améliorer son anglais.

ɔpɔʁtynite

He made use of the opportunity to improve his English.

2475 officiellement — **officially**

adv

La langue officielle de la Thaïlande est le thaï.

ɔfisjɛlmɑ̃

Thai is the official language in Thailand.

2476 fixe — **fixed, set; base salary**

adj, nm

Nos vendeurs reçoivent un salaire fixe plus une commission.

fiks

Our salespeople get a fixed salary plus a commission.

2477 fasciner — **to fascinate**

verb

Le spectacle de cirque a fasciné le public.

fasine

The circus show fascinated the audience.

2478 menu — **menu, slender, slim, minor**

nm, adv, adj

Tom consulta le menu puis décida de commander un plat de poisson.

məny

Tom looked at the menu and decided to order a fish dish.

2479 plancher — **floor**

nm, verb

Il faut demander un balai pour balayer le plancher.

plɑ̃ʃe

We must ask for a broom to sweep the floor.

2480	**subir**	**to undergo, be subjected to, suffer**
	verb	Le chirurgien m'a convaincue de subir une opération de transplantation.
	sybiʁ	*The surgeon persuaded me to undergo an organ transplant operation.*
2481	**saigner**	**to bleed**
	verb	Vous ne saignerez pas jusqu'à ce que mort s'ensuive.
	seɲe	*You won't bleed to death.*
2482	**dentiste**	**dentist**
	nm, nf	Je n'arrive pas à trouver une bonne excuse pour mon retard chez le dentiste.
	dɑ̃tist	*I can't come up with a good excuse for being late for the dentist.*
2483	**légal**	**legal**
	adj	Ce n'est pas simplement parce que quelque chose est légal qu'il est éthique.
	legal	*Just because something is legal, it doesn't mean that it's ethical.*
2484	**civilisation**	**civilization**
	nf	Il y a une tendance à employer l'espace souterrain pour les fins les moins ornementales de la civilisation.
	sivilizasjɔ̃	*There is a tendency to utilize underground space for the less ornamental purposes of civilization.*
2485	**avertissement**	**warning**
	nm	Je lui ai donné un avertissement auquel il n'a prêté aucune attention.
	avɛʁtismɑ̃	*I gave him a warning, to which he paid no attention.*
2486	**tache**	**stain, spot, mark**
	nf	Sur sa chemise se trouvait une tache de sauce.
	taʃ	*On his shirt there was a sauce stain.*
2487	**antenne**	**antenna**
	nf	L'antenne de télé a été cassée par l'orage la nuit dernière.
	ɑ̃tɛn	*The TV antenna broke away in last night's storm.*
2488	**confier**	**to entrust**
	verb	Je confie mes secrets uniquement à ma meilleure amie.
	kɔ̃fje	*I only entrust my secrets to my best friend.*
2489	**onde**	**wave**
	nf	L'appareil mesure l'amplitude des ondes sonores.
	ɔ̃d	*The device measures the amplitude of the sound waves.*
2490	**assaut**	**assault, attack, bout**
	nm	Le commandant a donné l'ordre à ses troupes de commencer l'assaut.
	aso	*The commander ordered his troops to begin the assault.*
2491	**fiche**	**card, sheet, slip, form**
	nf	Les deux dernières colonnes de l'exemple de contrôle de cette fiche constituent les indicateurs.
	fiʃ	*The two last columns of the example for recording data on this sheet are the indicators.*
2492	**épisode**	**episode**
	nf	Y a-t-il d'autres épisodes intéressants dans l'histoire ?
	epizɔd	*Are there any other interesting episodes in history?*
2493	**anneau**	**ring**

	nm	Cet anneau est un objet magique qui donne un grand pouvoir à celui qui l'utilise.
	ano	*This ring is a magic item that gives great power to its user.*
2494	**maquillage**	**makeup**
	nf	J'aime son sens du style. Ses vêtements et son maquillage sont toujours jolis.
	makijaʒ	*I like her sense of style. Her clothes and makeup always look good.*
2495	**doue**	**talented, gifted**
	adj	Avez-vous suivi une formation de cuisinière ou ètes-vous naturellement douée ?
	du	*Did you ever have training as a cook or are you just naturally gifted?*
2496	**enregistrer**	**to record, check in**
	verb	Merci de vous enregistrer au moins une heure avant de partir.
	ãʁəʒistʁe	*Please check in at least an hour before leaving.*
2497	**impact**	**impact**
	nm	Ce n'est pas mon objectif d'enquêter sur l'impact de la théorie d'Emmet sur la biologie.
	ɛ̃pakt	*It is not my purpose to investigate the impact of Emmet's theory on biology.*
2498	**effacer**	**to erase, clean**
	verb	Le professeur a effacé le tableau noir à la fin du cours.
	efase	*The teacher erased the blackboard at the end of the class.*
2499	**zone**	**area**
	nf	Il y a beaucoup de zones au Canada où il est interdit d'abattre des arbres.
	zon	*In Canada, there are many areas where it is illegal to log trees.*
2500	**loger**	**to put up, accomodate, stay**
	verb	L´hotel peut loger vingt personne.
	lɔʒe	*The hotel can accomodate twenty people.*
2501	**conflit**	**conflict**
	nm	Il y a toujours des conflits avec en entre des muslims.
	kɔ̃fli	*There are always confcts with and between muslims.*

A. Adjectives

Rank	French	PoS	English
10	un, une, des	adj, det, nm, pron	a, an, one
28	bien	adj(i), adv, nm	well
31	tout	adv, det, nm, adj, pron	all, very
44	sur	adj, prep	on, upon
63	bon	adj, adv, int, nm	good
66	même	adj(f), adv, pron	same, even, self
70	chose	adj(f), nf	thing
74	autre	adj(f), pron	other
84	juste	adv, nm, adj(f)	just, only; fair
86	quelque	adv, adj, det	some
97	sûr	adj, prep	on, upon
98	leur	det, adj(f), pron	them, their, theirs
99	avant	adj(i), adv, nm, prep	before
105	vrai	adv, nm, adj	true
107	mal	adj(i), adv, nm	bad, sore
110	mort	adj, nf	dead; death
112	mieux	adj(i)[pl], adv, nm	better
113	petit	adv, nm, adj	small, little
120	quel	det, adj, pron	which, what
139	désolé	adj	sorry, afraid
141	seul	adj	alone, only
151	chose	adj(f), nf	thing
154	bas	adv, nm&f, adj[pl], nm[pl]	low; bass; stockings
155	moins	adj(i)[pl], adv, nm[pl], prep	less
157	passe	nf, adj, prep	pass, past
160	grand	adv, nm/f, adj	great, older girl or boy, tall
166	enfant	nm, nf, adj(f)	child
175	ami	nm/f, adj	friend
200	vieux	adj[pl], nm[pl]	old
213	nouveau	adj, nm	new
222	beau	adj, nm	handsome, fine, right
228	super	adj(i), nm	great
229	chaque	det, adj	each, every
238	aucun	det, adj, pron	none, either, neither, not any
243	arrivé	adj	arrived, happen
249	fin	adj, adv, nf, nm	end; gist, clever person
251	jeune	nmf, adj(f)	young
252	chéri	noun, adj	darling, love, dear
253	premier	det, nm&f, adj	first, premier, first,
255		adj, adv, nm	right
259	feu	adj(f), nm	fire
262	gros	adv, nm, adj[pl]	big, whoiesale, heavy
265	dernier	nm&f, adj	last
272	fort	adv, adj, nm	strong
275	affaire	nf, adj	case, matter, business

278	**fou**	*adj, nm*	mad, crazy
280	**prêt**	*adj, nm*	ready
287	**boulot**	*adj, nm*	work, job
293	**haut**	*adv, adj*	top, high
295	**bébé**	*nmf, adj(f)*	baby
296	**possible**	*adj(f)*	possible
298	**plein**	*adv, nm, adj, prep*	full
312	**instant**	*adj, nm*	instant, moment
318	**meilleur**	*nmf, adj, adv*	best, better,
325	**dur**	*adv, nm&f, adj*	hard
328	**important**	*nm, adj*	important
339	**ferme**	*adj*	shut, closed, locked
341	**heureux**	*adj[pl]*	happy, lucky, fortunate
346	**calme**	*nm, adj(f)*	composure, calm
347	**parent**	*nm&f, adj*	parent
355	**parfait**	*nm, adj, int*	perfect
360	**pauvre**	*nmf, adj(f)*	poor
362	**drôle**	*adj(f), nm*	funny, strange
368	**impossible**	*nm, adj(f)*	impossible
370	**facile**	*adj(f)*	easy
372	**mauvais**	*adv, nm, adj[pl]*	bad, wrong
373	**général**	*nm, adj*	general
383	**gentil**	*adj*	nice, kind
386	**malade**	*nmf, adj(f)*	mental patient; ill, sick
393	**cher**	*adj, adv*	expensive
399	**plan**	*adj, nm*	plan
402	**propre**	*nm, adj(f)*	particular; clean, proper
409	**génial**	*adj*	inspired, great, brilliant
411	**tôt**	*adj(i), adv*	early
416	**difficile**	*adj(f)*	difficult

419	**pire**	*adj(f), nm*	worse, worst
420	**simple**	*adj(f)*	simple, single
426	**sale**	*adj(f)*	dirty
428	**sauf**	*adj, prep*	except
434	**noir**	*nmf adj*	black (wo)man), black
441	**inquiet**	*adj*	worried, anxious
443	**sérieux**	*nm, adj[pl]*	seriousness, serious
450	**grave**	*adv, adj(f), nm*	serious, grave
452	**courant**	*adj, nm*	current
455	**con**	*adj, nmf*	stupid
456	**gauche**	*nf, adj(f)*	left
457	**content**	*adj*	glad, pleased, happy
459	**rouge**	*nm, adj(f)*	red
463	**prochain**	*adj, nm*	next; fellow man
467	**long**	*adv, adj, nm*	long, lengthy, length
469	**idiot**	*nmf, adj*	idiot, fool, stupid
473	**continu**	*adj*	continuous
477	**certain**	*adj, det, nm, pron*	certain, sure
484	**bienvenue**	*nf, adj*	welcome
490	**arme**	*adj*	armed
492	**bizarre**	*adj(f)*	strange, odd
500	**froid**	*nm, adj*	cold
502	**secret**	*nm, adj*	secret
504	**second**	*adj, det, nm*	second
505	**cru**	*adj*	vintage, raw, crude
513	**joli**	*adj*	pretty, attractive
518	**libre**	*adj(f)*	free
521	**neuf**	*det, adj, num*	nine; new
522	**faux**	*adv, adj[pl], nm[pl], nf[pl]*	false; scythe
529	**intérieur**	*nm adj*	interior, inside

532	**incroyable**	*adj(f)*	incredible, amazing, unbelievable
534	**présent**	*nm, adj*	present
545	**magnifique**	*adj(f)*	magnificent
549	**tranquille**	*adj(f)*	quiet
550	**chaud**	*adv, nm, adj*	warm, hot
553	**pareil**	*adj, nm*	similar, likewise; peer, equal; the same
556	**anniversaire**	*nm, adj(f)*	anniversary, birthday
557	**blanc**	*adj, nm*	white
559	**moyen**	*adj, nm*	means, way; medium
562	**clair**	*adv, adj*	clear
585	**anglais**	*nm, adj[pl]*	English
590	**exact**	*adj*	exact, correct
608	**dangereux**	*adj[pl]*	dangerous
613	**fou**	*adj, nm*	mad, crazy
619	**arriere**	*adj(i), adv, nm*	back, rear
622	**radio**	*adj(i), nm, nf*	radio
632	**triste**	*adj(f)*	sad
633	**tel**	*adj, det, pron*	such
635	**plusieurs**	*det, adj, pron*	several
639	**étrange**	*adj(f)*	strange, odd
647	**merveilleux**	*adj[pl]*	marvellous, wonderful
652	**sud**	*adj(i), nm*	south
660	**public**	*nm, adj*	public, audience
664	**bête**	*nf, adj(f)*	animal, beast; stupid
668	**amoureux**	*nmf, adj[pl]*	lover; in love, amorous
670	**normal**	*adj*	normal
682	**sympa**	*adj*	friendly, nice, kind
688	**nord**	*adj(i), nm*	north
694	**terrible**	*adj(f)*	terrible, dreadful

702	**stupide**	*adj(f)*	stupid, silly, bemused
723	**dingue**	*adj*	crazy, mad, wild, nutty
724	**inutile**	*adj(f)*	useless
725	**nul**	*adj, det, pron*	nil, null
727	**différent**	*adj*	different
741	**ennemi**	*nmf, adj*	enemy
752	**blessé**	*adj, nmf*	injured; injured person, causualty
753	**humain**	*nm, adj*	human
755	**coupable**	*nmf, adj(f)*	guilty
763	**lâche**	*adj*	loose
767	**directeur**	*nmf, adj*	director
772	**américain**	*adj, nm*	American, American English,
781	**riche**	*adj(f)*	rich
785	**ridicule**	*nm, adj(f)*	ridiculousness, silly
788	**intéressant**	*adj*	interesting
790	**rose**	*adj(f), nf*	pink; rose
792	**vide**	*adj(f), nm*	empty; vacuum
793	**responsable**	*adj(f), nmf*	responsible
795	**capable**	*adj(f)*	able, capable
801	**fier**	*adj, v*	to rely on; proud
811	**longue**	*adj*	long
813	**formidable**	*adj(f)*	tremendous, considerable, great
822	**monstre**	*nm adj(f)*	monster
825	**francais**	*nm, adj[pl]*	French
834	**ouest**	*adj(i), nm*	west
841	**superbe**	*nf, adj(f)*	arrogance; superb, magnificent
843	**horrible**	*adj(f)*	horrible, terrible, dreadful, hideous

844	**court**	*adj, adv, nm*	short	1016	**proche**	*adv, noun, adj(f), prep*	nearby, close
854	**excellent**	*adj*	excellent				
861	**joyeux**	*adj[pl]*	merry, joyful, happy	1019	**ancien**	*adj, nm*	ancient; former
869	**règle**	*adj*	regular, steady, well-ordered, ruled	1024	**cassé**	*adj*	broken
				1040	**chinois**	*noun, adj[pl]*	Chinese
870	**animal**	*nm, adj*	animal	1047	**étranger**	*noun, adj*	foreigner; foreign
872	**imbécile**	*adj, nf*	imbecile, fool				
881	**contraire**	*nm, adj(f)*	opposite, contrary	1058	**fantastique**	*noun, adj(f)*	fantastic, terrific, great, weird, eerie
884	**politique**	*nm, nf, adj(f)*	politician; politics; political				
				1063	**règle**	*adj*	regular, steady, well-ordered, ruled
885	**fait**	*adj, nm*	done, fact				
887	**entier**	*nm, adj*	whole, full	1068	**suivant**	*noun, adj, prep*	following
894	**rapide**	*adj(f), nm*	fast, quick; rapids, fast train				
				1071	**passager**	*noun, adj*	passenger, temporary
895	**frais**	*adj[pl], adv, nm[pl]*	cool, fresh; fee, expense	1080	**vidéo**	*adj(i), nf*	video
				1085	**futur**	*noun, adj*	future
901	**spécial**	*adj*	special				
912	**sacré**	*adj*	sacred	1088	**attendu**	*adj*	expected
915	**nécessaire**	*nm, adj(f)*	necessary, required	1090	**faible**	*noun, adj(f)*	weak
923	**personnel**	*noun, adj*	personnel, personal	1096	**utile**	*adj(f)*	useful
				1099	**voleur**	*noun, adj*	thief, light-fingered
925	**mignon**	*adj*	cute				
931	**malin**	*noun, adj*	smart, shrewd, cunning	1103	**gâteau**	*noun, adj*	cake
				1106	**vif**	*noun, adj*	lively
937	**doux**	*adv, noun, adj[pl]*	soft, sweet				
				1107	**assassin**	*noun, adj*	murderer, assassin
945	**enceinte**	*adjf, nf*	pregnant; enclosure	1111	**militaire**	*noun, adj(f)*	military
947	**bleu**	*adj, nm*	blue	1119	**puissant**	*noun, adj*	powerful
959	**failli**	*adj*	bankrupt				
969	**énorme**	*adj(f)*	enormous, huge	1121	**vert**	*noun, adj*	green
975	**moindre**	*adj(f)*	lesser, least, slightest	1126	**célèbre**	*adj(f)*	famous
				1136	**charmant**	*adj*	charming
976	**censé**	*adj*	supposed	1139	**agréable**	*noun, adj(f)*	pleasant, nice, agreeable
981	**unique**	*adj(f)*	unique				
998	**honnête**	*adj(f)*	honest, decent, fair	1145	**saint**	*noun, adj*	saint, holy
1001	**aveugle**	*noun, adj(f)*	blind	1146	**marrant**	*noun, adj*	funny, funny guy

1158	**nerveux**	*noun, adj[pl]*	nervous, irritable	1278	**soudain**	*adj, adv*	sudden, suddenly
1160	**direct**	*noun, adj*	direct	1287	**portable**	*adj(f), nm*	portable, wearable; cell phone
1164	**aise**	*noun, adj(f)*	comfort, joy, pleasure, ease	1295	**bref**	*adj, adv, nm*	brief, short
1171	**champion**	*noun, adj*	champion	1296	**réel**	*noun, adj*	real
1175	**extérieur**	*noun, adj*	exterior	1301	**plat**	*adj, nm*	dish, flat
1176	**désert**	*adj, nm*	desert, wilderness	1330	**affreux**	*noun, adj[pl]*	dreadful, awful, horrible
1177	**intelligent**	*adj*	intelligent, clever, bright, smart	1331	**ours**	*adj(i), nm[pl]*	bear
1183	**sage**	*noun, adj(f)*	wise, good, sound, sensible	1333	**prisonnier**	*noun, adj*	prisoner, captive
1187	**vache**	*adj(f), nf*	cow	1337	**demi**	*adj(i), adv, nm*	half
1189	**ordinateur**	*noun, adj*	computer	1339	**alerte**	*adj(f), nf*	agile, alert, warning
1192	**russe**	*noun, adj(f)*	Russian	1343	**prudent**	*adj*	prudent, careful, cautious
1194	**amusant**	*noun, adj*	funny, amusing, entertaining	1345	**donne**	*adj*	given
1196	**ouvert**	*adj*	open	1351	**tenu**	*adj*	tenuous, slender, held
1197	**nombreux**	*adj[pl]*	numerous	1356	**sec**	*adj, adv, nm*	dry
1199	**mince**	*adj(f), int*	thin, slim, slender	1361	**vierge**	*noun, adj(f)*	virgin
1203	**moteur**	*noun, adj*	motor	1364	**suspect**	*noun, adj*	suspicious, suspect
1215	**artiste**	*noun, adj(f)*	artist	1375	**immeuble**	*noun, adj(f)*	building
1228	**japonais**	*noun, adj[pl]*	Japanese	1383	**curieux**	*noun, adj[pl]*	curious
1246	**allemand**	*noun, adj*	German	1387	**uniforme**	*adj(f), nm*	uniform, steady, regular
1248	**policier**	*noun, adj*	policeman	1388	**marine**	*adj, nf*	marine, navy
1249	**innocent**	*noun, adj*	innocent	1413	**brave**	*noun, adj*	brave, worthy, good, brave man
1250	**véritable**	*adj(f)*	real, TRUE	1415	**sale**	*noun, adj(f)*	dirty
1253	**patient**	*noun, adj*	patient	1416	**roule**	*adj*	rolled
1262	**juif**	*noun, adj*	Jew, Jewish	1417	**extraordinaire**	*adj(f)*	extraordinary
1263	**chouette**	*nf, adj, int*	owl, nice, awesome!	1424	**net**	*adj, nm*	clear; Internet, web
1267	**chocolat**	*adj(i), nm*	chocolate	1425	**vivant**	*noun, adj*	alive, living

#	Word	Type	Meaning
1426	**compliqué**	noun, adj	complicated, complex
1427	**fiancé**	noun, adj	fiancé, engaged
1430	**sombre**	adj(f)	dark
1432	**voisin**	noun, adj	neighbor
1433	**lourd**	adj	heavy
1443	**égal**	noun, adj	equal
1444	**sport**	adj(i), nm	sport
1447	**adorable**	adj	adorable, sweet
1450	**gardien**	noun, adj	guardian, keeper
1456	**joueur**	noun, adj	player
1458	**commun**	noun, adj	common
1459	**tien(s)**	noun, adj[pl], int	ah, well
1461	**crâne**	adj(f), nm	skull
1466	**délicieux**	adj	delicious
1482	**liquide**	noun, adj(f)	liquid
1484	**marin**	noun, adj	sea, marine, sailor
1488	**jaloux**	noun, adj	jealous
1490	**physique**	noun, adj(f)	physical, physics
1492	**infirmier**	noun, adj	nurse
1497	**particulier**	noun, adj	particular, peculiar; person
1508	**matériel**	noun, adj	material, equipment
1511	**jaune**	adv, noun, adj(f)	yellow
1514	**rare**	adj(f)	rare
1516	**magique**	adj(f)	magic; magical
1517	**rat**	adj(f), nm	rat
1524	**romantique**	noun, adj(f)	romantic
1531	**inconnu**	noun, adj	unknown
1535	**panique**	noun, adj(f)	panic
1536	**criminel**	noun, adj	criminal
1537	**sauvage**	noun, adj(f)	savage, wild
1540	**complet**	adj, nm	full, complete, full
1543	**principal**	noun, adj	principal
1547	**cochon**	noun, adj	pig
1555	**profond**	adv, noun, adj	deep
1556	**malheureux**	noun, adj[pl]	unhappy, miserable
1558	**roman**	adj, nm	novel
1570	**indien**	noun, adj	Indian
1571	**meurtrier**	noun, adj	murderer, deadly, lethal
1580	**logique**	noun, adj(f)	logic, logical
1586	**courageux**	noun, adj[pl]	courageous
1600	**sable**	adj(i), nm	sand
1604	**pratique**	noun, adj(f)	practice, practical
1617	**pur**	adj, nmf	pure; hard-liner
1622	**idéal**	nm, adj	ideal
1624	**élève**	adj	high, heavy, tall
1629	**ordinaire**	adv, nm, adj(f)	ordinary
1632	**naturel**	nm, adj	naturalness, natural
1637	**central**	adj, nm	central; exchange
1642	**chic**	adj	chic, luxurious
1651	**correct**	adj	correct
1653	**national**	adj, nf	national; road, state highway
1656	**raisonnable**	adj(f)	reasonable, fair
1660	**étudiant**	nm/f, adj	student
1661	**créme**	adj(i), nf	cream

1665	nu	nm, adj	naked, nude	1804	classique	nm, adj(f)	classic
1668	couvert	adj, nm	covered, overcast; place, seat, cutlery	1813	incapable	adj	incapable, incompetent
1670	technique	nf, adj(f)	technique, technics, technical	1821	précieux	adj [pl]	precious
				1828	échec	adj(i), nm	failure
1673	doué	adj	gifted	1831	précis	adj[pl, noun	precise; noun
1683	noble	adj(f, nmf	noble, noble(wo)man	1833	objectif	adj, nm	objective, aim, goal; lens
1684	large	adj(f), adv, nm	wide, width	1843	électrique	adj(f)	electric
1685	urgent	adj	urgent	1849	las	adj	tired, weary
1686	digne	adj(f)	dignified, worthy	1852	producteur	nm/f, adj	producer
1690	plaisant	adj	pleasant	1854	critique	adj(f), nmf	criticism, critical, critic
1696	absurde	nm, adj(f)	absurd	1864	italien	nm/f, adj	Italian
1699	maximum	nm, adj	maximum	1868	moral	adj, nm	moral, morale
1706	pair	adj, nm	peer, pair, even	1869	supérieur	adj, nmf	superior
1707	moche	adj	ugly	1871	tendre	adj(f)	tender, soft
1708	blond	nmf, adj	blond, fair-haired	1874	ivre	adj	drunk, intoxicated
1714	scientifique	adj(f), nmf	scientific; scientist	1876	gagnant	nmf, adj	winner, winning
1715	traître	nm, adj	traitor, treacherous	1883	assis	adj	seated
				1894	final	nm, adj	final
1718	cave	adj(f), nm, nf	cellar, basement	1905	expert	nm, adj	expert
				1911	moderne	adj	modern
1722	minable	adj	seedy, shabby	1916	sensible	adj(f)	sensitive
1744	aimable	adj(f)	pleasant, kind, nice	1920	fonce	adj	dark
1747	adulte	nmf, adj(f)	adult	1945	sourd	adj, nmf	deaf, deaf person
1752	vague	adj(f); nf	vague; wave	1948	injuste	adj(f)	unfair, unjust
1758	géant	nmf, adj	giant, gigantic	1952	fidèle	adj	faithful
1771	orange	adj(i), nf	orange	1956	total	adj, nm	total
1783	professionnel	nmf, adj	professional	1957	réservé	adj	reserved
1784	incident	adj, nm	incident	1959	espagnol	nm, adj	Spanish
1789	exprès	adj[pl], adv	deliberately, on purpose, intentionally	1960	solide	nm, adj(f)	solid
1791	rond	adj, nm, nf	round, circle, patrol,	1970	veuf	nmf, adj	widow, widowed, widower
1793	fichu	adj	damn, rotten	1978	timide	adj(f)	timid, shy, bashful
1799	furieux	adj	furious, raging, violent, mad	1979	fermé	adj	shut, closed, locked

1982	**célibataire**	*adj, nf, nm*	single
1990	**mondial**	*adj*	world, global
1992	**généreux**	*adj*	generous
2009	**pervers**	*nmf; adj[pl]*	pervert; perverse, perverted
2012	**immense**	*adj(f)*	immense
2017	**manuel**	*adj, nm*	manual
2018	**cruel**	*adj*	cruel, ferocious, bitter
2020	**méchant**	*adj*	bad, mean
2024	**léger**	*adj*	light, slight, thin
2026	**publique**	*adj, nf*	public
2033	**nucléaire**	*adj, nm*	nuclear, nuclear power
2034	**populaire**	*adj(f)*	popular
2037	**nue**	*adj*	naked
2044	**issu**	*adj*	descended from, come from
2051	**mortel**	*nmf, adj*	mortal, deadly, lethal
2058	**sain**	*adj*	healthy, sane
2063	**impressionnant**	*adj*	impressive, upsetting
2071	**solitaire**	*adj(f, nmf*	solitary, lone, lonely, loner
2075	**original**	*nm, adj*	original
2076	**trompe**	*adj*	horn, trunk
2080	**clinique**	*adj(f), nf*	clinical, private hospital
2083	**suprême**	*adj*	supreme
2084	**sincère**	*adj*	sincere
2086	**violent**	*adj*	violent
2089	**franc**	*adj, adv, adj, nm*	frank; franc
2091	**excitant**	*adj*	exciting
2097	**splendide**	*adj*	magnificent, wonderful
2105	**efficace**	*adj(f)*	efficient, effective
2110	**divin**	*adj, nm*	divine, heavenly
2112	**négatif**	*adj, nm*	negative
2115	**invisible**	*adj(f)*	invisible
2131	**prime**	*noun, adj(f), nf*	free gift, premium, bonus
2148	**remarquable**	*adj(f)*	remarkable, outstanding
2151	**ennuyeux**	*adj*	boring, annoying, dull
2152	**ouvrier**	*nmf, adj*	worker, working-class
2161	**complexe**	*nm, adj(f)*	complex
2173	**fabuleux**	*adj*	fabulous
2175	**illégal**	*adj*	illegal
2186	**plastique**	*nm, adj(f)*	plastic
2193	**chanceux**	*adj*	fortunate, lucky
2201	**chagrin**	*adj, nm*	grief, sorrow
2204	**gratuit**	*adj*	free, gratuitous, unwarranted
2205	**britannique**	*adj(f)*	British
2206	**social**	*adj*	social
2208	**vire**	*adj*	fired
2216	**sexuel**	*adj*	sexual
2223	**reconnaissant**	*adj*	grateful
2238	**gris**	*nm, adj[pl]*	gray
2244	**armé**	*adj*	armed
2246	**communiste**	*adj(f, nmf*	communist
2251	**essentiel**	*nm, adj*	essential
2272	**pourvu**	*adj; adv*	equiped with; so long as, provided
2281	**mobile**	*adj(f), nm*	mobile, portable; motive
2303	**royal**	*adj*	royal
2305	**officiel**	*adj, nmf*	official
2327	**quitte**	*adj*	to be clear off, quits
2334	**ravissant**	*adj*	delightful, ravishing
2337	**lave**	*adj*	washed
2342	**capital**	*nm, nf, adj*	major, chief, principal; capital, assets
2345	**suisse**	*adj(f)*	Swiss

2357	**médical**	*adj*	medical		2428	**égoïste**	*adj, nm, nf*	selfish, egoist
2359	**guerrier**	*nmf, adj*	warrior; warlike		2438	**commercial**	*adj, nm*	commercial, marketeer
2373	**dégueulasse**	*adj*	disgusting, filthy		2444	**éternel**	*adj*	eternal
2390	**vain**	*adj*	vain		2460	**civil**	*adj, nm*	civil; civilian
2392	**parent**	*nmf, adj*	parent		2462	**gras**	*adj[pl], adv, nm[pl]*	fatty, fat, greasy
2400	**fameux**	*adj[pl]*	famous					
2402	**nègre**	*nm, adj*	negro		2465	**pompier**	*adj, nm*	fireman, firefighter
2403	**catholique**	*nmf, adj(f)*	catholic		2467	**tragique**	*adj(f), nm*	tragic, tragedy
2405	**misérable**	*nmf, adj*	miserable, wretched		2476	**fixe**	*adj, nm*	fixed, set; base salary
2411	**meuble**	*nm, adj(f)*	piece of furniture		2478	**menu**	*nm, adv, adj*	menu, slender, slim, minor
2412	**foutu**	*adj*	fucking, damned					
2426	**volontaire**	*nmf, adj(f)*	volunteer; voluntary		2483	**légal**	*adj*	legal
					2495	**doue**	*adj*	talented, gifted

B. Adverbs

Rank	French	PoS	English
4	**pas**	*adv, nm[pl]*	not; footstep
7	**là**	*adv, int*	there, here
9	**que, qu'**	*adv, conj, pron*	that, which, who, whom, as
15	**ne, n´**	*adv*	not
17	**en**	*adv, prep, pron*	in, by
24	**mais**	*adv, conj, int*	but
25	**y**	*adv, ni, pron*	there
28	**bien**	*adj(i), adv, nm*	well
30	**si**	*adv, conj, ni*	if, whether
31	**tout**	*adv, det, nm, adj, pron*	all, very
32	**plus**	*adv*	more, no
33	**non**	*adv, ni*	no, not
38	**oui**	*adv, ni*	yes
43	**comme**	*adv, conj*	like, as
46	**ici**	*adv*	here
50	**là**	*adv, int*	there, here
51	**rien**	*adv, nm, pron*	nothing
53	**où**	*adv, pron*	where
55	**pourquoi**	*adv, conj, ni*	why
56	**quand**	*adv, conj*	when
61	**alors**	*adv*	then, so
62	**comment**	*adv, conj, int, ni*	how
63	**bon**	*adj, adv, int, nm*	good
64	**ou**	*adv, pron*	where
65	**très**	*adv*	very
66	**même**	*adj(f), adv, pron*	same, even, self
68	**jamais**	*adv*	never
69	**aussi**	*adv, conj*	too, also, as
75	**maintenant**	*adv*	now
76	**encore**	*adv*	again, yet
77	**peu**	*adv*	little
78	**vraiment**	*adv*	truly, really, very
80	**toujours**	*adv*	always
84	**juste**	*adv, nm, adj(f)*	just, only; fair
86	**quelque**	*adv, adj, det*	some
90	**trop**	*adv*	too much, too many
99	**avant**	*adj(i), adv, nm, prep*	before
105	**vrai**	*adv, nm, adj*	true
107	**mal**	*adj(i), adv, nm*	bad, sore
109	**après**	*adv*	after
112	**mieux**	*adj(i)[pl], adv, nm*	better
113	**petit**	*adv, nm, adj*	small, little
114	**beaucoup**	*adv*	much, a lot of, many
117	**depuis**	*adv, prep*	since, for , in
122	**déjà**	*adv*	already, ever
143	**vite**	*adv*	fast, quickly
146	**soit**	*adv, conj*	either...or

154	**bas**	adv, nm&f, adj[pl], nm[pl]	low; bass; stockings
155	**moins**	adj(i)[pl], adv, nm[pl], prep	less
158	**demain**	adv, nm	tomorrow
160	**grand**	adv, nm/f, adj	great, older girl or boy, tall
167	**assez**	adv	enough
171	**puis**	adv	then, so
172	**tard**	adv	late
181	**combien**	adv, conj	how much, how many
182	**tant**	adv	so much, so many
194	**contre**	adv, nm, prep	against
221	**longtemps**	adv	a long time, a long while
224	**seulement**	adv	only
234	**ensemble**	adv, nm	together
242	**devant**	adv, nm, prep	in front, ahead
247	**dessus**	adv, nm[pl], prep	above, on top
249	**fin**	adj, adv, nf, nm	end; gist, clever person
255		adj, adv, nm	right
258	**loin**	adv, nm	far
262	**gros**	adv, nm, adj[pl]	big, whoiesale, heavy
268	**enfin**	adv	at last, finally
272	**fort**	adv, adj, nm	strong
284	**point**	adv, nm	point
285	**dehors**	adv, nm[pl], prep	outside
286	**hier**	adv	yesterday
289	**près**	adv, prep	near, nearby, close by
292	**ainsi**	adv	thus
293	**haut**	adv, adj	top, high
298	**plein**	adv, nm, adj, prep	full
304	**plutôt**	adv	rather
311	**bientôt**	adv	soon
314	**tellement**	adv	so much
315	**derrière**	adv, nm, prep	last; behind
317	**presque**	adv	almost
318	**meilleur**	nmf, adj, adv	best, better,
325	**dur**	adv, nm&f, adj	hard
329	**ben**	adv	well
348	**dedans**	adv, nm[pl], prep	inside, indoors
353	**autant**	adv	as much, as many
363	**parfois**	adv	sometimes
367	**ci**	adv, pron	this one, here
372	**mauvais**	adv, nm, adj[pl]	bad, wrong
380	**exactement**	adv	exactly
392	**partout**	adv	everywhere, all over the place
393	**cher**	adj, adv	expensive
411	**tôt**	adj(i), adv	early
415	**surtout**	adv, nm	especially, above all
418	**ensuite**	adv	next
427	**souvent**	adv	often
430	**sûrement**	adv	surely
446	**force**	adv, nf	force
450	**grave**	adv, adj(f), nm	serious, grave
467	**long**	adv, adj, nm	long, lengthy, length

498	ailleurs	*adv*	elsewhere, somewhere else
522	faux	*adv, adj[pl], nm[pl], nf[pl]*	false; scythe
526	debout	*adv*	standing
535	absolument	*adv*	absolutely
550	chaud	*adv, nm, adj*	warm, hot
552	doucement	*adv*	gently, softly
561	complètement	*adv*	completely, fully
562	clair	*adv, adj*	clear
593	autour	*adv, nm*	around
598	simplement	*adv*	simply, just
619	arriere	*adj(i), adv, nm*	back, rear
626	pourtant	*adv*	yet, nonetheless, nevertheless
656	hors	*adv, prep*	except, outside
721	probablement	*adv*	probably
756	environ	*adv, prep, nm*	about, thereabouts, or so
818	immediatement	*adv*	immediately
830	certainement	*adv*	certainly
844	court	*adj, adv, nm*	short
895	frais	*adj[pl], adv, nm[pl]*	cool, fresh; fee, expense
937	doux	*adv, noun, adj[pl]*	soft, sweet
965	force	*adv, nf*	force
973	finalement	*adv*	finally, eventually
978	justement	*adv*	exactly, rightly, precisely
1016	proche	*adv, noun, adj(f), prep*	nearby, close
1032	lors	*adv*	at the time of, during

1038	dessous	*adv, nm[pl], prep*	underneath, below, bottom, underside
1056	attendant	*adv*	meanwhile
1074	parfaitement	*adv*	perfectly
1093	cesse	*adv*	constantly, always
1110	sérieusement	*adv*	seriously
1115	autrement	*adv*	differently, something else, otherwise
1143	apparemment	*adv*	apparently
1174	désormais	*adv*	from now on, henceforth
1182	pis	*adv, nm[pl]*	worse
1198	également	*adv*	also, too, as well, equally
1205	franchement	*adv*	frankly
1241	rapidement	*adv*	quickly, rapidly
1266	malheureusement	*adv*	unfortunately
1275	totalement	*adv*	totally
1278	soudain	*adj, adv*	sudden, suddenly
1279	heureusement	*adv*	fortunately, luckily
1295	bref	*adj, adv, nm*	brief, short
1314	piano	*adv, nm*	piano
1323	évidemment	*adv*	obviously
1327	delà	*adv*	beyond, above, over
1334	directement	*adv*	directly
1337	demi	*adj(i), adv, nm*	half

1356	**sec**	*adj, adv, nm*	dry
1359	**facilement**	*adv*	easily
1414	**évident**	*adv*	obviously, of course
1422	**davantage**	*adv*	more
1467	**quant**	*adv*	as for
1477	**lentement**	*adv*	slowly
1487	**auprès**	*adv*	nearby, close to, next to
1511	**jaune**	*adv, noun, adj(f)*	yellow
1534	**cependant**	*adv, conj*	however
1555	**profond**	*adv, noun, adj*	deep
1561	**récemment**	*adv*	recently
1629	**ordinaire**	*adv, nm, adj(f)*	ordinary
1634	**autrefois**	*adv*	in the past
1638	**forcément**	*adv*	without question, inevitably
1684	**large**	*adj(f), adv, nm*	wide, width
1688	**uniquement**	*adv*	only
1705	**réellement**	*adv*	really
1733	**naturellement**	*adv*	naturally
1789	**exprès**	*adj[pl], adv*	deliberately, on purpose, intentionally
1798	**clairement**	*adv*	clearly
1812	**tandis**	*adv*	while
1816	**auparavant**	*adv*	beforehand
1834	**profondément**	*adv*	profoundly, deeply
1837	**entièrement**	*adv*	entirely, completely
1858	**concernant**	*adv, prep*	concerning
1870	**personnellement**	*adv*	personally
1924	**extrêmement**	*adv*	extremely
1964	**normalement**	*adv*	normally
2004	**suffisamment**	*adv*	sufficiently
2089	**franc**	*adj, adv, adj, nm*	frank; franc
2092	**guère**	*adv*	hardly
2144	**rarement**	*adv*	rarely, seldom
2217	**honnêtement**	*adv*	honestly
2224	**particulièrement**	*adv*	particulary
2236	**jusque**	*adv, prep*	to, up to, until, till
2241	**pratiquement**	*adv*	practically
2257	**volontiers**	*adv*	with pleasure, willingly, gladly
2272	**pourvu**	*adj; adv*	equiped with; so long as, provided
2286	**terriblement**	*adv*	terribly, awfully
2346	**énormément**	*adv*	enormously
2365	**carrément**	*adv*	completely, directly, straight out
2372	**certes**	*adv*	indeed, certainly, of course
2394	**etc**	*adv*	et cetera , etc.

2407	**sincèrement**	*adv*	truly, sincerely
2410	**actuellement**	*adv*	at present, at the moment
2419	**précisément**	*adv*	precisely
2422	**correctement**	*adv*	properly
2455	**partant**	*adv*	thus, consequencly, therefore
2462	**gras**	*adj[pl], adv, nm[pl]*	fatty, fat, greasy
2475	**officiellement**	*adv*	officially
2478	**menu**	*nm, adv, adj*	menu, slender, slim, minor

220

C. Conjunctions

Rank	French	PoS	English
9	que, qu'	adv, conj, pron	that, which, who, whom, as
12	et	conj	and
24	mais	adv, conj, int	but
30	si	adv, conj, num	if, whether
43	comme	adv, conj	like, as
55	pourquoi	adv, conj, num	why
56	quand	adv, conj	when
62	comment	adv, conj, int, num	how
69	aussi	adv, conj	too, also, as
111	parce que	conj	because
124	donc	conj	so, then, therefore, thus
146	soit	adv, conj	either...or
181	combien	adv, conj	how much, how many
193	num	conj	nor
227	car	conj, nm	because
397	sinon	conj	otherwise, or else, or
431	or	conj, nm	gold; hence, thus
506	allô	conj	hello
840	lorsque	conj	when
908	puisque	conj	since
1534	cependant	adv, conj	however

D. Determiners

Rank	French	PoS	English
1	**de, du, de la, de l', des**	*det, prep*	of, from, some, any
5	**le, la, les, l´**	*det, pron*	the; him, her, it, them
10	**un, une, des**	*adj, det, nm, pron*	a, an, one
13	**à, au, aux**	*det, prep*	to, at, in
16	**ce, cet, cette, ces**	*det, pron*	this, that
31	**tout**	*adv, det, nm, adj, pron*	all, very
34	**mon, ma, mes**	*det*	my
54	**votre**	*det*	your
58	**son, sa, ses**	*det, nm*	his, her, its; sound; bran
59	**ton, ta, tes**	*det, nm*	your; tone
72	**deux**	*det, num*	two, couple
81	**notre**	*det*	our
86	**quelque**	*adv, adj, det*	some
98	**leur**	*det, adj(f), pron*	them, their, theirs
120	**quel**	*det, adj, pron*	which, what
149	**trois**	*det, num*	three
229	**chaque**	*det, adj*	each, every
238	**aucun**	*det, adj, pron*	none, either, neither, not any
253	**premier**	*det, nm&f, adj*	first, premier, first,
290	**cinq**	*det, nm[pl]*	five
303	**quatre**	*det, num*	four
366	**six**	*det, num*	six
408	**dix**	*det, num*	ten
477	**certain**	*adj, det, nm, pron*	certain, sure
504	**second**	*adj, det, nm*	second
521	**neuf**	*det, adj, num*	nine; new
586	**sept**	*det, num*	seven
621	**huit**	*det, num*	eight
633	**tel**	*adj, det, pron*	such
635	**plusieurs**	*det, adj, pron*	several
683	**mille**	*det, nm, num*	thousand
687	**seconde**	*det, nf*	second
725	**nul**	*adj, det, pron*	nil, null
802	**deuxième**	*det, nm, nf*	second
852	**cent**	*det, nm*	one hundred, cent
995	**troisième**	*det, nm, nf*	third
1055	**vôtre**	*det*	your (form & pl)
1212	**vingt**	*det, num*	twenty
1625	**douze**	*det, num*	twelve
1675	**nôtre**	*det*	our
1774	**quinze**	*det, num*	fifteen
1842	**trente**	*det, num*	thirty
2243	**cinquante**	*det, num*	fifty
2450	**onze**	*det, num*	eleven

E. Interjections

Rank	French	PoS	English
7	là	adv, int	there, here
24	mais	adv, conj, int	but
50	là	adv, int	there, here
62	comment	adv, conj, int, num	how
63	bon	adj, adv, int, nm	good
67	merci	int, nm, nf	thank you; favor
83	oh	int	oh
95	dieu	int, nm	god
127	ouais	int	yeah
134	merde	int, nf	sh*t, crap
140	salut	int, nm	salute, hi, bye
153	ah	int	ah, oh
163	hein	int	eh, huh
174	eh	int	hey, uh
355	parfait	nm, adj, int	perfect
483	euh	int	er, um, uh
536	dame	int, nf	lady
579	diable	int, nm	devil
634	bravo	int, nm	bravo, well done
768	adieu	int, nm	goodbye, farewell, adieu
832	ha	int	oh
943	stop	nm, int	stop
1043	gare	int, nf	station, railway station; beware
1178	hum	int	um, uh, Hmm
1199	mince	adj(f), int	thin, slim, slender
1263	chouette	nf, adj, int	owl, nice, awesome!
1371	dame	int, nf	lady
1459	tien(s)	noun, adj[pl], int	ah, well
1500	chut	int	hush
1710	ouah	int	wow!
2088	coucou	int	hello
2134	zut	int	heck

F. Nouns

Rank	French	PoS	English
3	être	nm, v	to be; being
4	pas	adv, nm[pl]	not; footstep
10	un, une, des	adj, det, nm, pron	a, an, one
14	avoir	nm, v	asset, to have
21	moi	nm, pron	me
28	bien	adj(i), adv, nm	well
31	tout	adv, det, nm, adj, pron	all, very
39	aller	nm, v	to go
40	toi	nm, pron	you, yourself
41	faire	nm, v	to do, make
44	sur	adj, prep	on, upon
47	savoir	nm, v	to know
49	vouloir	nm, v	to want
51	rien	adv, nm, pron	nothing
52	dire	nm, v	to say
58	son, sa, ses	det, nm	his, her, its; sound; bran
59	ton, ta, tes	det, nm	your; tone
60	pouvoir	nm, v	can, to be able to
63	bon	adj, adv, int, nm	good
66	même	adj(f), adv, pron	same, even, self
67	merci	int, nm, nf	thank you; favor
70	chose	adj(f), nf	thing
74	autre	adj(f), pron	other
79	temps	nm[pl]	time
82	vie	nf	life
84	juste	adv, nm, adj(f)	just, only; fair
86	quelque	adv, adj, det	some
87	monde	nm	world, people
88	accord	nm	agreement
89	fois	nf[pl]	time, times
93	devoir	nm, v	to have to, owe; duty
94	père	nm	father
95	dieu	int, nm	god
96	homme	nm	man
97	sûr	adj, prep	on, upon
98	leur	det, adj(f), pron	them, their, theirs
99	avant	adj(i), adv, nm, prep	before
100	besoin	nm	need
101	femme	nf	woman, wife
102	personne	nf, pron	person, people, anybody, anyone nobody, no-one
105	vrai	adv, nm, adj	true
106	an	nm	year
107	mal	adj(i), adv, nm	bad, sore
108	parler	nm, v	to speak, talk
110	mort	adj, nf	dead; death
112	mieux	adj(i)[pl], adv, nm	better
113	petit	adv, nm, adj	small, little
115	monsieur	nm	mister, sir, gentleman
119	mère	nf	mother

120	**quel**	*det, adj, pron*	which, what
121	**fille**	*nf*	girl, daughter
123	**gens**	*nmpl*	people
125	**jour**	*nm*	day
126	**soir**	*nm*	evening
128	**argent**	*nm*	money, silver
129	**maison**	*nf*	house
130	**nom**	*nm*	name
131	**bonjour**	*nm*	hello
132	**penser**	*nm, v*	to think
133	**nuit**	*nf*	night
134	**merde**	*int, nf*	sh*t, crap
135	**papa**	*nm*	dad, daddy
136	**maman**	*nf*	mom
138	**peur**	*nf*	fear
139	**désolé**	*adj*	sorry, afraid
140	**salut**	*int, nm*	salute, hi, bye
141	**seul**	*adj*	alone, only
147	**air**	*nm*	air, appearance
151	**chose**	*adj(f), nf*	thing
152	**fil**	*nm*	thread, wire
154	**bas**	*adv, nm&f, adj[pl], nm[pl]*	low; bass; stockings
155	**moins**	*adj(i)[pl], adv, nm[pl], prep*	less
157	**passe**	*nf, adj, prep*	pass, past
158	**demain**	*adv, nm*	tomorrow
160	**grand**	*adv, nm/f, adj*	great, older girl or boy, tall
161	**tête**	*nf*	head
165	**raison**	*nf*	reason
166	**enfant**	*nm, nf, adj(f)*	child
168	**moment**	*nm*	moment
169	**amour**	*nm*	love
170	**heure**	*nf*	hour
175	**ami**	*nm/f, adj*	friend
179	**gars**	*nm[pl]*	guy
180	**chance**	*nf*	luck; chance
183	**part**	*nf*	share
184	**voiture**	*nf*	car
185	**problème**	*nm*	problem
186	**coup**	*nm*	coup, blow, knock, stroke
187	**porte**	*nf*	door
188	**travail**	*nm*	work
189	**famille**	*nf*	family
190	**sens**	*nm[pl]*	sense, meaning
191	**putain**	*nf*	whore, bitch; stupid
192	**idée**	*nf*	idea
194	**contre**	*adv, nm, prep*	against
200	**vieux**	*adj[pl], nm[pl]*	old
201	**attention**	*nf*	attention
206	**sang**	*nm*	blood
207	**histoire**	*nf*	history, story
209	**question**	*nf*	question
210	**frère**	*nm*	brother
211	**ville**	*nf*	city
213	**nouveau**	*adj, nm*	new
215	**truc**	*nm*	trick; (that) thing (what I can't recall)
217	**œil**	*nm*	eye
218	**moi**	*nm, pron*	me
220	**mec**	*nm*	guy
222	**beau**	*adj, nm*	handsome, fine, right
223	**police**	*nf*	police
226	**eau**	*nf*	water
227	**car**	*conj, nm*	because
228	**super**	*adj(i), nm*	great
229	**chaque**	*det, adj*	each, every
230	**cas**	*nm[pl]*	case
231	**terre**	*nf*	earth, world, soil, land
233	**main**	*nf*	hand
234	**ensemble**	*adv, nm*	together

235	type	nm	type; guy
236	pardon	nm	forgiveness
237	vers	nm[pl], prep	toward; verse
238	aucun	det, adj, pron	none, either, neither, not any
239	guerre	nf	war
240	suite	nf	result, follow-up, rest
242	devant	adv, nm, prep	in front, ahead
243	arrivé	adj	arrived, happen
245	matin	nm	morning
246	aide	nm, nf	help, assistance
247	dessus	adv, nm[pl], prep	above, on top
248	genre	nm	type, kind, sort
249	fin	adj, adv, nf, nm	end; gist, clever person
251	jeune	nmf adj(f)	young
252	chéri	noun, adj	darling, love, dear
253	premier	det, nm&f, adj	first, premier, first,
255		adj, adv, nm	right
256	côté	nf	coast
257	chambre	nf	bedroom, chamber
258	loin	adv, nm	far
259	feu	adj(f), nm	fire
261	train	nm	train
262	gros	adv, nm, adj[pl]	big, whoiesale, heavy
265	dernier	nm&f, adj	last
266	minute	nf	minute
267	mari	nm	husband
269	madame	nf	madam, lady
270	façon	nf	way, manner

271	film	nm	film, movie
272	fort	adv, adj, nm	strong
273	écoute	nf	listening
274	pays	nm[pl]	country
275	affaire	nf, adj	case, matter, business
276	endroit	nm	place, spot
277	corps	nm[pl]	body
278	fou	adj, nm	mad, crazy
279	vivre	nm, v	to live
280	prêt	adj, nm	ready
283	cause	nf	cause
284	point	adv, nm	point
285	dehors	adv, nm[pl], prep	outside
287	boulot	adj, nm	work, job
288	garçon	nm	boy
290	cinq	det, nm[pl]	five
291	chef	nm	head, leader, chief
293	haut	adv, adj	top, high
295	bébé	nmf, adj(f)	baby
296	possible	adj(f)	possible
297	école	nf	school
298	plein	adv, nm, adj, prep	full
299	année	nf	year
300	manger	nm, v	to eat
301	docteur	nm	doctor
302	tour	nm, nf	tower; turn; tour
306	semaine	nf	week
307	vérité	nf	truth
309	capitaine	nm	captain
310	affaire	nf	business, matter
312	instant	adj, nm	instant, moment
315	derrière	adv, nm, prep	last; behind
318	meilleur	nmf, adj, adv	best, better,

319	**numéro**	*nm*	number
320	**journée**	*nf*	day
321	**dollar**	*nm*	dollar
322	**confiance**	*nf*	confidence, trust
323	**garde**	*nm, nf*	guard
324	**souvenir**	*nm, v*	memory; to remember
325	**dur**	*adv, nm&f, adj*	hard
326	**bureau**	*nm*	office, desk
327	**abord**	*nm*	manner; approach, access, environs
328	**important**	*nm, adj*	important
331	**cours**	*nfpl, nm[pl]*	course
332	**seigneur**	*nm*	lord
334	**route**	*nf*	road
335	**cul**	*nm*	bum, arse, ass
336	**minute**	*nf*	minute
337	**bonsoir**	*nm*	good evening
338	**jeu**	*nm*	game
339	**ferme**	*adj*	shut, closed, locked
340	**plaisir**	*nm*	pleasure
341	**heureux**	*adj[pl]*	happy, lucky, fortunate
342	**mot**	*nm*	word
343	**musique**	*nf*	music
344	**chien**	*nm*	dog
345	**messieurs**	*nmpl*	gentlemen
346	**calme**	*nm, adj(f)*	composure, calm
347	**parent**	*nm&f, adj*	parent
348	**dedans**	*adv, nm[pl], prep*	inside, indoors
349	**mariage**	*nm*	marriage, wedding
352	**lit**	*nm*	bed
355	**parfait**	*nm, adj, int*	perfect
356	**cœur**	*nm*	heart
358	**service**	*nm*	service

360	**pauvre**	*nmf, adj(f)*	poor
361	**mademoiselle**	*nf*	Miss
362	**drôle**	*adj(f), nm*	funny, strange
364	**retour**	*nm*	return
365	**verre**	*nm*	glass
368	**impossible**	*nm, adj(f)*	impossible
370	**facile**	*adj(f)*	easy
371	**maître**	*nm*	master
372	**mauvais**	*adv, nm, adj[pl]*	bad, wrong
373	**général**	*nm, adj*	general
374	**doute**	*nm*	doubt
375	**prison**	*nf*	prison, jail
377	**faute**	*nf*	mistake, error, fault
379	**bras**	*nm[pl]*	arm
382	**café**	*nm*	coffee, café
383	**gentil**	*adj*	nice, kind
385	**lieu**	*nm*	place
386	**malade**	*nmf, adj(f)*	mental patient; ill, sick
388	**roi**	*nm*	king
390	**président**	*nm*	president
393	**cher**	*adj, adv*	expensive
396	**équipe**	*nf*	team
398	**esprit**	*nm*	mind, spirit
399	**plan**	*adj, nm*	plan
401	**boire**	*nm, v*	to drink
402	**propre**	*nm, adj(f)*	particular; clean, proper
403	**état**	*nm*	state
404	**bois**	*nm[pl]*	wood
409	**génial**	*adj*	inspired, great, brilliant
410	**sécurité**	*nf*	security, safety, health
411	**tôt**	*adj(i), adv*	early
414	**avis**	*nm[pl]*	opinion, mind
415	**surtout**	*adv, nm*	especially, above all
416	**difficile**	*adj(f)*	difficult

419	pire	adj(f), nm	worse, worst
420	simple	adj(f)	simple, single
421	paix	nf[pl]	peace
422	sujet	nm	subject, topic
423	retard	nm	delay, late
424	livre	nm, nf	book; pound
426	sale	adj(f)	dirty
428	sauf	adj, prep	except
429	choix	nm[pl]	choice
431	or	conj, nm	gold; hence, thus
432	visage	nm	face
433	ordre	nm	order
434	noir	nmf adj	black (wo)man), black
435	dîner	nm, v	dinner; to dine
436	âge	nm	age
437	chemin	nm	path, way
439	face	nf	front, side, face
440	rue	nf	street
441	inquiet	adj	worried, anxious
442	photo	nf	photo
443	sérieux	nm, adj[pl]	seriousness, serious
444	ciel	nm	sky
445	honneur	nm	honor
446	force	adv, nf	force
449	million	nm	million
450	grave	adv, adj(f), nm	serious, grave
451	voix	nf[pl]	voice
452	courant	adj, nm	current
453	propos	nm[pl]	remark
454	bateau	nm	boat, ship
455	con	adj, nmf	stupid
456	gauche	nf, adj(f)	left
457	content	adj	glad, pleased, happy
458	prix	nm[pl]	price; prize
459	rouge	nm, adj(f)	red

460	faim	nf	hungry
461	avion	nm	plane
462	devenir	nm, v	to become
463	prochain	adj, nm	next; fellow man
465	voyage	nm	trip, journey
466	sorte	nf	sort, kind
467	long	adv, adj, nm	long, lengthy, length
468	espèce	nf	species
469	idiot	nmf, adj	idiot, fool, stupid
470	gueule	nf	mouth, trap
471	début	nm	beginning
473	continu	adj	continuous
474	hôpital	nm	hospital
475	grâce	nf	thanks, grace, favor
476	message	nm	message
477	certain	adj, det, nm, pron	certain, sure
478	patron	nm	boss
482	oncle	nm	uncle
484	bienvenue	nf, adj	welcome
486	camp	nm	camp
488	soleil	nm	sun
489	cheveu	nm	hair
490	arme	adj	armed
491	salle	nf	room
492	bizarre	adj(f)	strange, odd
496	pièce	nf	piece, part, component; room
497	erreur	nf	mistake, error
499	rapport	nm	relationship, report
500	froid	nm, adj	cold
501	scène	nf	scene
502	secret	nm, adj	secret
503	sac	nm	bag, sack
504	second	adj, det, nm	second
505	cru	adj	vintage, raw, crude
508	hôtel	nm	hotel
509	soirée	nf	evening

510	sœur	nf	sister
511	pied	nm	foot
512	carte	nf	card
513	joli	adj	pretty, attractive
514	groupe	nm	group
516	agent	nm, nf	agent
517	effet	nm	effect
518	libre	adj(f)	free
519	foutre	v, nm	to f*ck, shove off, piss off
520	bordel	nm	brothel, mess, chaos
521	neuf	det, adj, num	nine; new
522	faux	adv, adj[pl], nm[pl], nf[pl]	false; scythe
523	situation	nf	situation
525	lumière	nf	light
527	Noël	nm	Christmas
528	cheval	nm	horse
529	intérieur	nm adj	interior, inside
531	loi	nf	law
532	incroyable	adj(f)	incredible, amazing, unbelievable
533	lettre	nf	letter
534	présent	nm, adj	present
536	dame	int, nf	lady
537	professeur	nm, nf	professor, teacher
538	fric	nm	cash, money, dough
540	coin	nm	corner
541	table	nf	table
542	colonel	nm	colonel
543	âme	nf	soul
544	dos	nm[pl]	back
545	magnifique	adj(f)	magnificent
549	tranquille	adj(f)	quiet
550	chaud	adv, nm, adj	warm, hot
553	pareil	adj, nm	similar, likewise; peer, equal; the same
554	accident	nm	accident
555	appel	nm	call, phone call
556	anniversaire	nm, adj(f)	anniversary, birthday
557	blanc	adj, nm	white
558	risque	nm	risk
559	moyen	adj, nm	means, way; medium
562	clair	adv, adj	clear
563	meurtre	nm	murder
564	toucher	nm, v	to touch
565	dejeuner	nm, v	lunch, to eat lunch
567	lire	nf, v	to read; italian lira
568	avance	nf	advance
570	forme	nf	form
571	bord	nm	edge, side
573	mer	nf	sea
574	medecin	nm	physician, doctor
575	midi	nm	noon
576	porter	nm, v	to wear, carry
578	silence	nm	silence
579	diable	int, nm	devil
580	cadeau	nm	present, gift
582	flic	nm, nf	cop
583	avocat	nm	lawyer
585	anglais	nm, adj[pl]	English
587	moitié	nf	half
590	exact	adj	exact, correct
592	télé	nf	TV
593	autour	adv, nm	around
595	ligne	nf	line
597	arrivée	nf	arrival
599	mission	nf	mission
600	balle	nf	ball, bullet
603	classe	nf	class
604	pari	nm	bet, wager
605	peuple	nm	people
606	habitude	nf	habit

607	voie	nf	road, lane, route, track, way
608	dangereux	adj[pl]	dangerous
609	pote	nm	mate
610	contrôle	nm	control
611	honte	nf	shame
612	impression	nf	impression
613	fou	adj, nm	mad, crazy
617	chanson	nf	song, tune
618	trou	nm	hole
619	arriere	adj(i), adv, nm	back, rear
620	poste	nm, nf	post, position, job; post office
622	radio	adj(i), nm, nf	radio
624	attaque	nf	attack
625	baiser	nm, v	to kiss
627	réponse	nf	answer, response
628	connard	nm	shithead, asshole
629	pute	nf	whore, bitch, prostitute
630	bande	nf	band, strip
631	enfer	nm	hell
632	triste	adj(f)	sad
633	tel	adj, det, pron	such
634	bravo	int, nm	bravo, well done
635	plusieurs	det, adj, pron	several
637	rire	nm, v	to laugh
638	compagnie	nf	company
639	étrange	adj(f)	strange, odd
640	exemple	nm	example
641	combat	nm	fight, combat, battle
642	secours	nm[pl]	help, aid, assistance
643	connerie	nf	crap, bullsh*t, stupidity
645	coucher	nm, v	lie down, sleep
647	merveilleux	adj[pl]	marvellous, wonderful
650	lune	nf	moon
651	bouche	nf	mouth
652	sud	adj(i), nm	south
654	ennui	nm	boredom, trouble, worry
655	but	nm	goal, aim, objective, purpose
657	sortie	nf	exit
658	boîte	nf	box
659	vol	nm	flight, theft
660	public	nm, adj	public, audience
661	lieutenant	nm	lieutenant
662	système	nm	system
663	époque	nf	era, period
664	bête	nf, adj(f)	animal, beast; stupid
666	avenir	nm	future
667	santé	nf	health
668	amoureux	nmf, adj[pl]	lover; in love, amorous
669	cuisine	nf	cooking, kitchen
670	normal	adj	normal
671	danger	nm	danger
672	gouvernement	nm	government
673	village	nm	village
676	journal	nm	newspaper, paper
677	approche	nf	approach
678	dommage	nm	damage, harm; too bad, a pity
679	peau	nf	skin
680	nez	nm[pl]	nose
682	sympa	adj	friendly, nice, kind
683	mille	det, nm, num	thousand
684	héros	nm[pl]	hero
685	banque	nf	bank
686	clé	nf	key
687	seconde	det, nf	second
688	nord	adj(i), nm	north

689	inspecteur	nm	inspector
690	liberté	nf	liberty, freedom
691	salaud	nm	bastard
692	cour	nf	yard, court
693	juge	nm, nf	judge
694	terrible	adj(f)	terrible, dreadful
696	crime	nm	crime
698	thé	nm	tea
699	bonheur	nm	happiness
700	tas	nm[pl]	pile, lots of, heap
701	travers	nm[pl]	breadth, across; fault, amiss
702	stupide	adj(f)	stupid, silly, bemused
703	blague	nf	joke
705	conseil	nm	advice, counsel, council
707	rêve	nm	dream
708	pitié	nf	pity, mercy
709	vin	nm	wine
710	don	nm	gift
711	sol	nm	floor, ground
712	vent	nm	wind
713	club	nm	club
714	gamin	nm	kid
715	tante	nf	aunt
716	bar	nm	bar
717	milieu	nm	middle
718	reine	nf	queen
720	centre	nm	center, centre
722	bière	nf	beer, coffin
723	dingue	adj	crazy, mad, wild, nutty
724	inutile	adj(f)	useless
725	nul	adj, det, pron	nil, null
727	différent	adj	different
729	vêtement	nm	garment, item or article of clothing
730	liste	nf	list
732	société	nf	society
733	soin	nm	care
734	pierre	nf	stone
738	parole	nf	word
740	départ	nm	departure
741	ennemi	nmf, adj	enemy
742	spectacle	nm	sight, show
743	recherche	nf	research, search
745	intérêt	nm	interest
747	rôle	nm	role
748	félicitations	nf	congratulations
751	position	nf	position
752	blessé	adj, nmf	injured; injured person, causualty
753	humain	nm, adj	human
754	match	nm	match, game
755	coupable	nmf, adj(f)	guilty
756	environ	adv, prep, nm	about, thereabouts, or so
757	art	nm	art
758	espoir	nm	hope
759	mur	nm	wall
760	église	nf	church
761	salope	nf	slut
762	beauté	nf	beauty
763	lâche	adj	loose
766	colère	nf	anger, wrath
767	directeur	nmf, adj	director
768	adieu	int, nm	goodbye, farewell, adieu
770	tort	nm	wrong
772	américain	adj, nm	American, American English,
773	revenu	nm	income
774	justice	nf	justice
775	soldat	nm	soldier
776	expérience	nf	experience
777	cerveau	nm	brain
778	fenêtre	nf	window
779	quartier	nm	district, quarter
780	prince	nm	prince

781	**riche**	*adj(f)*	rich
782	**fleur**	*nf*	flower
784	**presse**	*nf*	press
785	**ridicule**	*nm, adj(f)*	ridiculousness, silly
786	**preuve**	*nf*	proof
788	**intéressant**	*adj*	interesting
789	**gosse**	*nm, nf*	kid
790	**rose**	*adj(f), nf*	pink; rose
791	**nature**	*nf*	nature
792	**vide**	*adj(f), nm*	empty; vacuum
793	**responsable**	*adj(f), nmf*	responsible
794	**courage**	*nm*	courage
795	**capable**	*adj(f)*	able, capable
796	**cinéma**	*nm*	cinema
797	**décision**	*nf*	decision
798	**taxi**	*nm*	taxi
801	**fier**	*adj, v*	to rely on; proud
802	**deuxième**	*det, nm, nf*	second
803	**appartement**	*nm*	apartment, flat
804	**contact**	*nm*	contact
807	**manière**	*nf*	manner, way
808	**jambe**	*nf*	leg
809	**occasion**	*nf*	chance, opportunity
810	**défense**	*nf*	defence
811	**longue**	*adj*	long
813	**formidable**	*adj(f)*	tremendous, considerable, great
814	**base**	*nf*	base
815	**glace**	*nf*	ice, ice cream; mirror
816	**dent**	*nf*	tooth
819	**paie**	*nf*	pay, payroll
820	**machine**	*nf*	machine
821	**vacance**	*nf*	vacancy; vacation ; holiday
822	**monstre**	*nm, adj(f)*	monster
823	**tueur**	*nm*	killer, hit man
825	**francais**	*nm, adj[pl]*	French
826	**course**	*nf*	race, shopping
827	**majeste**	*nf*	majesty
829	**type**	*nm*	type; guy
833	**importance**	*nf*	importance
834	**ouest**	*adj(i), nm*	west
835	**chat**	*nm*	cat; chat
839	**joie**	*nf*	joy
841	**superbe**	*nf, adj(f)*	arrogance; superb, magnificent
842	**bain**	*nm*	bath, bathing
843	**horrible**	*adj(f)*	horrible, terrible, dreadful, hideous
844	**court**	*adj, adv, nm*	short
846	**bombe**	*nf*	bomb
848	**realite**	*nf*	reality
850	**camion**	*nm*	truck
852	**cent**	*det, nm*	one hundred, cent
853	**rencontre**	*nm*	meeting
854	**excellent**	*adj*	excellent
855	**respect**	*nm*	respect
856	**terrain**	*nm*	ground, terrain
857	**projet**	*nm*	project
859	**poisson**	*nm*	fish
861	**joyeux**	*adj[pl]*	merry, joyful, happy
863	**envers**	*nm[pl], prep*	towards
864	**kilometre**	*nm*	kilometer
865	**ange**	*nm*	angel
866	**copine**	*nf*	girlfriend
867	**chaussure**	*nf*	shoe, sneakers
868	**dossier**	*nm*	file, record; case
869	**règle**	*adj*	regular, steady, well-ordered, ruled
870	**animal**	*nm, adj*	animal
871	**langue**	*nf*	language, tongue
872	**imbécile**	*adj, nf*	imbecile, fool

873	princesse	nf	princess
874	zone	nf	zone, area
876	charge	nf	to charge, load
877	enfoiré	nm	bastard
878	nourriture	nf	food
879	pont	nm	bridge
881	contraire	nm, adj(f)	opposite, contrary
883	douleur	nf	pain
884	politique	nm, nf, adj(f)	politician; politics; political
885	fait	adj, nm	done, fact
886	magasin	nm	store, shop
887	entier	nm, adj	whole, full
888	chapeau	nm	hat
891	papier	nm	paper
892	action	nf	action
894	rapide	adj(f), nm	fast, quick; rapids, fast train
895	frais	adj[pl], adv, nm[pl]	cool, fresh; fee, expense
896	réunion	nf	meeting, reunion
897	île	nf	island
898	toilette	nf	washing, toilet, lavatory, bathroom, restroom
900	opération	nf	operation
901	spécial	adj	special
902	planète	nf	planet
903	champ	nm	field, realm
904	couleur	nf	color
905	pain	nm	bread
906	destin	nm	fate, destiny
910	vaisseau	nm	ship, vessel
911	sexe	nm	sex
912	sacré	adj	sacred
913	repas	nm[pl]	meal
914	contrat	nm	contract
915	nécessaire	nm, adj(f)	necessary, required
916	client	nm	client, customer
918	lait	nm	milk
919	mémoire	nm, nf	memory
921	copain	nm	friend, buddy, mate
922	reste	nm	rest
923	personnel	noun, adj	personnel, personal
925	mignon	adj	cute
926	couteau	nm	knife
927	témoin	nm	witness
928	foi	nf	faith
930	direction	nf	direction, management
931	malin	noun, adj	smart, shrewd, cunning
932	niveau	nm	level
936	procès	nm[pl]	trial, proceedings
937	doux	adv, noun, adj[pl]	soft, sweet
938	solution	nf	solution
940	goût	nm	taste
942	différence	nf	difference
943	stop	nm, int	stop
945	enceinte	adjf, nf	pregnant; enclosure
946	université	nf	university, college
947	bleu	adj, nm	blue
948	mètre	nm	meter
949	marre	nf	fed up, to have enough
953	officier	nm, nf, v	officer; officiate
954	espace	nm, nf	space
955	sourire	nm, v	smile; to smile
956	mérite	nm	merit
957	lettre	nf	letter
959	failli	adj	bankrupt
960	angleterre	nf	England
961	vitesse	nf	speed
962	jambe	nf	leg
963	camera	nf	camera
964	arbre	nm	tree
965	force	adv, nf	force

#	Word	Type	Meaning
966	trésor	nm	treasure, treasury
967	victime	nf	victim
968	énergie	nf	energy
969	énorme	adj(f)	enormous, huge
975	moindre	adj(f)	lesser, least, slightest
976	censé	adj	supposed
977	image	nf	picture, image
980	chasse	nf	chase, hunt, hunting
981	unique	adj(f)	unique
982	arrêt	nm	stop
984	balle	nf	ball, bullet
985	dimanche	nm	Sunday
986	lycée	nm	high school
987	fil	nm	thread, wire
988	morceau	nm	piece, bit
991	doigt	nm	finger
993	appareil	nm	apparatus, device
994	piste	nf	track, trail, path
995	troisième	det, nm, nf	third
997	programme	nm	program
998	honnête	adj(f)	honest, decent, fair
999	voiture	nf	car
1001	aveugle	noun, adj(f)	blind
1002	présence	nf	presence
1003	crise	nf	crisis
1008	pluie	nf	rain
1011	souris	nf[pl]	mouse
1013	regard	nm	look, glance
1014	intention	nf	intention
1015	cou	nm	neck
1016	proche	adv, noun, adj(f), prep	nearby, close
1017	urgence	nf	emergency
1018	folie	nf	madness, folly, insanity
1019	ancien	adj, nm	ancient; former
1020	relation	nf	relationship
1021	bouteille	nf	bottle
1022	étager	nm	floor
1024	cassé	adj	broken
1025	jardin	nm	garden
1027	oiseau	nm	bird
1028	frappé	nf	strike, striking, stamp, impression, punch
1029	nombre	nm	number
1030	sentiment	nm	feeling
1031	toit	nm	roof
1033	métier	nm	job, occupation, trade
1034	maladie	nf	illness, disease
1035	poche	nf	pocket
1037	succès	nm[pl]	success
1038	dessous	adv, nm[pl], prep	underneath, below, bottom, underside
1039	théâtre	nm	theater
1040	chinois	noun, adj[pl]	Chinese
1043	gare	int, nf	station, railway

			station; beware	1078	signal	*nm*	signal
1044	**billet**	*nm*	ticket	1079	**crétin**	*nm*	dumbass
1046	**paradis**	*nm[pl]*	paradise, heaven	1080	**vidéo**	*adj(i), nf*	video
1047	**étranger**	*noun, adj*	foreigner; foreign	1081	**coffrer**	*nm*	trunk, boot, chest
1048	**campagne**	*nf*	countryside	1082	**pression**	*nf*	pressure
1049	**alcool**	*nm*	alcohol	1083	**costume**	*nm*	suit, costume, dress
1050	**samedi**	*nm*	Saturday	1084	**information**	*nf*	information
1054	**odeur**	*nf*	smell, odor	1085	**futur**	*noun, adj*	future
1057	**montagne**	*nf*	mountain	1086	**univers**	*nm[pl]*	universe
1058	**fantastique**	*noun, adj(f)*	fantastic, terrific, great, weird, eerie	1087	**volonté**	*nf*	will
1059	**victoire**	*nf*	victory	1088	**attendu**	*adj*	expected
1060	**carrière**	*nf*	career	1089	**excuse**	*nf*	excuse, apology
1063	**règle**	*adj*	regular, steady, well-ordered, ruled	1090	**faible**	*noun, adj(f)*	weak
1065	**queue**	*nf*	tail, handle, stalk, stem, rear	1094	**ministre**	*nm, nf*	minister
				1095	**naissance**	*nf*	birth
1066	**viande**	*nf*	meat	1096	**utile**	*adj(f)*	useful
1067	**rivière**	*nf*	river	1097	**gaz**	*nm[pl]*	gas
1068	**suivant**	*noun, adj, prep*	following	1098	**bataille**	*nf*	battle
1070	**fusil**	*nm*	rifle, gun	1099	**voleur**	*noun, adj*	thief, light-fingered
1071	**passager**	*noun, adj*	passenger, temporary	1100	**poids**	*nm[pl]*	weight
1072	**hasard**	*nm*	chance, luck	1102	**star**	*nf*	star
1073	**neige**	*nf*	snow	1103	**gâteau**	*noun, adj*	cake
1075	**journal**	*nm*	newspaper, paper	1104	**ventre**	*nm*	belly, stomach
1077	**plage**	*nf*	beach	1105	**connaissance**	*nf*	knowledge
				1106	**vif**	*noun, adj*	lively

1107	assassin	noun, adj	murderer, assassin	1141	bal	nm	ball
1108	vendredi	nm	Friday	1142	oreille	nf	ear
1109	couple	nm, nf	couple	1144	zéro	nm	zero
1111	militaire	noun, adj(f)	military	1145	saint	noun, adj	saint, holy
1112	date	nf	date	1146	marrant	noun, adj	funny, funny guy
1113	titre	nm	title	1147	joue	nf	cheek
1114	génie	nm	genius	1148	salon	nm	lounge, living room
1117	os	nm[pl]	bone	1149	lève	nf	survey
1118	valeur	nf	value, worth	1150	conversation	nf	conversation
1119	puissant	noun, adj	powerful	1152	fer	nm	iron
1120	style	nm	style	1153	gorge	nf	throat
1121	vert	noun, adj	green	1154	victime	nf	victim
1122	fortune	nf	fortune	1155	détail	nm	detail
1123	poulet	nm	chicken	1157	violence	nf	violence
1125	genou	nm	knee	1158	nerveux	noun, adj[pl]	nervous, irritable
1126	célèbre	adj(f)	famous	1159	aéroport	nm	airport
1128	cousin	nm	cousin	1160	direct	noun, adj	direct
1129	conscience	nf	conscience, consciousness	1161	tribunal	nm	court
1131	article	nm	article	1162	paquet	nm	packet
1132	étoile	nf	star	1164	aise	noun, adj(f)	comfort, joy, pleasure, ease
1133	millier	nm	thousand	1167	lance	nf	lance, spear
1135	mine	nf	appearance, look, skin	1168	usiner	nf	factory
1136	charmant	adj	charming	1170	forêt	nf	forest
1139	agréable	noun, adj(f)	pleasant, nice, agreeable	1171	champion	noun, adj	champion
1140	château	nm	castle	1172	horreur	nf	horror

1173	**test**	*nm*	test
1175	**extérieur**	*noun, adj*	exterior
1176	**désert**	*adj, nm*	desert, wilderness
1177	**intelligent**	*adj*	intelligent, clever, bright, smart
1179	**compte**	*nm*	account, count
1180	**mode**	*nm, nf*	mode, way, fashion
1181	**série**	*nf*	series
1182	**pis**	*adv, nm[pl]*	worse
1183	**sage**	*noun, adj(f)*	wise, good, sound, sensible
1187	**vache**	*adj(f), nf*	cow
1188	**repos**	*nm[pl]*	rest
1189	**ordinateur**	*noun, adj*	computer
1190	**rock**	*nm*	rock music
1191	**ombre**	*nm, nf*	shade, shadow
1192	**russe**	*noun, adj(f)*	Russian
1193	**minuit**	*nm*	midnight
1194	**amusant**	*noun, adj*	funny, amusing, entertaining
1195	**membre**	*nm*	member
1196	**ouvert**	*adj*	open
1197	**nombreux**	*adj[pl]*	numerous
1199	**mince**	*adj(f), int*	thin, slim, slender
1200	**essence**	*nf*	gas, petrol
1201	**maire**	*nm*	mayor
1202	**lundi**	*nm*	Monday
1203	**moteur**	*noun, adj*	motor
1206	**cigarette**	*nf*	cigarette
1208	**puissance**	*nf*	power
1209	**hiver**	*nm*	winter
1210	**souffle**	*nm*	breath, puff
1213	**miracle**	*nm*	miracle
1215	**artiste**	*noun, adj(f)*	artist
1217	**lac**	*nm*	lake
1218	**sommeil**	*nm*	sleep, sleepiness
1220	**leçon**	*nf*	lesson
1221	**chemise**	*nf*	shirt, folder
1222	**fantôme**	*nm*	ghost, phantom
1223	**acteur**	*nm*	actor
1224	**parc**	*nm*	park
1225	**chair**	*nf*	flesh
1226	**rue**	*nf*	street
1228	**japonais**	*noun, adj[pl]*	Japanese
1230	**semblant**	*nm*	semblance, pretence
1232	**échange**	*nm*	exchange
1237	**gouverneur**	*nm, nf*	governor
1238	**mark**	*nm*	mark
1239	**chauffeur**	*nm*	driver, chauffeur
1242	**unité**	*nf*	unity; unit
1244	**souci**	*nm*	worry, concern, care
1245	**manteau**	*nm*	coat, overcoat

1246	**allemand**	*noun, adj*	German		1273	**étude**	*nf*	study
1247	**pantalon**	*nm*	trousers, pants		1274	**faveur**	*nf*	favor
1248	**policier**	*noun, adj*	policeman		1276	**pause**	*nf*	break, pause
1249	**innocent**	*noun, adj*	innocent		1277	**mai**	*nm*	May
1250	**véritable**	*adj(f)*	real, TRUE		1278	**soudain**	*adj, adv*	sudden, suddenly
1251	**caisse**	*nf*	till, cash desk, cashier		1280	**choc**	*nm*	shock, clash
1252	**lunette(s)**	*nf*	sg: telescope; pl: glasses		1281	**note**	*nf*	note, grade
1253	**patient**	*noun, adj*	patient		1283	**malheur**	*nm*	misfortune
1254	**menteur**	*nm*	liar		1285	**mars**	*nm[pl]*	March; Mars
1255	**perte**	*nf*	loss		1287	**portable**	*adj(f), nm*	portable, wearable; cell phone
1256	**menace**	*nf*	threat		1288	**secrétaire**	*nm, nf*	secretary
1257	**émission**	*nf*	transmision, broadcasting, programme		1289	**mensonge**	*nm*	lie
1259	**permission**	*nf*	permission, leave		1291	**gloire**	*nf*	glory, fame
1260	**herbe**	*nf*	grass, herb		1292	**accès**	*nm[pl]*	access
1261	**front**	*nm*	front, forehead		1293	**changement**	*nm*	change
1262	**juif**	*noun, adj*	Jew, Jewish		1294	**poupée**	*nf*	doll, dolly, puppet
1263	**chouette**	*nf, adj, int*	owl, nice, awesome!		1295	**bref**	*adj, adv, nm*	brief, short
1264	**chaise**	*nf*	chair		1296	**réel**	*noun, adj*	real
1267	**chocolat**	*adj(i), nm*	chocolate		1297	**ballon**	*nm*	ball
1268	**mouvement**	*nm*	movement		1298	**abri**	*nm*	shelter
1269	**identité**	*nf*	identity		1299	**corde**	*nf*	rope, cord, string
1270	**douche**	*nf*	shower, douche		1301	**plat**	*adj, nm*	dish, flat
1271	**chaleur**	*nf*	heat		1302	**emploi**	*nm*	employment, work, use
1272	**lèvre**	*nf*	lip		1304	**attrape**	*nf*	catch

1305	**foule**	*nf*	crowd
1306	**larme**	*nf*	tear
1307	**siècle**	*nm*	century
1309	**veste**	*nf*	jacket
1310	**couverture**	*nf*	blanket
1311	**fac**	*nf*	uni, university
1313	**lancer**	*nm, v*	to throw, launch, start
1314	**piano**	*adv, nm*	piano
1315	**source**	*nf*	source, spring
1316	**camarade**	*nm, nf*	friend, comrade, pal, mate
1317	**couche**	*nf*	layer, coat
1318	**prêtre**	*nm*	priest
1319	**saison**	*nf*	season
1322	**supporter**	*nm, v*	to support, endure
1324	**image**	*nf*	picture, image
1325	**distance**	*nf*	distance
1329	**somme**	*nm, nf*	amount, sum; nap
1330	**affreux**	*noun, adj[pl]*	dreadful, awful, horrible
1331	**ours**	*adj(i), nm[pl]*	bear
1332	**geste**	*nm*	gesture
1333	**prisonnier**	*noun, adj*	prisoner, captive
1335	**tableau**	*nm*	frame, picture, painting, panel
1337	**demi**	*adj(i), adv, nm*	half
1338	**commissaire**	*nm, nf*	superintendent, commissioner
1339	**alerte**	*adj(f), nf*	agile, alert, warning
1342	**singe**	*nm*	monkey
1343	**prudent**	*adj*	prudent, careful, cautious
1345	**donne**	*adj*	given
1347	**aube**	*nf*	dawn, daybreak
1348	**propriétaire**	*nm, nf*	owner
1349	**laisse**	*nf*	leash, lead
1351	**tenu**	*adj*	tenuous, slender, held
1352	**bite**	*nf*	cock
1353	**étoile**	*nf*	star
1354	**frontière**	*nf*	border
1356	**sec**	*adj, adv, nm*	dry
1360	**porc**	*nm*	pig, pork
1361	**vierge**	*noun, adj(f)*	virgin
1364	**suspect**	*noun, adj*	suspicious, suspect
1365	**station**	*nf*	station
1368	**bagage**	*nm*	luggage, baggage
1369	**protection**	*nf*	protection
1370	**tir**	*nm*	fire, shot, launch
1371	**dame**	*int, nf*	lady
1372	**empereur**	*nm*	emperor
1373	**océan**	*nm*	ocean
1374	**concert**	*nm*	concert
1375	**immeuble**	*noun, adj(f)*	building
1377	**chaîne**	*nf*	chain, channel

1378	**enfance**	*nf*	childhood
1380	**cauchemar**	*nm*	nightmare, bad dream
1381	**amitié**	*nf*	friendship
1382	**partenaire**	*nm, nf*	partner
1383	**curieux**	*noun, adj[pl]*	curious
1384	**patte**	*nf*	paw, foot, leg
1385	**lendemain**	*nm*	next day
1386	**soupe**	*nf*	soup
1387	**uniforme**	*adj(f), nm*	uniform, steady, regular
1388	**marine**	*adj, nf*	marine, navy
1389	**reserve**	*nf*	reserve
1390	**chine**	*nf*	China
1391	**désir**	*nm*	desire
1392	**objet**	*nm*	objective; object
1396	**humanité**	*nf*	humanity
1397	**lapin**	*nm*	rabbit
1401	**bâtiment**	*nm*	building
1402	**chèque**	*nm*	check
1403	**palais**	*nm[pl]*	palace, palate
1404	**valise**	*nf*	suitcase
1406	**haine**	*nf*	hatred, hate
1407	**assurance**	*nf*	insurance, confidence
1408	**navire**	*nm*	ship
1409	**foyer**	*nm*	home, hearth
1410	**printemps**	*nm[pl]*	spring
1412	**personnage**	*nm*	character, individual
1413	**brave**	*noun, adj*	brave, worthy, good, brave man
1415	**sale**	*noun, adj(f)*	dirty
1416	**roule**	*adj*	rolled
1417	**extraordinaire**	*adj(f)*	extraordinary
1418	**explosion**	*nf*	explosion
1419	**sucre**	*nm*	sugar
1420	**procureur**	*nm*	prosecutor
1421	**opinion**	*nf*	opinion
1423	**gardé**	*nm, nf*	guard
1424	**net**	*adj, nm*	clear; Internet, web
1425	**vivant**	*noun, adj*	alive, living
1426	**compliqué**	*noun, adj*	complicated, complex
1427	**fiancé**	*noun, adj*	fiancé, engaged
1430	**sombre**	*adj(f)*	dark
1431	**hâte**	*nf*	haste, impatience
1432	**voisin**	*noun, adj*	neighbor
1433	**lourd**	*adj*	heavy
1435	**comte**	*nm*	count
1437	**réputation**	*nf*	reputation
1439	**créature**	*nf*	creature
1442	**soif**	*nf*	thirst
1443	**égal**	*noun, adj*	equal
1444	**sport**	*adj(i), nm*	sport
1445	**résultat**	*nm*	result, follow-up

1446	siège	nm	seat, bench	1476	péché	nf	fishing; peach
1447	adorable	adj	adorable, sweet	1478	empire	nm	empire
1449	canon	nm	gun, cannon	1479	débile	nm	debile, daft person
1450	gardien	noun, adj	guardian, keeper	1481	imagination	nf	imagination
1452	terme	nm	term, deadline	1482	liquide	noun, adj(f)	liquid
1453	troupe	nf	troop	1484	marin	noun, adj	sea, marine, sailor
1454	théorie	nf	theory	1486	humeur	nf	mood, temper
1456	joueur	noun, adj	player	1488	jaloux	noun, adj	jealous
1457	région	nf	region	1489	temple	nm	temple
1458	commun	noun, adj	common	1490	physique	noun, adj(f)	physical, physics
1459	tien(s)	noun, adj[pl], int	ah, well	1492	infirmier	noun, adj	nurse
1460	médicament	nm	drug, medication	1493	secteur	nm	sector
1461	crâne	adj(f), nm	skull	1496	cirque	nm	circus; cirque
1462	traduction	nf	translation	1497	particulier	noun, adj	particular, peculiar; person
1463	studio	nm	studio, studio apartment	1501	vision	nf	vision, view
1465	responsabilité	nf	responsibility	1502	cloche	nf	bell
1466	délicieux	adj	delicious	1503	croix	nf[pl]	cross
1468	trace	nf	trace, mark, track	1504	vente	nf	sale
1470	modèle	nm	model	1505	démon	nm	demon, fiend, devil
1471	cellule	nf	cell	1507	aventure	nf	adventure
1472	gêne	nm	gene	1508	matériel	noun, adj	material, equipment
1473	pêcher	nm, v	to fish, go fishing; peach tree	1509	surface	nf	surface
1474	poule	nf	hen, chick	1510	télévision	nf	television, TV
1475	sénateur	nm	senator	1511	jaune	adv, noun, adj(f)	yellow

1513	**boutique**	*nf*	shop
1514	**rare**	*adj(f)*	rare
1515	**journaliste**	*nm, nf*	journalist, reporter
1516	**magique**	*adj(f)*	magic; magical
1517	**rat**	*adj(f), nm*	rat
1518	**cri**	*nm*	shout, cry
1519	**patience**	*nf*	patience
1520	**ménage**	*nm*	housekeeping, housework
1521	**comité**	*nm*	committee
1524	**romantique**	*noun, adj(f)*	romantic
1525	**port**	*nm*	harbor, port
1526	**science**	*nf*	science
1527	**bouffe**	*nf*	food, grub
1528	**crédit**	*nm*	credit
1530	**promesse**	*nf*	promise
1531	**inconnu**	*noun, adj*	unknown
1533	**ambulance**	*nf*	ambulance
1535	**panique**	*noun, adj(f)*	panic
1536	**criminel**	*noun, adj*	criminal
1537	**sauvage**	*noun, adj(f)*	savage, wild
1538	**donnée**	*nf*	fact, datum
1539	**royaume**	*nm*	kingdom, state
1540	**complet**	*adj, nm*	full, complete, full
1541	**centaine**	*nf*	hundred
1542	**scénario**	*nm*	scenario, script
1543	**principal**	*noun, adj*	principal
1544	**jus**	*nm*	juice, sauce
1545	**pot**	*nm*	jar, pot
1546	**divorce**	*nm*	divorce
1547	**cochon**	*noun, adj*	pig
1548	**cadavre**	*nm*	corpse
1549	**révolution**	*nf*	revolution
1550	**existence**	*nf*	existence
1552	**lien**	*nm*	link, bond
1553	**fromage**	*nm*	cheese
1554	**période**	*nm, nf*	period
1555	**profond**	*adv, noun, adj*	deep
1556	**malheureux**	*noun, adj[pl]*	unhappy, miserable
1558	**roman**	*adj, nm*	novel
1559	**poussière**	*nf*	dust
1560	**passion**	*nf*	passion
1562	**maitre**	*nm*	master
1563	**lutte**	*nf*	struggle, fight, conflict
1566	**cap**	*nm*	cape
1567	**version**	*nf*	version
1568	**entraînement**	*nm*	training
1569	**mardi**	*nm*	Tuesday
1570	**indien**	*noun, adj*	Indian
1571	**meurtrier**	*noun, adj*	murderer, deadly, lethal
1572	**examen**	*nm*	exam

1573	**septembre**	*nm*	September	1604	**pratique**	*noun, adj(f)*	practice, practical
1576	**serpent**	*nm*	snake	1605	**écran**	*nm*	screen
1577	**bouton**	*nm*	button, knob, spot	1607	**ceinture**	*nf*	belt, waist
1578	**piscine**	*nf*	swimming pool	1609	**miel**	*nm*	honey
1579	**courrier**	*nm*	mail, post	1611	**estomac**	*nm*	stomach
1580	**logique**	*noun, adj(f)*	logic, logical	1612	**salaire**	*nm*	salary, wage
1581	**rythme**	*nm*	rhythm, rate	1616	**incendie**	*nm*	fire, blaze
1582	**cancer**	*nm*	cancer	1617	**pur**	*adj, nmf*	pure; hard-liner
1584	**peinture**	*nf*	painting, paint, picture	1619	**prénom**	*nm*	first name
1585	**jeudi**	*nm*	Thursday	1620	**fuite**	*nf*	escape
1586	**courageux**	*noun, adj[pl]*	courageous	1621	**invite**	*nm*	guest
1588	**camarade**	*nm, nf*	friend, comrade, pal, mate	1622	**idéal**	*nm, adj*	ideal
1589	**hall**	*nm*	foyer, lobby	1623	**condition**	*nf*	condition
1591	**ascenseur**	*nm*	elevator	1624	**élève**	*adj*	high, heavy, tall
1592	**garage**	*nm*	garage	1626	**virus**	*nm[pl]*	virus
1594	**traitement**	*nm*	treatment, salary, wage	1627	**poil**	*nm*	hair, bristle
1595	**sein**	*nm*	breast, bosom	1628	**jeunesse**	*nf*	youth
1596	**nation**	*nf*	nation	1629	**ordinaire**	*adv, nm, adj(f)*	ordinary
1597	**propriété**	*nf*	property	1630	**agence**	*nf*	agency
1598	**labo**	*nm*	lab	1631	**loup**	*nm*	wolf
1599	**machine**	*nf*	machine	1632	**naturel**	*nm, adj*	naturalness, natural
1600	**sable**	*adj(i), nm*	sand	1633	**bombe**	*nf*	bomb
1601	**commission**	*nf*	commission	1635	**équipage**	*nm*	crew, gear
1602	**section**	*nf*	section	1636	**tempête**	*nf*	storm, gale, turmoil
				1637	**central**	*adj, nm*	central; exchange

1639	**acteur**	*nm*	actor		1669	**couloir**	*nm*	corridor, aisle
1641	**miroir**	*nm*	mirror		1670	**technique**	*nf, adj(f)*	technique, technics, technical
1642	**chic**	*adj*	chic, luxurious		1671	**œuf**	*nm*	egg
1643	**jury**	*nm*	jury, board of examiners		1672	**réaction**	*nf*	reaction
1647	**cérémonie**	*nf*	ceremony		1673	**doué**	*adj*	gifted
1648	**tasse**	*nf*	cup		1674	**attente**	*nf*	wait
1649	**absence**	*nf*	absence		1676	**race**	*nf*	breed, race
1650	**comportement**	*nm*	behavior		1677	**bêtise**	*nf*	foolishness, rubbish
1651	**correct**	*adj*	correct		1679	**colle**	*nf*	glue, adhesive
1653	**national**	*adj, nf*	national; road, state highway		1680	**poitrine**	*nf*	chest, breast, breasts, bosom
1654	**carte**	*nf*	card		1681	**enterrement**	*nm*	burial, funeral
1655	**masque**	*nm*	mask		1683	**noble**	*adj(f, nmf*	noble, noble(wo)man
1656	**raisonnable**	*adj(f)*	reasonable, fair		1684	**large**	*adj(f), adv, nm*	wide, width
1657	**bijou**	*nm*	jewel		1685	**urgent**	*adj*	urgent
1658	**mystère**	*nm*	mystery		1686	**digne**	*adj(f)*	dignified, worthy
1659	**cabine**	*nf*	hut, cubicle, booth, box, room, cabin		1687	**être**	*nm*	human being
1660	**étudiant**	*nm/f, adj*	student		1689	**riz**	*nm*	rice
1661	**créme**	*adj(i), nf*	cream		1690	**plaisant**	*adj*	pleasant
1662	**parfum**	*nm*	perfume, scent, fragrance		1692	**puce**	*nf*	chip
1664	**vengeance**	*nf*	revenge		1693	**ex**	*nmfi*	ex
1665	**nu**	*nm, adj*	naked, nude		1694	**origine**	*nf*	origin, source
1667	**qualité**	*nf*	quality		1695	**attitude**	*nf*	attitude
1668	**couvert**	*adj, nm*	covered, overcast; place, seat, cutlery		1696	**absurde**	*nm, adj(f)*	absurd
					1697	**union**	*nf*	union

1698	bagnole	*nf*	wagon, car	1728	rang	*nm*	rank, row
1699	maximum	*nm, adj*	maximum	1732	humour	*nm*	humor
1700	effort	*nm*	effort	1735	commandement	*nm*	command, order, commandment
1701	chambre	*nf*	bedroom, chamber, room	1737	mandat	*nm*	term, mandate
1702	vélo	*nm*	bike, bicycle	1738	milliard	*nm*	billion, thousand million
1703	esclave	*nmf*	slave	1739	fruit	*nm*	fruit
1704	éducation	*nf*	education	1741	partage	*nm*	division, cutting, sharing
1706	pair	*adj, nm*	peer, pair, even	1742	bourse	*nf*	purse, scholarship, grant
1707	moche	*adj*	ugly	1743	jungle	*nf*	jungle
1708	blond	*nmf, adj*	blond, fair-haired	1744	aimable	*adj(f)*	pleasant, kind, nice
1709	boule	*nf*	ball	1747	adulte	*nmf, adj(f)*	adult
1711	déclaration	*nf*	declaration	1748	pomme	*nf*	apple
1713	site	*nm*	site	1749	auteur	*nm, nf*	author
1714	scientifique	*adj(f), nmf*	scientific; scientist	1750	jugement	*nm*	judgement
1715	traître	*nm, adj*	traitor, treacherous	1751	organisation	*nf*	organization
1716	panne	*nf*	breakdown, failure	1752	vague	*adj(f); nf*	vague; wave
1718	cave	*adj(f), nm, nf*	cellar, basement	1753	légende	*nf*	legend, caption, key
1719	cassette	*nf*	cassette, tape	1755	barbe	*nf*	beard
1720	essai	*nm*	attempt, try, test	1756	territoire	*nm*	territory
1721	musée	*nf*	museum	1757	blessure	*nf*	injury, wound
1722	minable	*adj*	seedy, shabby	1758	géant	*nmf, adj*	giant, gigantic
1723	sommet	*nm*	summit	1759	moto	*nm*	motorbike
1725	aile	*nf*	wing, sail, blade	1760	communauté	*nf*	community
1726	bagarre	*nf*	fight				
1727	production	*nf*	production				

1761	**cage**	nf	cage		1795	**domaine**	nm	domain, field
1763	**rayon**	nm	ray, beam, radius; department, section, shelf		1797	**religion**	nf	religion
					1799	**furieux**	adj	furious, raging, violent, mad
1764	**sorcier**	nm	sorcerer, witch		1801	**circonstance**	nf	circumstance
1765	**pile**	nf	pile, stack, battery, tails		1802	**excellence**	nf	excellence
1766	**kilo**	nm	kilo		1803	**cimetière**	nm	cemetary, graveyard
1767	**écrivain**	nm	writer		1804	**classique**	nm, adj(f)	classic
1770	**limite**	nf	limit		1805	**arrestation**	nf	arrest
1771	**orange**	adj(i), nf	orange		1807	**cabinet**	nm	cabinet, agency, office
1776	**conseiller**	nm, v	adviser, to advise		1808	**comédie**	nf	comedy, playacting
1777	**ligne**	nf	line		1809	**bond**	nm	leap, rebound
1778	**escalier**	nm	stairs, staircase		1810	**tunnel**	nm	tunnel
1779	**explication**	nf	explanation		1811	**amant**	nm	lover
1783	**professionnel**	nmf, adj	professional		1813	**incapable**	adj	incapable, incompetent
1784	**incident**	adj, nm	incident		1814	**drapeau**	nm	flag
1785	**colline**	nf	hill		1818	**magazine**	nm	magazine
1786	**autorisation**	nf	authorization, permission, permit		1821	**précieux**	adj [pl]	precious
1788	**ministère**	nm, nf	minister		1822	**éternité**	nf	eternity, lifetime
1789	**exprès**	adj[pl], adv	deliberately, on purpose, intentionally		1824	**huile**	nf	oil
					1825	**proposition**	nf	proposition, proposal
1790	**football**	nm	football, soccer		1826	**soutien**	nm	support
1791	**rond**	adj, nm, nf	round, circle, patrol,		1827	**hauteur**	nf	height
1792	**exercice**	nm	exercise,		1828	**échec**	adj(i), nm	failure
1793	**fichu**	adj	damn, rotten		1830	**culture**	nf	culture
1794	**vote**	nm	vote		1831	**précis**	adj[pl, noun	precise; noun

1832	**langage**	*nm*	language
1833	**objectif**	*adj, nm*	objective, aim, goal; lens
1835	**souffrance**	*nf*	suffering
1836	**pétrole**	*nm*	crude oil, petroleum
1838	**épreuve**	*nf*	test, ordeal, trial
1840	**bibliothèque**	*nf*	library
1843	**électrique**	*adj(f)*	electric
1844	**ranger**	*nm, v*	to tidy up, put away
1847	**vallée**	*nf*	valley
1848	**golf**	*nm*	golf, golf course
1849	**las**	*adj*	tired, weary
1851	**loyer**	*nm*	rent
1852	**producteur**	*nm/f, adj*	producer
1853	**quart**	*nm*	quarter
1854	**critique**	*adj(f), nmf*	criticism, critical, critic
1855	**acte**	*nm*	act
1856	**plateau**	*nm*	plateau, tray, set, stage
1857	**auto**	*nm, nf*	car
1859	**conférence**	*nf*	conference
1860	**charme**	*nm*	charm
1861	**fièvre**	*nf*	fever
1862	**réception**	*nf*	reception
1863	**duc**	*nm*	duke
1864	**italien**	*nm/f, adj*	Italian
1865	**fenêtre**	*nf*	window

1867	**cervelle**	*nf*	brain, brains
1868	**moral**	*adj, nm*	moral, morale
1869	**supérieur**	*adj, nmf*	superior
1871	**tendre**	*adj(f)*	tender, soft
1872	**discussion**	*nf*	discussion
1874	**ivre**	*adj*	drunk, intoxicated
1876	**gagnant**	*nmf, adj*	winner, winning
1877	**beurre**	*nm*	butter
1878	**commerce**	*nm*	trade, commerce
1879	**fleuve**	*nm*	river
1880	**nerf**	*nm*	nerve
1882	**pédé**	*nf*	homosexual, queer
1883	**assis**	*adj*	seated
1885	**liaison**	*nf*	liaison, connection
1886	**document**	*nm*	document
1887	**salopard**	*nm*	bastard
1888	**place**	*nf*	room, space, seat, square, place
1889	**nuage**	*nm*	cloud
1891	**avenue**	*nf*	avenue
1892	**guitare**	*nf*	guitar
1894	**final**	*nm, adj*	final
1895	**brise**	*nf*	breeze, air
1896	**réseau**	*nm*	network
1897	**prière**	*nf*	prayer

1898	réalisateur	*nmf*	director	1926	collier	*nm*	necklace
1899	surveillance	*nf*	surveillance, monitoring	1927	alliance	*nf*	alliance
1900	épaule	*nf*	shoulder	1928	congé	*nm*	time off, leave
1901	placard	*nm*	cupboard, locker	1929	portefeuille	*nm*	wallet
1902	mercredi	*nm*	Wednesday	1932	terroriste	*nm, nf*	terrorist
1903	chiffre	*nm*	figure, number	1933	clan	*nm*	clan
1904	lampe	*nf*	lamp, light	1934	exécution	*nf*	execution
1905	expert	*nm, adj*	expert	1938	invitation	*nf*	invitation
1906	autorité	*nf*	authority	1939	électricité	*nf*	electricity
1907	destruction	*nf*	destruction	1941	avril	*nm*	April
1908	congrès	*nm*	congres, convention, conference	1943	acier	*nm*	steel
1909	poudre	*nf*	powder, dust	1945	sourd	*adj, nmf*	deaf, deaf person
1910	juillet	*nm*	July	1946	degré	*nm*	degree
1911	moderne	*adj*	modern	1947	instruction	*nf*	instruction, direction
1912	stade	*nm*	stadium, stage	1948	injuste	*adj(f)*	unfair, unjust
1913	serment	*nm*	oath, vow	1949	division	*nf*	division
1914	dette	*nf*	debt	1950	fierté	*nf*	pride
1916	sensible	*adj(f)*	sensitive	1952	fidèle	*adj*	faithful
1918	expression	*nf*	expression	1955	renseignement	*nm*	information
1919	métro	*nm*	metro, subway	1956	total	*adj, nm*	total
1920	fonce	*adj*	dark	1957	réservé	*adj*	reserved
1921	chat	*nm*	cat; chat	1958	tare	*nf*	defect
1923	balance	*nf*	scales, balance	1959	espagnol	*nm, adj*	Spanish
1925	séance	*nf*	meeting	1960	solide	*nm, adj(f)*	solid
				1961	avantage	*nm*	advantage

1962	**habitant**	*nm*	inhabitant		1999	**tension**	*nf*	tension
1963	**rage**	*nf*	rage, fury, rabies		2000	**serviette**	*nf*	towel, napkin
1966	**neveu**	*nm*	nephew		2003	**passeport**	*nm*	passport
1968	**ouverture**	*nf*	opening		2005	**échelle**	*nf*	ladder
1970	**veuf**	*nmf, adj*	widow, widowed, widower		2006	**cercle**	*nm*	circle, cycle
1971	**munition**	*nf*	ammunition, supplies		2008	**citoyen**	*nmf*	citizen
1973	**juin**	*nm*	June		2009	**pervers**	*nmf; adj[pl]*	pervert; perverse, perverted
1977	**bâton**	*nm*	stick, rod		2010	**tentative**	*nf*	attempt
1978	**timide**	*adj(f)*	timid, shy, bashful		2011	**règlement**	*nm*	settlement, solution
1979	**fermé**	*adj*	shut, closed, locked		2012	**immense**	*adj(f)*	immense
1980	**caractère**	*nm*	nature, character		2013	**comté**	*nm*	count
1982	**célibataire**	*adj, nf, nm*	single		2014	**crainte**	*nf*	fear
1983	**pasteur**	*nm*	minister, clergyman, pastor		2017	**manuel**	*adj, nm*	manual
1984	**progrès**	*nm*	progress		2018	**cruel**	*adj*	cruel, ferocious, bitter
1985	**ordure**	*nf*	filth		2019	**octobre**	*nm*	October
1986	**matière**	*nf*	matter		2020	**méchant**	*adj*	bad, mean
1987	**puits**	*nm[pl]*	well, shaft, pit		2021	**dessin**	*nm*	drawing, pattern, design
1988	**bonté**	*nf*	kindness		2022	**inde**	*nf*	India
1990	**mondial**	*adj*	world, global		2024	**léger**	*adj*	light, slight, thin
1991	**intelligence**	*nf*	intelligence		2025	**diamant**	*nm*	diamond
1992	**généreux**	*adj*	generous		2026	**publique**	*adj, nf*	public
1994	**température**	*nf*	temperature		2028	**asile**	*nm*	shelter, asylum, hospital
1995	**fête**	*nf*	party		2030	**sou**	*nm*	penny
1996	**saloperie**	*nf*	trash, junk, filth		2032	**tournage**	*nm*	shooting

2033	**nucléaire**	adj, nm	nuclear, nuclear power
2034	**populaire**	adj(f)	popular
2036	**couronne**	nf	crown, wreath
2037	**nue**	adj	naked
2038	**vedette**	nf	star, patrol boat
2040	**garce**	nf	bitch
2041	**formation**	nf	training
2042	**audience**	nf	audience, hearing
2044	**issu**	adj	descended from, come from
2045	**procédure**	nf	procedure
2048	**mouche**	nf	fly
2049	**conséquence**	nf	result, consequence
2050	**groupe**	nm	group
2051	**mortel**	nmf, adj	mortal, deadly, lethal
2052	**collègue**	nm, nf	colleague
2053	**objection**	nf	objection
2058	**sain**	adj	healthy, sane
2059	**tradition**	nf	tradition
2061	**département**	nm	department
2063	**impressionnant**	adj	impressive, upsetting
2064	**accusation**	nf	accusation, indictment
2065	**disque**	nm	disc, disk
2067	**entretien**	nm	interview, discussion, maintenance
2069	**chasseur**	nm	hunter, fighter, page, messenger
2071	**solitaire**	adj(f, nmf	solitary, lone, lonely, loner
2073	**micro**	nm	mike, micro, microphone
2074	**technologie**	nf	technology
2075	**original**	nm, adj	original
2076	**trompe**	adj	horn, trunk
2078	**patrie**	nf	homeland, home country
2079	**tuyau**	nm	pipe, tube
2080	**clinique**	adj(f), nf	clinical, private hospital
2081	**régime**	nf	diet, regime
2082	**album**	nm	album
2083	**suprême**	adj	supreme
2084	**sincère**	adj	sincere
2085	**pipe**	nf	pipe
2086	**violent**	adj	violent
2087	**émotion**	nm	emotion
2089	**franc**	adj, adv, adj, nm	frank; franc
2090	**remarque**	nf	remark
2091	**excitant**	adj	exciting
2093	**sel**	nm	salt
2094	**canapé**	nf	couch, sofa
2097	**splendide**	adj	magnificent, wonderful
2098	**promotion**	nf	promotion, advertising
2099	**scandale**	nm	scandal, uproar

2100	cran	nm	guts, notch	2140	cravete	nf	necktie
2102	élément	nm	element	2141	frigo	nm	fridge
2105	efficace	adj(f)	efficient, effective	2142	traîne	nf	train
2106	événement	nm	event	2143	câble	nm	cable
2107	personnalité	nf	personality	2148	remarquable	adj(f)	remarkable, outstanding
2109	rumeur	nf	rumor	2149	exception	nf	exception
2110	divin	adj, nm	divine, heavenly	2150	gant	nm	glove
2111	dégât	pl, nm	damage	2151	ennuyeux	adj	boring, annoying, dull
2112	négatif	adj, nm	negative	2152	ouvrier	nmf, adj	worker, working-class
2115	invisible	adj(f)	invisible	2153	record	nm	record
2116	signature	nf	signature	2155	enseigne	nf	sign
2120	canard	nm	duck	2156	angle	nm	angle, point of view
2121	stylo	nm	pen	2157	instinct	nm	instinct
2122	possibilité	nf	possibility	2158	impôt	nm	tax
2123	réveil	nm	the waking up, alarm clock	2161	complexe	nm, adj(f)	complex
2125	ère	nf	era	2162	méthode	nf	method
2127	étape	nf	stage, step, phase	2164	tigre	nm	tiger
2131	prime	noun, adj(f), nf	free gift, premium, bonus	2165	tragédie	nf	tragedy
2132	renfort	nm	help, back-up, support	2166	torture	nf	torture
2133	publicité	nf	publicity	2167	industrie	nf	industry
2135	séjour	nm	stay	2168	population	nf	population
2136	tabac	nm	tobacco	2169	adaptation	nf	adaptation
2137	chaos	nm[pl]	chaos	2171	autoroute	nf	motorway, highway, freeway
2139	tarte	nf	pie	2172	obscurité	nf	darkness, obscurity

2173	**fabuleux**	*adj*	fabulous
2174	**linge**	*nf*	linen, cloth
2175	**illégal**	*adj*	illegal
2176	**rigole**	*nf*	laugh
2178	**fauteuil**	*nm*	armchair, seat
2179	**vendeur**	*nm*	salesman, seller
2180	**novembre**	*nm*	November
2181	**collection**	*nf*	collection, series
2182	**tonne**	*nf*	metric ton, tonne
2183	**accent**	*nm*	accent
2186	**plastique**	*nm, adj(f)*	plastic
2187	**marche**	*nf*	walk, step, march
2188	**commande**	*nf*	order, control
2189	**lot**	*nm*	share, prize, lot
2190	**trahison**	*nf*	betrayal, treachery, treason
2191	**sensation**	*nf*	sensation
2192	**mesure**	*nf*	measure
2193	**chanceux**	*adj*	fortunate, lucky
2194	**boue**	*nf*	mud
2195	**cabane**	*nf*	hut, cabine
2196	**merveille**	*nf*	marvel, wonder
2197	**poing**	*nm*	fist, punch
2198	**sacrifice**	*nm*	sacrifice
2199	**communication**	*nf*	communication
2201	**chagrin**	*adj, nm*	grief, sorrow
2203	**drogue**	*nf*	drug
2204	**gratuit**	*adj*	free, gratuitous, unwarranted
2205	**britannique**	*adj(f)*	British
2206	**social**	*adj*	social
2207	**coïncidence**	*nf*	coincidence
2208	**vire**	*adj*	fired
2209	**août**	*nm*	August
2210	**malédiction**	*nf*	curse
2211	**pension**	*nf*	pension; room and board, boarding school
2212	**ténèbre**	*nf*	darkness
2213	**phase**	*nf*	phase, round
2214	**noix**	*nf*	nuts
2215	**boum**	*nm*	bang
2216	**sexuel**	*adj*	sexual
2218	**défi**	*nm*	challenge
2220	**désastre**	*nm*	disaster
2221	**feuille**	*nf*	leaf, sheet
2223	**reconnaissant**	*adj*	grateful
2225	**solitude**	*nf*	solitude, loneliness
2227	**jouet**	*nm*	toy
2229	**ingénieur**	*nm*	engineer
2230	**chant**	*nm*	song
2231	**ongle**	*nf*	nail, fingernail
2232	**trafic**	*nm*	traffic, circulation

2233	**activité**	*nf*	activity		2267	**survie**	*nf*	survival
2234	**reconnaissance**	*nf*	recognition, gratitude		2268	**batterie**	*nf*	battery; drum set
2235	**foie**	*nm*	liver		2270	**manche**	*nm, nf*	handle, sleeve
2237	**cercueil**	*nm*	coffin		2272	**pourvu**	*adj; adv*	equiped with; so long as, provided
2238	**gris**	*nm, adj[pl]*	gray		2275	**principe**	*nm*	principle
2239	**livraison**	*nf*	delivery		2278	**masse**	*nf*	mass
2240	**pilule**	*nf*	pill		2279	**luxe**	*nm*	luxury
2244	**armé**	*adj*	armed		2280	**terreur**	*nf*	terror, dread
2245	**chapitre**	*nm*	chapter		2281	**mobile**	*adj(f), nm*	mobile, portable; motive
2246	**communiste**	*adj(f, nmf*	communist		2282	**sagesse**	*nf*	wisdom, moderation
2247	**commissariat**	*nm*	police station		2289	**décembre**	*nm*	December
2248	**trouille**	*nf*	(avoir la trouille: to be scared stiff		2291	**usage**	*nm*	use, usage
2250	**pisse**	*nf*	piss		2292	**collège**	*nm*	secondary school, body
2251	**essentiel**	*nm, adj*	essential		2293	**symbole**	*nm*	symbol
2252	**génération**	*nm*	generation		2294	**aile**	*nf*	wing, fender
2254	**écriture**	*nf*	writing, entry		2295	**flamme**	*nf*	flame, fire, fervor, brilliance
2256	**massacre**	*nm*	massacre, slaughter		2296	**bloc**	*nm*	block
2258	**phrase**	*nf*	sentence, phrase		2297	**règne**	*nm*	reign
2259	**poème**	*nm*	poem		2298	**orage**	*nm*	storm, thunderstorm
2260	**pénis**	*nm*	penis		2299	**poste**	*nm, nf*	post, position; post office
2261	**singe**	*nm*	monkey		2303	**royal**	*adj*	royal
2263	**époux**	*nm*	husband		2304	**texte**	*nm*	text
2264	**automne**	*nm*	fall, autumn		2305	**officiel**	*adj, nmf*	official
2265	**brigade**	*nf*	team, squad, brigade					

2306	**pompe**	*nf*	pump
2307	**poubelle**	*nf*	trash can, garbage
2308	**patrouille**	*nf*	patrol
2309	**équippement**	*nm*	equipment
2310	**taux**	*nm*	rate
2311	**taudis**	*nm*	slum
2312	**métal**	*nm*	metal
2313	**destination**	*nf*	destination
2315	**pique**	*nf;nm*	pike, critique; spade
2316	**accueil**	*nm*	welcome, reception
2317	**roue**	*nf*	wheel
2318	**économie**	*nf*	economy
2319	**tombe**	*nf*	grave, tomb
2320	**charité**	*nf*	charity
2323	**cuisine**	*nf*	cooking, kitchen
2324	**laboratoire**	*nm*	laboratory
2325	**déconner**	*nm*	to talk crap, to screw around, mess around
2326	**plaisanterie**	*nf*	joke
2327	**quitte**	*adj*	to be clear off, quits
2328	**culotte**	*nf*	pants, panties
2329	**boisson**	*nf*	drink, beverage
2330	**saut**	*nm*	jump, leap
2331	**matinée**	*nf*	morning
2333	**otage**	*nm*	hostage
2334	**ravissant**	*adj*	delightful, ravishing
2336	**tireur**	*nm*	shooter
2337	**lave**	*adj*	washed
2338	**ambassadeur**	*nm*	ambassador
2339	**atmosphère**	*nf*	atmosphere
2341	**casier**	*nm*	locker
2342	**capital**	*nm, nf, adj*	major, chief, principal; capital, assets
2343	**cendre**	*nf*	ash
2344	**syndicat**	*nm*	union
2345	**suisse**	*adj(f)*	Swiss
2347	**outil**	*nm*	tool
2348	**testament**	*nm*	will
2349	**poète**	*nm*	poet
2350	**combinaison**	*nf*	combination
2354	**lecture**	*nf*	reading
2355	**processus**	*nm[pl]*	process
2357	**médical**	*adj*	medical
2358	**atelier**	*nm*	workshop, studio
2359	**guerrier**	*nmf, adj*	warrior; warlike
2360	**pouce**	*nm*	thumb, inch
2361	**entraîneur**	*nm*	coach, trainer
2363	**panier**	*nm*	basket
2364	**pétrin**	*nm*	mess, spot, pickle
2366	**tonnerre**	*nf*	thunder

2367	témoignage	nm	testimony, evidence, witness
2369	indice	nm	indication, sign, clue, hint
2370	création	nf	creation
2371	environnement	nm	environment
2373	dégueulasse	adj	disgusting, filthy
2375	dose	nf	dose, amount
2377	môme	nm, nf	kid
2378	curiosité	nf	curiosity
2379	administration	nf	administration
2380	misère	nf	misery, poverty
2381	cuir	nm	leather
2382	transport	nm	transportation
2384	savon	nm	soap
2385	pipi	nm	pee, wee
2387	plante	nf	plant
2388	viol	nm	rape
2389	douceur	nf	softness, smoothness, mildness, gentleness, sweetness
2390	vain	adj	vain
2392	parent	nmf, adj	parent
2395	écart	nm	space, gap
2397	fonction	nf	function
2399	machin	nm	thingy
2400	fameux	adj[pl]	famous
2401	talent	nm	talent
2402	nègre	nm, adj	negro
2403	catholique	nmf, adj(f)	catholic
2405	misérable	nmf, adj	miserable, wretched
2406	requin	nm	shark
2408	affection	nf	affection, ailment
2409	adversaire	nm, nf	opponent, adversary
2411	meuble	nm, adj(f)	piece of furniture
2412	foutu	adj	fucking, damned
2413	dignité	nf	dignity
2415	rat	nf	rat
2418	dépression	nm	depression
2420	circuit	nm	circuit
2421	voile	nm, nf	veil, sail
2426	volontaire	nmf, adj(f)	volunteer; voluntary
2427	fumier	nm	manure
2428	égoïste	adj, nm, nf	selfish, egoist
2429	brouillard	nm	fog, mist, haze
2430	construction	nf	construction, building
2431	météo	nf	weather forecast, weather report
2432	fillette	nf	little girl, girl
2433	motif	nm	motive, purpose
2435	loyauté	nf	loyalty
2436	évidence	nf	evidence

2437	mouton	nm	sheep
2438	commercial	adj, nm	commercial, marketeer
2440	remède	nf	remedy
2442	catastrophe	nf	catastrophe, disaster
2443	disparition	nf	disappearance
2444	éternel	adj	eternal
2445	drap	nm	sheet
2447	coco	nm	mate, coconut
2448	éclair	nm	flash, spark
2451	feuille	nf	leaf, sheet, slip
2453	nichon	nm	boob, tit, breast
2454	interview	nf	interview
2456	promenade	nf	walk, stroll
2457	association	nf	association
2458	leader	nm, nf	leader
2459	discipline	nf	discipline
2460	civil	adj, nm	civil; civilian
2461	lancement	nm	launch
2462	gras	adj[pl], adv, nm[pl]	fatty, fat, greasy
2463	transfert	nm	transfer
2464	satellite	nm	satellite
2465	pompier	adj, nm	fireman, firefighter
2467	tragique	adj(f), nm	tragic, tragedy
2468	enregistrement	nm	recording, registration, check-in, logging
2469	circulation	nf	circulation, traffic
2470	casque	nf	helmet
2471	compétition	nm	competition
2472	caution	nf	deposit, guarantee, bail
2473	adn	nm	DNA
2474	opportunité	nf	opportunity, appropriateness
2476	fixe	adj, nm	fixed, set; base salary
2478	menu	nm, adv, adj	menu, slender, slim, minor
2479	plancher	nm, v	floor
2482	dentiste	nm, nf	dentist
2483	légal	adj	legal
2484	civilisation	nf	civilization
2485	avertissement	nm	warning
2486	tache	nf	stain, spot, mark
2487	antenne	nf	antenna
2489	onde	nf	wave
2490	assaut	nm	assault, attack, bout
2491	fiche	nf	card, sheet, slip, form
2493	anneau	nm	ring
2494	maquillage	nf	makeup
2495	doue	adj	talented, gifted
2497	impact	nm	impact
2499	zone	nf	area
2501	conflit	nm	conflict

G. Numerals

Rank	French	PoS	English
10	un, une	adj, det, nm, pron, num	a, an, one
72	deux	num	two, couple
149	trois	num	three
303	quatre	num	four
366	six	num	six
408	dix	num	ten
521	neuf	adj, num	nine; new
586	sept	num	seven
621	huit	num	eight
683	mille	nm, num	thousand
1212	vingt	num	twenty
1625	douze	num	twelve
1774	quinze	num	fifteen
1842	trente	num	thirty
2243	cinquante	num	fifty
2450	onze	num	eleven

H. Prepositions

Rank	French	PoS	English
1	**de, du, de la, de l', des**	det, prep	of, from, some, any
13	**à, au, aux**	det, prep	to, at, in
17	**en**	adv, prep, pron	in, by
20	**pour**	prep	to, for, in order to,
27	**dans**	prep	in, into, from
37	**avec**	prep	with
44	**sur**	adj, prep	on, upon
57	**par**	prep	by
85	**sans**	prep	without
97	**sûr**	adj, prep	on, upon
99	**avant**	adj(i), adv, nm, prep	before
104	**chez**	prep	at, with
116	**voilà**	prep	right, there, here; that's
117	**depuis**	adv, prep	since, for , in
155	**moins**	adj(i)[pl], adv, nm[pl], prep	less
156	**entre**	prep	between
157	**passe**	nf, adj, prep	pass, past
194	**contre**	adv, nm, prep	against
204	**sous**	prep	under
205	**voici**	prep	here is, here are, this is, these are
237	**vers**	nm[pl], prep	toward; verse
242	**devant**	adv, nm, prep	in front, ahead
247	**dessus**	adv, nm[pl], prep	above, on top
285	**dehors**	adv, nm[pl], prep	outside
289	**près**	adv, prep	near, nearby, close by
298	**plein**	adv, nm, adj, prep	full
315	**derrière**	adv, nm, prep	last; behind
348	**dedans**	adv, nm[pl], prep	inside, indoors
406	**dès**	prep	from, as soon
428	**sauf**	adj, prep	except
602	**selon**	prep	according to
656	**hors**	adv, prep	except, outside
756	**environ**	adv, prep, nm	about, thereabouts, or so
817	**parmi**	prep	among
863	**envers**	nm[pl], prep	towards
989	**durant**	prep	during, for
1016	**proche**	adv, noun, adj(f), prep	nearby, close
1026	**malgré**	prep	despite, in spite of
1038	**dessous**	adv, nm[pl], prep	underneath, below, bottom, underside
1068	**suivant**	noun, adj, prep	following
1858	**concernant**	adv, prep	concerning
2236	**jusque**	adv, prep	to, up to, until, till

I. Pronouns

Rank	French	PoS	English
2	je, j´	pron	I
5	le, la, les, l´	det, pron	the; him, her, it, them
6	vous	pron	you (form & pl)
8	tu	pron	you (fam)
9	que, qu'	adv, conj, pron	that, which, who, whom, as
10	un, une, des	adj, det, nm, pron	a, an, one
11	il	pron	he, it
16	ce, cet, cette, ces	det, pron	this, that
17	en	adv, prep, pron	in, by
18	on	pron	one, we
19	cela	pron	that, it
21	moi	nm, pron	me
22	qui	pron	who, whom
23	nous	pron	we, us
25	y	adv, num, pron	there
26	me, m'	pron	me, to me, myself
29	elle	pron	she, her
31	tout	adv, det, nm, adj, pron	all, very
36	te, t´	pron	you, to you, from you
40	toi	nm, pron	you, yourself
42	se, s´	pron	oneself, himself, herself, itself, themselves
45	quoi	pron	what
48	lui	pron	him, her
51	rien	adv, nm, pron	nothing
53	où	adv, pron	where
64	ou	adv, pron	where
66	même	adj(f), adv, pron	same, even, self
74	autre	adj(f), pron	other
98	leur	det, adj(f), pron	them, their, theirs
102	personne	nf, pron	person, people, anybody, anyone nobody, no-one
120	quel	det, adj, pron	which, what
214	eux	pron	them
218	moi	nm, pron	me
238	aucun	det, adj, pron	none, either, neither, not any
281	dont	pron	whose, of which
294	celui	pron	that, the one, he, him
357	ceci	pron	this
367	ci	adv, pron	this one, here
477	certain	adj, det, nm, pron	certain, sure
589	chacun	pron	each
633	tel	adj, det, pron	such
635	plusieurs	det, adj, pron	several
725	nul	adj, det, pron	nil, null
736	lequel	pron	who, whom, which
828	mien	pron	mine
1358	soi	num, pron	one, oneself, self
1565	quiconque	pron	whoever, anyone who

2434   **sien**   *pron*   his, hers

J. Verbs

Rank	French	PoS	English
3	être	nm, v	to be; being
14	avoir	nm, v	asset, to have
35	suivre	v	to follow
39	aller	nm, v	to go
41	faire	nm, v	to do, make
47	savoir	nm, v	to know
49	vouloir	nm, v	to want
52	dire	nm, v	to say
60	pouvoir	nm, v	can, to be able to
71	voir	v	to see
73	falloir	v	to take, require, need
91	venir	v	to come
92	croire	v	to believe
93	devoir	nm, v	to have to, owe; duty
103	aimer	v	to like, love, wish
108	parler	nm, v	to speak, talk
118	devoir	v	must, have to
132	penser	nm, v	to think
137	rester	v	to stay
142	arriver	v	to arrive, happen
144	prendre	v	to take
145	regarder	v	to look, watch
148	passer	v	to pass, go
150	plaire	v	to please, like
159	appeler	v	to call
162	arrêter	v	to stop, arrest
164	attendre	v	to wait
173	tuer	v	to kill
176	partir	v	to leave
177	connaître	v	to know
178	aider	v	to help, assist
195	revoir	v	to see again, revise, meet
196	entendre	v	to hear
197	comprendre	v	to understand
198	pendre	v	to hang down
199	trouver	v	to find
202	demander	v	to ask for
203	chercher	v	to look for
208	sortir	v	to go out, leave
212	finir	v	to finish
216	tenir	v	to hold
219	laisser	v	to leave
225	importer	v	to import; to be important
232	placer	v	to place
241	prier	v	to pray
244	mettre	v	to put, place
250	perdre	v	to lose
254	donner	v	to give
260	jouer	v	to play
263	compter	v	to count
264	mourir	v	to die
279	vivre	nm, v	to live
282	espérer	v	to hope
300	manger	nm, v	to eat
305	marcher	v	to walk
308	envier	v	to envy
313	essayer	v	to try
316	tomber	v	to fall
324	souvenir	nm, v	memory; to remember
330	peiner	v	to toil, labor, struggle
333	suffire	v	to be sufficient, suffice
350	entrer	v	to enter, go in, come in, get in
351	rentrer	v	to go in, come in, come back, return
354	revenir	v	to come back
359	téléphoner	v	to telephone, phone, call
369	payer	v	to pay
376	adorer	v	to adore, worship
378	oublier	v	to forget

381	**fêter**	*v*	to celebrate
384	**valoir**	*v*	to be worth
387	**changer**	*v*	to change
389	**commencer**	*v*	to begin, start
391	**travailler**	*v*	to work
394	**rendre**	*v*	to render, return, yield, give up
395	**écrire**	*v*	to write
400	**montrer**	*v*	to show
401	**boire**	*nm, v*	to drink
405	**essayer**	*v*	to try
407	**sembler**	*v*	to seem
412	**rêver**	*v*	to dream
413	**armer**	*v*	to arm
417	**dormir**	*v*	to sleep
425	**apprendre**	*v*	to learn
435	**dîner**	*nm, v*	dinner; to dine
438	**bouillir**	*v*	to boil
447	**garder**	*v*	to keep
448	**tirer**	*v*	to pull, fire
462	**devenir**	*nm, v*	to become
464	**acheter**	*v*	to buy
472	**bouger**	*v*	to move, shift, budge
479	**recevoir**	*v*	to receive
480	**ouvrir**	*v*	to open
481	**promettre**	*v*	to promise
485	**occuper**	*v*	to occupy
487	**manquer**	*v*	to miss
493	**gagner**	*v*	to win, earn
494	**fondre**	*v*	to melt, merge
495	**sauver**	*v*	to rescue, save
507	**battre**	*v*	to beat, hit
515	**monter**	*v*	to go up, rise, assemble
519	**foutre**	*v, nm*	to f*ck, shove off, piss off
524	**taire**	*v*	to keep quiet, hold ones tongue
530	**écouter**	*v*	to listen to
539	**retrouver**	*v*	to find, recall
546	**rencontrer**	*v*	to meet
547	**réussir**	*v*	to succeed
548	**rappeler**	*v*	to recall, call back, remember
551	**agir**	*v*	to act
560	**terminer**	*v*	to finish, end,
564	**toucher**	*nm, v*	to touch
565	**dejeuner**	*nm, v*	lunch, to eat lunch
566	**envoyer**	*v*	to send
567	**lire**	*nf, v*	to read; italian lira
569	**detester**	*v*	to hate, detest
572	**decider**	*v*	to decide
576	**porter**	*nm, v*	to wear, carry
577	**ignorer**	*v*	to ignore
581	**supposer**	*v*	to suppose, assume
584	**jurer**	*v*	to swear
588	**surprendre**	*v*	to surprise
591	**commander**	*v*	to order, command
594	**disparaître**	*v*	to disappear, vanish
596	**expliquer**	*v*	to explain
601	**quitter**	*v*	to leave
614	**suivre**	*v*	to follow
615	**retourner**	*v*	to return, go back
616	**offrir**	*v*	to offer
623	**ressembler**	*v*	to look like, resemble
625	**baiser**	*nm, v*	to kiss
636	**exister**	*v*	to exist
637	**rire**	*nm, v*	to laugh
644	**visiter**	*v*	to visit
645	**coucher**	*nm, v*	lie down, sleep
646	**imaginer**	*v*	to imagine
648	**continuer**	*v*	to continue
649	**voler**	*v*	to steal, rob
653	**danser**	*v*	to dance
665	**vendre**	*v*	to sell

#	Word	POS	Meaning
674	poser	v	to put, pose, ask
675	ouvrir	v	to open
681	servir	v	to serve
695	paraître	v	to appear
697	asseoir	v	to sit
704	préférer	v	to prefer
706	protéger	v	to protect
719	signer	v	to sign
726	sentir	v	to feel, smell
728	emmener	v	to take
731	unir	v	to unite, come to terms with
735	utiliser	v	to use
737	ficher	v	to file; to make fun of, not care, not give a damn
739	marier	v	to marry
744	choisir	v	to choose
746	intéresser	v	to interest, involve
749	descendre	v	to go down, come down
750	tourner	v	to turn, to spin
764	adresser	v	to address
765	sauter	v	to jump
769	parier	v	to bet
771	conduire	v	to lead, drive
783	présenter	v	to present
787	épouser	v	to marry, wed
799	chanter	v	to sing
800	excuser	v	to excuse
801	fier	adj, v	to rely on; proud
805	cacher	v	to hide
806	répondre	v	to answer
812	jeter	v	to throw
824	naitre	v	to be born
831	couper	v	to cut
836	degager	v	to free, clear
837	chier	v	to sh*t, piss off, get pissed off
838	ravir	v	to delight, rob
845	deranger	v	to disturb, bother
847	ramener	v	to bring back, return, take back
849	enqueter	v	to investigate, hold inquiry, conduct a survey
851	signifier	v	to mean
858	eviter	v	to avoid
862	empecher	v	to prevent
875	droguer	v	to drug, take drugs
880	refuser	v	to refuse
882	enchanter	v	to delight, enchant, rejoice
889	raconter	v	to tell
890	discuter	v	to discuss, debate; to question
893	permettre	v	to allow
899	coder	v	to code, encode
907	découvrir	v	to discover, find out
909	tailler	v	to cut, carve, engrave, sharpen, trim
917	détruire	v	to destroy
920	pleurer	v	to cry
924	doubler	v	to double, pass; to dub
929	remercier	v	to thank
933	remettre	v	to deliver, replace, set, put back
934	habiter	v	to live
935	apporter	v	to bring
939	fermer	v	to close, shut
941	amuser	v	to amuse
944	réfléchir	v	to reflect
950	mentir	v	to lie
951	courir	v	to run
952	arranger	v	to arrange

953	**officier**	*nm, nf, v*	officer; officiate
955	**sourire**	*nm, v*	smile; to smile
958	**accepter**	*v*	to accept, admit
970	**appartenir**	*v*	to belong
971	**préparer**	*v*	to prepare
972	**regretter**	*v*	to regret
974	**inviter**	*v*	to invite
979	**enlever**	*v*	to remove, to take off
983	**filer**	*v*	to spin, run, get out
990	**casser**	*v*	to break
992	**vérifier**	*v*	to check, verify
996	**dépendre**	*v*	to depend
1000	**régler**	*v*	to pay, adjust, settle
1004	**amener**	*v*	to bring
1005	**interdire**	*v*	to forbid, prohibit, ban
1006	**lever**	*v*	to lift, raise
1007	**obtenir**	*v*	to get, obtain
1009	**récupérer**	*v*	to get back, recover, recuperate
1010	**prouver**	*v*	to prove
1012	**restaurer**	*v*	to restore, feed
1023	**rejoindre**	*v*	to rejoin, reunite
1036	**frapper**	*v*	to hit, strike, knock
1041	**craindre**	*v*	to fear, be afraid of
1045	**remarquer**	*v*	to remark; to notice, point out
1051	**produire**	*v*	to product
1052	**répéter**	*v*	to repeat
1053	**souhaiter**	*v*	to wish
1061	**fatiguer**	*v*	to tire, get
1062	**rater**	*v*	to miss, misfire
1064	**assurer**	*v*	to assure, insure
1069	**obliger**	*v*	to require, force, oblige, to have to
1076	**échapper**	*v*	to escape
1091	**attraper**	*v*	to catch, get, pick up
1092	**inquiéter**	*v*	to worry, disturb
1101	**discourir**	*v*	to discuss, to discourse, ramble
1116	**amener**	*v*	to bring
1124	**embrasser**	*v*	to kiss, embrace
1127	**cibler**	*v*	to target
1130	**prévenir**	*v*	to prevent, warn; to notify
1134	**reprendre**	*v*	to resume, recover, start again, take back
1137	**reposer**	*v*	to rest
1138	**noter**	*v*	to note, notice, write down
1151	**piloter**	*v*	to fly, pilot, drive
1156	**priver**	*v*	to deprive
1163	**fumer**	*v*	to smoke
1165	**emmerder**	*v*	to bug, bother
1166	**joindre**	*v*	to join
1169	**défendre**	*v*	to defend, forbid
1184	**concerner**	*v*	to concern
1185	**grandir**	*v*	to grow, increase, expand
1186	**pousser**	*v*	to push
1204	**réparer**	*v*	to repair, fix, correct, make up
1207	**partager**	*v*	to share
1211	**tenter**	*v*	to tempt, try
1214	**apprécier**	*v*	to appreciate
1216	**créer**	*v*	to create
1219	**réveiller**	*v*	to wake up

1227	reculer	v	to move back, back up, move backward
1229	coûter	v	to cost
1231	annoncer	v	to announce
1233	payer	v	to pay
1234	débarrasser	v	to clear, get rid of
1235	fuir	v	to flee
1236	supplier	v	to beg, implore, plead
1240	marquer	v	to mark
1243	fesser	v	to spank
1258	abandonner	v	to give up, abandon
1265	suicider	v	to commit suicide
1282	piéger	v	to trap, booby-trap
1284	attaquer	v	to attack
1286	fonctionner	v	to function, work
1290	nettoyer	v	to clean
1300	respirer	v	to breathe
1303	ennuyer	v	to bore, worry, bother
1308	atteindre	v	to reach
1312	mener	v	to lead, live
1313	lancer	nm, v	to throw, launch, start
1320	mesurer	v	to measure
1321	entreprendre	v	to begin, start, undertake
1322	supporter	nm, v	to support, endure
1326	commettre	v	to commit
1328	laver	v	to wash, clean
1336	reconnaître	v	to recognize
1340	plaisanter	v	to joke
1341	crier	v	to shout, scream, cry out
1344	ressentir	v	to feel
1346	convaincre	v	to convince

1350	coincer	v	to jam, hinder, get stuck
1355	remonter	v	to go back up
1357	diriger	v	to lead, direct
1362	réserver	v	to book, to reserve
1363	haïr	v	to detest, hate, abhor
1366	tromper	v	to deceive
1367	souffrir	v	to suffer
1376	virer	v	to turn, change, transfer, kick out
1379	maudire	v	to curse
1393	tracer	v	to draw, write, mark out
1394	recommencer	v	to resume, start again, start over
1395	traverser	v	to cross, traverse
1398	sonner	v	to ring
1399	baguer	v	to ring, tag
1400	survivre	v	to survive
1405	charger	v	to load, charge
1411	voiler	v	to veil
1428	accuser	v	to accuse
1429	construire	v	to build, construct
1434	retirer	v	to remove, withdraw
1436	contrôler	v	to control, check, inspect, monitor
1438	exploser	v	to explode, blow up
1440	étudier	v	to study
1441	brûler	v	to burn
1448	cingler	v	to whip, to slash
1451	représenter	v	to represent
1455	surveiller	v	to watch

1464	**libérer**	v	to free, liberate, release
1469	**traiter**	v	to treat, handle, deal with
1473	**pêcher**	nm, v	to fish, go fishing; peach tree
1480	**deviner**	v	to guess, solve
1483	**avancer**	v	to advance, move forward
1485	**plaire**	v	to please
1491	**bosser**	v	to work, bash on
1494	**tâcher**	v	to endeavor, strive
1495	**enfuir**	v	to run away, flee
1498	**engager**	v	to hire, involve
1499	**réaliser**	v	to realize, achieve
1506	**barrer**	v	to close, block, bar, cross
1512	**veiller**	v	to look after, stay up
1522	**baisser**	v	to lower, turn down, bend down
1523	**combattre**	v	to fight
1529	**abrutir**	v	stupefy, dumb down
1532	**concourir**	v	compete, participate
1551	**accompagner**	v	to accompany
1557	**nommer**	v	to call, name, appoint
1564	**briser**	v	to break
1574	**élever**	v	to grow, lift, raise
1575	**profiter**	v	to take advantage, profit
1583	**proposer**	v	to propose
1587	**œuvrer**	v	to work
1590	**figurer**	v	to represent, appear
1593	**approcher**	v	to approach
1603	**nager**	v	to swim
1606	**chuter**	v	to fall
1608	**briller**	v	to shine
1610	**crever**	v	to burst, puncture
1613	**inventer**	v	to invent
1614	**étonner**	v	to astonish, amaze, surprise
1615	**nourrir**	v	to feed, nourish
1618	**refaire**	v	to redo, make again
1640	**calmer**	v	to calm down
1644	**pardonner**	v	to forgive, excuse
1645	**affronter**	v	to confront, face
1646	**lâcher**	v	to let go, release
1652	**récompenser**	v	to reward, recompense
1663	**avouer**	v	to admit
1666	**presser**	v	to squeeze, press
1678	**moquer**	v	to mock, make fun of
1682	**installer**	v	to install
1691	**condamner**	v	to condemn
1712	**chasser**	v	to hunt, chase away
1717	**traîner**	v	to drag, pull
1724	**blesser**	v	to hurt
1729	**livrer**	v	to deliver
1730	**venger**	v	to avenge, take revenge
1731	**flotter**	v	to float, hang, stream
1734	**résoudre**	v	to solve, resolve
1736	**remplacer**	v	to replace
1740	**plaindre**	v	to pity, feel sorry for, complain

1745	**guider**	*v*	to guide
1746	**gâcher**	*v*	to waste, spoil
1754	**botter**	*v*	to kick
1762	**désirer**	*v*	to desire, to want
1768	**forcer**	*v*	to force
1769	**respecter**	*v*	to respect
1772	**associer**	*v*	to associate
1773	**bénir**	*v*	to bless
1775	**posséder**	*v*	to possess, own, have
1776	**conseiller**	*nm, v*	adviser, to advise
1780	**voyager**	*v*	to travel
1781	**attirer**	*v*	to attract
1782	**poursuivre**	*v*	to pursue
1787	**assassiner**	*v*	to murder, assassinate
1796	**retenir**	*v*	to retain, hold back, remember
1800	**pisser**	*v*	to piss
1806	**taper**	*v*	to beat, slam, bang, type, tap
1815	**échouer**	*v*	to fail
1817	**risquer**	*v*	to risk
1819	**remplir**	*v*	to fill, fulfill, fill out
1820	**véhiculer**	*v*	to transport, convey
1823	**citer**	*v*	to quote
1829	**fâcher**	*v*	to anger, make angry, get angry
1839	**copier**	*v*	to copy, reproduce
1841	**énerver**	*v*	to annoy, get on someone nerves
1844	**ranger**	*nm, v*	to tidy up, put away
1845	**enterrer**	*v*	to bury, lay aside
1846	**assister**	*v*	to attend; assist, help
1850	**soigner**	*v*	to treat, look after, take care for
1866	**couvrir**	*v*	to cover
1873	**alarmer**	*v*	to alarm
1875	**héler**	*v*	to hail, call out
1881	**séparer**	*v*	to separate
1884	**employer**	*v*	to use, employ
1893	**portraire**	*v*	to portray
1915	**entraîner**	*v*	to train
1917	**ajouter**	*v*	to add
1922	**durer**	*v*	to last
1930	**trahir**	*v*	to betray, give away
1931	**repartir**	*v*	to distribute, spread out, share out, divide
1935	**convenir**	*v*	to suit, to agree on
1936	**pourrir**	*v*	to rot
1937	**juger**	*v*	to judge
1940	**admettre**	*v*	to admit
1942	**convier**	*v*	to invite
1944	**promener**	*v*	to take for a walk, go for a walk
1951	**exprimer**	*v*	to express
1953	**causer**	*v*	to cause; to chat
1954	**couler**	*v*	to flow, run, sink
1965	**cesser**	*v*	to cease, stop
1967	**emprunter**	*v*	to borrow
1969	**habiller**	*v*	to dress, get dressed
1972	**écraser**	*v*	to crush
1974	**dégoûter**	*v*	to disgust
1975	**démarrer**	*v*	to start
1976	**louer**	*v*	to rent, praise
1981	**dépêcher**	*v*	to hurry, to dispatch

1989	**déposer**	v	to deposit, to leave, to put down
1993	**gérer**	v	to manage
1997	**rapporter**	v	to bring back, report
1998	**filmer**	v	to film, shoot
2001	**guérir**	v	to cure
2002	**rouler**	v	to roll
2007	**exiger**	v	to require, demand
2015	**plaquer**	v	to tackle, drop, ditch, dump
2016	**réunir**	v	to reunite
2023	**demeurer**	v	to remain, live
2027	**emporter**	v	to take, remove
2029	**organiser**	v	to organise, throw
2031	**oser**	v	to dare
2035	**orchestrer**	v	to orchestrate
2039	**renvoyer**	v	to send back, dismiss
2043	**participer**	v	to participate
2046	**brancher**	v	to plug in, connect
2047	**influencer**	v	to influence
2054	**éteindre**	v	to switch off, to turn off, to extinguish
2055	**allumer**	v	to switch on, light up, turn on
2056	**obéir**	v	to obey
2057	**sabrer**	v	to cut
2060	**décevoir**	v	to dissapoint
2062	**résister**	v	to resist
2066	**piquer**	v	to sting, bite, prick, be hot; to steal
2068	**accueillir**	v	to welcome, greet, accommodate
2070	**examiner**	v	to examine
2072	**goutter**	v	to drip
2077	**dépasser**	v	to exceed, to overtake
2095	**abattre**	v	to pull down, kill, beat, cut down
2096	**déclarer**	v	to declare, disclose
2101	**mêler**	v	to mix, get mixed up with
2103	**arracher**	v	to pull up, tear up
2104	**interroger**	v	to question, interrogate
2108	**buter**	v	to stumble, trip, run into, prop up, score
2113	**éclater**	v	to burst, to shatter
2114	**viser**	v	to aim
2117	**user**	v	to wear out, wear away, use up
2118	**insister**	v	to insist
2119	**autoriser**	v	to authorize, allow
2124	**pleuvoir**	v	to rain
2126	**conclure**	v	to conclude
2128	**contacter**	v	to contact, get in touch with
2129	**identifier**	v	to identify
2130	**attacher**	v	to attach
2138	**enfermer**	v	to shut, lock in
2145	**goûter**	v	to taste
2146	**disputer**	v	to dispute, contest
2147	**impliquer**	v	to imply, implicate
2154	**délirer**	v	to rave, to be delirious
2159	**rompre**	v	to break, to break up
2160	**rattraper**	v	to recapture, recover, catch up, make up for
2163	**suggérer**	v	to suggest

2170	admirer	v	to admire
2177	opérer	v	to operate
2184	déplacer	v	to move, to put off, to displace
2185	serrer	v	to tighten, squeeze
2200	appuyer	v	to lean, support
2202	concentrer	v	to concentrate
2219	estimer	v	to estimate; to consider, deem
2222	éliminer	v	to eliminate
2226	débrouiller	v	to untangle, to sort out
2228	tarder	v	to delay
2242	diplômer	v	to graduate
2249	analyser	v	to analyse
2253	adjoindre	v	to add sth to, to appoint
2255	annuler	v	to cancel
2262	statuer	v	to rule
2266	éloigner	v	to remove
2269	ordonner	v	to ordain, organize, order
2271	creuser	v	to dig
2273	mordre	v	to bite, overlap into
2274	contenir	v	to contain
2276	bourrer	v	to stuff
2277	rembourser	v	to reimburse, pay back, pay off, repay
2283	rigoler	v	to laugh,
2284	informer	v	to inform, notify
2285	saluer	v	to greet, salute
2287	satisfaire	v	to satisfy
2288	avaler	v	to swallow
2290	planter	v	to plant, pitch
2300	destiner	v	to intend, be used
2301	renoncer	v	to give up, renounce
2302	gréver	v	to put strain on, encumber
2314	accomplir	v	to accomplish
2321	mélanger	v	to mix, mix up, confuse
2322	endormir	v	to put to sleep, fall asleep
2332	relever	v	to raise , lift
2335	fabriquer	v	to manufacture, invent, make
2340	menacer	v	to threaten
2351	transformer	v	to transform
2352	ramasser	v	to pick up, collect, gather
2353	avertir	v	to warn
2356	vaincre	v	to beat, defeat, overcome, conquer
2362	peindre	v	to paint, depict, portray
2368	douter	v	to doubt
2374	enseigner	v	to teach
2376	effrayer	v	to frighten, scare
2383	prêter	v	to lend
2386	fouiller	v	to search, frisk, go through, rummage through
2391	détendre	v	to loosen, to relax
2393	interrompre	v	to interrupt
2396	pester	v	pester contre: to curse
2398	élire	v	to elect
2404	indiquer	v	to indicate, signal
2414	ramer	v	to row
2416	patienter	v	to wait
2417	vomir	v	to throw up, to vomit

2423	**fringuer**	v	to dress
2424	**améliorer**	v	to improve
2425	**observer**	v	to observe, watch
2439	**lier**	v	to link, join, tie to
2441	**maintenir**	v	to maintain
2446	**envelopper**	v	to wrap, surround, veil
2449	**témoigner**	v	to bear witness, to testify
2452	**embêter**	v	to bother
2477	**fasciner**	v	to fascinate

2479	**plancher**	nm, v	floor
2480	**subir**	v	to undergo, be subjected to, suffer
2481	**saigner**	v	to bleed
2488	**confier**	v	to entrust
2496	**enregistrer**	v	to record, check in
2498	**effacer**	v	to erase, clean
2500	**loger**		to put up, accomodate, stay
		v	

5. French – English Alphabetical Dictionary

Rank	French	PoS	English
	A		
FREQ.			
13	**à, au, aux**	det, prep	to, at, in
1258	**abandonner**	v	to give up, abandon
2095	**abattre**	v	to pull down, kill, beat, cut down
327	**abord**	nm	manner; approach, access, environs
1298	**abri**	nm	shelter
1529	**abrutir**	v	stupefy, dumb down
1649	**absence**	nf	absence
535	**absolument**	adv	absolutely
1696	**absurde**	nm, adj(f)	absurd
2183	**accent**	nm	accent
958	**accepter**	v	to accept, admit
1292	**accès**	nm[pl]	access
554	**accident**	nm	accident
1551	**accompagner**	v	to accompany
2314	**accomplir**	v	to accomplish
88	**accord**	nm	agreement
2316	**accueil**	nm	welcome, reception
2068	**accueillir**	v	to welcome, greet, accommodate
2064	**accusation**	nf	accusation, indictment
1428	**accuser**	v	to accuse
464	**acheter**	v	to buy
1943	**acier**	nm	steel
1855	**acte**	nm	act
1223	**acteur**	nm	actor
1639	**acteur**	nm	actor
892	**action**	nf	action
2233	**activité**	nf	activity
2410	**actuellement**	adv	at present, at the moment
2169	**adaptation**	nf	adaptation
768	**adieu**	int, nm	goodbye, farewell, adieu
2253	**adjoindre**	v	to add sth to, to appoint
1940	**admettre**	v	to admit
2379	**administration**	nf	administration
2170	**admirer**	v	to admire
2473	**adn**	nm	DNA
1447	**adorable**	adj	adorable, sweet
376	**adorer**	v	to adore, worship
764	**adresser**	v	to address
1747	**adulte**	nmf, adj(f)	adult
2409	**adversaire**	nm, nf	opponent, adversary
1159	**aéroport**	nm	airport
275	**affaire**	nf, adj	case, matter, business
310	**affaire**	nf	business, matter

2408	affection	nf	affection, ailment	1927	alliance	nf	alliance
1330	affreux	noun, adj[pl]	dreadful, awful, horrible	506	allô	conj	hello
1645	affronter	v	to confront, face	2055	allumer	v	to switch on, light up, turn on
1042	afin	in	order to, so that, so as	61	alors	adv	then, so
436	âge	nm	age	1811	amant	nm	lover
1630	agence	nf	agency	2338	ambassadeur	nm	ambassador
516	agent	nm, nf	agent	1533	ambulance	nf	ambulance
551	agir	v	to act	543	âme	nf	soul
1139	agréable	noun, adj(f)	pleasant, nice, agreeable	2424	améliorer	v	to improve
153	ah	int	ah, oh	1004	amener	v	to bring
246	aide	nm, nf	help, assistance	1116	amener	v	to bring
178	aider	v	to help, assist	772	américain	adj, nm	American, American English,
1725	aile	nf	wing, sail, blade	175	ami	nm/f, adj	friend
2294	aile	nf	wing, fender	1381	amitié	nf	friendship
498	ailleurs	adv	elsewhere, somewhere else	169	amour	nm	love
1744	aimable	adj(f)	pleasant, kind, nice	668	amoureux	nmf, adj[pl]	lover; in love, amorous
103	aimer	v	to like, love, wish	1194	amusant	noun, adj	funny, amusing, entertaining
292	ainsi	adv	thus	941	amuser	v	to amuse
147	air	nm	air, appearance	106	an	nm	year
1164	aise	noun, adj(f)	comfort, joy, pleasure, ease	2249	analyser	v	to analyse
1917	ajouter	v	to add	1019	ancien	adj, nm	ancient; former
1873	alarmer	v	to alarm	865	ange	nm	angel
2082	album	nm	album	585	anglais	nm, adj[pl]	English
1049	alcool	nm	alcohol	2156	angle	nm	angle, point of view
1339	alerte	adj(f), nf	agile, alert, warning	960	angleterre	nf	England
1246	allemand	noun, adj	German	870	animal	nm, adj	animal
39	aller	nm, v	to go	2493	anneau	nm	ring
				299	année	nf	year

556	**anniversaire**	nm, adj(f)	anniversary, birthday
1231	**annoncer**	v	to announce
2255	**annuler**	v	to cancel
2487	**antenne**	nf	antenna
2209	**août**	nm	August
993	**appareil**	nm	apparatus, device
1143	**apparemment**	adv	apparently
803	**appartement**	nm	apartment, flat
970	**appartenir**	v	to belong
555	**appel**	nm	call, phone call
159	**appeler**	v	to call
935	**apporter**	v	to bring
1214	**apprécier**	v	to appreciate
425	**apprendre**	v	to learn
677	**approche**	nf	approach
1593	**approcher**	v	to approach
2200	**appuyer**	v	to lean, support
109	**après**	adv	after
964	**arbre**	nm	tree
128	**argent**	nm	money, silver
490	**arme**	adj	armed
2244	**armé**	adj	armed
413	**armer**	v	to arm
2103	**arracher**	v	to pull up, tear up
952	**arranger**	v	to arrange
1805	**arrestation**	nf	arrest
982	**arrêt**	nm	stop
162	**arrêter**	v	to stop, arrest
619	**arriere**	adj(i), adv, nm	back, rear
243	**arrivé**	adj	arrived, happen
597	**arrivée**	nf	arrival
142	**arriver**	v	to arrive, happen
757	**art**	nm	art
1131	**article**	nm	article
1215	**artiste**	noun, adj(f)	artist
1591	**ascenseur**	nm	elevator
2028	**asile**	nm	shelter, asylum, hospital
1107	**assassin**	noun, adj	murderer, assassin
1787	**assassiner**	v	to murder, assassinate
2490	**assaut**	nm	assault, attack, bout
697	**asseoir**	v	to sit
167	**assez**	adv	enough
1883	**assis**	adj	seated
1846	**assister**	v	to attend; assist, help
2457	**association**	nf	association
1772	**associer**	v	to associate
1407	**assurance**	nf	insurance, confidence
1064	**assurer**	v	to assure, insure
2358	**atelier**	nm	workshop, studio
2339	**atmosphère**	nf	atmosphere
2130	**attacher**	v	to attach
624	**attaque**	nf	attack
1284	**attaquer**	v	to attack
1308	**atteindre**	v	to reach
1056	**attendant**	adv	meanwhile
164	**attendre**	v	to wait
1088	**attendu**	adj	expected

1674	**attente**	*nf*	wait
2011	**attention**	*nf*	attention
1781	**attirer**	*v*	to attract
1695	**attitude**	*nf*	attitude
1304	**attrape**	*nf*	catch
1091	**attraper**	*v*	to catch, get, pick up
1347	**aube**	*nf*	dawn, daybreak
238	**aucun**	*det, adj, pron*	none, either, neither, not any
2042	**audience**	*nf*	audience, hearing
1816	**auparavant**	*adv*	beforehand
1487	**auprès**	*adv*	nearby, close to, next to
69	**aussi**	*adv, conj*	too, also, as
353	**autant**	*adv*	as much, as many
1749	**auteur**	*nm, nf*	author
1857	**auto**	*nm, nf*	car
2264	**automne**	*nm*	fall, autumn
1786	**autorisation**	*nf*	authorization, permission, permit
2119	**autoriser**	*v*	to authorize, allow
1906	**autorité**	*nf*	authority
2171	**autoroute**	*nf*	motorway, highway, freeway
593	**autour**	*adv, nm*	around
74	**autre**	*adj(f), pron*	other
1634	**autrefois**	*adv*	in the past
1115	**autrement**	*adv*	differently, something else, otherwise
2288	**avaler**	*v*	to swallow
568	**avance**	*nf*	advance
1483	**avancer**	*v*	to advance, move forward
99	**avant**	*adj(i), adv, nm, prep*	before
1961	**avantage**	*nm*	advantage
37	**avec**	*prep*	with
666	**avenir**	*nm*	future
1507	**aventure**	*nf*	adventure
1891	**avenue**	*nf*	avenue
2353	**avertir**	*v*	to warn
2485	**avertissement**	*nm*	warning
1001	**aveugle**	*noun, adj(f)*	blind
461	**avion**	*nm*	plane
414	**avis**	*nm[pl]*	opinion, mind
583	**avocat**	*nm*	lawyer
14	**avoir**	*nm, v*	asset, to have
1663	**avouer**	*v*	to admit
1941	**avril**	*nm*	April

B

1368	**bagage**	*nm*	luggage, baggage
1726	**bagarre**	*nf*	fight
1698	**bagnole**	*nf*	wagon, car
1399	**baguer**	*v*	to ring, tag
842	**bain**	*nm*	bath, bathing
625	**baiser**	*nm, v*	to kiss

1522	**baisser**	v	to lower, turn down, bend down		1877	**beurre**	nm	butter
1141	**bal**	nm	ball		1840	**bibliothèque**	nf	library
1923	**balance**	nf	scales, balance		28	**bien**	adj(i), adv, nm	well
600	**balle**	nf	ball, bullet		311	**bientôt**	adv	soon
984	**balle**	nf	ball, bullet		484	**bienvenue**	nf, adj	welcome
1297	**ballon**	nm	ball		722	**bière**	nf	beer, coffin
630	**bande**	nf	band, strip		1657	**bijou**	nm	jewel
685	**banque**	nf	bank		1044	**billet**	nm	ticket
716	**bar**	nm	bar		1352	**bite**	nf	cock
1755	**barbe**	nf	beard		492	**bizarre**	adj(f)	strange, odd
1506	**barrer**	v	to close, block, bar, cross		703	**blague**	nf	joke
					557	**blanc**	adj, nm	white
154	**bas**	adv, nm&f, adj[pl], nm[pl]	low; bass; stockings		752	**blessé**	adj, nmf	injured; injured person, causualty
814	**base**	nf	base		1724	**blesser**	v	to hurt
1098	**bataille**	nf	battle		1757	**blessure**	nf	injury, wound
454	**bateau**	nm	boat, ship		947	**bleu**	adj, nm	blue
1401	**bâtiment**	nm	building		2296	**bloc**	nm	block
1977	**bâton**	nm	stick, rod		1708	**blond**	nmf, adj	blond, fair-haired
2268	**batterie**	nf	battery; drum set		401	**boire**	nm, v	to drink
507	**battre**	v	to beat, hit		404	**bois**	nm[pl]	wood
222	**beau**	adj, nm	handsome, fine, right		2329	**boisson**	nf	drink, beverage
114	**beaucoup**	adv	much, a lot of, many		658	**boîte**	nf	box
					846	**bombe**	nf	bomb
762	**beauté**	nf	beauty		1633	**bombe**	nf	bomb
295	**bébé**	nmf, adj(f)	baby		63	**bon**	adj, adv, int, nm	good
329	**ben**	adv	well		1809	**bond**	nm	leap, rebound
1773	**bénir**	v	to bless		699	**bonheur**	nm	happiness
100	**besoin**	nm	need		131	**bonjour**	nm	hello
664	**bête**	nf, adj(f)	animal, beast; stupid		337	**bonsoir**	nm	good evening
					1988	**bonté**	nf	kindness
1677	**bêtise**	nf	foolishness, rubbish		571	**bord**	nm	edge, side

520	**bordel**	*nm*	brothel, mess, chaos		2205	**britannique**	*adj(f)*	British
1491	**bosser**	*v*	to work, bash on		2429	**brouillard**	*nm*	fog, mist, haze
1754	**botter**	*v*	to kick		1441	**brûler**	*v*	to burn
651	**bouche**	*nf*	mouth		326	**bureau**	*nm*	office, desk
2194	**boue**	*nf*	mud		655	**but**	*nm*	goal, aim, objective, purpose
1527	**bouffe**	*nf*	food, grub					
472	**bouger**	*v*	to move, shift, budge		2108	**buter**	*v*	to stumble, trip, run into, prop up, score
438	**bouillir**	*v*	to boil					
1709	**boule**	*nf*	ball			**c**		
287	**boulot**	*adj, nm*	work, job					
2215	**boum**	*nm*	bang		1659	**cabine**	*nf*	hut, cubicle, booth, box, room, cabin
2276	**bourrer**	*v*	to stuff		1807	**cabinet**	*nm*	cabinet, agency, office
1742	**bourse**	*nf*	purse, scholarship, grant		2143	**câble**	*nm*	cable
1021	**bouteille**	*nf*	bottle		805	**cacher**	*v*	to hide
1513	**boutique**	*nf*	shop		1548	**cadavre**	*nm*	corpse
1577	**bouton**	*nm*	button, knob, spot		580	**cadeau**	*nm*	present, gift
2046	**brancher**	*v*	to plug in, connect		382	**café**	*nm*	coffee, café
379	**bras**	*nm[pl]*	arm		1761	**cage**	*nf*	cage
1413	**brave**	*noun, adj*	brave, worthy, good, brave man		1251	**caisse**	*nf*	till, cash desk, cashier
634	**bravo**	*int, nm*	bravo, well done		346	**calme**	*nm, adj(f)*	composure, calm
1295	**bref**	*adj, adv, nm*	brief, short		1640	**calmer**	*v*	to calm down
2265	**brigade**	*nf*	team, squad, brigade		1316	**camarade**	*nm, nf*	friend, comrade, pal, mate
1608	**briller**	*v*	to shine		1588	**camarade**	*nm, nf*	friend, comrade, pal, mate
1895	**brise**	*nf*	breeze, air		963	**camera**	*nf*	camera
1564	**briser**	*v*	to break		850	**camion**	*nm*	truck
					486	**camp**	*nm*	camp
					1048	**campagne**	*nf*	countryside

2094	**canapé**	nf	couch, sofa
2120	**canard**	nm	duck
1582	**cancer**	nm	cancer
1449	**canon**	nm	gun, cannon
1566	**cap**	nm	cape
795	**capable**	adj(f)	able, capable
309	**capitaine**	nm	captain
2342	**capital**	nm, nf, adj	major, chief, principal; capital, assets
227	**car**	conj, nm	because
1980	**caractère**	nm	nature, character
2365	**carrément**	adv	completely, directly, straight out
1060	**carrière**	nf	career
512	**carte**	nf	card
1654	**carte**	nf	card
230	**cas**	nm[pl]	case
2341	**casier**	nm	locker
2470	**casque**	nf	helmet
1024	**cassé**	adj	broken
990	**casser**	v	to break
1719	**cassette**	nf	cassette, tape
2442	**catastrophe**	nf	catastrophe, disaster
2403	**catholique**	nmf, adj(f)	catholic
1380	**cauchemar**	nm	nightmare, bad dream
283	**cause**	nf	cause
1953	**causer**	v	to cause; to chat
2472	**caution**	nf	deposit, guarantee, bail
1718	**cave**	adj(f), nm, nf	cellar, basement
16	**ce, cet, cette, ces**	det, pron	this, that
357	**ceci**	pron	this
1607	**ceinture**	nf	belt, waist
19	**cela**	pron	that, it
1126	**célèbre**	adj(f)	famous
1982	**célibataire**	adj, nf, nm	single
1471	**cellule**	nf	cell
294	**celui**	pron	that, the one, he, him
2343	**cendre**	nf	ash
976	**censé**	adj	supposed
852	**cent**	det, nm	one hundred, cent
1541	**centaine**	nf	hundred
1637	**central**	adj, nm	central; exchange
720	**centre**	nm	center, centre
1534	**cependant**	adv, conj	however
2006	**cercle**	nm	circle, cycle
2237	**cercueil**	nm	coffin
1647	**cérémonie**	nf	ceremony
477	**certain**	adj, det, nm, pron	certain, sure
830	**certainement**	adv	certainly
2372	**certes**	adv	indeed, certainly, of course
777	**cerveau**	nm	brain
1867	**cervelle**	nf	brain, brains
1093	**cesse**	adv	constantly, always
1965	**cesser**	v	to cease, stop
589	**chacun**	pron	each

2201	**chagrin**	*adj, nm*	grief, sorrow
1377	**chaîne**	*nf*	chain, channel
1225	**chair**	*nf*	flesh
1264	**chaise**	*nf*	chair
1271	**chaleur**	*nf*	heat
257	**chambre**	*nf*	bedroom, chamber
1701	**chambre**	*nf*	bedroom, chamber, room
903	**champ**	*nm*	field, realm
1171	**champion**	*noun, adj*	champion
180	**chance**	*nf*	luck; chance
2193	**chanceux**	*adj*	fortunate, lucky
1293	**changement**	*nm*	change
387	**changer**	*v*	to change
617	**chanson**	*nf*	song, tune
2230	**chant**	*nm*	song
799	**chanter**	*v*	to sing
2137	**chaos**	*nm[pl]*	chaos
888	**chapeau**	*nm*	hat
2245	**chapitre**	*nm*	chapter
229	**chaque**	*det, adj*	each, every
876	**charge**	*nf*	to charge, load
1405	**charger**	*v*	to load, charge
2320	**charité**	*nf*	charity
1136	**charmant**	*adj*	charming
1860	**charme**	*nm*	charm
980	**chasse**	*nf*	chase, hunt, hunting
1712	**chasser**	*v*	to hunt, chase away
2069	**chasseur**	*nm*	hunter, fighter, page, messenger
835	**chat**	*nm*	cat; chat
1921	**chat**	*nm*	cat; chat
1140	**château**	*nm*	castle
550	**chaud**	*adv, nm, adj*	warm, hot
1239	**chauffeur**	*nm*	driver, chauffeur
867	**chaussure**	*nf*	shoe, sneakers
291	**chef**	*nm*	head, leader, chief
437	**chemin**	*nm*	path, way
1221	**chemise**	*nf*	shirt, folder
1402	**chèque**	*nm*	check
393	**cher**	*adj, adv*	expensive
203	**chercher**	*v*	to look for
252	**chéri**	*noun, adj*	darling, love, dear
528	**cheval**	*nm*	horse
489	**cheveu**	*nm*	hair
104	**chez**	*prep*	at, with
1642	**chic**	*adj*	chic, luxurious
344	**chien**	*nm*	dog
837	**chier**	*v*	to sh*t, piss off, get pissed off
1903	**chiffre**	*nm*	figure, number
1390	**chine**	*nf*	China
1040	**chinois**	*noun, adj[pl]*	Chinese
1280	**choc**	*nm*	shock, clash
1267	**chocolat**	*adj(i), nm*	chocolate
744	**choisir**	*v*	to choose
429	**choix**	*nm[pl]*	choice
70	**chose**	*adj(f), nf*	thing
151	**chose**	*adj(f), nf*	thing

1263	chouette	nf, adj, int	owl, nice, awesome!
1500	chut	int	hush
1606	chuter	v	to fall
367	ci	adv, pron	this one, here
1127	cibler	v	to target
444	ciel	nm	sky
1206	cigarette	nf	cigarette
1803	cimetière	nm	cemetary, graveyard
796	cinéma	nm	cinema
1448	cingler	v	to whip, to slash
290	cinq	det, nm[pl]	five
2243	cinquante	det, num	fifty
1801	circonstance	nf	circumstance
2420	circuit	nm	circuit
2469	circulation	nf	circulation, traffic
1496	cirque	nm	circus; cirque
1823	citer	v	to quote
2008	citoyen	nmf	citizen
2460	civil	adj, nm	civil; civilian
2484	civilisation	nf	civilization
562	clair	adv, adj	clear
1798	clairement	adv	clearly
1933	clan	nm	clan
603	classe	nf	class
1804	classique	nm, adj(f)	classic
686	clé	nf	key
916	client	nm	client, customer
2080	clinique	adj(f), nf	clinical, private hospital
1502	cloche	nf	bell
713	club	nm	club
1547	cochon	noun, adj	pig
2447	coco	nm	mate, coconut
899	coder	v	to code, encode
356	cœur	nm	heart
1081	coffrer	nm	trunk, boot, chest
540	coin	nm	corner
1350	coincer	v	to jam, hinder, get stuck
2207	coïncidence	nf	coincidence
766	colère	nf	anger, wrath
1679	colle	nf	glue, adhesive
2181	collection	nf	collection, series
2292	collège	nm	secondary school, body
2052	collègue	nm, nf	colleague
1926	collier	nm	necklace
1785	colline	nf	hill
542	colonel	nm	colonel
641	combat	nm	fight, combat, battle
1523	combattre	v	to fight
181	combien	adv, conj	how much, how many
2350	combinaison	nf	combination
1808	comédie	nf	comedy, playacting
1521	comité	nm	committee
2188	commande	nf	order, control

1735	**commandement**	*nm*	command, order, commandment	263	**compter**	*v*	to count
591	**commander**	*v*	to order, command	1435	**comte**	*nm*	count
43	**comme**	*adv, conj*	like, as	2013	**comté**	*nm*	count
389	**commencer**	*v*	to begin, start	455	**con**	*adj, nmf*	stupid
62	**comment**	*adv, conj, int*	how	2202	**concentrer**	*v*	to concentrate
1878	**commerce**	*nm*	trade, commerce	1858	**concernant**	*adv, prep*	concerning
2438	**commercial**	*adj, nm*	commercial, marketeer	1184	**concerner**	*v*	to concern
1326	**commettre**	*v*	to commit	1374	**concert**	*nm*	concert
1338	**commissaire**	*nm, nf*	superintendent, commissioner	2126	**conclure**	*v*	to conclude
2247	**commissariat**	*nm*	police station	1532	**concourir**	*v*	compete, participate
1601	**commission**	*nf*	commission	1691	**condamner**	*v*	to condemn
1458	**commun**	*noun, adj*	common	1623	**condition**	*nf*	condition
1760	**communauté**	*nf*	community	771	**conduire**	*v*	to lead, drive
2199	**communication**	*nf*	communication	1859	**conférence**	*nf*	conference
2246	**communiste**	*adj(f, nmf*	communist	322	**confiance**	*nf*	confidence, trust
638	**compagnie**	*nf*	company	2488	**confier**	*v*	to entrust
2471	**compétition**	*nm*	competition	2501	**conflit**	*nm*	conflict
1540	**complet**	*adj, nm*	full, complete, full	1928	**congé**	*nm*	time off, leave
561	**complètement**	*adv*	completely, fully	1908	**congrès**	*nm*	congres, convention, conference
2161	**complexe**	*nm, adj(f)*	complex	1105	**connaissance**	*nf*	knowledge
1426	**compliqué**	*noun, adj*	complicated, complex	177	**connaître**	*v*	to know
1650	**comportement**	*nm*	behavior	628	**connard**	*nm*	shithead, asshole
197	**comprendre**	*v*	to understand	643	**connerie**	*nf*	crap, bullsh*t, stupidity
1179	**compte**	*nm*	account, count	1129	**conscience**	*nf*	conscience, consciousness
				705	**conseil**	*nm*	advice, counsel, council

1776	conseiller	nm, v	adviser, to advise
2049	conséquence	nf	result, consequence
2430	construction	nf	construction, building
1429	construire	v	to build, construct
804	contact	nm	contact
2128	contacter	v	to contact, get in touch with
2274	contenir	v	to contain
457	content	adj	glad, pleased, happy
473	continu	adj	continuous
648	continuer	v	to continue
881	contraire	nm, adj(f)	opposite, contrary
914	contrat	nm	contract
194	contre	adv, nm, prep	against
610	contrôle	nm	control
1436	contrôler	v	to control, check, inspect, monitor
1346	convaincre	v	to convince
1935	convenir	v	to suit, to agree on
1150	conversation	nf	conversation
1942	convier	v	to invite
921	copain	nm	friend, buddy, mate
1839	copier	v	to copy, reproduce
866	copine	nf	girlfriend
1299	corde	nf	rope, cord, string
277	corps	nm[pl]	body
1651	correct	adj	correct
2422	correctement	adv	properly
1083	costume	nm	suit, costume, dress
256	côté	nf	coast
1015	cou	nm	neck
1317	couche	nf	layer, coat
645	coucher	nm, v	lie down, sleep
2088	coucou	int	hello
1954	couler	v	to flow, run, sink
904	couleur	nf	color
1669	couloir	nm	corridor, aisle
186	coup	nm	coup, blow, knock, stroke
755	coupable	nmf, adj(f)	guilty
831	couper	v	to cut
1109	couple	nm, nf	couple
692	cour	nf	yard, court
794	courage	nm	courage
1586	courageux	noun, adj[pl]	courageous
452	courant	adj, nm	current
951	courir	v	to run
2036	couronne	nf	crown, wreath
1579	courrier	nm	mail, post
331	cours	nfpl, nm[pl]	course
826	course	nf	race, shopping
844	court	adj, adv, nm	short
1128	cousin	nm	cousin
926	couteau	nm	knife
1229	coûter	v	to cost
1668	couvert	adj, nm	covered, overcast; place, seat, cutlery

1310	**couverture**	*nf*	blanket
1866	**couvrir**	*v*	to cover
1041	**craindre**	*v*	to fear, be afraid of
2014	**crainte**	*nf*	fear
2100	**cran**	*nm*	guts, notch
1461	**crâne**	*adj(f), nm*	skull
2140	**cravete**	*nf*	necktie
2370	**création**	*nf*	creation
1439	**créature**	*nf*	creature
1528	**crédit**	*nm*	credit
1216	**créer**	*v*	to create
1661	**créme**	*adj(i), nf*	cream
1079	**crétin**	*nm*	dumbass
2271	**creuser**	*v*	to dig
1610	**crever**	*v*	to burst, puncture
1518	**cri**	*nm*	shout, cry
1341	**crier**	*v*	to shout, scream, cry out
696	**crime**	*nm*	crime
1536	**criminel**	*noun, adj*	criminal
1003	**crise**	*nf*	crisis
1854	**critique**	*adj(f), nmf*	criticism, critical, critic
92	**croire**	*v*	to believe
1503	**croix**	*nf[pl]*	cross
505	**cru**	*adj*	vintage, raw, crude
2018	**cruel**	*adj*	cruel, ferocious, bitter

2381	**cuir**	*nm*	leather
669	**cuisine**	*nf*	cooking, kitchen
2323	**cuisine**	*nf*	cooking, kitchen
335	**cul**	*nm*	bum, arse, ass
2328	**culotte**	*nf*	pants, panties
1830	**culture**	*nf*	culture
1383	**curieux**	*noun, adj[pl]*	curious
2378	**curiosité**	*nf*	curiosity

D

536	**dame**	*int, nf*	lady
671	**danger**	*nm*	danger
608	**dangereux**	*adj[pl]*	dangerous
27	**dans**	*prep*	in, into, from
653	**danser**	*v*	to dance
1112	**date**	*nf*	date
1422	**davantage**	*adv*	more
1234	**débarrasser**	*v*	to clear, get rid of
1479	**débile**	*nm*	debile, daft person
1	**de, du, de la, de l', des**	*det, prep*	of, from, some, any
526	**debout**	*adv*	standing
2226	**débrouiller**	*v*	to untangle, to sort out
471	**début**	*nm*	beginning
2289	**décembre**	*nm*	December
2060	**décevoir**	*v*	to dissapoint
572	**decider**	*v*	to decide
797	**décision**	*nf*	decision
1711	**déclaration**	*nf*	declaration
2096	**déclarer**	*v*	to declare, disclose

2325	**déconner**	*nm*	to talk crap, to screw around, mess around
907	**découvrir**	*v*	to discover, find out
348	**dedans**	*adv, nm[pl], prep*	inside, indoors
1169	**défendre**	*v*	to defend, forbid
810	**défense**	*nf*	defence
2218	**défi**	*nm*	challenge
836	**degager**	*v*	to free, clear
2111	**dégât**	*pl, nm*	damage
1974	**dégoûter**	*v*	to disgust
1946	**degré**	*nm*	degree
2373	**dégueulasse**	*adj*	disgusting, filthy
285	**dehors**	*adv, nm[pl], prep*	outside
122	**déjà**	*adv*	already, ever
565	**dejeuner**	*nm, v*	lunch, to eat lunch
1327	**delà**	*adv*	beyond, above, over
1466	**délicieux**	*adj*	delicious
2154	**délirer**	*v*	to rave, to be delirious
158	**demain**	*adv, nm*	tomorrow
202	**demander**	*v*	to ask for
1975	**démarrer**	*v*	to start
2023	**demeurer**	*v*	to remain, live
1337	**demi**	*adj(i), adv, nm*	half
1505	**démon**	*nm*	demon, fiend, devil
816	**dent**	*nf*	tooth
2482	**dentiste**	*nm, nf*	dentist
740	**départ**	*nm*	departure
2061	**département**	*nm*	department
2077	**dépasser**	*v*	to exceed, to overtake
1981	**dépêcher**	*v*	to hurry, to dispatch
996	**dépendre**	*v*	to depend
2184	**déplacer**	*v*	to move, to put off, to displace
1989	**déposer**	*v*	to deposit, to leave, to put down
2418	**dépression**	*nm*	depression
117	**depuis**	*adv, prep*	since, for , in
845	**deranger**	*v*	to disturb, bother
265	**dernier**	*nm&f, adj*	last
315	**derrière**	*adv, nm, prep*	last; behind
406	**dès**	*prep*	from, as soon
2220	**désastre**	*nm*	disaster
749	**descendre**	*v*	to go down, come down
1176	**désert**	*adj, nm*	desert, wilderness
1391	**désir**	*nm*	desire
1762	**désirer**	*v*	to desire, to want
1391	**désolé**	*adj*	sorry, afraid
1174	**désormais**	*adv*	from now on, henceforth
2021	**dessin**	*nm*	drawing, pattern, design
1038	**dessous**	*adv, nm[pl], prep*	underneath, below, bottom, underside
247	**dessus**	*adv, nm[pl], prep*	above, on top

906	**destin**	*nm*	fate, destiny	1334	**directement**	*adv*	directly
2313	**destination**	*nf*	destination	767	**directeur**	*nmf, adj*	director
2300	**destiner**	*v*	to intend, be used	930	**direction**	*nf*	direction, management
1907	**destruction**	*nf*	destruction	1357	**diriger**	*v*	to lead, direct
1155	**détail**	*nm*	detail	2459	**discipline**	*nf*	discipline
2391	**détendre**	*v*	to loosen, to relax	1101	**discourir**	*v*	to discuss, to discourse, ramble
569	**detester**	*v*	to hate, detest	1872	**discussion**	*nf*	discussion
917	**détruire**	*v*	to destroy	890	**discuter**	*v*	to discuss, debate; to question
1914	**dette**	*nf*	debt				
72	**deux**	*det, num*	two, couple	594	**disparaître**	*v*	to disappear, vanish
802	**deuxième**	*det, nm, nf*	second	2443	**disparition**	*nf*	disappearance
242	**devant**	*adv, nm, prep*	in front, ahead	2146	**disputer**	*v*	to dispute, contest
462	**devenir**	*nm, v*	to become	2065	**disque**	*nm*	disc, disk
1480	**deviner**	*v*	to guess, solve	1325	**distance**	*nf*	distance
93	**devoir**	*nm, v*	to have to, owe; duty	2110	**divin**	*adj, nm*	divine, heavenly
118	**devoir**	*v*	must, have to	1949	**division**	*nf*	division
579	**diable**	*int, nm*	devil	1546	**divorce**	*nm*	divorce
2025	**diamant**	*nm*	diamond	408	**dix**	*det, num*	ten
95	**dieu**	*int, nm*	god	301	**docteur**	*nm*	doctor
942	**différence**	*nf*	difference	1886	**document**	*nm*	document
727	**différent**	*adj*	different	991	**doigt**	*nm*	finger
416	**difficile**	*adj(f)*	difficult	321	**dollar**	*nm*	dollar
1686	**digne**	*adj(f)*	dignified, worthy	1795	**domaine**	*nm*	domain, field
2413	**dignité**	*nf*	dignity	678	**dommage**	*nm*	damage, harm; too bad, a pity
985	**dimanche**	*nm*	Sunday				
435	**dîner**	*nm, v*	dinner; to dine	710	**don**	*nm*	gift
723	**dingue**	*adj*	crazy, mad, wild, nutty	124	**donc**	*conj*	so, then, therefore, thus
2242	**diplômer**	*v*	to graduate				
52	**dire**	*nm, v*	to say				
1160	**direct**	*noun, adj*	direct				

1345	**donne**	*adj*	given	1863	**duc**	*nm*	duke
1538	**donnée**	*nf*	fact, datum	325	**dur**	*adv, nm&f, adj*	hard
254	**donner**	*v*	to give				
281	**dont**	*pron*	whose, of which	989	**durant**	*prep*	during, for
				1922	**durer**	*v*	to last
417	**dormir**	*v*	to sleep				
544	**dos**	*nm[pl]*	back		**E**		
2375	**dose**	*nf*	dose, amount				
868	**dossier**	*nm*	file, record; case	226	**eau**	*nf*	water
924	**doubler**	*v*	to double, pass; to dub	2395	**écart**	*nm*	space, gap
552	**doucement**	*adv*	gently, softly	1232	**échange**	*nm*	exchange
2389	**douceur**	*nf*	softness, smoothness, mildness, gentleness, sweetness	1076	**échapper**	*v*	to escape
				1828	**échec**	*adj(i), nm*	failure
				2005	**échelle**	*nf*	ladder
1270	**douche**	*nf*	shower, douche	1815	**échouer**	*v*	to fail
2495	**doue**	*adj*	talented, gifted	2448	**éclair**	*nm*	flash, spark
1673	**doué**	*adj*	gifted	2113	**éclater**	*v*	to burst, to shatter
883	**douleur**	*nf*	pain	297	**école**	*nf*	school
374	**doute**	*nm*	doubt	2318	**économie**	*nf*	economy
2368	**douter**	*v*	to doubt	273	**écoute**	*nf*	listening
937	**doux**	*adv, noun, adj[pl]*	soft, sweet	530	**écouter**	*v*	to listen to
				1605	**écran**	*nm*	screen
1625	**douze**	*det, num*	twelve	1972	**écraser**	*v*	to crush
2445	**drap**	*nm*	sheet	395	**écrire**	*v*	to write
1814	**drapeau**	*nm*	flag	2254	**écriture**	*nf*	writing, entry
2203	**drogue**	*nf*	drug	1767	**écrivain**	*nm*	writer
875	**droguer**	*v*	to drug, take drugs	1704	**éducation**	*nf*	education
255	**droit**	*adj, adv, nm*	right	2498	**effacer**	*v*	to erase, clean
362	**drôle**	*adj(f), nm*	funny, strange	517	**effet**	*nm*	effect
				2105	**efficace**	*adj(f)*	efficient, effective

1700	**effort**	*nm*	effort		1884	**employer**	*v*	to use, employ
2376	**effrayer**	*v*	to frighten, scare		2027	**emporter**	*v*	to take, remove
1443	**égal**	*noun, adj*	equal		1967	**emprunter**	*v*	to borrow
1198	**également**	*adv*	also, too, as well, equally		17	**en**	*adv, prep, pron*	in, by
760	**église**	*nf*	church					
2428	**égoïste**	*adj, nm, nf*	selfish, egoist		945	**enceinte**	*adjf, nf*	pregnant; enclosure
174	**eh**	*int*	hey, uh		882	**enchanter**	*v*	to delight, enchant, rejoice
1939	**électricité**	*nf*	electricity					
1843	**électrique**	*adj(f)*	electric		76	**encore**	*adv*	again, yet
2102	**élément**	*nm*	element		2322	**endormir**	*v*	to put to sleep, fall asleep
					2	232 = PLACER		
1624	**élève**	*adj*	high, heavy, tall		276	**endroit**	*nm*	place, spot
					968	**énergie**	*nf*	energy
1574	**élever**	*v*	to grow, lift, raise		1841	**énerver**	*v*	to annoy, get on someone nerves
2222	**éliminer**	*v*	to eliminate					
2398	**élire**	*v*	to elect		1378	**enfance**	*nf*	childhood
29	**elle**	*pron*	she, her		166	**enfant**	*nm, nf, adj(f)*	child
2266	**éloigner**	*v*	to remove		631	**enfer**	*nm*	hell
2452	**embêter**	*v*	to bother		2138	**enfermer**	*v*	to shut, lock in
1124	**embrasser**	*v*	to kiss, embrace		268	**enfin**	*adv*	at last, finally
1257	**émission**	*nf*	transmision, broadcasting, programme		877	**enfoiré**	*nm*	bastard
					1495	**enfuir**	*v*	to run away, flee
					1498	**engager**	*v*	to hire, involve
728	**emmener**	*v*	to take		979	**enlever**	*v*	to remove, to take off
1165	**emmerder**	*v*	to bug, ANNOY#3 bother					
2087	**émotion**	*nm*	emotion		741	**ennemi**	*nmf, adj*	enemy
862	**empecher**	*v*	to prevent		654	**ennui**	*nm*	boredom, trouble, worry
1372	**empereur**	*nm*	emperor					
1478	**empire**	*nm*	empire		1303	**ennuyer**	*v*	to bore, worry, bother
1302	**emploi**	*nm*	employment, work, use		2151	**ennuyeux**	*adj*	boring, annoying, dull
					969	**énorme**	*adj(f)*	enormous, huge

2346	**énormément**	*adv*	enormously
849	**enqueter**	*v*	to investigate, hold inquiry, conduct a survey
2468	**enregistrement**	*nm*	recording, registration, check-in, logging
2496	**enregistrer**	*v*	to record, check in
2155	**enseigne**	*nf*	sign
2374	**enseigner**	*v*	to teach
2342	**ensemble**	*adv, nm*	together
418	**ensuite**	*adv*	next
196	**entendre**	*v*	to hear
1681	**enterrement**	*nm*	burial, funeral
1845	**enterrer**	*v*	to bury, lay aside
887	**entier**	*nm, adj*	whole, full
1837	**entièrement**	*adv*	entirely, completely
1568	**entraînement**	*nm*	training
1915	**entraîner**	*v*	to train
2361	**entraîneur**	*nm*	coach, trainer
156	**entre**	*prep*	between
1321	**entreprendre**	*v*	to begin, start, undertake
350	**entrer**	*v*	to enter, go in, come in, get in
2067	**entretien**	*nm*	interview, discussion, maintenance
2446	**envelopper**	*v*	to wrap, surround, veil
863	**envers**	*nm[pl], prep*	towards
308	**envier**	*v*	to envy

[IN ROUTLEDGE]
1185   ENTRETENIR - TALK TO ; TO MAINTAIN
= 1433 IN ROUTLEDGE]

756	**environ**	*adv, prep, nm*	about, thereabouts, or so
2371	**environnement**	*nm*	environment
566	**envoyer**	*v*	to send
1900	**épaule**	*nf*	shoulder
2492	**épisode**	*nf*	episode
663	**époque**	*nf*	era, period
787	**épouser**	*v*	to marry, wed
2263	**époux**	*nm*	husband
1838	**épreuve**	*nf*	test, ordeal, trial
1635	**équipage**	*nm*	crew, gear
396	**équipe**	*nf*	team
2309	**équippement**	*nm*	equipment
2125	**ère**	*nf*	era
497	**erreur**	*nf*	mistake, error
1778	**escalier**	*nm*	stairs, staircase
1703	**esclave**	*nmf*	slave
954	**espace**	*nm, nf*	space
1959	**espagnol**	*nm, adj*	Spanish
468	**espèce**	*nf*	species
282	**espérer**	*v*	to hope
758	**espoir**	*nm*	hope
398	**esprit**	*nm*	mind, spirit
1720	**essai**	*nm*	attempt, try, test
313	**essayer**	*v*	to try
405	**essayer**	*v*	to try
1200	**essence**	*nf*	gas, petrol
2251	**essentiel**	*nm, adj*	essential
2219	**estimer**	*v*	to estimate; to consider, deem
1611	**estomac**	*nm*	stomach
12	**et**	*conj*	and

1022	**étager**	*nm*	floor
2127	**étape**	*nf*	stage, step, phase
403	**état**	*nm*	state
2394	**etc**	*adv*	et cetera , etc.
2054	**éteindre**	*v*	to switch off, to turn off, to extinguish
2444	**éternel**	*adj*	eternal
1822	**éternité**	*nf*	eternity, lifetime
1132	**étoile**	*nf*	star
1353	**étoile**	*nf*	star
1614	**étonner**	*v*	to astonish, amaze, surprise
639	**étrange**	*adj(f)*	strange, odd
1047	**étranger**	*noun, adj*	foreigner; foreign
3	**être**	*nm, v*	to be; being
1687	**être**	*nm*	human being
1273	**étude**	*nf*	study
1660	**étudiant**	*nm/f, adj*	student
1440	**étudier**	*v*	to study
483	**euh**	*int*	er, um, uh
214	**eux**	*pron*	them
2106	**événement**	*nm*	event
1323	**évidemment**	*adv*	obviously
2436	**évidence**	*nf*	evidence
1414	**évident**	*adv*	obviously, of course
858	**eviter**	*v*	to avoid
1693	**ex**	*nmfi*	ex
590	**exact**	*adj*	exact, correct
380	**exactement**	*adv*	exactly
1572	**examen**	*nm*	exam
2070	**examiner**	*v*	to examine
1802	**excellence**	*nf*	excellence
854	**excellent**	*adj*	excellent
2149	**exception**	*nf*	exception
2091	**excitant**	*adj*	exciting
1089	**excuse**	*nf*	excuse, apology
800	**excuser**	*v*	to excuse
1934	**exécution**	*nf*	execution
640	**exemple**	*nm*	example
1792	**exercice**	*nm*	exercise,
2007	**exiger**	*v*	to require, demand
1550	**existence**	*nf*	existence
636	**exister**	*v*	to exist
776	**expérience**	*nf*	experience
1905	**expert**	*nm, adj*	expert
1779	**explication**	*nf*	explanation
596	**expliquer**	*v*	to explain
1438	**exploser**	*v*	to explode, blow up
1418	**explosion**	*nf*	explosion
1789	**exprès**	*adj[pl], adv*	deliberately, on purpose, intentionally
1918	**expression**	*nf*	expression
1951	**exprimer**	*v*	to express
1175	**extérieur**	*noun, adj*	exterior
1417	**extraordinaire**	*adj(f)*	extraordinary
1924	**extrêmement**	*adv*	extremely

F

2335	**fabriquer**	v	to manufacture, invent, make
2173	**fabuleux**	adj	fabulous
1311	**fac**	nf	uni, university
439	**face**	nf	front, side, face
1829	**fâcher**	v	to anger, make angry, get angry
370	**facile**	adj(f)	easy
1359	**facilement**	adv	easily
270	**façon**	nf	way, manner
1090	**faible**	noun, adj(f)	weak
959	**failli**	adj	bankrupt
460	**faim**	nf	hungry
41	**faire**	nm, v	to do, make
885	**fait**	adj, nm	done, fact
73	**falloir**	v	to take, require, need
2400	**fameux**	adj[pl]	famous
189	**famille**	nf	family
1058	**fantastique**	noun, adj(f)	fantastic, terrific, great, weird, eerie
1222	**fantôme**	nm	ghost, phantom
2477	**fasciner**	v	to fascinate
1061	**fatiguer**	v	to tire, get
377	**faute**	nf	mistake, error, fault
2178	**fauteuil**	nm	armchair, seat
522	**faux**	adv, adj[pl], nm[pl], nf[pl]	false; scythe
1274	**faveur**	nf	favor
748	**félicitations**	nf	congratulations
101	**femme**	nf	woman, wife
778	**fenêtre**	nf	window
1865	**fenêtre**	nf	window
1152	**fer**	nm	iron
339	**ferme**	adj	shut, closed, locked
1979	**fermé**	adj	shut, closed, locked
939	**fermer**	v	to close, shut
1243	**fesser**	v	to spank
1995	**fête**	nf	party
381	**fêter**	v	to celebrate
259	**feu**	adj(f), nm	fire
2221	**feuille**	nf	leaf, sheet
2451	**feuille**	nf	leaf, sheet, slip
1427	**fiancé**	noun, adj	fiancé, engaged
1890	**fiancer**	fiance	to get engaged, to betroth
2491	**fiche**	nf	card, sheet, slip, form
737	**ficher**	v	to file; to make fun of, not care, not give a damn
1793	**fichu**	adj	damn, rotten
1952	**fidèle**	adj	faithful
801	**fier**	adj, v	to rely on; proud
1950	**fierté**	nf	pride
1861	**fièvre**	nf	fever
1590	**figurer**	v	to represent, appear
152	**fil**	nm	thread, wire
987	**fil**	nm	thread, wire
983	**filer**	v	to spin, run, get out
121	**fille**	nf	girl, daughter

2432	**fillette**	*nf*	little girl, girl	2041	**formation**	*nf*	training
271	**film**	*nm*	film, movie	570	**forme**	*nf*	form
1998	**filmer**	*v*	to film, shoot	813	**formidable**	*adj(f)*	tremendous, considerable, great
249	**fin**	*adj, adv, nf, nm*	end; gist, clever person	272	**fort**	*adv, adj, nm*	strong
1894	**final**	*nm, adj*	final	1122	**fortune**	*nf*	fortune
973	**finalement**	*adv*	finally, eventually	278	**fou**	*adj, nm*	mad, crazy
212	**finir**	*v*	to finish	613	**fou**	*adj, nm*	mad, crazy
2476	**fixe**	*adj, nm*	fixed, set; base salary	2386	**fouiller**	*v*	to search, frisk, go through, rummage through
2295	**flamme**	*nf*	flame, fire, fervor, brilliance	1305	**foule**	*nf*	crowd
782	**fleur**	*nf*	flower	519	**foutre**	*v, nm*	to f*ck, shove off, piss off
1879	**fleuve**	*nm*	river	2412	**foutu**	*adj*	fucking, damned
582	**flic**	*nm, nf*	cop	1409	**foyer**	*nm*	home, hearth
1731	**flotter**	*v*	to float, hang, stream	895	**frais**	*adj[pl], adv, nm[pl]*	cool, fresh; fee, expense
928	**foi**	*nf*	faith	2089	**franc**	*adj, adv, adj, nm*	frank; franc
2235	**foie**	*nm*	liver	825	**francais**	*nm, adj[pl]*	French
89	**fois**	*nf[pl]*	time, times	1205	**franchement**	*adv*	frankly
1018	**folie**	*nf*	madness, folly, insanity	1028	**frappé**	*nf*	strike, striking, stamp, impression, punch
1920	**fonce**	*adj*	dark	1036	**frapper**	*v*	to hit, strike, knock
2397	**fonction**	*nf*	function	210	**frère**	*nm*	brother
1286	**fonctionner**	*v*	to function, work	538	**fric**	*nm*	cash, money, dough
494	**fondre**	*v*	to melt, merge	2141	**frigo**	*nm*	fridge
1790	**football**	*nm*	football, soccer	2423	**fringuer**	*v*	to dress
446	**force**	*adv, nf*	force	500	**froid**	*nm, adj*	cold
965	**force**	*adv, nf*	force				
1638	**forcément**	*adv*	without question, inevitably				
1768	**forcer**	*v*	to force				
1170	**forêt**	*nf*	forest				

1553	**fromage**	*nm*	cheese		1103	**gâteau**	*noun, adj*	cake
1261	**front**	*nm*	front, forehead		456	**gauche**	*nf, adj(f)*	left
1354	**frontière**	*nf*	border		1097	**gaz**	*nm[pl]*	gas
1739	**fruit**	*nm*	fruit		1758	**géant**	*nmf, adj*	giant, gigantic
1235	**fuir**	*v*	to flee		1472	**gêne**	*nm*	gene
1620	**fuite**	*nf*	escape		373	**général**	*nm, adj*	general
1163	**fumer**	*v*	to smoke		2252	**génération**	*nm*	generation
2427	**fumier**	*nm*	manure		1992	**généreux**	*adj*	generous
1799	**furieux**	*adj*	furious, raging, violent, mad		409	**génial**	*adj*	inspired, great, brilliant
1070	**fusil**	*nm*	rifle, gun		1114	**génie**	*nm*	genius
1085	**futur**	*noun, adj*	future		1125	**genou**	*nm*	knee
					248	**genre**	*nm*	type, kind, sort
	G				123	**gens**	*nmpl*	people
					383	**gentil**	*adj*	nice, kind
1746	**gâcher**	*v*	to waste, spoil		1993	**gérer**	*v*	to manage
1876	**gagnant**	*nmf, adj*	winner, winning		1332	**geste**	*nm*	gesture
493	**gagner**	*v*	to win, earn		815	**glace**	*nf*	ice, ice cream; mirror
714	**gamin**	*nm*	kid		1291	**gloire**	*nf*	glory, fame
2150	**gant**	*nm*	glove		1848	**golf**	*nm*	golf, golf course
1592	**garage**	*nm*	garage		1153	**gorge**	*nf*	throat
2040	**garce**	*nf*	bitch		789	**gosse**	*nm, nf*	kid
288	**garçon**	*nm*	boy		940	**goût**	*nm*	taste
323	**garde**	*nm, nf*	guard		2145	**goûter**	*v*	to taste
1423	**gardé**	*nm, nf*	guard		2072	**goutter**	*v*	to drip
447	**garder**	*v*	to keep		672	**gouvernement**	*nm*	government
1450	**gardien**	*noun, adj*	guardian, keeper		1237	**gouverneur**	*nm, nf*	governor
1043	**gare**	*int, nf*	station, railway station; beware		475	**grâce**	*nf*	thanks, grace, favor
179	**gars**	*nm[pl]*	guy		160	**grand**	*adv, nm/f, adj*	great, older girl or boy, tall

1185	**grandir**	*v*	to grow, increase, expand		1589	**hall**	*nm*	foyer, lobby
2462	**gras**	*adj[pl], adv, nm[pl]*	fatty, fat, greasy		1072	**hasard**	*nm*	chance, luck
2204	**gratuit**	*adj*	free, gratuitous, unwarranted		1431	**hâte**	*nf*	haste, impatience
					293	**haut**	*adv, adj*	top, high
450	**grave**	*adv, adj(f), nm*	serious, grave		1827	**hauteur**	*nf*	height
2302	**gréver**	*v*	to put strain on, encumber		1635	**hein**	*int*	eh, huh
					1875	**héler**	*v*	to hail, call out
2238	**gris**	*nm, adj[pl]*	gray		1260	**herbe**	*nf*	grass, herb
262	**gros**	*adv, nm, adj[pl]*	big, whoiesale, heavy		684	**héros**	*nm[pl]*	hero
					170	**heure**	*nf*	hour
514	**groupe**	*nm*	group		1279	**heureusement**	*adv*	fortunately, luckily
2050	**groupe**	*nm*	group		341	**heureux**	*adj[pl]*	happy, lucky, fortunate
2092	**guère**	*adv*	hardly		286	**hier**	*adv*	yesterday
2001	**guérir**	*v*	to cure		207	**histoire**	*nf*	history, story
239	**guerre**	*nf*	war		1209	**hiver**	*nm*	winter
2359	**guerrier**	*nmf, adj*	warrior; warlike		96	**homme**	*nm*	man
470	**gueule**	*nf*	mouth, trap		998	**honnête**	*adj(f)*	honest, decent, fair
1745	**guider**	*v*	to guide		2217	**honnêtement**	*adv*	honestly
1892	**guitare**	*nf*	guitar		445	**honneur**	*nm*	honor
					611	**honte**	*nf*	shame
	H				474	**hôpital**	*nm*	hospital
					1172	**horreur**	*nf*	horror
832	**ha**	*int*	oh		843	**horrible**	*adj(f)*	horrible, terrible, dreadful, hideous
1969	**habiller**	*v*	to dress, get dressed		656	**hors**	*adv, prep*	except, outside
1962	**habitant**	*nm*	inhabitant		508	**hôtel**	*nm*	hotel
934	**habiter**	*v*	to live		1824	**huile**	*nf*	oil
606	**habitude**	*nf*	habit		621	**huit**	*det, num*	eight
1406	**haine**	*nf*	hatred, hate		1178	**hum**	*int*	um, uh, Hmm
1363	**haïr**	*v*	to detest, hate, abhor		753	**humain**	*nm, adj*	human

1396	**humanité**	*nf*	humanity	2158	**impôt**	*nm*	tax
1486	**humeur**	*nf*	mood, temper	612	**impression**	*nf*	impression
1732	**humour**	*nm*	humor	2063	**impressionnant**	*adj*	impressive, upsetting
				1813	**incapable**	*adj*	incapable, incompetent
	I			1616	**incendie**	*nm*	fire, blaze
46	**ici**	*adv*	here	1784	**incident**	*adj, nm*	incident
1622	**idéal**	*nm, adj*	ideal	1531	**inconnu**	*noun, adj*	unknown
192	**idée**	*nf*	idea	532	**incroyable**	*adj(f)*	incredible, amazing, unbelievable
2129	**identifier**	*v*	to identify				
1269	**identité**	*nf*	identity	2022	**inde**	*nf*	India
469	**idiot**	*nmf, adj*	idiot, fool, stupid	2369	**indice**	*nm*	indication, sign, clue, hint
577	**ignorer**	*v*	to ignore				
11	**il**	*pron*	he, it	1570	**indien**	*noun, adj*	Indian
897	**île**	*nf*	island	2404	**indiquer**	*v*	to indicate, signal
2175	**illégal**	*adj*	illegal	2167	**industrie**	*nf*	industry
977	**image**	*nf*	picture, image	1492	**infirmier**	*noun, adj*	nurse
1324	**image**	*nf*	picture, image	2047	**influencer**	*v*	to influence
1481	**imagination**	*nf*	imagination	1084	**information**	*nf*	information
646	**imaginer**	*v*	to imagine	2284	**informer**	*v*	to inform, notify
872	**imbécile**	*adj, nf*	imbecile, fool	2229	**ingénieur**	*nm*	engineer
818	**immediatement**	*adv*	immediately	1948	**injuste**	*adj(f)*	unfair, unjust
2012	**immense**	*adj(f)*	immense	1249	**innocent**	*noun, adj*	innocent
1375	**immeuble**	*noun, adj(f)*	building	441	**inquiet**	*adj*	worried, anxious
2497	**impact**	*nm*	impact	1092	**inquiéter**	*v*	to worry, disturb
2147	**impliquer**	*v*	to imply, implicate	2118	**insister**	*v*	to insist
833	**importance**	*nf*	importance	689	**inspecteur**	*nm*	inspector
328	**important**	*nm, adj*	important	1682	**installer**	*v*	to install
225	**importer**	*v*	to import; to be important				
368	**impossible**	*nm, adj(f)*	impossible				

312	**instant**	*adj, nm*	instant, moment
215 7	**instinct**	*nm*	instinct
194 7	**instruction**	*nf*	instruction, direction
199 1	**intelligence**	*nf*	intelligence
117 7	**intelligent**	*adj*	intelligent, clever, bright, smart
101 4	**intention**	*nf*	intention
100 5	**interdire**	*v*	to forbid, prohibit, ban
788	**intéressant**	*adj*	interesting
746	**intéresser**	*v*	to interest, involve
745	**intérêt**	*nm*	interest
529	**intérieur**	*nm adj*	interior, inside
210 4	**interroger**	*v*	to question, interrogate
239 3	**interrompre**	*v*	to interrupt
245 4	**interview**	*nf*	interview
724	**inutile**	*adj(f)*	useless
161 3	**inventer**	*v*	to invent
211 5	**invisible**	*adj(f)*	invisible
193 8	**invitation**	*nf*	invitation
162 1	**invite**	*nm*	guest
974	**inviter**	*v*	to invite
204 4	**issu**	*adj*	descended from, come from
186 4	**italien**	*nm/f, adj*	Italian
187 4	**ivre**	*adj*	drunk, intoxicated

J

| 148 8 | **jaloux** | *noun, adj* | jealous |
| 68 | **jamais** | *adv* | never |

808	**jambe**	*nf*	leg
962	**jambe**	*nf*	leg
122 8	**japonais**	*noun, adj[pl]*	Japanese
102 5	**jardin**	*nm*	garden
151 1	**jaune**	*adv, noun, adj(f)*	yellow
2	**je, j´**	*pron*	I
812	**jeter**	*v*	to throw
338	**jeu**	*nm*	game
158 5	**jeudi**	*nm*	Thursday
251	**jeune**	*nmf adj(f)*	young
162 8	**jeunesse**	*nf*	youth
839	**joie**	*nf*	joy
116 6	**joindre**	*v*	to join
513	**joli**	*adj*	pretty, attractive
114 7	**joue**	*nf*	cheek
260	**jouer**	*v*	to play
222 7	**jouet**	*nm*	toy
145 6	**joueur**	*noun, adj*	player
125	**jour**	*nm*	day
676	**journal**	*nm*	newspaper, paper
107 5	**journal**	*nm*	newspaper, paper
151 5	**journaliste**	*nm, nf*	journalist, reporter
320	**journée**	*nf*	day
861	**joyeux**	*adj[pl]*	merry, joyful, happy
693	**juge**	*nm, nf*	judge
175 0	**jugement**	*nm*	judgement
193 7	**juger**	*v*	to judge
126 2	**juif**	*noun, adj*	Jew, Jewish
191 0	**juillet**	*nm*	July

1973	**juin**	*nm*	June
1743	**jungle**	*nf*	jungle
584	**jurer**	*v*	to swear
1643	**jury**	*nm*	jury, board of examiners
1544	**jus**	*nm*	juice, sauce
2236	**jusque**	*adv, prep*	to, up to, until, till
84	**juste**	*adv, nm, adj(f)*	just, only; fair
978	**justement**	*adv*	exactly, rightly, precisely
774	**justice**	*nf*	justice

K

1766	**kilo**	*nm*	kilo
864	**kilometre**	*nm*	kilometer

L

7	**là**	*adv, int*	there, here
50	**là**	*adv, int*	there, here
1598	**labo**	*nm*	lab
2324	**laboratoire**	*nm*	laboratory
1217	**lac**	*nm*	lake
763	**lâche**	*adj*	loose
1646	**lâcher**	*v*	to let go, release
1349	**laisse**	*nf*	leash, lead
219	**laisser**	*v*	to leave
918	**lait**	*nm*	milk
1904	**lampe**	*nf*	lamp, light
1167	**lance**	*nf*	lance, spear
2461	**lancement**	*nm*	launch
1313	**lancer**	*nm, v*	to throw, launch, start
1832	**langage**	*nm*	language
871	**langue**	*nf*	language, tongue
1397	**lapin**	*nm*	rabbit
1684	**large**	*adj(f), adv, nm*	wide, width
1306	**larme**	*nf*	tear
1849	**las**	*adj*	tired, weary
2337	**lave**	*adj*	washed
1328	**laver**	*v*	to wash, clean
5	**le, la, les, l´**	*det, pron*	the; him, her, it, them
2458	**leader**	*nm, nf*	leader
1220	**leçon**	*nf*	lesson
2354	**lecture**	*nf*	reading
2483	**légal**	*adj*	legal
1753	**légende**	*nf*	legend, caption, key
2024	**léger**	*adj*	light, slight, thin
1385	**lendemain**	*nm*	next day
1477	**lentement**	*adv*	slowly
736	**lequel**	*pron*	who, whom, which
533	**lettre**	*nf*	letter
957	**lettre**	*nf*	letter
98	**leur**	*det, adj(f), pron*	them, their, theirs
1149	**lève**	*nf*	survey
1006	**lever**	*v*	to lift, raise
1272	**lèvre**	*nf*	lip

FREQ

1885	liaison	nf	liaison, connection	2189	lot	nm	share, prize, lot
1464	libérer	v	to free, liberate, release	1976	louer	v	to rent, praise
690	liberté	nf	liberty, freedom	1631	loup	nm	wolf
518	libre	adj(f)	free	1433	lourd	adj	heavy
1552	lien	nm	link, bond	2435	loyauté	nf	loyalty
2439	lier	v	to link, join, tie to	1851	loyer	nm	rent
385	lieu	nm	place	48	lui	pron	him, her
661	lieutenant	nm	lieutenant	525	lumière	nf	light
595	ligne	nf	line	1202	lundi	nm	Monday
1777	ligne	nf	line	650	lune	nf	moon
1770	limite	nf	limit	1252	lunette(s)	nf	sg: telescope; pl: glasses
2174	linge	nf	linen, cloth	1563	lutte	nf	struggle, fight, conflict
1482	liquide	noun, adj(f)	liquid	2279	luxe	nm	luxury
567	lire	nf, v	to read; italian lira	986	lycée	nm	high school
730	liste	nf	list		**M**		
352	lit	nm	bed				
2239	livraison	nf	delivery	2399	machin	nm	thingy
424	livre	nm, nf	book; pound	820	machine	nf	machine
1729	livrer	v	to deliver	1599	machine	nf	machine
2500	loger	v	to put up, accomodate, stay	269	madame	nf	madam, lady
				361	mademoiselle	nf	Miss
1580	logique	noun, adj(f)	logic, logical	886	magasin	nm	store, shop
531	loi	nf	law	1818	magazine	nm	magazine
258	loin	adv, nm	far	1516	magique	adj(f)	magic; magical
467	long	adv, adj, nm	long, lengthy, length	545	magnifique	adj(f)	magnificent
221	longtemps	adv	a long time, a long while	1277	mai	nm	May
811	longue	adj	long	233	main	nf	hand
1032	lors	adv	at the time of, during	75	maintenant	adv	now
				2441	maintenir	v	to maintain
840	lorsque	conj	when	1201	maire	nm	mayor

24	**mais**	*adv, conj, int*	but		739	**marier**	*v*	to marry
129	**maison**	*nf*	house		1484	**marin**	*noun, adj*	sea, marine, sailor
1562	**maitre**	*nm*	master		1388	**marine**	*adj, nf*	marine, navy
371	**maître**	*nm*	master		1238	**mark**	*nm*	mark
827	**majeste**	*nf*	majesty		1240	**marquer**	*v*	to mark
107	**mal**	*adj(i), adv, nm*	bad, sore		1146	**marrant**	*noun, adj*	funny, funny guy
386	**malade**	*nmf, adj(f)*	mental patient; ill, sick		949	**marre**	*nf*	fed up, to have enough
1034	**maladie**	*nf*	illness, disease		1285	**mars**	*nm[pl]*	March; Mars
2210	**malédiction**	*nf*	curse		1655	**masque**	*nm*	mask
1026	**malgré**	*prep*	despite, in spite of		2256	**massacre**	*nm*	massacre, slaughter
1283	**malheur**	*nm*	misfortune		2278	**masse**	*nf*	mass
1266	**malheureusement**	*adv*	unfortunately		754	**match**	*nm*	match, game
1556	**malheureux**	*noun, adj[pl]*	unhappy, miserable		1508	**matériel**	*noun, adj*	material, equipment
931	**malin**	*noun, adj*	smart, shrewd, cunning		1986	**matière**	*nf*	matter
136	**maman**	*nf*	mom		245	**matin**	*nm*	morning
2270	**manche**	*nm, nf*	handle, sleeve		2331	**matinée**	*nf*	morning
1737	**mandat**	*nm*	term, mandate		1379	**maudire**	*v*	to curse
300	**manger**	*nm, v*	to eat		372	**mauvais**	*adv, nm, adj[pl]*	bad, wrong
807	**manière**	*nf*	manner, way		1699	**maximum**	*nm, adj*	maximum
487	**manquer**	*v*	to miss		26	**me, m'**	*pron*	me, to me, myself
1245	**manteau**	*nm*	coat, overcoat		220	**mec**	*nm*	guy
2017	**manuel**	*adj, nm*	manual		2020	**méchant**	*adj*	bad, mean
2494	**maquillage**	*nf*	makeup		574	**medecin**	*nm*	physician, doctor
2187	**marche**	*nf*	walk, step, march		2357	**médical**	*adj*	medical
305	**marcher**	*v*	to walk		1460	**médicament**	*nm*	drug, medication
1569	**mardi**	*nm*	Tuesday		318	**meilleur**	*nmf, adj, adv*	best, better,
267	**mari**	*nm*	husband					
349	**mariage**	*nm*	marriage, wedding					

2321	**mélanger**	*v*	to mix, mix up, confuse					weather report
2101	**mêler**	*v*	to mix, get mixed up with	2162	**méthode**	*nf*	method
1195	**membre**	*nm*	member	1033	**métier**	*nm*	job, occupation, trade
66	**même**	*adj(f), adv, pron*	same, even, self	948	**mètre**	*nm*	meter
				1919	**métro**	*nm*	metro, subway
919	**mémoire**	*nm, nf*	memory	244	**mettre**	*v*	to put, place
1256	**menace**	*nf*	threat	2411	**meuble**	*nm, adj(f)*	piece of furniture
2340	**menacer**	*v*	to threaten	563	**meurtre**	*nm*	murder
1520	**ménage**	*nm*	housekeeping, housework	1571	**meurtrier**	*noun, adj*	murderer, deadly, lethal
1312	**mener**	*v*	to lead, live	2073	**micro**	*nm*	mike, micro, microphone
1289	**mensonge**	*nm*	lie	575	**midi**	*nm*	noon
1254	**menteur**	*nm*	liar	1609	**miel**	*nm*	honey
950	**mentir**	*v*	to lie	828	**mien**	*pron*	mine
2478	**menu**	*nm, adv, adj*	menu, slender, slim, minor	112	**mieux**	*adj(i)[pl], adv, nm*	better
573	**mer**	*nf*	sea	925	**mignon**	*adj*	cute
67	**merci**	*int, nm, nf*	thank you; favor	717	**milieu**	*nm*	middle
1902	**mercredi**	*nm*	Wednesday	1111	**militaire**	*noun, adj(f)*	military
134	**merde**	*int, nf*	sh*t, crap	683	**mille**	*det, nm, num*	thousand
119	**mère**	*nf*	mother	1738	**milliard**	*nm*	billion, thousand million
956	**mérite**	*nm*	merit	1133	**millier**	*nm*	thousand
2196	**merveille**	*nf*	marvel, wonder	449	**million**	*nm*	million
647	**merveilleux**	*adj[pl]*	marvellous, wonderful	1722	**minable**	*adj*	seedy, shabby
476	**message**	*nm*	message	1199	**mince**	*adj(f), int*	thin, slim, slender
345	**messieurs**	*nmpl*	gentlemen	1135	**mine**	*nf*	appearance, look, skin
2192	**mesure**	*nf*	measure	1788	**ministère**	*nm, nf*	minister
1320	**mesurer**	*v*	to measure	1094	**ministre**	*nm, nf*	minister
2312	**métal**	*nm*	metal	1193	**minuit**	*nm*	midnight
2431	**météo**	*nf*	weather forecast,	266	**minute**	*nf*	minute

336	**minute**	*nf*	minute
1213	**miracle**	*nm*	miracle
1641	**miroir**	*nm*	mirror
2405	**misérable**	*nmf, adj*	miserable, wretched
2380	**misère**	*nf*	misery, poverty
599	**mission**	*nf*	mission
2281	**mobile**	*adj(f), nm*	mobile, portable; motive
1707	**moche**	*adj*	ugly
1180	**mode**	*nm, nf*	mode, way, fashion
1470	**modèle**	*nm*	model
1911	**moderne**	*adj*	modern
21	**moi**	*nm, pron*	me
218	**moi**	*nm, pron*	me
975	**moindre**	*adj(f)*	lesser, least, slightest
155	**moins**	*adj(i)[pl], adv, nm[pl], prep*	less
587	**moitié**	*nf*	half
2377	**môme**	*nm, nf*	kid
168	**moment**	*nm*	moment
34	**mon, ma, mes**	*det*	my
87	**monde**	*nm*	world, people
1990	**mondial**	*adj*	world, global
115	**monsieur**	*nm*	mister, sir, gentleman
822	**monstre**	*nm adj(f)*	monster
1057	**montagne**	*nf*	mountain
515	**monter**	*v*	to go up, rise, assemble
400	**montrer**	*v*	to show
1678	**moquer**	*v*	to mock, make fun of
1868	**moral**	*adj, nm*	moral, morale
988	**morceau**	*nm*	piece, bit
2273	**mordre**	*v*	to bite, overlap into
110	**mort**	*adj, nf*	dead; death
2051	**mortel**	*nmf, adj*	mortal, deadly, lethal
342	**mot**	*nm*	word
1203	**moteur**	*noun, adj*	motor
2433	**motif**	*nm*	motive, purpose
1759	**moto**	*nm*	motorbike
2048	**mouche**	*nf*	fly
264	**mourir**	*v*	to die
2437	**mouton**	*nm*	sheep
1268	**mouvement**	*nm*	movement
559	**moyen**	*adj, nm*	means, way; medium
1971	**munition**	*nf*	ammunition, supplies
759	**mur**	*nm*	wall
1721	**musée**	*nf*	museum
343	**musique**	*nf*	music
1658	**mystère**	*nm*	mystery

N

1603	**nager**	*v*	to swim
1095	**naissance**	*nf*	birth
824	**naitre**	*v*	to be born
1596	**nation**	*nf*	nation
1653	**national**	*adj, nf*	national; road, state highway
791	**nature**	*nf*	nature
1632	**naturel**	*nm, adj*	naturalness, natural

1733	**naturellement**	*adv*	naturally
1408	**navire**	*nm*	ship
15	**ne, n´**	*adv*	not
915	**nécessaire**	*nm, adj(f)*	necessary, required
2112	**négatif**	*adj, nm*	negative
2402	**nègre**	*nm, adj*	negro
1073	**neige**	*nf*	snow
1880	**nerf**	*nm*	nerve
1158	**nerveux**	*noun, adj[pl]*	nervous, irritable
1424	**net**	*adj, nm*	clear; Internet, web
1290	**nettoyer**	*v*	to clean
521	**neuf**	*det, adj, num*	nine; new
1966	**neveu**	*nm*	nephew
680	**nez**	*nm[pl]*	nose
193	**ni**	*conj, adv*	nor
2453	**nichon**	*nm*	boob, tit, breast
932	**niveau**	*nm*	level
1683	**noble**	*adj(f, nmf*	noble, noble(wo)man
527	**Noël**	*nm*	Christmas
434	**noir**	*nmf adj*	black (wo)man), black
2214	**noix**	*nf*	nuts
130	**nom**	*nm*	name
1029	**nombre**	*nm*	number
1197	**nombreux**	*adj[pl]*	numerous
1557	**nommer**	*v*	to call, name, appoint
33	**non**	*adv*	no, not
688	**nord**	*adj(i), nm*	north
670	**normal**	*adj*	normal

1964	**normalement**	*adv*	normally
1281	**note**	*nf*	note, grade
1138	**noter**	*v*	to note, notice, write down
81	**notre**	*det*	our
1675	**nôtre**	*det*	our
1615	**nourrir**	*v*	to feed, nourish
878	**nourriture**	*nf*	food
23	**nous**	*pron*	we, us
213	**nouveau**	*adj, nm*	new
2180	**novembre**	*nm*	November
1665	**nu**	*nm, adj*	naked, nude
1889	**nuage**	*nm*	cloud
2033	**nucléaire**	*adj, nm*	nuclear, nuclear power
2037	**nue**	*adj*	naked
133	**nuit**	*nf*	night
725	**nul**	*adj, det, pron*	nil, null
319	**numéro**	*nm*	number

O

2056	**obéir**	*v*	to obey
1833	**objectif**	*adj, nm*	objective, aim, goal; lens
2053	**objection**	*nf*	objection
1392	**objet**	*nm*	objective; object
1069	**obliger**	*v*	to require, force, oblige, to have to
2172	**obscurité**	*nf*	darkness, obscurity
2425	**observer**	*v*	to observe, watch
1007	**obtenir**	*v*	to get, obtain

809	**occasion**	*nf*	chance, opportunity
485	**occuper**	*v*	to occupy
1373	**océan**	*nm*	ocean
2019	**octobre**	*nm*	October
1054	**odeur**	*nf*	smell, odor
217	**œil**	*nm*	eye
1671	**œuf**	*nm*	egg
1587	**œuvrer**	*v*	to work
2305	**officiel**	*adj, nmf*	official
2475	**officiellement**	*adv*	officially
953	**officier**	*nm, nf, v*	officer; officiate
616	**offrir**	*v*	to offer
83	**oh**	*int*	oh
1027	**oiseau**	*nm*	bird
1191	**ombre**	*nm, nf*	shade, shadow
18	**on**	*pron*	one, we
482	**oncle**	*nm*	uncle
2489	**onde**	*nf*	wave
2231	**ongle**	*nf*	nail, fingernail
2450	**onze**	*det, num*	eleven
900	**opération**	*nf*	operation
2177	**opérer**	*v*	to operate
1421	**opinion**	*nf*	opinion
2474	**opportunité**	*nf*	opportunity, appropriateness
431	**or**	*conj, nm*	gold; hence, thus
2298	**orage**	*nm*	storm, thunderstorm
1771	**orange**	*adj(i), nf*	orange

2035	**orchestrer**	*v*	to orchestrate
1629	**ordinaire**	*adv, nm, adj(f)*	ordinary
1189	**ordinateur**	*noun, adj*	computer
2269	**ordonner**	*v*	to ordain, organize, order
433	**ordre**	*nm*	order
1985	**ordure**	*nf*	filth
1142	**oreille**	*nf*	ear
1751	**organisation**	*nf*	organization
2029	**organiser**	*v*	to organise, throw
2075	**original**	*nm, adj*	original
1694	**origine**	*nf*	origin, source
1117	**os**	*nm[pl]*	bone
2031	**oser**	*v*	to dare
2333	**otage**	*nm*	hostage
64	**ou**	*adv, pron*	where
53	**où**	*adv, pron*	where
1710	**ouah**	*int*	wow!
127	**ouais**	*int*	yeah
378	**oublier**	*v*	to forget
834	**ouest**	*adj(i), nm*	west
38	**oui**	*adv*	yes
1331	**ours**	*adj(i), nm[pl]*	bear
2347	**outil**	*nm*	tool
1196	**ouvert**	*adj*	open
1968	**ouverture**	*nf*	opening
2152	**ouvrier**	*nmf, adj*	worker, working-class
480	**ouvrir**	*v*	to open

675	ouvrir	v	to open

P

819	paie	nf	pay, payroll
905	pain	nm	bread
1706	pair	adj, nm	peer, pair, even
421	paix	nf[pl]	peace
1403	palais	nm[pl]	palace, palate
2363	panier	nm	basket
1535	panique	noun, adj(f)	panic
1716	panne	nf	breakdown, failure
1247	pantalon	nm	trousers, pants
135	papa	nm	dad, daddy
891	papier	nm	paper
1162	paquet	nm	packet
57	par	prep	by
1046	paradis	nm[pl]	paradise, heaven
695	paraître	v	to appear
1224	parc	nm	park
111	parce que	conj	because
236	pardon	nm	forgiveness
1644	pardonner	v	to forgive, excuse
553	pareil	adj, nm	similar, likewise; peer, equal; the same
347	parent	nm&f, adj	parent
2392	parent	nmf, adj	parent
355	parfait	nm, adj, int	perfect
1074	parfaitement	adv	perfectly
363	parfois	adv	sometimes
1662	parfum	nm	perfume, scent, fragrance

604	pari	nm	bet, wager
769	parier	v	to bet
108	parler	nm, v	to speak, talk
817	parmi	prep	among
738	parole	nf	word
183	part	nf	share
1741	partage	nm	division, cutting, sharing
1207	partager	v	to share
2455	partant	adv	thus, consequencly, therefore
1382	partenaire	nm, nf	partner
2043	participer	v	to participate
1497	particulier	noun, adj	particular, peculiar; person
2224	particulièrement	adv	particulary
176	partir	v	to leave
392	partout	adv	everywhere, all over the place
4	pas	adv, nm[pl]	not; footstep
1071	passager	noun, adj	passenger, temporary
157	passe	nf, adj, prep	pass, past
2003	passeport	nm	passport
148	passer	v	to pass, go
1560	passion	nf	passion
1983	pasteur	nm	minister, clergyman, pastor
1519	patience	nf	patience
1253	patient	noun, adj	patient
2416	patienter	v	to wait
2078	patrie	nf	homeland, home country

478	**patron**	nm	boss
2308	**patrouille**	nf	patrol
1384	**patte**	nf	paw, foot, leg
1276	**pause**	nf	break, pause
360	**pauvre**	nmf, adj(f)	poor
369	**payer**	v	to pay
1233	**payer**	v	to pay
274	**pays**	nm[pl]	country
679	**peau**	nf	skin
1476	**péché**	nf	fishing; peach
1473	**pêcher**	nm, v	to fish, go fishing; peach tree
1882	**pédé**	nf	homosexual, queer
2362	**peindre**	v	to paint, depict, portray
330	**peiner**	v	to toil, labor, struggle
1584	**peinture**	nf	painting, paint, picture
198	**pendre**	v	to hang down
2260	**pénis**	nm	penis
132	**penser**	nm, v	to think
2211	**pension**	nf	pension; room and board, boarding school
250	**perdre**	v	to lose
94	**père**	nm	father
1554	**période**	nm, nf	period
893	**permettre**	v	to allow
1259	**permission**	nf	permission, leave
1412	**personnage**	nm	character, individual
2107	**personnalité**	nf	personality
102	**personne**	nf, pron	person, people, anybody, anyone nobody, no-one
923	**personnel**	noun, adj	personnel, personal
1870	**personnellement**	adv	personally
1255	**perte**	nf	loss
2009	**pervers**	nmf; adj[pl]	pervert; perverse, perverted
2396	**pester**	v	pester contre: to curse
113	**petit**	adv, nm, adj	small, little
2364	**pétrin**	nm	mess, spot, pickle
1836	**pétrole**	nm	crude oil, petroleum
77	**peu**	adv	little
605	**peuple**	nm	people
138	**peur**	nf	fear
2213	**phase**	nf	phase, round
442	**photo**	nf	photo
2258	**phrase**	nf	sentence, phrase
1490	**physique**	noun, adj(f)	physical, physics
1314	**piano**	adv, nm	piano
496	**pièce**	nf	piece, part, component; room
511	**pied**	nm	foot
1282	**piéger**	v	to trap, booby-trap
734	**pierre**	nf	stone
1765	**pile**	nf	pile, stack, battery, tails
1151	**piloter**	v	to fly, pilot, drive
2240	**pilule**	nf	pill

2085	**pipe**	*nf*	pipe		2290	**planter**	*v*	to plant, pitch
2385	**pipi**	*nm*	pee, wee		2015	**plaquer**	*v*	to tackle, drop, ditch, dump
2315	**pique**	*nf;nm*	pike, critique; spade		2186	**plastique**	*nm, adj(f)*	plastic
2066	**piquer**	*v*	to sting, bite, prick, be hot; to steal		1301	**plat**	*adj, nm*	dish, flat
419	**pire**	*adj(f), nm*	worse, worst		1856	**plateau**	*nm*	plateau, tray, set, stage
1182	**pis**	*adv, nm[pl]*	worse		298	**plein**	*adv, nm, adj, prep*	full
1578	**piscine**	*nf*	swimming pool		920	**pleurer**	*v*	to cry
2250	**pisse**	*nf*	piss		2124	**pleuvoir**	*v*	to rain
1800	**pisser**	*v*	to piss		1008	**pluie**	*nf*	rain
994	**piste**	*nf*	track, trail, path		860	**plupart**	*most,*	the majority , most
708	**pitié**	*nf*	pity, mercy		32	**plus**	*adv*	more, no
1901	**placard**	*nm*	cupboard, locker		635	**plusieurs**	*det, adj, pron*	several
1888	**place**	*nf*	room, space, seat, square, place		304	**plutôt**	*adv*	rather
2322	**placer**	*v*	to place		1035	**poche**	*nf*	pocket
1077	**plage**	*nf*	beach		2259	**poème**	*nm*	poem
1740	**plaindre**	*v*	to pity, feel sorry for, complain		2349	**poète**	*nm*	poet
1500	**plaire**	*v*	to please, like		1100	**poids**	*nm[pl]*	weight
1485	**plaire**	*v*	to please		1627	**poil**	*nm*	hair, bristle
1690	**plaisant**	*adj*	pleasant		2197	**poing**	*nm*	fist, punch
1340	**plaisanter**	*v*	to joke		284	**point**	*adv, nm*	point
2326	**plaisanterie**	*nf*	joke		859	**poisson**	*nm*	fish
340	**plaisir**	*nm*	pleasure		1680	**poitrine**	*nf*	chest, breast, breasts, bosom
399	**plan**	*adj, nm*	plan		223	**police**	*nf*	police
2479	**plancher**	*nm, v*	floor		1248	**policier**	*noun, adj*	policeman
902	**planète**	*nf*	planet		884	**politique**	*nm, nf, adj(f)*	politician; politics; political
2387	**plante**	*nf*	plant		1748	**pomme**	*nf*	apple

2306	**pompe**	*nf*	pump		1294	**poupée**	*nf*	doll, dolly, puppet
2465	**pompier**	*adj, nm*	fireman, firefighter		20	**pour**	*prep*	to, for, in order to,
879	**pont**	*nm*	bridge		55	**pourquoi**	*adv, conj*	why
2034	**populaire**	*adj(f)*	popular		1936	**pourrir**	*v*	to rot
2168	**population**	*nf*	population		1782	**poursuivre**	*v*	to pursue
1360	**porc**	*nm*	pig, pork		626	**pourtant**	*adv*	yet, nonetheless, nevertheless
1525	**port**	*nm*	harbor, port		2272	**pourvu**	*adj; adv*	equiped with; so long as, provided
1287	**portable**	*adj(f), nm*	portable, wearable; cell phone		1186	**pousser**	*v*	to push
187	**porte**	*nf*	door		1559	**poussière**	*nf*	dust
1929	**portefeuille**	*nm*	wallet		60	**pouvoir**	*nm, v*	can, to be able to
576	**porter**	*nm, v*	to wear, carry		1604	**pratique**	*noun, adj(f)*	practice, practical
1893	**portraire**	*v*	to portray		2241	**pratiquement**	*adv*	practically
674	**poser**	*v*	to put, pose, ask		1821	**précieux**	*adj [pl]*	precious
751	**position**	*nf*	position		1831	**précis**	*adj[pl, noun*	precise; noun
1775	**posséder**	*v*	to possess, own, have		2419	**précisément**	*adv*	precisely
2122	**possibilité**	*nf*	possibility		704	**préférer**	*v*	to prefer
296	**possible**	*adj(f)*	possible		253	**premier**	*det, nm&f, adj*	first, premier, first,
620	**poste**	*nm, nf*	post, position, job; post office		144	**prendre**	*v*	to take
2299	**poste**	*nm, nf*	post, position; post office		1619	**prénom**	*nm*	first name
1545	**pot**	*nm*	jar, pot		971	**préparer**	*v*	to prepare
609	**pote**	*nm*	mate		289	**près**	*adv, prep*	near, nearby, close by
2307	**poubelle**	*nf*	trash can, garbage		1002	**présence**	*nf*	presence
2360	**pouce**	*nm*	thumb, inch		534	**présent**	*nm, adj*	present
1909	**poudre**	*nf*	powder, dust		783	**présenter**	*v*	to present
1474	**poule**	*nf*	hen, chick		390	**président**	*nm*	president
1123	**poulet**	*nm*	chicken		317	**presque**	*adv*	almost
					784	**presse**	*nf*	press

1666	**presser**	v	to squeeze, press	1852	**producteur**	nm/f, adj	producer
1082	**pression**	nf	pressure	1727	**production**	nf	production
280	**prêt**	adj, nm	ready	1051	**produire**	v	to product
2383	**prêter**	v	to lend	537	**professeur**	nm, nf	professor, teacher
1318	**prêtre**	nm	priest	1783	**professionnel**	nmf, adj	professional
786	**preuve**	nf	proof	1575	**profiter**	v	to take advantage, profit
1130	**prévenir**	v	to prevent, warn; to notify	1555	**profond**	adv, noun, adj	deep
241	**prier**	v	to pray	1834	**profondément**	adv	profoundly, deeply
1897	**prière**	nf	prayer	997	**programme**	nm	program
2131	**prime**	noun, adj(f), nf	free gift, premium, bonus	1984	**progrès**	nm	progress
780	**prince**	nm	prince	857	**projet**	nm	project
873	**princesse**	nf	princess	2456	**promenade**	nf	walk, stroll
1543	**principal**	noun, adj	principal	1944	**promener**	v	to take for a walk, go for a walk
2275	**principe**	nm	principle				
1410	**printemps**	nm[pl]	spring	1530	**promesse**	nf	promise
375	**prison**	nf	prison, jail	481	**promettre**	v	to promise
1333	**prisonnier**	noun, adj	prisoner, captive	2098	**promotion**	nf	promotion, advertising
1156	**priver**	v	to deprive	453	**propos**	nm[pl]	remark
458	**prix**	nm[pl]	price; prize	1583	**proposer**	v	to propose
721	**probablement**	adv	probably	1825	**proposition**	nf	proposition, proposal
185	**problème**	nm	problem				
2045	**procédure**	nf	procedure	402	**propre**	nm, adj(f)	particular; clean, proper
936	**procès**	nm[pl]	trial, proceedings	1348	**propriétaire**	nm, nf	owner
2355	**processus**	nm[pl]	process	1597	**propriété**	nf	property
463	**prochain**	adj, nm	next; fellow man	1369	**protection**	nf	protection
1016	**proche**	adv, noun, adj(f), prep	nearby, close	706	**protéger**	v	to protect
1420	**procureur**	nm	prosecutor	1010	**prouver**	v	to prove

1343	**prudent**	*adj*	prudent, careful, cautious
660	**public**	*nm, adj*	public, audience
2133	**publicité**	*nf*	publicity
2026	**publique**	*adj, nf*	public
1692	**puce**	*nf*	chip
171	**puis**	*adv*	then, so
908	**puisque**	*conj*	since
1208	**puissance**	*nf*	power
1119	**puissant**	*noun, adj*	powerful
1987	**puits**	*nm[pl]*	well, shaft, pit
1617	**pur**	*adj, nmf*	pure; hard-liner
191	**putain**	*nf*	whore, bitch; stupid
629	**pute**	*nf*	whore, bitch, prostitute

Q

1667	**qualité**	*nf*	quality
56	**quand**	*adv, conj*	when
1467	**quant**	*adv*	as for
1853	**quart**	*nm*	quarter
779	**quartier**	*nm*	district, quarter
303	**quatre**	*det, num*	four
9	**que, qu'**	*adv, conj, pron*	that, which, who, whom, as
120	**quel**	*det, adj, pron*	which, what
86	**quelque**	*adv, adj, det*	some
209	**question**	*nf*	question

1065	**queue**	*nf*	tail, handle, stalk, stem, rear
22	**qui**	*pron*	who, whom
1565	**quiconque**	*pron*	whoever, anyone who
1774	**quinze**	*det, num*	fifteen
2327	**quitte**	*adj*	to be clear off, quits
601	**quitter**	*v*	to leave
45	**quoi**	*pron*	what

R

1676	**race**	*nf*	breed, race
889	**raconter**	*v*	to tell
622	**radio**	*adj(i), nm, nf*	radio
1963	**rage**	*nf*	rage, fury, rabies
165	**raison**	*nf*	reason
1656	**raisonnable**	*adj(f)*	reasonable, fair
2352	**ramasser**	*v*	to pick up, collect, gather
847	**ramener**	*v*	to bring back, return, take back
2414	**ramer**	*v*	to row
1728	**rang**	*nm*	rank, row
1844	**ranger**	*nm, v*	to tidy up, put away
894	**rapide**	*adj(f), nm*	fast, quick; rapids, fast train
1241	**rapidement**	*adv*	quickly, rapidly
548	**rappeler**	*v*	to recall, call back, remember
499	**rapport**	*nm*	relationship, report
1997	**rapporter**	*v*	to bring back, report

1514	**rare**	*adj(f)*	rare	1227	**reculer**	*v*	to move back, back up, move backward
2144	**rarement**	*adv*	rarely, seldom				
1517	**rat**	*adj(f), nm*	rat	1009	**récupérer**	*v*	to get back, recover, recuperate
2415	**rat**	*nf*	rat				
1062	**rater**	*v*	to miss, misfire	1296	**réel**	*noun, adj*	real
2160	**rattraper**	*v*	to recapture, recover, catch up, make up for	1705	**réellement**	*adv*	really
				1618	**refaire**	*v*	to redo, make again
838	**ravir**	*v*	to delight, rob	944	**réfléchir**	*v*	to reflect
				880	**refuser**	*v*	to refuse
2334	**ravissant**	*adj*	delightful, ravishing	1013	**regard**	*nm*	look, glance
1763	**rayon**	*nm*	ray, beam, radius; department, section, shelf	145	**regarder**	*v*	to look, watch
				2081	**régime**	*nf*	diet, regime
1672	**réaction**	*nf*	reaction	1457	**région**	*nf*	region
1898	**réalisateur**	*nmf*	director	869	**règle**	*adj*	regular, steady, well-ordered, ruled
1499	**réaliser**	*v*	to realize, achieve	1063	**règle**	*adj*	regular, steady, well-ordered, ruled
848	**realite**	*nf*	reality				
1561	**récemment**	*adv*	recently	2011	**règlement**	*nm*	settlement, solution
1862	**réception**	*nf*	reception	1000	**régler**	*v*	to pay, adjust, settle
479	**recevoir**	*v*	to receive	2297	**règne**	*nm*	reign
743	**recherche**	*nf*	research, search	972	**regretter**	*v*	to regret
1394	**recommencer**	*v*	to resume, start again, start over	718	**reine**	*nf*	queen
				1023	**rejoindre**	*v*	to rejoin, reunite
1652	**récompenser**	*v*	to reward, recompense	1020	**relation**	*nf*	relationship
2234	**reconnaissance**	*nf*	recognition, gratitude	2332	**relever**	*v*	to raise , lift
2223	**reconnaissant**	*adj*	grateful	1797	**religion**	*nf*	religion
1336	**reconnaître**	*v*	to recognize	2148	**remarquable**	*adj(f)*	remarkable, outstanding
2153	**record**	*nm*	record	2090	**remarque**	*nf*	remark

1045	**remarquer**	*v*	to remark; to notice, point out	1188	**repos**	*nm[pl]*	rest
2277	**rembourser**	*v*	to reimburse, pay back, pay off, repay	1137	**reposer**	*v*	to rest
				1134	**reprendre**	*v*	to resume, recover, start again, take back
2440	**remède**	*nf*	remedy				
929	**remercier**	*v*	to thank	1451	**représenter**	*v*	to represent
933	**remettre**	*v*	to deliver, replace, set, put back	1437	**réputation**	*nf*	reputation
				2406	**requin**	*nm*	shark
1355	**remonter**	*v*	to go back up	1896	**réseau**	*nm*	network
1736	**remplacer**	*v*	to replace	1389	**reserve**	*nf*	reserve
1819	**remplir**	*v*	to fill, fulfill, fill out	1957	**réservé**	*adj*	reserved
853	**rencontre**	*nm*	meeting	1362	**réserver**	*v*	to book, to reserve
546	**rencontrer**	*v*	to meet				
394	**rendre**	*v*	to render, return, yield, give up	2062	**résister**	*v*	to resist
				1734	**résoudre**	*v*	to solve, resolve
2132	**renfort**	*nm*	help, back-up, support	855	**respect**	*nm*	respect
2301	**renoncer**	*v*	to give up, renounce	1769	**respecter**	*v*	to respect
				1300	**respirer**	*v*	to breathe
1955	**renseignement**	*nm*	information	1465	**responsabilité**	*nf*	responsibility
351	**rentrer**	*v*	to go in, come in, come back, return	793	**responsable**	*adj(f), nmf*	responsible
				623	**ressembler**	*v*	to look like, resemble
2039	**renvoyer**	*v*	to send back, dismiss	1344	**ressentir**	*v*	to feel
1204	**réparer**	*v*	to repair, fix, correct, make up	1012	**restaurer**	*v*	to restore, feed
1931	**repartir**	*v*	to distribute, spread out, share out, divide	922	**reste**	*nm*	rest
				137	**rester**	*v*	to stay
913	**repas**	*nm[pl]*	meal	1445	**résultat**	*nm*	result, follow-up
1052	**répéter**	*v*	to repeat	423	**retard**	*nm*	delay, late
806	**répondre**	*v*	to answer	1796	**retenir**	*v*	to retain, hold back, remember
627	**réponse**	*nf*	answer, response				

1434	**retirer**	*v*	to remove, withdraw
364	**retour**	*nm*	return
615	**retourner**	*v*	to return, go back
539	**retrouver**	*v*	to find, recall
896	**réunion**	*nf*	meeting, reunion
2016	**réunir**	*v*	to reunite
547	**réussir**	*v*	to succeed
707	**rêve**	*nm*	dream
2123	**réveil**	*nm*	the waking up, alarm clock
1219	**réveiller**	*v*	to wake up
354	**revenir**	*v*	to come back
773	**revenu**	*nm*	income
412	**rêver**	*v*	to dream
195	**revoir**	*v*	to see again, revise, meet
1549	**révolution**	*nf*	revolution
781	**riche**	*adj(f)*	rich
785	**ridicule**	*nm, adj(f)*	ridiculousness, silly
51	**rien**	*adv, nm, pron*	nothing
2176	**rigole**	*nf*	laugh
2283	**rigoler**	*v*	to laugh,
637	**rire**	*nm, v*	to laugh
558	**risque**	*nm*	risk
1817	**risquer**	*v*	to risk
1067	**rivière**	*nf*	river
1689	**riz**	*nm*	rice
1190	**rock**	*nm*	rock music
388	**roi**	*nm*	king
747	**rôle**	*nm*	role
1558	**roman**	*adj, nm*	novel
1524	**romantique**	*noun, adj(f)*	romantic
2159	**rompre**	*v*	to break, to break up
1791	**rond**	*adj, nm, nf*	round, circle, patrol,
790	**rose**	*adj(f), nf*	pink; rose
2317	**roue**	*nf*	wheel
459	**rouge**	*nm, adj(f)*	red
1416	**roule**	*adj*	rolled
2002	**rouler**	*v*	to roll
334	**route**	*nf*	road
2303	**royal**	*adj*	royal
1539	**royaume**	*nm*	kingdom, state
440	**rue**	*nf*	street
1226	**rue**	*nf*	street
2109	**rumeur**	*nf*	rumor
1192	**russe**	*noun, adj(f)*	Russian
1581	**rythme**	*nm*	rhythm, rate

S

1600	**sable**	*adj(i), nm*	sand
2057	**sabrer**	*v*	to cut
503	**sac**	*nm*	bag, sack
912	**sacré**	*adj*	sacred
2198	**sacrifice**	*nm*	sacrifice
1183	**sage**	*noun, adj(f)*	wise, good, sound, sensible
2282	**sagesse**	*nf*	wisdom, moderation
2481	**saigner**	*v*	to bleed
2058	**sain**	*adj*	healthy, sane
1145	**saint**	*noun, adj*	saint, holy

1319	**saison**	*nf*	season		42	**se, s´**	*pron*	oneself, himself, herself, itself, themselves
1612	**salaire**	*nm*	salary, wage					
691	**salaud**	*nm*	bastard		1925	**séance**	*nf*	meeting
426	**sale**	*adj(f)*	dirty		1356	**sec**	*adj, adv, nm*	dry
1415	**sale**	*noun, adj(f)*	dirty		504	**second**	*adj, det, nm*	second
491	**salle**	*nf*	room					
1148	**salon**	*nm*	lounge, living room		687	**seconde**	*det, nf*	second
					642	**secours**	*nm[pl]*	help, aid, assistance
1887	**salopard**	*nm*	bastard					
761	**salope**	*nf*	slut		502	**secret**	*nm, adj*	secret
1996	**saloperie**	*nf*	trash, junk, filth		1288	**secrétaire**	*nm, nf*	secretary
2285	**saluer**	*v*	to greet, salute		1493	**secteur**	*nm*	sector
140	**salut**	*int, nm*	salute, hi, bye		1602	**section**	*nf*	section
1050	**samedi**	*nm*	Saturday		410	**sécurité**	*nf*	security, safety, health
206	**sang**	*nm*	blood					
85	**sans**	*prep*	without		332	**seigneur**	*nm*	lord
667	**santé**	*nf*	health		1595	**sein**	*nm*	breast, bosom
2464	**satellite**	*nm*	satellite					
					2135	**séjour**	*nm*	stay
2287	**satisfaire**	*v*	to satisfy		2093	**sel**	*nm*	salt
428	**sauf**	*adj, prep*	except					
2330	**saut**	*nm*	jump, leap		602	**selon**	*prep*	according to
					306	**semaine**	*nf*	week
765	**sauter**	*v*	to jump		1230	**semblant**	*nm*	semblance, pretence
1537	**sauvage**	*noun, adj(f)*	savage, wild					
					407	**sembler**	*v*	to seem
495	**sauver**	*v*	to rescue, save		1475	**sénateur**	*nm*	senator
47	**savoir**	*nm, v*	to know		190	**sens**	*nm[pl]*	sense, meaning
2384	**savon**	*nm*	soap					
2099	**scandale**	*nm*	scandal, uproar		2191	**sensation**	*nf*	sensation
1542	**scénario**	*nm*	scenario, script		1916	**sensible**	*adj(f)*	sensitive
501	**scène**	*nf*	scene		1030	**sentiment**	*nm*	feeling
1526	**science**	*nf*	science		726	**sentir**	*v*	to feel, smell
1714	**scientifique**	*adj(f), nmf*	scientific; scientist		1881	**séparer**	*v*	to separate
					586	**sept**	*det, num*	seven

1573	**septembre**	*nm*	September
1181	**série**	*nf*	series
1110	**sérieusement**	*adv*	seriously
443	**sérieux**	*nm, adj[pl]*	seriousness, serious
1913	**serment**	*nm*	oath, vow
1576	**serpent**	*nm*	snake
2185	**serrer**	*v*	to tighten, squeeze
358	**service**	*nm*	service
2000	**serviette**	*nf*	towel, napkin
681	**servir**	*v*	to serve
141	**seul**	*adj*	alone, only
224	**seulement**	*adv*	only
911	**sexe**	*nm*	sex
2216	**sexuel**	*adj*	sexual
30	**si**	*adv, conj*	if, whether
1307	**siècle**	*nm*	century
1446	**siège**	*nm*	seat, bench
2434	**sien**	*pron*	his, hers
1078	**signal**	*nm*	signal
2116	**signature**	*nf*	signature
719	**signer**	*v*	to sign
851	**signifier**	*v*	to mean
578	**silence**	*nm*	silence
420	**simple**	*adj(f)*	simple, single
598	**simplement**	*adv*	simply, just
2084	**sincère**	*adj*	sincere
2407	**sincèrement**	*adv*	truly, sincerely
1342	**singe**	*nm*	monkey
2261	**singe**	*nm*	monkey

397	**sinon**	*conj*	otherwise, or else, or
1713	**site**	*nm*	site
523	**situation**	*nf*	situation
366	**six**	*det, num*	six
2206	**social**	*adj*	social
732	**société**	*nf*	society
510	**sœur**	*nf*	sister
1358	**soi**	*pron*	one, oneself, self
1442	**soif**	*nf*	thirst
1850	**soigner**	*v*	to treat, look after, take care for
733	**soin**	*nm*	care
126	**soir**	*nm*	evening
509	**soirée**	*nf*	evening
146	**soit**	*adv, conj*	either...or
711	**sol**	*nm*	floor, ground
775	**soldat**	*nm*	soldier
488	**soleil**	*nm*	sun
1960	**solide**	*nm, adj(f)*	solid
2071	**solitaire**	*adj(f, nmf*	solitary, lone, lonely, loner
2225	**solitude**	*nf*	solitude, loneliness
938	**solution**	*nf*	solution
1430	**sombre**	*adj(f)*	dark
1329	**somme**	*nm, nf*	amount, sum; nap
1218	**sommeil**	*nm*	sleep, sleepiness
1723	**sommet**	*nm*	summit
58	**son, sa, ses**	*det, nm*	his, her, its; sound; bran
1398	**sonner**	*v*	to ring
1764	**sorcier**	*nm*	sorcerer, witch
466	**sorte**	*nf*	sort, kind

657	**sortie**	*nf*	exit
208	**sortir**	*v*	to go out, leave
2030	**sou**	*nm*	penny
1244	**souci**	*nm*	worry, concern, care
1278	**soudain**	*adj, adv*	sudden, suddenly
1210	**souffle**	*nm*	breath, puff
1835	**souffrance**	*nf*	suffering
1367	**souffrir**	*v*	to suffer
1053	**souhaiter**	*v*	to wish
1386	**soupe**	*nf*	soup
1315	**source**	*nf*	source, spring
1945	**sourd**	*adj, nmf*	deaf, deaf person
955	**sourire**	*nm, v*	smile; to smile
1011	**souris**	*nf[pl]*	mouse
204	**sous**	*prep*	under
1826	**soutien**	*nm*	support
324	**souvenir**	*nm, v*	memory; to remember
427	**souvent**	*adv*	often
901	**spécial**	*adj*	special
742	**spectacle**	*nm*	sight, show
2097	**splendide**	*adj*	magnificent, wonderful
1444	**sport**	*adj(i), nm*	sport
1912	**stade**	*nm*	stadium, stage
1102	**star**	*nf*	star
1365	**station**	*nf*	station
2262	**statuer**	*v*	to rule
943	**stop**	*nm, int*	stop

1463	**studio**	*nm*	studio, studio apartment
702	**stupide**	*adj(f)*	stupid, silly, bemused
1120	**style**	*nm*	style
2121	**stylo**	*nm*	pen
2480	**subir**	*v*	to undergo, be subjected to, suffer
1037	**succès**	*nm[pl]*	success
1419	**sucre**	*nm*	sugar
652	**sud**	*adj(i), nm*	south
333	**suffire**	*v*	to be sufficient, suffice
2004	**suffisamment**	*adv*	sufficiently
2163	**suggérer**	*v*	to suggest
1265	**suicider**	*v*	to commit suicide
2345	**suisse**	*adj(f)*	Swiss
240	**suite**	*nf*	result, follow-up, rest
1068	**suivant**	*noun, adj, prep*	following
35	**suivre**	*v*	to follow
614	**suivre**	*v*	to follow
422	**sujet**	*nm*	subject, topic
228	**super**	*adj(i), nm*	great
841	**superbe**	*nf, adj(f)*	arrogance; superb, magnificent
1869	**supérieur**	*adj, nmf*	superior
1236	**supplier**	*v*	to beg, implore, plead
1322	**supporter**	*nm, v*	to support, endure
581	**supposer**	*v*	to suppose, assume

2083	**suprême**	*adj*	supreme	1812	**tandis**	*adv*	while
44	**sur**	*adj, prep*	on, upon	182	**tant**	*adv*	so much, so many
97	**sûr**	*adj, prep*	on, upon	715	**tante**	*nf*	aunt
430	**sûrement**	*adv*	surely	1806	**taper**	*v*	to beat, slam, bang, type, tap
1509	**surface**	*nf*	surface
588	**surprendre**	*v*	to surprise	172	**tard**	*adv*	late
415	**surtout**	*adv, nm*	especially, above all	2228	**tarder**	*v*	to delay
1899	**surveillance**	*nf*	surveillance, monitoring	1958	**tare**	*nf*	defect
1455	**surveiller**	*v*	to watch	2139	**tarte**	*nf*	pie
2267	**survie**	*nf*	survival	700	**tas**	*nm[pl]*	pile, lots of, heap
1400	**survivre**	*v*	to survive	1648	**tasse**	*nf*	cup
1364	**suspect**	*noun, adj*	suspicious, suspect	2311	**taudis**	*nm*	slum
2293	**symbole**	*nm*	symbol	2310	**taux**	*nm*	rate
682	**sympa**	*adj*	friendly, nice, kind	798	**taxi**	*nm*	taxi
2344	**syndicat**	*nm*	union	36	**te, t´**	*pron*	you, to you, from you
662	**système**	*nm*	system	1670	**technique**	*nf, adj(f)*	technique, technics, technical
	T			2074	**technologie**	*nf*	technology
2136	**tabac**	*nm*	tobacco	633	**tel**	*adj, det, pron*	such
541	**table**	*nf*	table	592	**télé**	*nf*	TV
1335	**tableau**	*nm*	frame, picture, painting, panel	359	**téléphoner**	*v*	to telephone, phone, call
2486	**tache**	*nf*	stain, spot, mark	1510	**télévision**	*nf*	television, TV
1494	**tâcher**	*v*	to endeavor, strive	314	**tellement**	*adv*	so much
909	**tailler**	*v*	to cut, carve, engrave, sharpen, trim	2367	**témoignage**	*nm*	testimoney, evidence, witness
524	**taire**	*v*	to keep quiet, hold ones tongue	2449	**témoigner**	*v*	to bear witness, to testify
2401	**talent**	*nm*	talent	927	**témoin**	*nm*	witness
				1994	**température**	*nf*	temperature

1636	**tempête**	*nf*	storm, gale, turmoil
1489	**temple**	*nm*	temple
79	**temps**	*nm[pl]*	time
1871	**tendre**	*adj(f)*	tender, soft
2212	**ténèbre**	*nf*	darkness
216	**tenir**	*v*	to hold
2466	**tennis**	*nf*	tennis
1999	**tension**	*nf*	tension
2010	**tentative**	*nf*	attempt
1211	**tenter**	*v*	to tempt, try
1351	**tenu**	*adj*	tenuous, slender, held
1452	**terme**	*nm*	term, deadline
560	**terminer**	*v*	to finish, end,
856	**terrain**	*nm*	ground, terrain
231	**terre**	*nf*	earth, world, soil, land
2280	**terreur**	*nf*	terror, dread
694	**terrible**	*adj(f)*	terrible, dreadful
2286	**terriblement**	*adv*	terribly, awfully
1756	**territoire**	*nm*	territory
1932	**terroriste**	*nm, nf*	terrorist
1173	**test**	*nm*	test
2348	**testament**	*nm*	will
161	**tête**	*nf*	head
2304	**texte**	*nm*	text
698	**thé**	*nm*	tea
1039	**théâtre**	*nm*	theater
1454	**théorie**	*nf*	theory

1459	**tien(s)**	*noun, adj[pl], int*	ah, well
2164	**tigre**	*nm*	tiger
1978	**timide**	*adj(f)*	timid, shy, bashful
1370	**tir**	*nm*	fire, shot, launch
448	**tirer**	*v*	to pull, fire
2336	**tireur**	*nm*	shooter
1113	**titre**	*nm*	title
40	**toi**	*nm, pron*	you, yourself
898	**toilette**	*nf*	washing, toilet, lavatory, bathroom, restroom
1031	**toit**	*nm*	roof
2319	**tombe**	*nf*	grave, tomb
316	**tomber**	*v*	to fall
59	**ton, ta, tes**	*det, nm*	your; tone
2182	**tonne**	*nf*	metric ton, tonne
2366	**tonnerre**	*nf*	thunder
770	**tort**	*nm*	wrong
2166	**torture**	*nf*	torture
411	**tôt**	*adj(i), adv*	early
1956	**total**	*adj, nm*	total
1275	**totalement**	*adv*	totally
564	**toucher**	*nm, v*	to touch
80	**toujours**	*adv*	always
302	**tour**	*nm, nf*	tower; turn; tour
2032	**tournage**	*nm*	shooting
750	**tourner**	*v*	to turn, to spin

31	**tout**	adv, det, nm, adj, pron	all, very	1842	**trente**	det, num	thirty
				65	**très**	adv	very
1468	**trace**	nf	trace, mark, track	966	**trésor**	nm	treasure, treasury
1393	**tracer**	v	to draw, write, mark out	1161	**tribunal**	nm	court
				632	**triste**	adj(f)	sad
2059	**tradition**	nf	tradition	149	**trois**	det, num	three
1462	**traduction**	nf	translation	995	**troisième**	det, nm, nf	third
2232	**trafic**	nm	traffic, circulation	2076	**trompe**	adj	horn, trunk
2165	**tragédie**	nf	tragedy	1366	**tromper**	v	to deceive
2467	**tragique**	adj(f), nm	tragic, tragedy	90	**trop**	adv	too much, too many
1930	**trahir**	v	to betray, give away	618	**trou**	nm	hole
2190	**trahison**	nf	betrayal, treachery, treason	2248	**trouille**	nf	(avoir la) trouille: to be scared stiff
				1453	**troupe**	nf	troop
261	**train**	nm	train				
2142	**traîne**	nf	train	199	**trouver**	v	to find
				215	**truc**	nm	trick; (that) thing (what I can't recall)
1717	**traîner**	v	to drag, pull				
1594	**traitement**	nm	treatment, salary, wage	8	**tu**	pron	you (fam)
				173	**tuer**	v	to kill
1469	**traiter**	v	to treat, handle, deal with	823	**tueur**	nm	killer, hit man
				1810	**tunnel**	nm	tunnel
1715	**traître**	nm, adj	traitor, treacherous				
				2079	**tuyau**	nm	pipe, tube
549	**tranquille**	adj(f)	quiet				
2463	**transfert**	nm	transfer	235	**type**	nm	type; guy
				829	**type**	nm	type; guy
2351	**transformer**	v	to transform				
2382	**transport**	nm	transportation		**U**		
188	**travail**	nm	work				
391	**travailler**	v	to work	10	**un, une, des**	adj, det, nm, pron, num	a, an, one
701	**travers**	nm[pl]	breadth, across; fault, amiss	1387	**uniforme**	adj(f), nm	uniform, steady, regular
1395	**traverser**	v	to cross, traverse	1697	**union**	nf	union

#	Word	Type	Definition
981	unique	adj(f)	unique
1688	uniquement	adv	only
731	unir	v	to unite, come to terms with unity; unit
1242	unité	nf	unity; unit
1086	univers	nm[pl]	universe
946	université	nf	university, college
1017	urgence	nf	emergency
1685	urgent	adj	urgent
2291	usage	nm	use, usage
2117	user	v	to wear out, wear away, use up
1168	usiner	nf	factory
1096	utile	adj(f)	useful
735	utiliser	v	to use

V

#	Word	Type	Definition
821	vacance	nf	vacancy; vacation ; holiday
1187	vache	adj(f), nf	cow
1752	vague	adj(f); nf	vague; wave
2390	vain	adj	vain
2356	vaincre	v	to beat, defeat, overcome, conquer
910	vaisseau	nm	ship, vessel
1118	valeur	nf	value, worth
1404	valise	nf	suitcase
1847	vallée	nf	valley
384	valoir	v	to be worth
2038	vedette	nf	star, patrol boat
1820	véhiculer	v	to transport, convey
1512	veiller	v	to look after, stay up
1702	vélo	nm	bike, bicycle
2179	vendeur	nm	salesman, seller
665	vendre	v	to sell
1108	vendredi	nm	Friday
1664	vengeance	nf	revenge
1730	venger	v	to avenge, take revenge
91	venir	v	to come
712	vent	nm	wind
1504	vente	nf	sale
1104	ventre	nm	belly, stomach
992	vérifier	v	to check, verify
1250	véritable	adj(f)	real, TRUE
307	vérité	nf	truth
365	verre	nm	glass
237	vers	nm[pl], prep	toward; verse
1567	version	nf	version
1121	vert	noun, adj	green
1309	veste	nf	jacket
729	vêtement	nm	garment, item or article of clothing
1970	veuf	nmf, adj	widow, widowed, widower
1066	viande	nf	meat
967	victime	nf	victim
1154	victime	nf	victim

1059	**victoire**	nf	victory
792	**vide**	adj(f), nm	empty; vacuum
1080	**vidéo**	adj(i), nf	video
82	**vie**	nf	life
1361	**vierge**	noun, adj(f)	virgin
200	**vieux**	adj[pl], nm[pl]	old
1106	**vif**	noun, adj	lively
673	**village**	nm	village
211	**ville**	nf	city
709	**vin**	nm	wine
1212	**vingt**	det, num	twenty
2388	**viol**	nm	rape
1157	**violence**	nf	violence
2086	**violent**	adj	violent
2208	**vire**	adj	fired
1376	**virer**	v	to turn, change, transfer, kick out
1626	**virus**	nm[pl]	virus
432	**visage**	nm	face
2114	**viser**	v	to aim
1501	**vision**	nf	vision, view
644	**visiter**	v	to visit
143	**vite**	adv	fast, quickly
961	**vitesse**	nf	speed
1425	**vivant**	noun, adj	alive, living
279	**vivre**	nm, v	to live
205	**voici**	prep	here is, here are, this is, these are
607	**voie**	nf	road, lane, route, track, way
116	**voilà**	prep	right, there, here; that's
2421	**voile**	nm, nf	veil, sail
1411	**voiler**	v	to veil
71	**voir**	v	to see
1432	**voisin**	noun, adj	neighbor
184	**voiture**	nf	car
999	**voiture**	nf	car
451	**voix**	nf[pl]	voice
659	**vol**	nm	flight, theft
649	**voler**	v	to steal, rob
1099	**voleur**	noun, adj	thief, light-fingered
2426	**volontaire**	nmf, adj(f)	volunteer; voluntary
1087	**volonté**	nf	will
2257	**volontiers**	adv	with pleasure, willingly, gladly
2417	**vomir**	v	to throw up, to vomit
1794	**vote**	nm	vote
54	**votre**	det	your
1055	**vôtre**	det	your (form & pl)
49	**vouloir**	nm, v	to want
6	**vous**	pron	you (form & pl)
465	**voyage**	nm	trip, journey
1780	**voyager**	v	to travel
105	**vrai**	adv, nm, adj	true
78	**vraiment**	adv	truly, really, very

Y

25	**y**	adv, pron	there

Z

1144	**zéro**	*nm*	zero
874	**zone**	*nf*	zone, area
2499	**zone**	*nf*	area
2134	**zut**	*int*	heck

6. Further Reading & Resources

For more tools, tips & tricks visit our site www.mostusedwords.com.

Bilingual books

In the beginning of the book I already spoke about the importance of reading when you're trying to acquire a new language.

We're creating a selection of multi-language texts, and our selection is ever expanding.

 Current bilingual texts available are English, Spanish, French, Portuguese, Spanish, Italian, Dutch and German

For more information, check www.mostusedwords.com/parallel-texts

Language learning methods

You'll find reviews of other 3rd party language learning applications, software, audiocourses and apps. There are so many available, and some are (much) better than others.

Check out our reviews at www.mostusedwords.com/reviews

Contact:

If you have any questions, you can contact me through e-mail info@mostusedwords.com.

First Printing, 2016

Jolie Laide LTD
12/F, 67 Percival Street, Hong Kong

www.MostUsedWords.com

Dedicated to my parents. It would not have been possible without you.

15633162R00197

Made in the USA
San Bernardino, CA
18 December 2018